A·N·N·U·A·L E·D·I·T·I·O·N·S

Drugs, Society, and Behavior

Twentieth Edition

05/06

EDITOR

Hugh T. Wilson

California State University-Sacramento

Hugh Wilson received his Bachelor of Arts degree from California State University, Sacramento, and a Master of Arts degree in Justice Administration and a Doctorate in Public Administration from Golden Gate University in San Francisco. Dr. Wilson is currently a professor of criminal justice at California State University, Sacramento. He has taught drug abuse recognition, enforcement, and policy to police officers and students of criminal justice for more than 20 years.

McGraw-Hill/Dushkin

2460 Kerper Blvd., Dubuque, IA 52001

Visit us on the Internet
http://www.dushkin.com

DEMCO

Credits

1. **Living With Drugs**
   Unit photo—© CORBIS/Royalty-Free
2. **Understanding How Drugs Work—Use, Dependency, and Addiction**
   Unit photo—© Getty Images/Scott T. Baxter
3. **The Major Drugs of Use and Abuse**
   Unit photo—© CORBIS/Royalty-Free
4. **Other Trends in Drug Use**
   Unit photo—PhotoDisc, Inc.
5. **Drugs and Crime**
   Unit photo—© Getty Images/Javier Pierini
6. **Measuring the Social Cost of Drugs**
   Unit photo—© Getty Images/PhotoLink?F. Schussler
7. **Creating and Sustaining Effective Drug Control Policy**
   Unit photo—© CORBIS/Royalty-Free
8. **Prevention, Treatment, and Education**
   Unit photo—© Getty Images/PhotoLink/D. Falconer

Copyright

Cataloging in Publication Data
Main entry under title: Annual Editions: Drugs, Society, and Behavior. 2005/2006.
1. Drugs, Society, and Behavior—Periodicals. I. Wilson, Hugh T., *comp*. II. Title: Drugs, Society, and Behavior.
ISBN 0–07–310824–3   658'.05   ISSN 1091–9945

Twentieth Edition

Cover image © Corbis/Royalty Free
Printed in the United States of America   1234567890QPDQPD0987654   Printed on Recycled Paper

Editors/Advisory Board

Members of the Advisory Board are instrumental in the final selection of articles for each edition of ANNUAL EDITIONS. Their review of articles for content, level, currentness, and appropriateness provides critical direction to the editor and staff. We think that you will find their careful consideration well reflected in this volume.

EDITOR

Hugh T. Wilson
California State University - Sacramento

ADVISORY BOARD

A. Michael Anch
St. Louis University

William T. Bailey
Indiana University

Valentine J. Belfiglio
Texas Woman's University

James W. Brown
Cornell College

Tyrone R. Burkett
Pennsylvania State University - Abington

W. William Chen
University of Florida - Gainesville

Michael R. Davey
Western Illinois University

Nancy T. Davis
The Richard Stockton College of New Jersey

Marc Gellman
University of Miami

Raymond Goldberg
SUNY at Cortland

Robert L. Hale
Shippensburg University

Bryan E. Hedrick
University of North Florida

Heath Hoffman
College of Charleston

Darrell D. Irwin
University of North Carolina at Wilmington

John Janowiak
Appalachian State University

Mary P. Lefkarites
Hunter College

Judith K. Muhammad
University of Phoenix - Detroit Campus

James Rothenberger
University of Minnesota - St. Paul

Stephen B. Thomas
Emory University

Alex Waigandt
University of Missouri - Columbia

William O. Walker
Florida International University

Staff

EDITORIAL STAFF

Larry Loeppke, Managing Editor
Susan Brusch, Senior Developmental Editor
Jay Oberbroeckling, Developmental Editor
Lenny J. Behnke, Permissions Coordinator
Lori Church, Permissions Coordinator
Shirley Lanners, Permissions Coordinator
Bonnie Coakley, Editorial Assistant

TECHNOLOGY STAFF

Luke David, eContent Coordinator

PRODUCTION STAFF

Beth Kundert, Production Manager
Trish Mish, Production Assistant
Jade Benedict, Production Assistant
Kari Voss, Lead Typesetter
Jean Smith, Typesetter
Karen Spring, Typesetter
Sandy Wille, Typesetter
Tara McDermott, Designer
Maggie Lytle, Cover Graphics

Preface

In publishing ANNUAL EDITIONS we recognize the enormous role played by the magazines, newspapers, and journals of the public press in providing current, first-rate educational information in a broad spectrum of interest areas. Many of these articles are appropriate for students, researchers, and professionals seeking accurate, current material to help bridge the gap between principles and theories and the real world. These articles, however, become more useful for study when those of lasting value are carefully collected, organized, indexed, and reproduced in a low-cost format, which provides easy and permanent access when the material is needed. That is the role played by ANNUAL EDITIONS.

It is difficult to define the framework by which Americans make decisions and develop perspectives on the use of drugs. There is no predictable expression of ideology. A wide range of individual and collective experience defines our national will towards drugs.

Despite drug prevention efforts, millions of Americans use illegal drugs on a monthly basis' and over 22 million are estimated to need drug treatment. Social costs from drugs are measured in the billions. Drugs impact almost every aspect of public and private life. Drugs are the subjects of presidential elections, congressional appointments, military interventions, and as observed this past year, the Olympic Games in Athens. Financial transactions from smuggling help sustain terrorist organizations. Drugs impact families, schools, health care systems, and governments in more places and in more ways than many believe imaginable.

Although it takes little effort to expose evil manifested by the abuse of drugs, there are tiny victories through which harm from drug abuse can be reduced. Scientific discovery relative to creating a new understanding of the processes of addiction is one. New treatment modalities, the successful use of drug courts, and the political support to expand these concepts has reduced drug-related impacts. In 2004 the Federal Government launched a 100 million dollar grant program to assist individuals in obtaining treatment and recovery services. The program included a proposal to double the amount in 2005. Although good evidence suggests that many of the most egregious forms of drug abuse have leveled off or been reduced, other disturbing trends—such as the non-medical use of prescription drugs—are emerging forcefully. Reducing harm is probably all that is possible. Drug abuse is a multifaceted problem requiring a multifaceted response. Complacency, encouraged by positive trends, has finally been recognized as a fatal mistake.

The articles contained in *Annual Editions: Drugs, Society, and Behavior 05/06* are a collection of facts, issues, and perspectives designed to provide the reader with a framework for examining current drug-related issues. The book is designed to offer students something to think about and something with which to think. It is a unique collection of materials of interest to the casual as well as the serious student of drug-related social phenomena. Unit 1 addresses the significance that drugs have in affecting diverse aspects of American life. It emphasizes the often-overlooked reality that drugs, legal and illegal, have remained a pervasive dimension of past as well as present American history. Unit 2 examines the ways that drugs affect the mind and body that result in dependence and addiction. Unit 3 examines the major drugs of use and abuse, along with issues relative to understanding the individual impacts of these drugs on society. This unit also illustrates the necessity to perceive the differences and similarities produced by the use of legal and illegal drugs. Unit 4 reviews the dynamic nature of drugs as it relates to changing patterns and trends of use. This unit gives special attention this year to designer drugs, particularly those that have fueled such controversy in sports this past year. Unit 5 focuses on the social costs of drug abuse and why the costs overwhelm many American institutions. Unit 6 illustrates the complexity and controversy in creating and implementing drug policy. Unit 7 concludes the book with discussions of current strategies for preventing and treating drug abuse. Can we deter people from harming themselves with drugs, and can we cure people addicted to drugs? What does work and what does not?

Annual Editions: Drugs, Society, and Behavior 05/06 contains a number of features that are designed to make the volume "user friendly." These include a *table of contents* with abstracts that summarize each article and key concepts in boldface, a *topic guide* to help locate articles on specific individuals or subjects, *World Wide Web links* that can be used to further explore the topics, and a comprehensive index.

We encourage your comments and criticisms on the articles provided and kindly ask for your review on the postage-paid rating form at the end of the book.

Hugh T. Wilson

Hugh T. Wilson
Editor

Contents

Preface   iv

Topic Guide   xii

Selected World Wide Web Sites   xiv

UNIT 1
Living with Drugs

Unit Overview   xvi

1. **Medicating Young Minds,** Jeffrey Kluger, *Time,* November 2, 2003
   Medications can ease the symptoms of such things as anxiety to attention deficit
   disorder. But the long-term effects of ***prescription pill-popping by kids*** are still
   unknown. Some physicians' argue it is out of control.   3

2. **Too Many Kids Smoke,** Dianna Gordon, *State Legislatures,* March
   2004
   Although teen smoking rates have fallen, more than ***2,000 American children
   between the ages of 12 and 17 become cigarette smokers every day***. The
   author argues that three factors: stress, boredom, and too much spending money
   are to blame.   8

3. **Drug Research and Children,** Michelle Meadows, *FDA Consumer,*
   January/February 2003
   Almost 80 percent of drugs have not been approved for pediatric use, but recent
   studies are providing important information about ***drug safety and effectiveness
   for children.*** Pediatricians say "it's about time."   10

4. **In Pursuit of Doped Excellence: The Lab Animal,** Michael
   Sokolove, *The New York Times Magazine,* January 12, 2004
   Elite athletes always have and always will pursue every competitive advantage—
   health and the law be damned. ***Is genetic manipulation next***?   15

5. **Is the Drug War Over? The Declining Proportion of Drug Offenders,**
   Graham Farrell and David E. Carter, *Corrections Compendium,* February 2003
   Is it possible that the drug war has not been the principal reason for recent ***prison
   population increases***? Could it be that one of the most infamous eras of incarceration in U.S. history is coming to a close? The authors examine the possible
   causes of the trends.   24

6. **So Here's to Privatizing the Public Costs of Alcohol Abuse,** Konrad Moore, *The Sacramento Bee,* May 2, 2004
   As matters of economic analysis, ***alcohol and tobacco carry high societal price
   tags***. But in California and other states, alcohol companies are immune from
   product liability. Many argue it is time for this to change.   29

7. **A Prescription for Abuse,** Russell Schanlaub, *Law and Order,* November 2003
   Most people who take prescription drugs use them in a responsible manner. More
   than nine million Americans, however, use ***prescription drugs for non-medical
   reasons***.   31

The concepts in bold italics are developed in the article. For further expansion, please refer to the Topic Guide and the Index.

UNIT 2
Understanding How Drugs Work—Use, Dependency, and Addiction

Unit Overview   **34**

8. **The Surprising Truth About Addiction,** Stanton Peele, *Psychology Today,* May/June 2004
   More people quit addictions than maintain them, and they do so on their own. This article discusses **what it takes to overcome bitter addictions**.   **37**

9. **The Addicted Brain,** Eric J. Nestler and Robert C. Malenka, *Scientific American,* March 2004
   Drug abuse produces long-term changes in the reward circuitry of the brain. Knowledge of the cellular and molecular details of these adaptations could lead to new treatments for **the compulsive behaviors that underlie addiction**.   **40**

10. **The End of Craving,** Michael Abrams, *Discover,* May 2003
    A controversial **new anti-addictive drug** is being studied. Made from the root bark of an African shrub, it may signal the end to craving.   **45**

11. **A New Treatment for Addiction,** Etienne Benson, *Monitor on Psychology,* June 2003
    The approval by the FDA of a new medication may reshape the landscape of **opiate addiction treatment.** Can it help the more than 1 million Americans who need it?   **47**

12. **More Than a Kick,** Kendall Morgan, *Science News,* March 22, 2003
    Scientists generally attribute nicotine's power to the activity it stimulates in the brain. This article discusses some of the latest scientific discoveries relative to this powerful drug.   **50**

13. **The Down Side of Up,** Alexis Jetter, *Health,* May 2004
    Paxil has made life worth living for people around the world; but **for those who want off**, this wonder drug can be frightening.   **53**

14. **Finding the Future Alcoholic,** Steven Stocker, *The Futurist,* May/June 2002
    Scientists may soon be able to **identify children who are likely to become alcoholics**. But Will society be able to prevent their addiction?   **58**

15. **Research Finds Alcohol Tolerance Gene,** Carl Hall, *The San Francisco Chronicle,* December 12, 2003
    Why is it that some people seem to handle their liquor better than others? Recent findings shed new light on **mankind's favorite drug of abuse**.   **62**

16. **In the Grip of a Deeper Pain,** Jerry Adler, *Newsweek,* October 20, 2003
    For people with **chronic pain,** synthetic **opioids** are a wonderful gift; for other people, they are a **prescription for abuse**.   **63**

UNIT 3
The Major Drugs of Use and Abuse

Unit Overview   **66**

17. **Alcohol's Deadly Triple Threat,** Karen Springen and Barbara Kantrowitz, *Newsweek,* May 10, 2004
    Women get addicted faster, seek help less often, and are more likely to die from the bottle. This article addresses the specific health issues related to women's use of alcohol.   **69**

The concepts in bold italics are developed in the article. For further expansion, please refer to the Topic Guide and the Index.

18. **When Drinking Helps,** Janet Raloff, *Science News,* March 8, 2003
One person's therapeutic nip may prove to be another's mistake. "With dozens of conflicting reports spilling out each year, is it any wonder that the public is confused about *alcohol and health*?"   71

19. **Binge Drinking Holds Steady: College Students Continue to Drink Despite Programs,** Alvin Powell, *Harvard University Gazette,* April 4, 2002
In spite of numerous programs targeting *drinking by college students*, the rate of binge drinking has stayed consistent for the past 10 years. This article discusses the forces that have long propelled this phenomenon.   74

20. **Dangerous Supplements Still at Large,** *Consumer Reports,* May 2004
If you can buy it at a clean, well-lighted store and it's "all-natural," it's not going to hurt you, right? This article discusses that some *dietary supplements are just too dangerous* to be on the market.   76

21. **Addicted to Anti-Depressants?,** Stephen Fried, *Glamour,* April 2003
Although for many patients Paxil, a top-selling anti-depressant, works amazingly well. Others say that *getting off the drug has involved true withdrawal.* Why weren't they warned?   82

22. **Stronger Pot, Bigger Worries,** David Wahlberg, *The Sacramento Bee,* May 5, 2004
It's not your parent's marijuana: *today's drug has nearly five times the level of THC than was in the pot of the 1970s.*   86

23. **Inside Dope,** Quentin Hardy, *Forbes,* November 10, 2003
Canada's 7 billion dollar marijuana production exceeds profits generated by cattle ranching, wheat farming, or forestry products. Only oil and gas are bigger.   88

24. **Heroin Hits Small-Town America,** Tim Jones, *Chicago Tribune,* May 4, 2003
This account of how the *drug trade* and *drug addiction* can destroy *family life* in a *small Ohio town* is just one snapshot of the rising tide of *heroin abuse* in *small towns* in the Midwest. Police in a 10-county area of northern Ohio blame it on proximity to larger cities.   93

25. **What You Need to Know About Club Drugs: Rave On,** Kerri Wachter, *Family Practice News,* November 15, 2003
In this article family practitioners discuss basic observations associated with the use of *popular club drugs such as Ecstacy and GHB.*   96

UNIT 4
Other Trends in Drug Use

Unit Overview   98

26. **Blowing the Whistle on Drugs,** Mark Starr, *Newsweek,* November 3, 2003
Many argue that an *epidemic of performance enhancing drug use* is at the heart of sports culture from pro sports to almost every Olympic venue. This article discusses how one raid on a California laboratory has changed sports history.   101

27. **Baseball Takes a Hit,** Richard Corliss, *Time,* March 15, 2004
Another steroid probe involving top players threatens to blight the game, anger fans, and alter the record books.   103

The concepts in bold italics are developed in the article. For further expansion, please refer to the Topic Guide and the Index.

28. **Designer Steroids: Ugly, Dangerous Things,** Ken Mannie, *Coach and Athletic Director,* April 2004
    Designer steroids are in the news and many ***athletes are running for cover****.* This collegiate strength and conditioning coach says the situation is getting uglier by the minute.   **105**

29. **Ever Farther, Ever Faster, Ever Higher?,** *The Economist,* August 7, 2004
    This past year has provided ample evidence that "doping" in sports is rife. This article presents details on how athletes at the summer Olympics in Athens were ***tested for drug doping****.*   **108**

30. **Life or Meth?,** *Outword Magazine,* March 13–27, 2003
    Methamphetamine—a powerful form of speed—delivers a euphoric high, much like that of heroin and cocaine. Known as "crystal meth," it is just as destructive and its use is growing among gay men.   **112**

31. **Teens Tell Truth About Drugs,** Michael Shaw, *The Times Educational Supplement,* September 19, 2003
    Cannabis before school and whisky during lessons—***students in London reveal all regarding their drug habits****.*   **116**

32. **Prescription Drug Abuse: FDA and SAMHSA Join Forces,** Michelle Meadows, *FDA Consumer,* March/April 2003
    When 19-year-old Kyle Moores of Manassas, Virginia, discovered that his abuse of the ***pain reliever oxycontin*** had left him in debt and unable to hold a job, he finally sought help for his addiction. He serves as one example in the government's new effort to control ***prescription drug abuse.*** Can it work?   **117**

33. **Adolescent OxyContin Abuse,** Debra A. Katz, M.D. and Lon R. Hays, M.D., *Journal of American Academy of Child and Adolescent Psychiatry,* February 2004
    Oxycontin*,* a powerful prescription pain reliever, has become a popular alternative to street drugs such as heroin. It is the number one prescribed Schedule 11 narcotic in the U.S. ***The authors discuss how kids get involved with it.***   **119**

34. **Warning Label: Teens Find a Dangerous, Cheap High in Over-the-Counter Cough Medicine,** Will Evans, *The Sacramento Bee,* January 29, 2004
    DXM, Dex, Skittles, Red Devils, Triple C, Robo—teens find a dangerous, ***cheap high in over-the-counter cough medicine****.*   **123**

UNIT 5
Measuring the Social Cost of Drugs

Unit Overview   **126**

35. **Policing a Rural Plague,** Dirk Johnson, *Newsweek,* March 8, 2004
    Since 1996, the police seizure of meth labs has gone up 500 percent to 9,368 last year. ***Meth is ravaging the Midwest. Why is it so hard to stop****?*   **129**

36. **About Face Program Turns Lives Around,** Mary Baldwin Kennedy, *Corrections Today,* April 2003
    Think ***steroids*** are just about making it in the pros? This high school user reveals how his search for speed and strength ended with a needle.   **131**

37. **Drug-Endangered Children,** Jerry Harris, *The FBI Law Enforcement Bulletin,* February 2004
    The number of children in the U.S. exposed to the inherently dangerous process of manufacturing methamphetamine has increased alarmingly. This article discusses the growing problem of ***children forced into association with methamphetamine****.*   **134**

The concepts in bold italics are developed in the article. For further expansion, please refer to the Topic Guide and the Index.

38. **Fetal Exposure to Drugs,** Tina Hesman, *The Press Democrat,* February 15, 2004

Research is shedding new light on the complex relationships between *fetal exposure to drugs and mental illness* later in life. As few as two drinks may kill fetal brain cells. **137**

39. **FDA Was Urged to Limit Kids' Antidepressants,** Rob Waters, *The San Francisco Chronicle,* April 16, 2004

Dr. Andrew Mosholder, an epidemiologist in the Office of Drug Safety, reported that *some antidepressants doubled the risk of suicide in children.* Do physicians have the necessary information to adequately consider the risk to children when prescribing antidepressants. **139**

40. **Date Rape Drugs,** John DePresca, *Law and Order,* October 2003

Roofies, saltwater, and Special K are not the ingredients to make a low fat, diet breakfast or the name of a new rock band. They are terms for *drugs used to render a victim defenseless to sexual assault.* This article discusses the relationship between these drugs and rape. **141**

UNIT 6
Creating and Sustaining Effective Drug Control Policy

Unit Overview **144**

41. **Queen Victoria's Cannabis Use: Or, How History Does and Does Not Get Used in Drug Policy Making,** Virginia Berridge, *Addiciton Research and Theory,* August 2003

The author of this article argues that historical policy analysis evolves as a reciprocal tool of policy makers—*what every policy maker should consider.* **147**

42. **Social Consequences of the War on Drugs: The Legacy of Failed Policy,** Eric L. Jensen, Jurg Gerber, and Clayton Mosher, *Criminal Justice Policy Review,* March 2004

This article argues that criminologists have failed to recognize many *significant implications of the drug war* while others argue that such negative implications have occurred in spite of the drug war, not becuase of it—which is correct? **149**

43. **How to Win the Drug War,** James Gray, *Liberty,* May 2003

James Gray argues that unless we change our approach, we will not be able to halt the *use and abuse of drugs.* **159**

44. **Tokin' Politics: Making Marijuana Law Reform An Election Issue,** Paul Armentano, *Heads,* May 2004

A pro-marijuana reform organization argues that neither George Bush nor John Kerry are for marijuana reform—does this article address *marijuana reform,* or something else? **162**

45. **Drug Legalization,** Douglas Husak, *Criminal Justice Ethics,* Winter/ Spring 2003

Philosopher Douglas Husak, in *support of legalizing drugs,* asserts that none of the standard arguments for criminalizing drugs are any good and that there is little evidence that drug laws deter drug use. Do you agree? **166**

46. **On the Decriminalization of Drugs,** George Sher, *Criminal Justice Ethics,* Winter/Spring 2003

Philosophy Professor George Sher argues against the theories expressed in the article by Douglas Husak. Sher asserts that the *reasonable theories of criminalization* do allow governments to criminalize some drug using behavior simply on the grounds that the behavior is risky, not only for the individual but for society. Do you agree? **174**

The concepts in bold italics are developed in the article. For further expansion, please refer to the Topic Guide and the Index.

47. Against the Legalization of Heroin, Peter De Marneffe, *Criminal Justice Ethics,* Winter/Spring 2003

In this third related article, philosopher Peter De Marneffe states that with respect to **heroin**, the social burdens associated with **prohibition** are justified—do you agree? 178

48. U.S., Canada Clash on Pot Laws, Donna Leinwand, *USA Today,* May 8, 2003

The Bush administration is hinting at sanctions if Canadian lawmakers do not act to prevent more **potent Canadian marijuana** from entering the United States. 184

UNIT 7
Prevention, Treatment, and Education

Unit Overview 186

49. Drug Treatment: The Willard Option, Melvin L. Williams, *Corrections Today,* April 2004

In drug treatment, everyone including the client must realize that drug abuse is a personal issue. For addicted inmates, however, accepting blame for one's plight has many connotations. This article discusses how one innovative treatment program is making progress in the **treatment of offenders with drug problems**. 189

50. Strategies to Improve Offender Outcomes in Treatment, Faye Taxman, *Corrections Today,* April 2004

Economic **costs associated with the incarceration of drug-related offenders** are in the billions. Many argue that not treating an offender's addiction produces a virtual guarantee for recidivism. This article discusses new strategies for addressing this costly problem. 194

51. Marijuana: Just Say No Again: The Old Failures of New and Improved Anti-drug Education, Renee Moilanen, *Reason,* January 2004

The mantra "Just Say No" became a national punch line for a reason: it didn't keep kids away from drugs. This article reviews current thinking on **drug education for teens**. 199

52. Binge Drinking: Not the Word of Choice, Fern Walter Goodhart, Linda C. Lederman, Lea P. Stewart, and Lisa Laitman, *Journal of American College Health,* July/August 2003

"Binge drinking" is a term commonly used to describe problem drinking by college students. The authors assert that students don't identify with this term and that **new ways of defining problem drinking are needed**. 204

53. A New Weapon in the War on Drugs: Family, Alexandra Marks, *The Christian Science Monitor,* April 30, 2003

A New York program that focuses on the family is a revolutionary **new model for drug treatment**. 207

54. National Survey Finds Strong Public Support for Treatment, *Alcoholism & Drug Abuse Weekly,* May 17, 2004

Results of a groundbreaking survey find **overwhelming public support for addiction treatment**. 209

55. Addicted, Neglectful Moms Offered Treatment, Custody, Henri E. Cauvin, *The Washington Post,* May 2, 2003

Henri Cauvin discusses some innovative ideas to address the difficult situation of **drug-dependent mothers** who wined up in Superior Court because they have neglected their children. 210

The concepts in bold italics are developed in the article. For further expansion, please refer to the Topic Guide and the Index.

56. **Consumer Direction, Self-Determination and Person-Centered Treatment,** *Alcoholism & Drug Abuse Weekly,* March 15, 2004
Alcohol, drug prevention, and treatment communities tend to be program-centered rather than *person-centered*. This article argues that it is time to rethink this position.   **211**

57. **SACHR: An Example of an Integrated, Harm Reduction Drug Treatment Program,** Bart Majoor and Joyce Rivera, *Journal of Substance Abuse Treatment,* March 2003
This article explains how the *concept of harm reduction*, as administered through the St. Ann's Corner of Harm Reduction in the Bronx, New York, exists as a viable option for deterring and treating drug abuse. Is this a successful role model and should it command wider attention in drug policy decision making in the U.S.?   **213**

Index   **218**
Test Your Knowledge Form   **222**
Article Rating Form   **223**

The concepts in bold italics are developed in the article. For further expansion, please refer to the Topic Guide and the Index.

Topic Guide

This topic guide suggests how the selections in this book relate to the subjects covered in your course. You may want to use the topics listed on these pages to search the Web more easily.

On the following pages a number of Web sites have been gathered specifically for this book. They are arranged to reflect the units of this *Annual Edition.* You can link to these sites by going to the DUSHKIN ONLINE support site at *http://www.dushkin.com/online/.*

ALL THE ARTICLES THAT RELATE TO EACH TOPIC ARE LISTED BELOW THE BOLD-FACED TERM.

Addiction

4. In Pursuit of Doped Excellence: The Lab Animal
7. A Prescription for Abuse
8. The Surprising Truth About Addiction
9. The Addicted Brain
10. The End of Craving
11. A New Treatment for Addiction
15. Research Finds Alcohol Tolerance Gene
16. In the Grip of a Deeper Pain
18. When Drinking Helps
19. Binge Drinking Holds Steady: College Students Continue to Drink Despite Programs
21. Addicted to Anti-Depressants?
22. Stronger Pot, Bigger Worries
24. Heroin Hits Small-Town America
30. Life or Meth?
55. Addicted, Neglectful Moms Offered Treatment, Custody

Alcoholism

6. So Here's to Privatizing the Public Costs of Alcohol Abuse
14. Finding the Future Alcoholic
18. When Drinking Helps
19. Binge Drinking Holds Steady: College Students Continue to Drink Despite Programs
38. Fetal Exposure to Drugs
52. Binge Drinking: Not the Word of Choice

Amphetamines

30. Life or Meth?
35. Policing a Rural Plague
37. Drug-Endangered Children
40. Date Rape Drugs

Anxiety

17. Alcohol's Deadly Triple Threat

Cocaine

45. Drug Legalization
46. On the Decriminalization of Drugs

College

19. Binge Drinking Holds Steady: College Students Continue to Drink Despite Programs

Depression

17. Alcohol's Deadly Triple Threat

Designer drugs

25. What You Need to Know About Club Drugs: Rave On
26. Blowing the Whistle on Drugs
27. Baseball Takes a Hit
28. Designer Steroids: Ugly, Dangerous Things
29. Ever Farther, Ever Faster, Ever Higher?
40. Date Rape Drugs

Drug abuse

17. Alcohol's Deadly Triple Threat

Drug economy

6. So Here's to Privatizing the Public Costs of Alcohol Abuse
19. Binge Drinking Holds Steady: College Students Continue to Drink Despite Programs
21. Addicted to Anti-Depressants?
23. Inside Dope
30. Life or Meth?
45. Drug Legalization

Drug policy

5. Is the Drug War Over? The Declining Proportion of Drug Offenders
40. Date Rape Drugs
42. Social Consequences of the War on Drugs: The Legacy of Failed Policy
43. How to Win the Drug War
44. Tokin' Politics: Making Marijuana Law Reform An Election Issue
45. Drug Legalization
46. On the Decriminalization of Drugs
47. Against the Legalization of Heroin
48. U.S., Canada Clash on Pot Laws

Drug treatment

10. The End of Craving
11. A New Treatment for Addiction
14. Finding the Future Alcoholic
36. About Face Program Turns Lives Around
49. Drug Treatment: The Willard Option
50. Strategies to Improve Offender Outcomes in Treatment
51. Marijuana: Just Say No Again: The Old Failures of New and Improved Anti-drug Education
52. Binge Drinking: Not the Word of Choice
53. A New Weapon in the War on Drugs: Family
54. National Survey Finds Strong Public Support for Treatment
55. Addicted, Neglectful Moms Offered Treatment, Custody
56. Consumer Direction, Self-Determination and Person-Centered Treatment

Epidemiology

4. In Pursuit of Doped Excellence: The Lab Animal
5. Is the Drug War Over? The Declining Proportion of Drug Offenders
8. The Surprising Truth About Addiction
9. The Addicted Brain
10. The End of Craving
13. The Down Side of Up
19. Binge Drinking Holds Steady: College Students Continue to Drink Despite Programs
26. Blowing the Whistle on Drugs
29. Ever Farther, Ever Faster, Ever Higher?
30. Life or Meth?
31. Teens Tell Truth About Drugs
32. Prescription Drug Abuse: FDA and SAMHSA Join Forces
33. Adolescent OxyContin Abuse
39. FDA Was Urged to Limit Kids' Antidepressants
45. Drug Legalization
46. On the Decriminalization of Drugs

Etiology

4. In Pursuit of Doped Excellence: The Lab Animal
7. A Prescription for Abuse
8. The Surprising Truth About Addiction
9. The Addicted Brain
13. The Down Side of Up
14. Finding the Future Alcoholic
15. Research Finds Alcohol Tolerance Gene
18. When Drinking Helps
19. Binge Drinking Holds Steady: College Students Continue to Drink Despite Programs

Gender and drug use

30. Life or Meth?
31. Teens Tell Truth About Drugs
40. Date Rape Drugs
55. Addicted, Neglectful Moms Offered Treatment, Custody

Heroin

11. A New Treatment for Addiction
16. In the Grip of a Deeper Pain
24. Heroin Hits Small-Town America
47. Against the Legalization of Heroin

Law enforcement

22. Stronger Pot, Bigger Worries
23. Inside Dope
24. Heroin Hits Small-Town America
30. Life or Meth?
35. Policing a Rural Plague
36. About Face Program Turns Lives Around
37. Drug-Endangered Children
40. Date Rape Drugs

Legalization

22. Stronger Pot, Bigger Worries
23. Inside Dope
45. Drug Legalization
46. On the Decriminalization of Drugs
47. Against the Legalization of Heroin

Marijuana

22. Stronger Pot, Bigger Worries
23. Inside Dope
31. Teens Tell Truth About Drugs
44. Tokin' Politics: Making Marijuana Law Reform An Election Issue
45. Drug Legalization
48. U.S., Canada Clash on Pot Laws
51. Marijuana: Just Say No Again: The Old Failures of New and Improved Anti-drug Education

Nicotine

2. Too Many Kids Smoke
12. More Than a Kick

Over-the-counter drugs

20. Dangerous Supplements Still at Large
34. Warning Label: Teens Find a Dangerous, Cheap High in Over-the-Counter Cough Medicine

Prescription drugs

1. Medicating Young Minds
3. Drug Research and Children
7. A Prescription for Abuse
13. The Down Side of Up
16. In the Grip of a Deeper Pain
21. Addicted to Anti-Depressants?
32. Prescription Drug Abuse: FDA and SAMHSA Join Forces
33. Adolescent OxyContin Abuse
39. FDA Was Urged to Limit Kids' Antidepressants

Prevention

14. Finding the Future Alcoholic

Prison

36. About Face Program Turns Lives Around

Race and drug use

29. Ever Farther, Ever Faster, Ever Higher?
31. Teens Tell Truth About Drugs
35. Policing a Rural Plague
37. Drug-Endangered Children

Research

3. Drug Research and Children
9. The Addicted Brain
10. The End of Craving
11. A New Treatment for Addiction
12. More Than a Kick
18. When Drinking Helps
29. Ever Farther, Ever Faster, Ever Higher?
30. Life or Meth?
38. Fetal Exposure to Drugs
39. FDA Was Urged to Limit Kids' Antidepressants
54. National Survey Finds Strong Public Support for Treatment

World Wide Web Sites

The following World Wide Web sites have been carefully researched and selected to support the articles found in this reader. The easiest way to access these selected sites is to go to our DUSHKIN ONLINE support site at *http://www.dushkin.com/online/*.

AE: Drugs, Society, & Behavior 05/06

The following sites were available at the time of publication. Visit our Web site—we update DUSHKIN ONLINE regularly to reflect any changes.

General Sources

Alcohol and Drug Links
http://www.realsolutions.org/druglink.htm

This set of Internet links provides information on Alcohol and Drug Use and Abuse. These links have been gathered by Real Solutions, a nonprofit organization dedicated to the needs of family and community.

Higher Education Center for Alcohol and Other Drug Prevention
http://www.edc.org/hec/

The U.S. Department of Education established the Higher Education Center for Alcohol and Other Drug Prevention to provide nationwide support for campus alcohol and other drug prevention efforts. The Center is working with colleges, universities, and preparatory schools throughout the country to develop strategies for changing campus culture, to foster environments that promote healthy lifestyles, and to prevent illegal alcohol and other drug use among students.

National Clearinghouse for Alcohol and Drug Information
http://www.health.org

This site provides information to teens about the problems and ramifications of drug use and abuse. There are numerous links to drug-related informational sites.

UNIT 1: Living with Drugs

National Council on Alcoholism and Drug Dependence, Inc.
http://www.ncadd.org

According to its Web site, The National Council on Alcoholism and Drug Dependence provides education, information, help, and hope in the fight against the chronic, and sometimes fatal, disease of alcoholism and other drug addictions.

UNIT 2: Understanding How Drugs Work—Use, Dependency, and Addiction

Centre for Addiction and Mental Health (CAMH)
http://www.camh.net

One of the largest addictions facilities in Canada, CAMH advances an understanding of addiction and translates this knowledge into resources that can be used to prevent problems and to provide effective treatments.

The National Center on Addiction and Substance Abuse at Columbia University
http://www.casacolumbia.org

The National Center on Addiction and Substance Abuse at Columbia University is a unique think/action tank that brings together all of the professional disciplines (health policy, medicine and nursing, communications, economics, sociology and anthropology, law and law enforcement, business, religion, and education) needed to study and combat all forms of substance abuse—illegal drugs, pills, alcohol, and tobacco—as they affect all aspects of society.

National Institute on Drug Abuse (NIDA)
http://www.nida.nih.gov

NIDA's mission is to lead the nation in bringing the power of science to bear on drug abuse and addiction.

UNIT 3: The Major Drugs of Use and Abuse

QuitNet
http://www.quitnet.org

The QuitNet helps smokers control their nicotine addiction. This site operates in association with the Boston University School of Public Health.

UNIT 4: Other Trends in Drug Use

Marijuana as a Medicine
http://mojo.calyx.net/~olsen/

This site promotes the concept of marijuana as medicine. This is a controversial issue that has been in the news quite a bit over the past few years. At this site, you will find numerous links to other sites that support this idea, as well as information developed specifically for this site.

UNIT 5: Measuring the Social Cost of Drugs

Drug Enforcement Administration
http://www.usdoj.gov/dea/

The mission of the Drug Enforcement Administration is to enforce the controlled substances laws and regulations of the United States.

The November Coalition
http://www.november.org

The November Coalition is a growing body of citizens whose lives have been gravely affected by the present drug policy. This group represents convicted prisoners, their loved ones, and others who believe that U.S. drug policies are unfair and unjust.

TRAC DEA Site
http://trac.syr.edu/tracdea/index.html

The Transactional Records Access Clearinghouse (TRAC) is a data gathering, data research, and data distribution organization associated with Syracuse University. According to its Web site, the purpose of TRAC is to provide the American people—and institutions of oversight such as Congress, news organizations, public interest groups, businesses, scholars, and lawyers—with comprehensive information about the activities of federal enforcement and regulatory agencies and the communities in which they take place.

UNIT 6: Creating and Sustaining Effective Drug

Control Policy

DrugText
http://www.drugtext.org

The DrugText library consists of individual drug-related libraries with independent search capabilities.

The National Organization on Fetal Alcohol Syndrome (NOFAS)
http://www.nofas.org

NOFAS is a nonprofit organization founded in 1990 dedicated to eliminating birth defects caused by alcohol consumption during pregnancy and improving the quality of life for those individuals and families affected. NOFAS is the only national organization focusing solely on fetal alcohol syndrome (FAS), the leading known cause of mental retardation.

National NORML Homepage
http://www.norml.org/

This is the home page for the National Organization for the Reform of Marijuana Laws.

UNIT 7: Prevention, Treatment, and Education

The Drug Reform Coordination Network (DRC)
http://www.drcnet.org

According to its home page, the DRC Network is committed to reforming current drug laws in the United States.

Drug Watch International
http://www.drugwatch.org

Drug Watch International is a volunteer nonprofit information network and advocacy organization that promotes the creation of healthy drug-free cultures in the world and opposes the legalization of drugs. The organization upholds a comprehensive approach to drug issues involving prevention, education, intervention/treatment, and law enforcement/interdiction.

United Nations International Drug Control Program (UNDCP)
http://www.undcp.org

The mission of UNDCP is to work with the nations and the people of the world to tackle the global drug problem and its consequences.

Marijuana Policy Project
http://www.mpp.org

The purpose of the Marijuana Policy Project is to develop and promote policies to minimize the harm associated with marijuana.

Office of National Drug Control Policy (ONDCP)
http://www.whitehousedrugpolicy.gov

The principal purpose of ONDCP is to establish policies, priorities, and objectives for the nation's drug control program, the goals of which are to reduce illicit drug use, manufacturing, and trafficking; drug-related crime and violence; and drug-related health consequences.

D.A.R.E.
http://www.dare-america.com

This year 33 million schoolchildren around the world—25 million in the United States—will benefit from D.A.R.E. (Drug Abuse Resistance Education), the highly acclaimed program that gives kids the skills they need to avoid involvement in drugs, gangs, or violence. D.A.R.E. was founded in 1983 in Los Angeles.

Hazelden
http://www.hazelden.org

Hazelden is a nonprofit organization providing high quality, affordable rehabilitation, education, prevention, and professional services and publications in chemical dependency and related disorders.

We highly recommend that you review our Web site for expanded information and our other product lines. We are continually updating and adding links to our Web site in order to offer you the most usable and useful information that will support and expand the value of your Annual Editions. You can reach us at: *http://www.dushkin.com/annualeditions/*.

UNIT 1
Living with Drugs

Unit Selections

1. **Medicating Young Minds**, Jeffrey Kluger
2. **Too Many Kids Smoke**, Dianna Gordon
3. **Drug Research and Children**, Michelle Meadows
4. **In Pursuit of Doped Excellence: The Lab Animal**, Michael Sokolove
5. **Is the Drug War Over? The Declining Proportion of Drug Offenders**, Graham Farrell and David E. Carter
6. **So Here's to Privatizing the Public Costs of Alcohol Abuse**, Konrad Moore
7. **A Prescription for Abuse**, Russell Schanlaub

Key Points to Consider

- Why is history important when attempting to understand contemporary drug-related events?

- What historical trends are expressed by the use of legal drugs versus illegal drugs?

- What are the historical drug-related landmarks of drug prohibition and control?

- How is the evolution of drug-related influence on American society like and unlike that occurring in other countries?

- What can we learn from these comparisons?

 **Links: www.dushkin.com/online/**
These sites are annotated in the World Wide Web pages.

National Council on Alcoholism and Drug Dependence, Inc.
http://www.ncadd.org

When attempting to define the American drug experience, one must examine the past as well as the present. Too often drug use and its associated phenomena are viewed through a contemporary looking glass relative to our personal views, biases, and perspectives. Although today's drug scene is definitely a product of the counterculture of the 1960s and 1970s, the crack trade of the 1980s, and the sophisticated, criminally syndicated, technologically efficient influence of the late 1980s and early 1990s, it is also a product of the more distant past. This past and the lessons it has generated, although largely unknown, forgotten, or ignored, provide one important perspective from which to assess our current status and to guide our future in terms of optimizing our efforts to manage the benefits and control the harm from legal and illegal drugs.

The American drug experience is often defined in terms of a million individual realities, all meaningful and all different. In fact, these realities often originated as pieces of our national, cultural, racial, religious, and personal past that combine to influence present-day drug-related phenomena significantly. The contemporary American drug experience is the product of centuries of human attempts to alter or sustain consciousness through the use of mind-altering drugs. Early American history

is replete with accounts of the exorbitant use of alcohol, opium, morphine, and cocaine.

Further review of this history clearly suggests the precedents for Americans' continuing pursuit of a vast variety of stimulant, depressant, and hallucinogenic drugs. Drug wars, drug epidemics, drug prohibitions, and escalating trends of alarming drug use patterns were present throughout the early history of the United States. During this period, the addictive properties of most drugs were largely unknown. Today, the addictive properties of almost all drugs are known. So why is it that so many drug-related lessons of the past repeat themselves in the face of such powerful new knowledge? Why is it that in 2005, Fetal Alcohol Syndrome remains as the leading preventable cause of mental retardation in infants? How is it that the pursuit of effects caused by drugs simply seems to defy the lessons of history? How big is the American drug problem and how is it measured? One important way of answering questions about drug abuse is by conducting research and analyzing data recovered through numerous reporting instruments. This data is in turn used to assess historical trends and make policy decisions in response to what has been learned.

An example of such data is from the leading source of information about drug use in America, the federal Substance Abuse and Mental Health Services Administration's National Survey on Drug Use and Health, released September of 2004, reports that there are 19.5 million Americans over 12 years of age who are current users of illicit drugs. The most widely used illicit drug is marijuana with 14.6 million users. Approximately 51 percent of Americans over 12 are drinkers of alcohol; 65 percent of full-time enrolled college students are binge drinkers (defined as consuming 5 or more drinks during a single drinking occasion). Approximately 30 percent of Americans over 12 use tobacco. The category consisting of 18–25 year olds represents the highest rate of tobacco use at 40.2 percent. Approximately 22 million people or 9.4 percent of the population, are believed to be drug-dependent on alcohol or illicit drugs. The size of the economy associated with drug use is staggering; Americans spent more than 70 billion dollars last year on illegal drugs alone.

Drugs impact our most powerful public institutions on many fronts. Drugs are *the* business of our criminal justice system, and drugs compete with terrorism, war, and other major national security concerns as demanding military issues. Many argue eloquently that drugs pose a "clear and present danger." Additional millions of dollars to fight drugs were pledged to South American countries this past year. Only terrorism and war distract the continuing military emphasis on drug fighting. As you read through the pages of this book, the pervasive nature of drug-related influences will become more apparent. Unfortunately, one of the most salient observations one can make is that drug use in our society is a topic about which many Americans have too little knowledge. History suggests that we have continually struggled to respond and react to the influence of drug use in our society. The lessons of our drug legacy are harsh, whether they are the subjects of public health or public policy. Turning an uninformed mind toward a social condition of such importance will only further our inability to address the dynamics of changing drug-related issues and problems.

Interestingly, since the September 11, 2001, terrorist bombings and the subsequent U.S. invasion of Iraq, research has identified certain drug trends also observed during previous national crises. The availability of illegal drugs, particularly heroin, declined in numerous reporting sites, apparently due to heightened security at U.S. airports and the borders. Heroin is now recognized as having surpassed crack as the drug associated with the most serious consequences. Oxycodone abuse, apparently influenced by heroin shortages, especially on the East Coast, has surged the past two years. The non-medical abuse of pain relievers is, in general, the most widely cited emerging drug problem and since September 11, the demand for drug treatment in such major Eastern cities such as New York City and Washington, D.C., has increased steadily.

The articles and graphics contained in this unit illustrate the multitude of issues influenced by the historical evolution of legal and illegal drug use in America. The historical development of drug-related phenomena is reflected within the character of all issues and controversies addressed by this book. Drug-related events of yesterday provide important meaning for understanding and addressing drug-related events of today and the future. Creating public policy and controlling crime surface immediately as examples with long-standing historical influences. As you read this and other literature on drug-related events, the dynamics of drug-related historical linkages will become apparent. As you read further, try to identify these historical linkages as they help define the focus at hand. For example, what are the implications for public health resulting from a historical lack of drug-related educational emphasis? What will history reflect twenty years from now? Is there a historical pattern of drug-related educational shortcomings that we should change?

MEDICATING YOUNG MINDS

Drugs have become increasingly popular for treating kids with mood and behavior problems. But how will that affect them in the long run?

By Jeffrey Kluger

GETTING BY IS HARD ENOUGH when you're 13. it's harder still when you've got other things on your mind—and Andrea Okeson had plenty to distract her. There were the constant stomach pains to consider; there was the nervousness, the distractibility, the overwhelming need to be alone. And, of course, there was the business of repeatedly checking the locks on the doors. All these things grew, inexplicably, to consume Andrea, until by the time she was through with the eighth grade, she seemed pretty much through with everything else too. "Andrea," said a teacher to her one day, "you look like death."

The problem, though neither Andrea nor her teacher knew it, was that her adolescent brain was being tossed by the neurochemical storms of generalized anxiety, obsessive-compulsive disorder (OCD) and attention-deficit/hyperactivity disorder (ADHD)—a decidedly lousy trifecta. If that was what eighth grade was, ninth was unimaginable.

But that was then. Andrea, now 18, is a freshman at the College of St. Catherine in St. Paul, Minn., enjoying her friends and her studies and looking forward to a career in fashion merchandising, all thanks to a bit of chemical stabilizing provided by a pair of pills: Lexapro, an antidepressant, and Adderall, a relatively new anti-ADHD drug. "I feel excited about things," Andrea says. "I feel like I got me back."

So a little medicine fixed what ailed a child. Good news all around, right? Well, yes—and no. Lexapro is the perfect an-swer for anxiety all right, provided you're willing to overlook the fact that it does its work by artificially manipulating the very chemicals responsible for feeling and thought. Adderall is the perfect answer for ADHD, provided you overlook the fact that it's a stimulant like Dexedrine. Oh, yes, you also have to overlook the fact that the Adderall has left Andrea with such side effects as weight loss and sleeplessness, and both drugs are being poured into a young brain that has years to go before it's finally fully formed. Still, says Andrea, "I'm just glad there were things that could be done."

Those things—whether Lexapro or Ritalin or Prozac or something else—are being done for more and more children in the U.S. and around the world. In fact, they are being done with such frequency that some people have justifiably begun to ask, Are we adults raising Generation R_x?

Just a few years ago, psychologists couldn't say with certainty that kids were even capable of suffering from depression the same way adults do. Now, according to PhRMA, a pharmaceutical trade group, up to 10% of all American kids may suffer from some mental illness. Perhaps twice that many have exhibited some symptoms of depression. Up to a million others may suffer from the alternately depressive and manic mood swings of bipolar disorder (BPD), one more condition that was thought until recently to be an affliction of adults alone. ADHD rates are exploding too.

According to a Mayo Clinic study, children between 5 and 19 have at least a 7.5% chance of being found to have ADHD, which amounts to nearly 5 million kids. Other children are receiving diagnoses and medication for obsessive-compulsive disorder, social-anxiety disorder, post-traumatic stress disorder (PTSD), pathological impulsiveness, sleeplessness, phobias and more.

Has the world—and Western societies in particular—simply become a more destabilizing place in which to raise children? Probably so. But other factors are at work, including sharp-eyed parents and doctors with a rising awareness of childhood mental illness and what can be done for it. "The scientific community thought that mental illness did not just start at 15 or 20 years old, but we didn't have the proper tools to diagnose it," says Rémi Quirion, director of the Institute of Neuroscience, Mental Health and Addiction of Canada. "Now we have developed more sophisticated tools and are more aware that these disorders could exist in young kids."

Also feeding the trend for more diagnoses is the arrival of whole new classes of psychotropic drugs with fewer side effects and greater efficacy than earlier medications, particularly the selective serotonin reuptake inhibitors (SSRIS), or antidepressants. While an earlier generation of antidepressants-tricyclics like Tofranil—didn't work in kids, SSRIS do. But the benefits of these SSRIS may not outweigh their risks. Last month British drug regulators recommended against the use of Paxil, Zoloft and three other SSRIS for children, citing links to suicidal thoughts and self-harm. Health Canada is now reviewing that link that has warned health-care professionals against prescribing Paxil to anyone 18 and under. It has also warned against the pediatric use of Effexor, a selective serotonin and norepinephrine reuptake inhibitor (SNRI).

> "OUR USAGE EXCEEDS OUR KNOWLEDGE BASE. **WE'RE LEARNING WHAT THESE DRUGS ARE** TO BE USED FOR, BUT LET'S FACE IT: **WE'RE EXPERIMENTING ON THESE KIDS."**
>
> —DR. GLEN ELLIOTT
> **UCSF Psychiatric Institute**

For now, nobody, not even the drug companies, argues that pills alone are the ideal answer to mental illness. Most experts believe that drugs are most effective when combined with talk therapy or other counseling. Nonetheless, the American Academy of Child and Adolescent Psychiatry now lists dozens of medications available for troubled kids, from the comparatively familiar Ritalin (for ADHD) to Zoloft and Celexa (for depression) to less familiar ones like Seroquel, Tegretol, Depakote (for bipolar disorder), and more are coming along all the time—though not all are approved for use in Canada. There are stimulants, mood stabilizers, sleep medications, antidepressants, anticonvulsants, antipsychotics, antianxieties and narrowcast drugs to deal with impulsiveness and post-traumatic flashbacks. A few of the newest meds were developed or approved specifically for kids. The majority have been okayed for adults only, but are being used "off label" for younger and younger patients. In 2002, for example, Canadian doctors made 141,000 recommendations for Paxil to patients under 19, says drug-policy researcher Alan Cassels, who calculated data provided by IMS Health Canada. The practice is common and perfectly legal but potentially risky, some believe. "For kids, we don't know as much about what

dose we should use and what could be the long-term impact of the treatment we're giving," says Quirion.

Within the medical community—to say nothing of the families of the troubled kids-concern is growing about what psychotropic drugs can do to still developing brains. Few people deny that mind pills help—ask the untold numbers who have climbed out of depressive pits or shaken off bipolar fits thanks to modern pharmacology. But few deny either that Western culture is a quick-fix culture, and if you give people a feel-good answer to a complicated problem, they will use it with little thought of long-term consequences.

"The problem," warns Dr. Glen Elliott, director of the Langley Porter Psychiatric Institute's children's center at the University of California, San Francisco, "is that our usage has outstripped our knowledge base. Let's face it, we're experimenting on these kids without tracking the results."

THE CASE FOR MEDICATION

THOSE EXPERIMENTS, HOWEVER, ARE OFTEN driven by dire need. When a child is suffering or suicidal, is it fair not to turn to the prescription pad in conjunction with therapy? Is it even safe? Untreated depression has a lifetime suicide rate of 15%—with still more deaths caused by related behaviors like self-medicating with alcohol and drugs. Kids with severe and untreated ADHD have been linked, according to some studies, to higher rates of substance abuse, dropping out of school and trouble with the law. Bipolar kids have a tendency to injure and kill themselves and others with uncontrolled behavior like brawling or reckless driving. They are also more prone to suicide.

Which is why Teresa Hatten of Fort Wayne, Ind., hesitated little when it came time to put her granddaughter Monica on medication. Hatten's grown daughter, Monica's mom, suffers from bipolar disorder, and so does Monica, 13. To give Monica a chance at a stable upbringing, Hatten took on the job of raising her, and one of the first things she had to do was get the violent mood swings of the bipolar disorder under con-

trol. It's been a long, tough slog. An initial drug combination of Ritalin and Prozac, prescribed when Monica was 6, simply collapsed her alternating depressed and manic moods into a single state with sad and wild features. By the time she was 8, her behavior was so unhinged, her school tried to expel her. Next Monica was switched to Zyprexa, an antipsychotic, that led to serious weight gain. "At 12 years old she had stretch marks," says Hatten. Now, a year later, Monica is taking a four-drug cocktail that includes Tegretol, an anticonvulsant, and Abilify, an antipsychotic. That, at last, seems to have solved the problem. "She's the best I've ever seen her," says Hatten. "She's smiling. Her moods are consistent. I'm cautiously optimistic." Monica agrees: "I'm in a better mood." Next up in the family's wellness campaign: Monica's 8-year-old cousin Jamari, who is on Zyprexa for a mood disorder.

Jonathan Singh, 18, of Toronto, has also come out of the darkness. "I had known for a long time something was wrong, but I didn't know what," he says. "I felt like there was this big, black fog in my brain that I couldn't fix." Exhausted and emaciated, Jonathan was finally given a diagnosis of major depression a year ago and was immediately put on Zoloft. Today, he has more energy and focus, his grades have improved, and he takes better care of himself. For his family, this has been a huge relief. "He has the look of someone who has come back to life," says his mother Jackie Beaurivage.

> "WE KNOW THAT FRONTAL LOBES, WHICH MANAGE BOTH FEELING AND THOUGHT, DON'T FULLY MATURE UNTIL AGE 30."
>
> —STEPHEN HINSHAW,
> **University of California**

All along the disorder spectrum there are such pharmacological success stories. In the October issue of the *Archives of General Psychiatry*, Dr. Mark Olfson of the New York State Psychiatric Institute reports that every time the use of antidepressants jumps 1%, suicide rates among kids 10 to 19 decrease, although

PILLS FOR CHILDREN HOW THEY WORK

Children are just as vulnerable as adults to mental illness. But though the pharmaceutical pantry is filling up with more medications designed and tested for kids, in some cases they still have to settle for smaller doses of drugs made for adults

	HOW IT WORKS	SIDE EFFECTS	TESTED/ APPROVED
ADDERALL	A once-a-day amphetamine, it puts the brake on areas of the brain responsible for organizing thoughts	Rapid heartbeat, high blood pressure and, in rare cases, overstimulation. It can also become addictive	✔ Approved to treat ADHD in children 3 and older
CONCERTA	It keeps neurons bathed in norepinephrine and dopamine, which reduce hyperactivity and inattention	Headache, stomach pain, sleeplessness and, in rare cases, overstimulation	✔ Approved for treatment of ADHD in children 6 to 12
STRATTERA	Approved in the U.S. a year ago, it's the first nonstimulant for ADHD: it enhances norepinephrine levels in the brain	Decreased appetite, fatigue, nausea, stomach pain	✔ Approved to treat ADHD in children 6 and older
RITALIN	Its active agent, methylphenidate, stimulates the brain to filter and prioritize incoming information	Headache, lack of appetite, irritability, nervousness, insomnia	✔ Approved to treat ADHD in children 6 and older
METHYPATCH	The patch form of the stimulant methylphenidate for ADHD, it delivers continuous low doses through the skin	Similar to those for oral methylphenidate	Not approved. In the U.S., the FDA has deemed the ADHD drug "unapprovable" until further study
PROZAC	Approved in the U.S. in 1987; the first antidepressant aimed at regulating serotonin, a brain chemical involved in mood	Insomnia, anxiety, nervousness, weight loss, mania	✔ Not approved for pediatric use but prescribed for children in Canada
ZOLOFT	It enhances the levels of serotonin in the brain to maintain feelings of satisfaction and stability	Upset stomach, dry mouth, agitation, decreased appetite	Not approved for kids. In Britain, regulators recently recommended against the use of SSRIs for children
PAXIL	Like Prozac and Zoloft, it elevates levels of serotonin in the brain	Nausea, drowsiness, insomnia	Not approved for kids. Health Canada has warned of an increase in suicidal thoughts for children on the drug
EFFEXOR	It targets two brain chemicals, serotonin and norepinephrine, to regulate mood	Nausea, constipation, nervousness, loss of appetite, drowsiness	Not approved for kids. Health Canada has warned of an increase in suicidal thoughts among children on the drug
DEPAKOTE	This antiseizure medication is particularly effective in treating the grandiose, hyperagitated state of mania	Liver and white blood cell abnormalities, headache, nausea, drowsiness	Not approved for kids, but used to treat childhood bipolar mania and seizures
ZYPREXA	It's a mood stabilizer designed to balance levels of serotonin and dopamine in the brain	Weight gain, drowsiness, dry mouth, seizures	Not approved for kids but prescribed pediatrically for bipolar disorder, psychotic depression and schizophrenia
LITHIUM	It stabilizes the episodes of elated, intensely joyous moods associated with mania	Nausea, loss of appetite, trembling of the hands	Not approved for kids but prescribed pediatrically for bipolar disorder and as an agent for suicide prevention

only slightly. But that doesn't include the nonsuicidal depressed kids whose misery is eased thanks to the same pills.

ARE ADULTS MEDDLING WITH NORMAL DEVELOPMENT?

FOR CHILDREN WITH LESS SEVERE problems—children who are somber but not depressed, antsy but not clinically hyperactive, who rely on some repetitive behaviors for comfort but are not patently obsessive compulsive—the pros and cons of using drugs are far less obvious. "Unless there is careful assessment, we might start medicating normal variations [in behavior]," says Stephen Hinshaw, chairman of psychology at the University of California, Berkeley.

The world would be a far less interesting place if all the eccentric kids were medicated toward some golden mean. Besides, there are just too many unanswered questions about giving mind drugs to kids to feel comfortable with ever broadening usage. What worries some doctors is that if you medicate a child's developing brain, you may be burning the village to save it. What does any kind of psychopharmacological meddling do, not just to brain chemistry but also to the acquisition of emotional skills-when, for example, antianxiety drugs are prescribed for a child who has not yet acquired the experience of managing stress without the meds? And what about side effects, from weight gain to jitteriness to flattened personality—all the things you don't want in the social crucible of grade school and, worse, high school.

Adding to the worries is a growing body of knowledge showing just how incompletely formed a child's brain truly is. "We now know from imaging studies that frontal lobes, which are vital to executive functions like managing feelings and thought, don't fully mature until age 30," says Hinshaw. That's a lot of time for drugs to muck around with cerebral clay.

For that reason, it may not always be worth pulling the pharmacological rip cord, particularly when symptoms are relatively mild. Child psychologists point out that often nonpharmaceutical treatments can reduce or eliminate the need for drugs. Anxiety disorders such as phobias can respond well to behavioral

therapy-in which patients are gently exposed to graduated levels of the very things they fear until the brain habituates to the escalating risk.

Depression too may respond to new, streamlined therapy techniques, especially cognitive therapy—a treatment aimed at helping patients reframe their view of the world so that setbacks and losses are put in less catastrophic perspective. "Cognitive behavioral therapy helps kids learn to manage their thoughts," says Dr. Miriam Kaufman, a professor of pediatrics at the University of Toronto and author of Helping Your Teen Overcome Depression: A Guide for Parents.

For kids with more serious symptoms, experts are worried that undermedicating is a bigger risk than overmedicating. "Say you've got a kid who's severely obsessive and literally can't leave the home because of the fears and rituals he's got to perform," says UCSF's Elliott. "Think about what anyone age 2 to age 16 has to learn to function in our society. Then think about losing two of those years to a disorder. Which two would you choose to lose?" Also on the side of intervention is the belief that treating more kids with mental illness could reduce its incidence in adults.

Dr. Kiki Chang at Stanford University is trying to show that this is true with bipolar kids. He recently published a study in the *Journal of Clinical Psychiatry* that looked at kids from bipolar families who had only early signs of the disease. Preemptive doses of Depakote eased early symptoms in 78% of cases before the illness ever had a chance to take hold. "You can sit and watch it develop or intervene and possibly prevent the disorder," says Chang. While the researcher is excited about his results, he admits that treating kids who are not yet truly sick is controversial. "There's a chance some of the kids might not develop bipolar at all," says Chang. "We need to have more genetics, more brain imaging, more biological markers to know which direction the kids are going."

HOW CAN WE MEASURE THE RESULT?

PREVENTING SYMPTOMS, OF COURSE, IS NOT everything. A sleep-

ing child is completely asymptomatic, for example, but that's not the same as being fully functioning. If the drugs that extinguish symptoms also alter the still developing brain, the cure may come at too high a price, at least for kids who are only mildly symptomatic. To determine if this kind of damage is being done, investigators have been turning more and more to brain scans such as magnetic resonance imaging (MRI). The results they're getting have been intriguing.

MRIs had already shown that the brain volumes of kids with ADHD are 3% smaller than those of unafflicted kids. That concerned researchers since nearly all those scans had been taken of children already being medicated for the disorder. Were the anatomical differences there to begin with, or were they caused by the drugs? Attempting to answer that, Dr. F. Xavier Castellanos of the New York University Child Studies Center took other scans, this time using only kids with ADHD and comparing those who were taking medication with those who were not. Reassuringly, he discovered that they all shared the same structural anomaly, a finding that seems to exonerate the drugs.

Dr. Steven Pliszka, chief of child psychiatry at the University of Texas Health Center in San Antonio, went further. He conducted scans that picked up not just the structure but the activity of the brains of untreated ADHD children, and compared these images with those from children who had been medicated for a year or more. The treated group showed no signs of any deficits in brain function as measured in blood flow. In fact, he says, "we saw hints of improvement toward normal."

What nobody denies is that more research is needed to resolve all these questions—and that it won't be easy to get it started. The first problem is one of time. It was only in the early 1990s that the antidepressant Prozac exploded into pharmacies. It's hard to do a lifetime of longitudinal studies on a drug that's been widely used for just over a decade. And each time the industry invents a new medication, the clock rewinds to zero for that particular pill.

Even if it were possible to conduct extended studies, getting volunteers for the work is difficult. The attrition rate is high in any years—-long research, especially so when the subjects are kids, who bore easily and, at any rate, eventually go away to college. On average, 40% of children will drop out of a long-term study before the work is done. And that assumes their parents will even sign them up in the first place. Some brain scans involve at least a little bit of radiation—something most parents are reluctant to expose their children to, particularly if those kids have no emotional disorders and are simply being used as a baseline to establish the look of a healthy brain. Getting good scans from kids who have diagnosable conditions isn't easy, as any radiologist who has ever tried to conduct a lengthy MRI on a child with ADHD can attest. "Holding still is not exactly what they do well," says Elliott.

"YOU CAN'T SCREEN FOR SIDE EFFECTS IN A 10-YEAR-OLD IN FIVE MINUTES. MANY DOCTORS DON'T LISTEN TO KIDS."

Ethical questions hamstring research too. Any gold-standard study requires that some of the kids who are suffering from a disorder receive no drugs so that they can be compared with the kids who

do. But if you believe the medications are helpful, how can you withhold them from a group of symptomatic children who need them?

Despite such obstacles, research is moving ahead, if haltingly. The U.S. National Institute of Mental Health is conducting a study called the Preschool ADHD Treatment Study, in which researchers will track ADHD kids between 3 and 8 years old to determine the benefits and side effects of stimulant medications. Castellanos and N.Y.U. colleague Rachel Klein are taking things further, calling back subjects who were enrolled in an ADHD-treatment study that began in 1970 to scan their now late-30s and early-40s brains for the long-term effects of drugs. Castellanos is also planning a study of young rats treated with varying amounts of psychotropic drugs, conducting dosing and anatomical studies that cannot be performed on humans.

THE RISK OF HASTY PRESCRIPTIONS

JUST AS IMPORTANT AS GETTING THE research rolling is fixing the health-care system on which kids rely. Like adults taking mind meds, Canadian children often get their drugs not from a specialist in psychiatry but from a pediatrician or family doctor. Part of the reason for the hurried drugging, experts say, is that there is a shortage of qualified

physicians in most regions of the country, particularly rural areas. In a perfect, or at least better, world more doctors would be trained in psychotherapy and more specialists and clinics would be located in remote areas. "We're probably at 20% of where we should be," says Dr. Tatyana Barankin, head of continuing medical education, division of child psychiatry, at the University of Toronto.

The pharmaceutical companies could be doing better too—and if they don't, governments must push them to do it. There is a lot of money to be made in developing the next Prozac, but there is less profit if you test it for longer than the law demands.

Until all these things happen, the heaviest lifting will, as always, be left to the family. Perhaps the most powerful medicine a suffering child needs is the educated instincts of a well-informed parent—one who has taken the time to study up on all the pharmaceutical and nonpharmaceutical options and pick the right ones. There will always be dangers associated with taking too many drugs-and also dangers from taking too few. "Like every other choice you make for your kids," says Chang, "you make right ones and wrong ones." When the health of a child's mind is on the line, getting it wrong is something that no parent wants.

TOO MANY KIDS SMOKE

Teen smoking rates have fallen, but there's still work to be done in trying to keep kids from becoming addicted to tobacco.

By Dianna Gordon

It is a good news/bad news scenario. The good news is that teen smoking rates have fallen, tapering off from 36.5 percent among high school seniors in 1997 to 26.7 percent in 2002, according to Michigan's Monitoring the Future Study, an annual survey of tobacco and drug use by high school students.

The bad news is that more than 2,000 Americans between 12 and 17 become new cigarette customers each day with 4.5 million under 18 considered "current smokers." Those are the figures behind the 26.7 percent of high school seniors who smoke, in part due to peer pressure and in part to the youthful sense of invulnerability, behavioral experts say.

Three factors—high stress, frequent boredom and too much spending money—contribute to teen use of cigarettes, alcohol and illegal drugs, according to the National Center on Addiction and Substance Abuse at Columbia University.

But there's a reason kids keep smoking: They quickly become addicted. A new McGill University study says that, contrary to what was once believed, it does not take several years of heavy or daily smoking to become dependent on nicotine. Kids become addicted earlier and faster than originally suspected.

STATE EFFORTS

The states spent $231 million in tobacco settlement money in 2003 for programs to educate adolescents about the dangers of tobacco, as well as an additional $265 million for tobacco use prevention.

Arizona's kid-oriented campaign that portrays tobacco use as a "tumor-causing, teeth-staining, smelly, puking habit" has raised teens' awareness about the ill effects of smoking and chewing, says Cathy Bischoff, head of the state health services department's tobacco education and prevention program. Since the campaign was launched in

---

FAST FACTS ON TEEN SMOKING

- 4.5 million kids under age 18 are current smokers.
- 10.7 percent of eighth graders and 17.7 percent of 10th graders are current smokers.
- 26.7 percent of teens are smokers by the time they graduate.
- More than half of all smokers begin before age 14.
- More than a third of kids who try smoking become daily smokers before leaving high school.
- More than 6.4 million kids under 18 alive today will eventually die from smoking-related diseases, unless current trends are reversed.
- 87 percent of teenagers prefer Marlboro, Camel and Newport—the three most heavily advertised brands.
- Teen smokers are three times more likely than nonsmokers to use alcohol, eight times more likely to use marijuana and 22 times more likely to use cocaine.
- Smoking by youngsters can hamper lung growth and the level of maximum lung function.
- Resting heart rates of young adult smokers are two to three beats per minute faster than those of nonsmokers.

Source: Campaign for Tobacco-Free Kids; Centers for Disease Control and Prevention

---

1996, close to 80 percent of Arizona's young people now say they know smoking affects their health.

Bischoff says the campaign continues to be refined. The newest angle targets girls, who were identified by the Columbia study to be more susceptible to stress and more likely to use spending money on cigarettes, alcohol or drugs. With the help of the Phoenix Mercury women's basketball team, the campaign is aimed not only at discouraging smoking, but building girls' self-esteem and body image by focusing on disciplined, skilled athletes.

"Hits" to the anti-tobacco campaign Web site between July and September rose from 101,000 to 182,000, "so we know we're communicating," Bischoff says.

California is working to make sure retailers know it's against the law to sell tobacco products to minors. Illegal sales to young people fell 12.2 percent after hitting a high of 19.3 percent in 2002 before the effort began. Policymakers also are moving toward a tobacco-free goal for the entire state. There are now few places people can legally smoke, making it less likely kids will take up the habit. It's working: Smoking among youngsters 12 to 17 has nearly halved from 11 percent in 1994 to 5.9 percent in 2001, according to California's youth tobacco survey.

Iowa has concentrated on thwarting teen efforts to buy tobacco products. Compliance checks by local law enforcement agencies using teen volunteers who tried to buy tobacco products showed that the kids were unsuccessful 95 percent of the time. Only 5 percent of the retailers visited by the teens did not comply with the state laws regarding sales to minors, down from the 11 percent rate of successful purchases in 2002 and 40 percent in 1997.

And in a move that has been shown to help deter kids from smoking, 14 states raised cigarette excise taxes this year, and 20 increased them last year. For every 10 percent increase in cigarette cost, there's a 4 percent to 7 percent drop in teen smoking rates, says Michael Berman, spokesman for Campaign for Tobacco-Free Kids.

Dianna Gordon is an assistant editor of State Legislatures magazine.

Drug Research and Children

Recent studies are providing important new information about drug safety and effectiveness for children. Pediatricians say it's about time.

By Michelle Meadows

Most drugs prescribed for children have not been tested in children. Only 20 percent to 30 percent of drugs approved by the Food and Drug Administration are labeled for pediatric use. So by necessity, doctors have routinely given drugs to children "off label," which means the drug hasn't been studied in children in adequate, well-controlled clinical trials approved by the agency.

To be well-controlled, a study should have an adequate number of people and a control group—people who are similar to the group taking the drug being studied, but who are receiving some different type of treatment, such as another drug or an inactive pill (placebo).

Experts say the historical lack of pediatric drug testing is due to a combination of reasons. The primary reason is that pharmaceutical companies generally have viewed children as a market that would only bring small financial benefits. The drugs that have been adequately studied in children—vaccines, some antibiotics, and some cough and cold medicines—have a large market.

"It's also harder to carry out studies in children," says Dianne Murphy, M.D., director of the FDA's Office of Pediatric Therapeutics. "You need child-friendly environments in every sense, from age-appropriate equipment and medical techniques to pediatric specialists who are sensitive to a child's fear."

Jeffrey Blumer, M.D., Ph.D., chief of pediatric pharmacology at Case Western Reserve University in Cleveland, says technical procedures that seem simple for adults, such as drawing blood or getting a urine sample, can be difficult with children.

The ethical issues are also stickier. For example, while adults can give informed consent to participate in a clinical trial, children can't because "consent" implies full understanding of potential risks and other considerations. Parents are involved in the decision to enroll children in a study, and children ages 7 or older can "assent" or "dissent," meaning they can agree or disagree to participate in a study.

Blumer says, "I've had parents who are enthusiastic about a study and then a 7-year-old who hears everything involved and says, 'No way!'"

Children Aren't Small Adults

But rather than avoiding pediatric research because of the challenges, experts say it's more important to build the foundation and resources needed to conduct the studies. Without them, children face significant risks.

In the absence of data, doctors use their medical judgment to decide on a particular drug and dose for children. "Some doctors stay away from drugs, which could deny needed treatment," Blumer says. "Generally, we take our best guess based on what's been done before."

A common approach has been to use data from adults and adjust the dose according to a child's weight. Experimenting over the years has taught doctors to use many drugs in children safely and effectively. But this trial-and-error approach has also resulted in tragedy, indicating that adult experiences with a drug aren't always a reliable predictor of how children will react.

For example, in the 1950s, the antibiotic chloramphenicol was widely used in adults to treat infections resistant to penicillin. But many newborn babies died after receiving the drug because their immature livers couldn't break down the antibiotic.

"Experience has shown us that we need to study drugs in children because they aren't small adults," says Ralph Kauffman, M.D., director of medical research at Children's Mercy Hospital in Kansas City, Mo. "It's not just about smaller weight," he says. "There are dynamics of growth and maturation of organs, changes in metabolism throughout infancy and childhood, changes in body proportion, and other developmental changes that affect how drugs are metabolized."

Proof Is in the Data

Fortunately, recent regulatory and legislative changes that give drug companies financial incentives to conduct drug studies in children have resulted in a dramatic increase in pediatric drug studies. "There have been more studies conducted in children in the last five years than in the previous 30 years combined," Kauffman says.

The information coming out of those studies has added pediatric information to the drug labeling for more than 40 drugs, and more changes are coming. Drug labeling is the guidance to doctors and other health-care providers on how to use a drug. "We knew that we needed science to determine proper dosing for children the same way we do with adults," says Dianne Murphy. "Now, we have confirmed it."

New discoveries have revealed underdosing, overdosing, ineffectiveness, and safety problems.

Ibuprofen, one of the most common over-the-counter drugs that parents rely on to reduce children's fevers, carried no dosing information for children younger than 2 years old until recently. Now, because of studies in thousands of young infants, the dose considered to be safe and effective for over-the-counter use has been established for children ages 6 months to 2 years.

The labeling has also been changed for Zantac (ranitidine), a drug used to treat gastroesophageal reflux. This condition can be life-threatening in infants. When reflux occurs, the stomach contents can flow up the esophagus and be aspirated into the lungs. This can harm the lungs of infants and result in breathing problems.

Studies have given doctors accurate dosing information for safer and more effective use of the drug to manage reflux in seriously ill infants. Richard Gorman, M.D., chairman of the Committee on Drugs at the American Academy of Pediatrics (AAP) and a pediatrician in Ellicott City, Md., says, "Now I can use ranitidine with as much information as doctors who use it in adults. I know the dose. I know the dosing interval."

With Neurontin (gabapentin), a drug used to control seizures, research has shown that higher doses are needed in children younger than 5 to control seizures. With Versed (midazolam), one of the most commonly used medicines to sedate children undergoing surgery, researchers found that children with congenital heart disease and pulmonary hypertension need to start therapy at a lower dose to prevent respiratory problems. Also, Versed formerly was available only by injection of the drug into a child's vein or muscle. But studies helped develop a new oral syrup, which is easier to give and less frightening to young children. (For more on label changes, see "Changing Drug Labels.")

New discoveries have revealed underdosing, overdosing, ineffectiveness, and safety problems. Gorman says, "Even though the best and brightest pediatric minds have helped us establish dosages for children, we're finding out that the dose is different than we thought in some cases. And that probably came as a surprise to most of us."

The FDA is working with the AAP to educate pediatricians about new physician labeling changes through an online continuing medical education program called PediaLink.

What's Spurring the Research?

The FDA has taken a carrot-and-stick approach to encourage pediatric studies, says William Rodriguez, M.D., the FDA's science director for pediatrics. The carrot is the voluntary pediatric exclusivity provision of the Food and Drug Administration Modernization Act of 1997 (FDAMA). And the stick has been the FDA's "pediatric rule," which required pediatric studies and was finalized in 1998. Here's an overview of each initiative:

The Pediatric Exclusivity Provision of FDAMA

The pediatric exclusivity provision has done more to spur pediatric studies than any other regulatory or legislative initiative so far. The provision extends patent protection to give companies an additional six months of marketing exclusivity if they do the studies in children requested by the FDA.

Patents protect a company's investment by giving it the sole right to sell a drug while the patent is in effect. When patents or other periods of exclusive marketing for brand-name drugs are close to expiring, other drug companies can apply to the FDA to sell generic versions, without having to repeat the original developer's clinical trials. So the trade-off is that by giving companies additional months of exclusivity, there is a delay in the availability of lower-cost generic drugs.

The FDA has interpreted the provision so that the six months of exclusivity isn't only added to the drug that was studied in the pediatric population, but also to any of the drug company's formulations, dosage forms, and indications that contain the same active part of a molecule (moiety) and have existing marketing exclusivity or patent life. So if a company markets an oral formulation and a topical cream containing the same moiety, the six months of marketing exclusivity will be added to any existing exclusivity or patent protection for both products.

The process can be initiated either by a drug company or the FDA. A drug company may submit a proposal to conduct pediatric studies to the FDA. If the FDA agrees that studying a drug may produce health benefits for children, the agency will issue a "Written Request" addressing the type of studies to be conducted, study design and goals, and the age groups to be studied. Or the agency may issue a Written Request on its own initiative when it identifies a need for pediatric data. No matter how the studies are initiated, if the FDA determines that the data submitted fairly respond to the Written Request, then the company will be granted six months of pediatric exclusivity.

The exclusivity provision also requires the FDA to publish an annual list of approved drugs for which additional pediatric information may produce health benefits.

More than 60 drugs have been granted exclusivity so far. As of Sept. 30, 2002, 601 studies had been requested and 256 Written Requests issued. The FDA estimates that about 80 percent of the studies outlined in Written Requests will be conducted.

Kauffman says the exclusivity is proof that economics plays a large role in the lack of pediatric studies. "Once the economic disincentive was removed," he says, "the dam broke completely open."

Diane Murphy, M.D., director of the FDA's Office of Pediatric Therapeutics, says "child-friendly environments"are needed when doing research on children. The office she oversees is mandated by the Best Pharmaceuticals for Children Act, signed into law in January 2002.

The exclusivity provision was renewed in January 2002 and extended through 2007 under the Best Pharmaceuticals for Children Act (BPCA). Some categories of drugs and age groups have remained inadequately studied. The incentive under FDAMA did not apply to old antibiotics and other drugs that lack marketing exclusivity or patent protection. For these products, the BPCA provides a contract mechanism through the NIH to fund pediatric studies. If a company that has a drug with existing exclusivity or patent protection chooses not to conduct the requested pediatric studies, this new mechanism through BPCA allows the Foundation for the National Institutes of Health to award grants so that third parties can conduct the needed studies.

The FDA's Pediatric Rule

In the early 1990s, the FDA implemented voluntary measures to encourage pediatric studies, but they were mostly unsuccessful. In 1997, the FDA published a proposed regulation that for the first time required manufacturers of new drug and biological products to conduct pediatric studies in some circumstances. The rule was finalized in 1998, and the first studies were required to be submitted starting December 2000.

But the rule had its critics. In December 2000, the Association of American Physicians and Surgeons, the Competitive Enterprise Institute and Consumer Alert filed a lawsuit against the pediatric rule, challenging the FDA's legal authority to require pediatric studies. And in October 2002, a federal district court overturned the pediatric rule.

HHS Secretary Tommy G. Thompson responded in mid-December 2002 by announcing that his department will push for rapid passage of legislation that would give the FDA authority to require pharmaceutical manufacturers to conduct appropriate pediatric clinical trials on drugs.

"The fastest and most decisive route for establishing clear authority in this area is to work with Congress for new legislation," Thompson said in a prepared statement. "Children need to have access to drugs that can benefit them, and these drugs need to be properly tested for pediatric use, not prescribed and sold without testing. Congress alone can speak clearly on the authority that FDA needs…"

Kauffman says turning the pediatric rule into law would be the ideal scenario. "The exclusivity provision sunsets again in 2007, with no guarantees of being renewed. We need something permanent so that we don't lose all the ground we've gained."

The pediatric rule was intended to address some of the gaps left by the pediatric exclusivity provision. Unlike the exclusivity provision, the pediatric rule was a requirement and covered both drugs and biologics—medical products derived from living sources such as vaccines, blood and blood derivatives, and new treatments for cancers.

Under the pediatric rule, the FDA could require pediatric studies of a drug submitted in a new drug application if the FDA determined the product was likely to be used in a substantial number of pediatric patients, or if the product would provide a meaningful benefit in the pediatric population over existing treatments. At the same time, the pediatric rule did not delay the availability of drugs for adults.

Changing Drug Labels

Recent pediatric drug studies have resulted in the addition of pediatric information to the labeling for more than 40 drugs. The drug labeling provides guidance for doctors and other health-care providers on how to use a drug. Here are examples of several changes that are considered significant for dosing and risk.

- **Luvox (fluvoxamine):** Treats obsessive-compulsive disorder. The dose of the drug may need to be increased up to the recommended adult dose in adolescents, but may need to be prescribed in lower than recommended doses for girls ages 8 to 11.
- **Neurontin (gabapentin):** Treats seizures. Safety and effectiveness have been established for children as young as 3. Children under 5 need higher doses than previously thought based on the studies conducted. New adverse effects not seen in adults, such as hostility and aggressive behavior, are now noted in the label.
- **Diprivan (propofol):** An anesthesia drug. A research study showed an increase in deaths when the drug was used for pediatric ICU sedation in comparison with standard sedative agents. Administration of propofol with the pain medication fentanyl may result in serious slowing of the heart rate.
- **BuSpar (buspirone):** Treats generalized anxiety disorder. Safety and effectiveness were not established in patients ages 6 to 17 at doses recommended for use in adults.
- **Versed (midazolam):** Used as a sedative. The drug was shown to have a higher risk of serious life-threatening adverse events for children with congenital heart disease and pulmonary hypertension. Research identified the need to begin therapy with doses at the lower end of the dosing range to prevent respiratory problems in this special pediatric population.
- **Lodine (etodolac):** Treats the signs and symptoms of juvenile rheumatoid arthritis. Research shows that the drug can be used in children ages 6 to 16 and that higher doses are needed in younger children.

"The exclusivity provision and the rule have worked in tandem," says the FDA's Dianne Murphy. "We have told sponsors who submit a new drug application and who are required under the rule to conduct pediatric studies that they also may qualify for pediatric exclusivity."

Gorman says the exclusivity provision is the one that has the drug industry's attention, but he has been most excited about the pediatric rule. "The exclusivity provision has been important for helping children play catch-up and that's important, but the pediatric rule puts children at the table very early in the development of drugs."

Building the Foundation

"There was no infrastructure for the research before," says Floyd R. Sallee, M.D., Ph.D., a child psychiatrist and director of the pediatric pharmacology research unit at Cincinnati Children's Hospital Medical Center. "I see the culture changing in industry and at FDA," he says. "Drug companies have hired pediatric experts and there is a larger network of expertise to draw from."

Sallee's center is part of the Pediatric Pharmacology Research Unit (PPRU) Network, a group of centers that conduct pediatric drug trials with support from the National Institute of Child Health and Human Development (NICHD). The network was established in 1994 and now includes 13 PPRUs.

Shirley Murphy, M.D., (no relation to Dianne Murphy) joined the FDA in September 2002 as director of the Division of Pediatric Drug Development. She says linkages between the FDA, NICHD, AAP, and other organizations have been important for building a foundation for pediatric research, and children are getting more and better drugs as a result.

"What it means for parents is that they can feel more secure knowing that their children are being treated appropriately," Shirley Murphy says. "FDA remains committed to keeping pediatric drug research a high priority."

Shirley Murphy cites pediatric oncology as another important area for the agency.

Several areas that will continue to receive the agency's attention include the ethics involved with studying drugs in children. The FDA's Pediatric Advisory Subcommittee has concluded that generally, pediatric studies should be conducted in subjects who may benefit from participation in the trial. Usually, this implies the subject has or is susceptible to the disease under study.

Debbie Birenbaum, M.D., an FDA pediatric team leader, says FDA experts think long and hard about the public health benefit before requesting pediatric studies. "We don't want to under study children and we don't want to over study them. It's our job to get information that will help them and protect them at the same time."

Shirley Murphy cites pediatric oncology as another important area for the agency. "The development of cancer drugs needs special consideration," she says. Differences in the biology of tumors in children and adults usually make it difficult to prescribe children drugs based on adult data. And it has been typical for new cancer drugs to reach children late—only after they have been tested in adults.

As a result of pediatric initiatives, there have been about 30 studies initiated on cancer drugs, which will help researchers gain access to potential new cancer therapies for children.

While it may be challenging to enroll children in clinical trials for some diseases, that's not the case with cancer. Most children receive their cancer therapy as part of a clinical trial. "Parents are desperate to have their children in these studies," says Patrick Reynolds, M.D., Ph.D., a pediatric oncologist with Childrens Hospital Los Angeles. "They know very well what the odds are and they want to take a chance to find life-saving treatment. They also want to help other children. They don't want to do nothing."

Reynolds is a member of the FDA's Pediatric Oncology Sub-committee, a group of outside experts who have met several times since 2000 to advise the agency on such questions as: In what phase of a drug development program should pediatric cancer studies begin? What trial designs should be used? How may data from adult studies be used in pediatric studies? How should adult and pediatric studies be coordinated when studying life-threatening diseases?

Reynolds calls both the pediatric rule and the exclusivity provision essential. "Children don't have a voice in this," he says. "Somebody has to stand up for them."

From *FDA Consumer*, January/February 2003, p. 36. Published by the U.S. Food and Drug Administration.

In Pursuit of Doped Excelence

The Lab Animal

By MICHAEL SOKOLOVE

On a brisk day last month, I was led through a warren of red brick buildings on the campus of the University of Pennsylvania in West Philadelphia and then up to a fifth-floor molecular physiology laboratory. I had come to visit some mice—and to get a peek at the future of sport.

I had heard about these mice, heard them called "mighty mice," but I was still shocked at the sight of them. There they were in several small cages, grouped with normal mice, all of them nibbling on mouse chow pellets. The mighty mice looked like a different animal. They were built like cattle, with thick necks and big haunches. They belonged in some kind of mouse rodeo.

The Penn researchers have used gene therapy on these mice to produce increased levels of IGF-1, or insulinlike growth factor-1, a protein that promotes muscle growth and repair. They have done this with mice before birth and with mice at four weeks of age. A result has been a sort of rodent fountain of youth. The mice show greater than normal muscle size and strength and do not lose it as they age. Rats altered in the same fashion and then put into physical training—they climb little ladders with weights strapped to their backs—have experienced a 35 percent strength gain in the targeted muscles and have not lost any of it "detraining," as a human being will when he quits going to the gym.

To the scientists, H. Lee Sweeney, chairman of Penn's department of physiology, and Elisabeth Barton, an assistant professor, the bizarre musculature of their lab specimens is exciting. This research could eventually be of immense benefit to the elderly and those with various "muscle wasting" diseases.

"Our impetus, going back to 1988, was to develop a therapy to stop people from getting weak when they get old," Sweeney, 50, explained. "They fall and injure themselves. We wanted to do something about that."

Barton, 39, has the broad shoulders and athletic build of the competitve cyclist and triathlete she once was. "You see children with muscular dystrophy, and their parents are just so broken up because it's so sad," she said. "You see grandparents who can't get out of bed. These are the people this is for."

But the Penn team has become acutely aware of a population impatient to see its research put into practice—the already strong, seeking to get stronger still. Sweeney gets their e-mail messages. One came from a high-school football coach in western Pennsylvania not long after Sweeney first presented his findings at a meeting of the American Society for Cell Biology. "This coach wanted me to treat his whole team," he said. "I told him it was not available for humans, and it may not be safe, and if I helped him we would all go to jail. I can only assume he didn't understand how investigational this is. Or maybe he wasn't winning, and his job was on the line."

Other calls and e-mail messages have come from weight lifters and bodybuilders. This kind of thing happens often after researchers publish in even the most arcane medical and scientific journals. A whole subculture of athletes and the coaches and chemists who are in the business of improving their performances is eager for the latest medical advances.

Sweeney knows that what he is doing works. The remaining question, the one that will require years of further research to answer, is how safe his methods are. But many athletes don't care about that. They want an edge now. They want money and acclaim. They want a payoff for their years of sweat and sacrifice, at whatever the cost.

"This was serious science, not sports science," Dr. Gary Wadler, a United States representative to the World Anti-Doping Agency, said when I spoke to him about the Penn experiments. "As soon as it gets into any legitimate publication, bango, these people get ahold of it and want to know how they can abuse it."

Sweeney's research will probably be appropriated before it is ever put to its intended medical purpose. Someone will use it to build a better sprinter or shot-putter.

There is a murky, "Casablanca"-like quality to sport at the moment. We are in a time of flux. No one is entirely clean. No one is entirely dirty. The rules are ambiguous. Everyone, and everything, is a little suspect.

Months before the great slugger Barry Bonds was summoned before a grand jury in December to answer questions about his association with the Bay Area Laboratory Co-Operative, known as Balco, which has been at the center of a spreading drug scandal after the discovery of a new "designer steroid," tetrahydrogestrinone (THG), a veteran American sprinter named Kelli White ran the track meet of her dreams at the World Championships in Paris. She captured the gold medal in the 100-meter and 200-meter races, the first American woman ever to win those sprints in tandem at an outdoor world championship. In both events, the 5-foot-4, 135-pound White, a tightly coiled ball of power and speed, exploded to career-best times.

On a celebratory shopping trip on the Champs-Elysees, White, 26, glimpsed her name in a newspaper headline and asked a Parisian to translate. She learned that she had flunked a postrace drug test and that her medals and $120,000 in prize money were in jeopardy. Later, she acknowledged that she had taken the stimulant modafinil, claiming that she needed it to treat narcolepsy but had failed to list it on a disclosure form. What she added after that was revealing, perhaps more so than she intended. "After a competition," she told reporters in Europe, "it's kind of hard to remember everything that you take during the day."

The THG scandal and the attention focused on Balco, which has advised dozens of top athletes (including Kelli White) on the use of dietary supplements, has opened the curtain on a seamy side of sport and on the fascinating cat-and-mouse game played between rogue chemists and the laboratory sleuths who try to police them.

But White's statement exposed another, deeper truth: elite athletes in many different sports routinely consume cocktails of vitamins, extracts and supplements, dozens of pills a day—the only people who routinely ingest more pills are AIDS patients—in the hope that their mixes of accepted drugs will replicate the effects of the banned substances taken by the cheaters. The cheaters and the noncheaters alike are science projects. They are the sum total of their innate athletic abilities and their dedication—and all the compounds and powders they ingest and inject.

A narrow tunnel leads to success at the very top levels of sport. This is especially so in Olympic nonteam events. An athlete who has devoted his life to sprinting, for example, must qualify for one of a handful of slots on his Olympic team. And to become widely known and make real money, he probably has to win one of the gold medals that is available every four years.

The temptation to cheat is human. In the realm of elite international sport, it can be irresistible.

After Kelli White failed her drug test, the United States Olympic Committee revealed that five other American athletes in track and field had tested positive this summer

for modafinil. Did they all suffer from narcolepsy? That would be hard to believe. More likely, word of modafinil and its supposed performance-enhancing qualities (perhaps along with the erroneous information that it was not detectable) went out on the circuit. It became the substance du jour.

For athletes, performance-enhancing drugs and techniques raise issues of health, fair play and, in some cases, legality. For sports audiences, the fans, the issues are largely philosophical and aesthetic.

On the most basic level, what are we watching, and why? If we equate achievement with determination and character, and that, after all, has always been part of our attachment to sport—to celebrate the physical expression of the human spirit—how do we recalibrate our thinking about sport when laboratories are partners in athletic success?

Major League Baseball, which came late to drug testing and then instituted a lenient program, seems to have decided that the power generated by bulked-up players is good for the game in the entertainment marketplace. The record-breaking sluggers Mark McGwire and Sammy Sosa have been virtual folk heroes and huge draws at the gate. Their runs at the record books became the dominant narratives of individual seasons. (Barry Bonds has been less popular only because of a sour public persona.) But the sport is much changed. Muscle Baseball is the near opposite of what I and many other fans over 30 were raised on, a game that involved strategy, bunting, stolen bases, the hit-and-run play—what is called Little Ball.

Professional basketball is not generally suspected of being drenched in steroids and other performance enhancers. But anyone who has seen even a few minutes of old games on the ESPN Classic network from, say, 20 years ago, is immediately struck by the evolution of players' physiques. Regardless of how it happened, today's N.B.A. players are heavier and markedly more muscled, and the game is tailored to their strengths. It is played according to a steroid aesthetic. What was once a sport of grace and geometry—athletes moving to open spaces on the floor, thinking in terms of passing angles—is now one primarily of power and aggression: players gravitate to the same space and try to go over or through one another.

But it is sports that have fixed standards and cherished records that present fans with the greatest conundrum. If what's exciting is to see someone pole vault to a new, unimaginable height—or become the "world's fastest human" or the first big-leaguer since Ted Williams to hit .400—how do we respond when our historical frame of reference is knocked askew by the suspicion, or known fact, that an athlete is powered by a banned substance?

IN ELITE SPORT, the associations of competitors who have never been sanctioned for drug use or known to fail a drug test can still raise questions. Marion Jones, the breathtaking sprinter and featured American performer of the 2000 Sydney Olympics, was married to the shot-putter C.J. Hunter—who was banned from those games after testing positive for the steroid nandralone. Jones later divorced Hunter, but then trained (briefly) with Charlie Francis, the disgraced ex-coach of Ben Johnson, the disgraced Canadian sprinter who was stripped of an Olympic gold medal. Carl Lewis, the greatest U.S. Olympian in history and a longtime crusader against performance-enhancing drugs—it was Lewis who was outsprinted by the steroid-fueled Ben Johnson at the 1988 Games in Seoul—has been accused of flunking a drug test of his own before the 1988 U.S. Olympic Trials. Lance Armstrong, brave cancer survivor, fierce and inspiring competitor, has kept up a long association with an Italian doctor in the thick of a sprawling drug scandal in Europe, although Armstrong himself has never come up positive on a drug test.

Even the substances themselves are murky. Because the $18-billion-a-year dietary-supplement industry is (at best) loosely regulated, some of the potions in the vitamin store at your local mall could well be tainted by steroids or growth hormones. The Food and Drug Administration just got around to banning the sale of ephedra last month, long after the herbal stimulant was blamed for numerous serious health problems, along with the sudden death last year of Steve Bechler, a Baltimore Orioles pitcher.

> **Once someone decided** to use gene therapy, 'you could change the endurance of the muscle or modulate the speed—all the performance characteristics.'

The whole situation cries out for a dose of clarity, but the closer you look, the fuzzier the picture. Start with the line between what's legal and illegal when it comes to enhancing performance. The line, already blurry, is likely over time to disappear entirely.

I visited a U.S. swimmer last September as technicians sealed up his bedroom, after which they installed equipment that reduced the amount of oxygen in his room and turned it into a high-altitude chamber. This is a common and legal training method that Ed Moses, America's best male breaststroker, said he hoped would increase his count of oxygen-carrying red blood cells. A whole team of long-distance runners sponsored by Nike lives in a much more elaborate simulated high-altitude dwelling in Portland, Ore. The desired effect of the so-called "live high, train low" method—sleep at altitude, train at sea level—is the same as you would get from taking erythropoietin, or EPO, which increases red-blood-cell production and is banned in sports.

Two other U.S. swimmers, in the lead-up to the Olympic Games in Sydney, were on a regimen of 25 pills a day, including minerals, proteins, amino acids and the nutritional supplement creatine, an effective but not necessarily safe builder of muscle mass. Much of the mix may well have been useless, but athletes tend to take what's put in front of them for fear of passing up the one magic pill.

"I like to think we're on the cutting edge of what can be done nutritionally and with supplements," the swimmers' coach, Richard Quick, said then as his athletes prepared for the 2000 games. "If you work hard consistently, with a high level of commitment, you can do steroidlike performances." One of his swimmers, Dara Torres, who increased her bench press from 105 pounds to 205 pounds and swam career-best times at the age of 33, said at the time that her goal was to "keep up with the people who are cheating without cheating."

And who are the cheaters? Everyone else. One primary motivation to cheat is the conviction that everyone else is cheating.

To draw the often arbitrary lines between performance enhancing and performance neutral, between health endangering and dicey but take it at your own risk—to ensure that sport remains "pure"—a vast worldwide bureaucracy has been enlisted.

At the lowest level are those who knock on the doors of athletes in their homes and apartments in the United States and Europe and in the mountain villages of Kenya and at the training sites in China and demand "out of competition" urine samples. Higher up on the pyramid are the laboratories around the world chosen to scan the urine (and blood) of elite athletes for the molecular signatures of any of hundreds of banned substances. At the top of the drug-fighting pyramid are the titans of international sport—the same people who cannot see to it that a figure skating competition is fairly judged.

The titans created the World Anti-Doping Agency, which works with governments and designated national organizations, including the United States Anti-Doping Agency. In combination with the urine-sample collectors, the various couriers in the chain of custody and the laboratories, W.A.D.A. is charged with making sure that the world's premier athletes are clean—and additionally that they have not concealed drug use through the use of various "masking agents." (The latest U.S.A.D.A. list specifically prohibits the following brand names: Defend, Test Free, Test Clean, UrinAid and Jamaica Me Clean.)

It is all an immensely complicated endeavor, one that requires W.A.D.A. to keep up with the onrushing science, to disseminate information to thousands of athletes, to navigate in different legal systems so that accused competitors get due process and, lastly, to manage the worldwide trafficking of urine samples. And it is all, in the end, quite possibly pointless.

Despite the hundreds of people and tens of millions of dollars devoted to the effort, international and national sports organizations may just lack the will to catch and sanction cheaters. The United States, specifically, has been singled out as negligent in its oversight. "The real issue is that USA Track and Field has become a complete and utter scofflaw," the W.A.D.A. president, Richard Pound, a Canadian, told me. "They have gone to extraordinary lengths to hide identities and data and to exonerate athletes who have tested positive."

Can you really have a serious antidoping effort without the full cooperation of the world's most powerful nation—and most powerful sports nation? It's hard to see how.

The tougher question is whether it will be scientifically possible to stay ahead of the cheaters. The rogue scientists and coach-gurus have been winning for years, and they have ever more tools available to them. THG, which set off the Balco inquiry, is only a slightly more clever version of an old thing: an anabolic steroid—the kind of blunt builder of muscle mass and strength prevalent in sports since the 1950's. But its discovery required an insider tip, and THG is child's play compared with what's coming in the near future (if, in fact, it is not here already): genetic manipulation in order to improve athletic performance.

Ultimately, the debate over athletic doping extends beyond sport. "The current doping agony," says John Hoberman, a University of Texas at Austin professor who has written extensively on performance drugs, "is a kind of very confused referendum on the future of human enhancement."

PETE ROSE was the prototypical "self-made" athlete, which is code for a sort of seeming nonathlete who makes the most of his meager abilities. But fans overlooked important genetic traits that made him baseball's all-time hits leader—chiefly, uncommon durability that allowed him to play 24 seasons virtually injury free. And what did Rose do to attain that? Nothing, really. As the son of a semipro athlete who played sandlot baseball and football into his early 40's, he came by that blocky, unbreakable body by way of genetic inheritance. In the off-season, Rose maintained himself by playing casual basketball a couple of times a week and eating greasy food and heaping bowls of potato chips.

When it comes to elite sport, there is no such thing as self-made. No amount of dedication can turn someone of average ability into a world-class sprinter, an N.B.A. player or a champion marathoner. You can't be an Olympic pistol shooter without some innate steadiness of hand or a Tour de France cyclist without a far-above-average efficiency at moving oxygen to muscles. Even a humdrum, physically unimpressive player on a major-league baseball team has something—usually extraordinary hand-eye coordination—that is not apparent to those who regard athletic gifts only in terms of great size, speed, endurance or power.

The former Olympic track coach Brooks Johnson once told me that sport at its highest level should be viewed as a competition waged among "genetic freaks." He mentioned Carl Lewis and Michael Jordan. But anyone who reaches the top echelon of Olympic competition or draws a paycheck for playing sports professionally should be considered in the same category. You cannot will yourself into an elite athlete, or get there through punishing workouts, without starting out way ahead of the rest of the human race.

You may, through pure dedication, be able to jump one level—from a middle-of-the-pack Olympic sprinter to the final heat, from a marginal N.F.L. prospect to a midround draft pick. Chemical enhancement can produce more significant improvements, but the principle is the same. You've got to start out as a member of the athletic elite.

At the 1996 Summer Olympics in Atlanta, a middling Irish swimmer named Michelle Smith de Bruin raised suspicions when she won three gold medals. She later flunked drug tests. But before the presumed cheating, she was already a competitor on the international swim scene, not a lap swimmer at the Dublin Y.

> **Is it possible to stay ahead of the cheaters? The rogue scientists and coach-gurus have been winning for years, and they have ever more tools available to them.**

The use and abuse of performance-enhancing drugs in elite sport, or doping, as it has been called since around 1900, is a mutant form of an exclusive competition. It is an effort by individuals who are already part of a thin slice of humanity—the genetic freaks—to gain an edge against one another, to exceed their physiological limits in a way that they could not through pure training. (The word itself is believed to derive from the Dutch word dop, an alcoholic beverage consumed by Zulu warriors before battle.)

While systematic doping—with the collaboration of chemists, doctors, coaches and trainers—is a modern phenomenon, scientific interest in athletes is not new. The medical establishment once viewed athletes with curiosity and occasionally with alarm. The act of training and pushing yourself to physical limits was considered dangerous or even a form of sickness. Sports science was observational, an opportunity to study the body in motion by looking at individuals at the extremes of human capacity.

The British physiologist A.V. Hill, a Nobel laureate in 1922, went to Cornell to study sprinters because, as he wrote, "matters of very great scientific interest can be found in the performances of that extraordinary machine, the human athlete." John Hoberman, the historian of sports doping, has written that scientists and doctors viewed the high-performance athlete as "a wonder of nature—a marvelous phenomenon that did not require improvement."

Certainly, athletes have long sought their own chemical and nutritional means to enhance performance. The ancient Greeks ran and wrestled in the nude because nothing, not even fabric, was supposed to interfere with the purity of sport, yet they ate mushrooms, sesame seeds, dried figs and herbs that were believed to give a precompetition energy boost. Marathoners and cyclists as recently as a century ago competed under the influence of strychnine, which is both a stimulant and a poison. Cyclists also used caffeine, cocaine, alcohol and even heroin.

What changed everything—what transformed performance-enhancing efforts from the realm of superstition into a true science—was the isolation of the male hormone testosterone in 1935. That led to the development by the late 30's of synthesized testosterone variants, or anabolic steroids. The difference between steroids and all previous performance enhancers was that steroids demonstrably worked—and they worked really well.

NEARLY EVERY drug used by athletes to boost performance started out as a therapeutic miracle.

Steroids are still prescribed for men with serious testosterone deficiencies. AIDS patients and others with muscle-wasting conditions are dosed with steroids.

Until the mid-80's, people suffering from severe anemia, as a result of chronic renal failure or other causes, had to undergo frequent blood transfusions. The development of recombinant human erythropoietin was a godsend. Instead of transfusions, anemics could get injections to boost their red-blood-cell count.

But what would the effect of EPO be on a person with a normal or better than normal red blood count? What could it do for an already genetically gifted, highly trained endurance athlete? Just what you would expect: make a superendurance athlete.

EPO swept the professional cycling circuit in Europe like a plague, nearly wrecking the sport. There were police raids, huge stockpiles of EPO confiscated from cyclists' hotel rooms, arrests, trials, wholesale suspensions of competitors. "Each racer had his little suitcase with dopes and syringes," a former doctor for European professional cycling teams told a British newspaper. "They did their own injections."

EPO migrated to other endurance sports, including cross-country skiing, marathoning and orienteering. Inevitably, it showed its fatal flip side.

"In simplest terms, EPO turns on the bone marrow to make more red blood cells," says Gary Wadler, the American delegate to W.A.D.A. "But there's a very delicate balance. You can have too much EPO. The body is a finely tuned instrument. It has feedback mechanisms to keep it in balance. What these athletes are often trying to do is get around the feedback, to trick their own bodies."

Between 1989 and 1992, seven Swedish competitors in orienteering—a mix of running and hiking that is sometimes called "cross country with brains"—died, apparently from heart attacks. Nearly all were in their 20's. As many as 18 Dutch and Belgian cyclists died under similarly mysterious circumstances between 1987 and 1990.

"At first they said it was some kind of virus, a respiratory virus," Wadler says. "But what kind of virus only knocks off the most fit individuals in their country? The autopsies were private. All the deaths were not definitively linked. But it was EPO. That was obvious to a lot of people."

For weight lifters and competitors in the "throwing" sports of shot-put, javelin, discus and hammer, the performance enhancer of choice has long been steroids. Anabolic steroids (anabolic means tissue building) increase muscle mass and enhance the explosiveness needed for a wide range of other athletic endeavors: sprinting, jumping, swimming, serving a tennis ball, swinging a baseball bat, delivering a hit on the football field. They afford an additional benefit in a violent sport like football because one of their side effects is aggressiveness or, in extreme cases, so-called roid rage.

Their use is starkly high risk, high reward. Other side effects include liver tumors, impotence, breast enlargement and shrunken testicles in men and male sexual characteristics in women. (Some of the side effects for women include enlargement of the clitoris, deepening of the voice, facial hair and male-pattern baldness.)

If you want a peek at the future of performance-enhanced sport—at what drug-laced athletes can accomplish—look back to the mid-80's, the apex of East Germany's shameful and ruthlessly effective doping program. The East Germans were not the only practitioners of extreme pharmacological sport, only the most flagrant and well organized. (East Germany is the only nation known to have systematically doped athletes, often minors, without their knowledge.)

"Things really got out of hand in the 1970's, 80's and 90's," Richard Pound of the W.A.D.A. says. Even as the science of detection improved, the International Olympic Committee and other global sports bodies were constrained, he says, by a "hesitancy to offend" either side while the world was still divided between East and West. "We looked away, and it snowballed."

Steroid usage works particularly well for women athletes, because they naturally make only a fraction of the testosterone that men produce. John Hoberman says: "In the 80's, what we saw was this new breed of monster athletes, particularly on the female side."

Certain records from this heyday of unpoliced steroid abuse—particularly in sports in which raw strength is a primary requirement—suggest that performances were achieved then that are unlikely to be matched by a clean competitor. The top 14 men's hammer throws in history occurred between 1984 and 1988. In the women's shot-put, you must go all the way down to the 35th farthest throw in history to find one that occurred after 1988.

Until last April, the top 10 men's shot-put throws in history occurred between 1975 and 1990. Then, at a competition in Kansas, the American shot-putter Kevin Toth finally broke into that elite group. His distance, 22.67 meters, was the farthest that anyone had put the shot in 13 years. Six months later, Toth's name was among the first to surface in the Balco scandal. Published reports said he had tested positive for THG, the new designer steroid.

In women's sprinting in the 80's, the star—and still the world-record holder in the 100- and 200-meter dashes—was Florence Griffith Joyner, FloJo. Americans loved her style, her body-hugging track suits, her long and fabulously decorated nails, her ebullience. Elsewhere in the world, and even in the United States among those with a knowledge of track and field, FloJo's exploits were viewed with more skepticism.

After Joyner died in 1998, at 38 (the cause was related to a seizure), a strange hybrid of a column appeared in the New York Times sports section. Written by Pat Connolly, who had coached Evelyn Ashford, the woman whose 100-meter record Joyner smashed, it was partly a tribute and partly a posthumous indictment. "Then, almost overnight, Florence's face changed—hardened along with her muscles that now bulged as if she had been born with a barbell in her crib," Connolly wrote. "It was difficult not to wonder if she had found herself an East German coach and was taking some kind of performance-enhancing drugs."

FloJo had been a very good, but never a champion, world-class sprinter. Her 1988 performance in Seoul was—in the damning parlance of international sport—anomalous.

We don't normally think of baseball in the context of hammer throwing, shot-putting or women's sprinting. But in terms of anomalous performance, baseball is East Germany in the 1980's: a frontier.

Just as in the steroid-drenched days of Olympic sport, a deep suspicion has attached itself to some of the latest records in baseball. This accompanies the grotesqueness of the appearance of some of the players. Curt Schilling, the All-Star pitcher, memorably told Sports Illustrated in 2002, "Guys out there look like Mr. Potato Head, with a head and arms and six or seven body parts that just don't look right."

I'm not sure whom, exactly, Schilling had in mind, but for me, his comment recalls a particular photograph taken in the 2002 season. The subjects are the home-run kings Barry Bonds and Sammy Sosa, sitting together, both of them with thick necks and bloated-looking faces. They look, well, freakish—as well as starkly different from their appearance as young players. Bonds entered baseball lean and wiry strong, much like his late father, the All-Star outfielder Bobby Bonds. Sosa, early in his ca-

reer, was not particularly big and showed little power at the plate.

The question of how many home runs it is possible to hit in one season is more open-ended than, say, the fastest possible time a person can achieve in the 100-meter dash. Factors like the size of the ballpark, liveliness of the ball and skill of opposing pitchers affect the outcome. Nevertheless, a century's worth of experience amounted to a pretty persuasive case that around 60 home runs, for whatever combination of reasons, was about the limit.

In 1927, Babe Ruth slugged 60, which remained the record until 1961, when Roger Maris (in a slightly longer season) hit 61. But in 1998 Mark McGwire of the St. Louis Cardinals obliterated Maris's record by hitting 70 home runs.

Late in that season, a reporter snooping around McGwire's locker spotted a bottle of androstenedione, or andro, a substance usually described as a steroid "precursor" that provides a steroidlike effect (and that is still unregulated in the major leagues). McGwire was forced to acknowledge that his strength was neither entirely "God given" nor acquired solely in the weight room. But at least McGwire entered baseball already big and as a prodigious home-run hitter; he hit 49 in his first big-league season, a record for rookies. Contrast that with the career arcs of Bonds and Sosa, which are unlike any in the game's long history.

Bonds had never hit more than 46 home runs until the 2000 season, and in most years his total was in the 30's. But at age 35, when players normally are on the downside of their production, he hit 49 home runs. The following season he turned into superman, breaking McGwire's record by hitting 73.

Bonds's totals in the next two seasons, 46 and 45, were artificially low because pitchers walked him a staggering 346 times. His new capabilities had thrown the balance between pitcher and hitter completely out of whack: the new Barry Bonds was too good for the game. He needed a league all his own.

Sosa's progression was even more unusual. In his first eight major-league seasons he averaged 22 home runs, although his totals did steadily increase and he hit 40 in 1996, then a career high. He was selected an All-Star exactly once. Unlike Bonds, he was not considered among baseball's elite players.

Then in 1998, McGwire's record-breaking year, Sammy Sosa hit 66 home runs—6 more than the great Babe Ruth had hit in his best season. Sosa wasn't done. The following year he hit 63, followed by seasons of 50, 64 and 49—the best five-year total in baseball history.

That there is rampant steroid use in baseball, at all levels, is undeniable. Ken Caminiti, the 1996 National League M.V.P., admitted his own use in a Sports Illustrated article in 2002 and estimated that at least half the players in the big leagues built strength with steroids. The former slugger Jose Canseco has acknowledged steroid use. In a 2002 USA Today survey of 556 big-league players, 44 percent said they felt pressure to take steroids.

Last year, The Washington Post published a sad series of stories revealing that teenage prospects in the baseball-rich Dominican Republic, the source of nearly one-fourth of all players signed to U.S. pro contracts, are taking veterinary steroids to try to get strong enough to attract the interest of scouts.

Whether Sosa and Bonds have built home-run power chemically cannot be known definitively. Nobody has presented evidence that they have, and both vehemently deny it. Sosa's name has not surfaced in the Balco case, and he has not testified before the grand jury.

Bonds did testify in December. The home of his personal trainer and boyhood friend, Greg Anderson, has been searched by federal agents. Bonds has acknowledged patronizing Balco, which under Victor Conte, its founder, has specialized in testing athletes' blood to determine the levels of elements like copper, chromium and magnesium and then recommending supplements. Experts I talked to say they consider Conte's theories medical mumbo jumbo, but he consulted with dozens of top athletes, including Marion Jones; Amy Van Dyken, an Olympic champion swimmer; and Bill Romanowski, a linebacker in the N.F.L. Jason Giambi of the Yankees was also a client and also testified before the grand jury.

In an article that appeared last June, Bonds told Muscle and Fitness magazine: "I visit Balco every three to six months. They check my blood to make sure my levels are where they should be. Maybe I need to eat more broccoli than I normally do. Maybe my zinc and magnesium intakes need to increase."

Bob Ryan, a veteran Boston Globe sports columnist, is among the baseball devotees who want to believe all Bonds is taking is broccoli and vitamins. But with both Bonds and Sosa, the presumption of innocence he would like to grant them clashes with the accumulation of circumstantial evidence and his own common sense.

"I knew every baseball benchmark from the time I was 10 or 11 years old," Ryan says. "I knew 60, and I knew 61. I knew 714 (the former career home-run mark held by Babe Ruth). Stats frame who a player is. They're part of the romance of the game, the enjoyment."

Bonds, with 658 career home runs, could surpass Hank Aaron's all-time total of 755 in just two or three more seasons. If he does, what will it mean? Will it carry the romance of other cherished baseball records? "Bonds was a leadoff man who could run early in his career, and now he is this hulking slugger," Ryan says. "Sammy, same thing. You want to believe it's all due to weight training and nutrition, but you have these guys hitting 40 home runs, maximum, and then well into their careers, they're in the 60's and 70's. It doesn't happen."

But Ryan is not seeking much new information on this subject. "I'm afraid of what you're going to tell me next," he says at one point in our conversation. "I'm living in some sort of denial. I'm afraid to look under the rock."

THE WORLD Anti-Doping Agency, imperfect as it may be, is generally considered an improvement over the patchwork approach to drug enforcement that preceded it. Created in 1999 at the World Conference on Doping in Sport in Lausanne, Switzerland, the agency was intended to bring coherence to antidoping regulations and "harmonization" among all the different nations and sports bodies expected to enforce them. In theory, it is the ultimate authority on matters of drugs and sport—looming over national Olympic committees and the national and international federations of all the individual sports and making it more difficult for those parochial interests to protect athletes caught doping.

W.A.D.A.'s medical committee devoted several years to compiling an impressively voluminous list of banned substances. But the role of W.A.D.A. and its president, Richard Pound, is mainly bureaucratic and political. W.A.D.A. can't slow science down—or influence a culture that hungrily pursues human enhancements of all kinds.

"All of these issues are going to be moot in 20 or 30 years," says Paul Root Wolpe, a professor of psychiatry at Penn and the chief of bioethics at NASA. "We already are seeing a blurring of the line between foods and drugs, so-called nutraceuticals. In the future, it will be more common, accepted. We'll eat certain engineered foods to be sharp for a business meeting, to increase confidence, to enhance endurance before a race or competition."

Currently, in determining whether to put something on its banned list, W.A.D.A. considers whether a substance is performance enhancing, contrary to the spirit of sport or potentially dangerous to health. "If it meets two of the three criteria, we are likely to put it on the list," Pound says.

But the first two criteria are ambiguous. Steroids and EPO are clearly performance enhancing. But so might Gatorade be, if you believe its advertising and all the data on the "science of hydration" disseminated by the Gatorade Sports Science Institute. And plenty of sports drinks claim to do more than Gatorade. "You identify a line and draw it somewhere," Pound says. "Why is it the 100-meter dash and not the 97-meter dash? It just is."

Between Gatorade and anabolic steroids lie all those powders and pills and injectibles that elite athletes put into their bodies, in quantities and combinations that may enhance performance or may prove innocuous. In most cases, no one is quite sure.

Less open to interpretation is "potentially dangerous to health." Any medical or pseudo-medical activity that takes place underground or in the black market is, by definition, dangerous. Nearly everyone, regardless of how they feel about abortion, will agree that it's more dangerous when it occurs in a back alley. Steroid use, dicey in most situations, is certainly more so when it takes place in the dark.

So issues of health are the strongest rationale for W.A.D.A. and the whole antidoping effort: to protect athletes from their own worst instincts. (Though the sports world is selective about its concerns for athletes' health. Offensive lineman in the N.F.L. just keep on getting fatter. The typical career of a major-league pitcher usually involves the gradual deterioration of shoulder and elbow.) But safety is going to become less of an issue.

"Right now we have a crude way of enhancing muscle mass," Wolpe says. "Years from now we'll look back on it, and it will seem low tech. When it's all on the dining-room table, there will not be the same kind of health issues we are seeing now with the unregulated and illicit supplements and drugs."

WHAT I LEARNED during my visit to Lee Sweeney's lab at the University of Pennsylvania is that lifting his research for purposes of athletic enhancement is not from some sci-fi future. It's possible—now.

Sweeney and his team know for sure they can build muscle mass and strength. Their next step as they try to determine if their methods are safe for humans will be to experiment on larger animals, most likely dogs with muscular dystrophy.

I asked Elisabeth Barton what would happen if some rogue nation or outlaw conglomerate of athletes asked her to disregard scientific prudence and create a human version of the mighty mice. Could she do it?

"Could I?" she answered. "Oh, yeah, it's easy. It's doable. It's a routine method that's published. Anyone who can clone a gene and work with cells could do it. It's not a mystery."

Behind her, Sweeney nodded his head in agreement. "It's not like growing a third arm or something," he said. "You could get there if you worked at it."

Sweeney said that once someone decided to use gene therapy to enhance performance, "you would not be limited to what I'm doing. You could change the endurance of the muscle or modulate the speed—all the performance characteristics. All the biology is there. If someone said, 'Here's $10 million—I want you to do everything you can think of in terms of sports,' you could get pretty imaginative."

To strengthen leg muscles for a sprinter, Sweeney said, he would "put the whole leg on bypass. I would isolate the leg and put in the virus through the blood. It would be more efficient than injections, which you would need a lot of because you're dealing with large muscles. But this is nothing a vascular surgeon couldn't do."

Could one already be doing it? "I don't know that it's not happening."

IGF-1 is already available on the Internet in ingestible form. It is advertised as a component of various powders and pills, and in this form it falls somewhere in that vast, murky area of legal, quasi-legal, black-market and plainly illegal substances for sale in the semiregulated supplement industry.

But Sweeney says that any nongenetic transfer of the protein would be ineffective—it would not circulate in

the blood in levels high enough to build muscle—and unsafe, because to the extent that it does circulate, it would target nonskeletal muscle, including the heart. (The mighty mice have shown no signs of enlarged hearts or other organs and no sign at all that the IGF-1 is circulating in their bloodstreams.)

For the elite athlete, that would be one of the benefits of genetic IGF-1. It wouldn't circulate in the blood. It would be detectable only through a muscle biopsy. It took a long time for the world's athletes to agree to submit to blood tests; it's difficult to imagine them consenting to having investigatory needles stuck in their muscles.

W.A.D.A. INVITED geneticists and others involved in the latest medical research to a conference in 2002 on Long Island. The antidoping officials were (and still are) focused on the IGF-1 research at Penn, so Lee Sweeney was there. He listened as Richard Pound tried a very tough sell.

The W.A.D.A. president told the scientists that he certainly appreciated the work they were doing, knew that they approached it with single-minded dedication and understood full well that nothing was more important than seeking cures for dread diseases. He then talked about another "humanistic activity" that he said was already threatened by science of a certain kind—the current science of performance enhancement—and could be ruined by the misuse of their research. As they moved forward, Pound asked, could they somewhere keep in mind the interests of sport?

As Pound recalls, the initial responses he got were somewhat dismissive: "They said we work at the gene level. You can't really tell what was altered from what was there naturally."

Pound, a lawyer, then asked rhetorically: "What if I could assure the Nobel Prize in Medicine would be awarded to the person in this room who figured out how to make a test to determine if a competitor had been genetically enhanced? You could do it, right?"

Pound got an acknowledgment that detection might be possible with enough resources devoted to it.

Lee Sweeney generously consults with W.A.D.A. and other antidoping officials. He's sympathetic to their cause. He just says it's hopeless. "There will come a day when they just have to give up," he says. "It's maybe 20 years away, but it's coming."

There is a parallel from the past for the entire issue of performance-enhancing drugs, one tied to what was once another unwelcome substance in sports: money. Some casual followers of the Olympic movement may still not fully realize that nearly all of the participants are now paid professionals. There never was any big announcement that the cherished concept of amateurism—athletes competing for the pure love of sport—had been discarded. But over time, the changed reality has been accepted. Top athletes profiting from under-the-table payments? The public didn't care, and the ideal of amateurism expired, outdated and unenforceable.

One of the last things Pound said to me indicated that he knows, too, that W.A.D.A.'s mission has an expiration date pending. Maybe genetic enhancements really won't work for athletes, he speculated. "If you strengthen the muscle to three times its normal strength, what happens when you break out of the starting blocks? Do you rip the muscle right off the bone?"

Pound seemed to like the thought of this gruesome image. He paused, then extended the thought. "That would be nice if that happened," he said. "It would be self-regulating."

Michael Sokolove, a contributing writer for the magazine, is the author of "The Ticket Out: Darryl Strawberry and the Boys of Crenshaw," to be published in April.

From the *New York Times* Magazine, January 12, 2004, pages 28, 30-33, 48, 54, 58. Copyright © 2004 by Michael Sokolove. Distributed by The New York Times Special Features. Reprinted by permission.

Is the Drug War Over? The Declining Proportion of Drug Offenders

By Graham Farrell and David E. Carter

The explosion of the prison population, involving large increases in drug offenders as a consequence of the war on drugs, has arguably been the story of American criminal justice during the past 20 years.[1] Yet by 2000, the proportion of U.S. inmates sentenced for drug offenses had been fairly stable for a decade, with an overall decline in recent years. In 2000, the proportion of drug offenders was only 0.3 percent above its 1990 level. Is it possible that the war on drugs has not been the principal driver of prison increases for the better part of the past decade? If so, could it be that one of the more infamous eras of U.S. incarceration is coming to a close?

Blumstein and Beck's (1999) essay on trends in the prison population may well be the most recent definitive review. Blumstein is an internationally renowned expert on such issues, while Beck oversees prison-related data for the Bureau of Justice Statistics. Their 1999 review assessed trends up until 1996. It concluded that regarding the 200 percent increase in the prison population between 1980 and 1996, "the dominant factor is drug offending."

There is not necessarily any contradiction between that finding and the one suggested here, which is based on analysis of more recent data. The current study has two aims. The first is to document the fact that despite the previous long-term increases, the proportion of inmates sentenced for drug offenses was stable during most of the 1990s, and on average, declining for six years up to 2000 (for seven years to October 2001 for federal prisons, for which more recent data were available at the

time of this writing). The second aim is to outline possible explanations for the trend.

Drug Offender Trends

The analysis herein, including the data-related statement and charts, are derived from the BJS data listed in Table 1. There is little doubt why drug offenders have figured prominently in recent discourse about the prison system. From 1980 to 2000, the number of sentenced drug offenders increased more than 13 times, from 23,749 to 314,998. Between 1980 and 1990, the number of drug offenders in U.S. prisons increased annually by an average of 22.5 percent and never less than 10 percent. The increase was sharpest between 1987 and 1990, when it ranged from 27 percent to 48 percent. The war on drugs raged (see Figure 1).

The rapid rise in the number of drug offenders during the second half of the 1980s, and its continuation through the 1990s, is well-known. However, when viewed as a proportion of total inmates, the story of drug offenders is somewhat different. National trends largely reflect those of state prisons that contain the bulk of inmates, and from less than 10 percent in the early 1980s, drug offenders rose to, and stayed at a level around, one-quarter of sentenced inmates for the first half of the 1990s (see Figure 2). The fairly horizontal nature of the trend for all U.S. prisons shows that as a proportion of total sentenced inmates, the number of drug offenders changed little throughout the 1990s and declined in recent years. The proportion of the

Table 1: Total and Drug-Offense Inmates in State and Federal Prisons, 1980-2000

	State Prison Inmates		Federal Prison Inmates	
	Total	**Drug Offense**	**Total**	**Drug Offense**
1980	295,819	19,000	19,023	4,749
1981	333,251	21,700	19,765	5,076
1982	375,603	25,300	20,938	5,518
1983	394,953	26,600	26,027	7,201
1984	417,389	31,700	27,622	8,152
1985	451,812	38,900	27,623	9,491
1986	486,655	45,400	30,104	11,344
1987	520,336	57,900	33,246	13,897
1988	562,605	79,100	33,758	15,087
1989	629,995	120,100	37,758	18,852
1990	689,600	149,700	46,575	24,297
1991	728,605	155,200	52,176	29,667
1992	778,495	172,300	59,516	35,398
1993	828,566	186,000	68,183	41,393
1994	904,647	202,100	73,958	45,367
1995	989,007	224,900	76,947	46,669
1996	1,032,440	237,600	80,872	49,096
1997	1,074,809	222,100	87,294	52,059
1998	1,136,760	236,800	95,323	55,984
1999	1,189,800	251,200	104,500	60,399
2000	1,206,400	251,100	112,329	63,898

Source: Bureau of Justice Statistics

Figure 1: The Usual Suspects: Sentenced Drug-Offense Inmates, 1980-2000

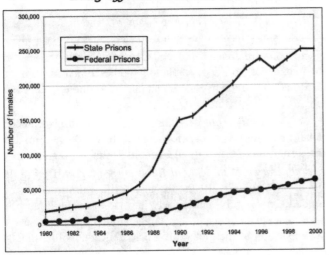

drug offenders in U.S. prisons in 2000 was the same as in 1990 (to within 0.3 percent).

Drug offenders were more prominent in the federal prison population than in the U.S. prison population as a whole. During the first half of the 1980s, approximately one-quarter of sentenced federal inmates were drug offenders. In 1990, for the first time, they surpassed the number of inmates for all other types of offenses—24,297, or 52 percent of all sentenced federal inmates, were drug offenders. That figure rose to a peak of 61.3 percent in 1994.

Distinguishing between the absolute and the relative number of drug offenders, although extraordinarily simple in analytic terms, produces two considerably different stories of the impact of the war on drugs. When absolute numbers are considered, the story of the 1990s appears similar to that of the 1980s. When relative numbers are considered, the trend across the 1990s is very different from that of the 1980s. This is because although the number of drug offenders increased in absolute terms, it did not increase relative to offenders for other crime types during the 1990s.

The trend that is the subject of this study is most apparent if the data are transformed one step further. When the annual change in the proportion of inmates is examined, an underlying trend in the makeup of the prison population is revealed. Figure 3 shows annual change grouped into five-year periods for visual clarity. The proportion of drug offenders was accelerating during the 1980s, particularly in the second half of that decade. The rate of growth slowed in the early 1990s. Since the mid-1990s, the proportion of drug offenders in U.S. prisons has decreased (see Figure 3).

The decreasing proportion of drug offenders was more marked and consistent in federal than in state prisons. In federal prisons, the proportion of drug offenders increased between 1990 and 1994, but at a declining rate. Since 1994, however, the proportion of federal drug offenders did not increase during any year. For the seven years until 2001, the proportion of federal inmates sentenced for drug offenses was either stable or decreasing. The proportion of sentenced federal inmates who were drug offenders fell 5.2 percent between 1995 and 2001. For the prison system as a whole, there was greater variation in the direction of change, but a similar tendency toward stability or a decrease in more recent years.

Skepticism: The First Response

Skepticism is a natural response to the unexpected: it is also a good research aid. The authors of this article were skeptical about the existence and significance of the trend discussed herein. The first main area of skepticism was the belief that such a trend would already be common knowledge. The second was that if it had not been widely known, perhaps that was because it was substantively insignificant?

Why Did So Few People Notice?

Several people will undoubtedly have noticed the decline in the proportion of drug offenders. Alert practitioners and analysts may have noticed it, particularly if it is more pronounced

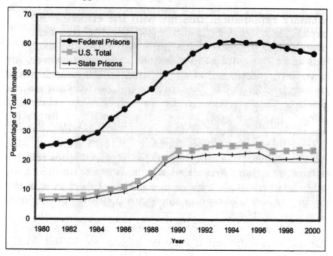

Figure 2: Prison Population: Percentage of Drug Offenders, 1980-2000

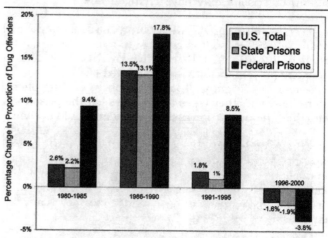

Figure 3: Percentage Change in Proportion of Drug Offenders in Sentenced Prison Population, 1980-2000 (5-Year Periods)

at the local levels (the national aggregates presented here will mask local and regional variations). However, a preliminary trawl of magazines and journals relating to prisons, combined with discussions among a small convenience sample of experts, suggest that there has been little attention paid to this underlying trend.[2] If the trend has been previously documented, then it does not appear to be a frequent subject of discussion among academic prison experts and is not prominently acknowledged in the academic or practitioner literature. Why would this be the case? Perhaps the trend is counterintuitive so that no one was looking for it, or those who noticed thought it an aberration that was too minor and brief to warrant exploration. It is more likely that it appeared trivial in light of the continuing massive increase in drug offenders.

Is It Important?

Is there any significance to the trend of a decreasing proportion of drug offenders? After all, the trend occurs in the context of continuing massive increases in the overall number of incarcerated drug offenders.

There may be much truth in the observation that the key issue is the continuing overall growth in drug offenders. However, noticing one trend does not preclude seeing another: When studying the economy, it is normal to examine overall output as well as growth, and output in different sectors and their relative growths, as well as at short- and long-term inflation and interest rates. Rates of change in economic indicators are examined to reveal underlying trends: A declining rate of increase in productivity, for example, may set off economic warning bells that go unnoticed when only output is examined. In truth, each statistical indicator provides different and complementary information. It is the same with prison statistics. Studying proportions of inmates in different categories and their relative rates of change in no way distracts from the importance of the overall trend. However, like ignoring the relative rate of annual change in the economy, ignoring the underlying dynamic of the compo-

sition of the prison population could cause certain issues to be overlooked. The issue in the current case is that the composition of the prison population has altered. More specifically, changes in the prison population have been driven less by drug offenders in recent years, and more by inmates for other offenses. Something, somewhere, has changed and it began to change quite some time ago. It may be difficult to tease out the implications that relate to the overly politicized issues of illicit drugs, the war on drugs and drug offenders. However, the fact that the trend may only be potentially significant does not detract from the need to draw the attention of a broader audience.

Rival Explanations

Why has the proportion of drug offenders been stable or declining? It is possible to speculate and develop rival explanations. Although it is unlikely to be an exhaustive list in this preliminary foray, several hypotheses are presented below. The possibility that there are multiple and overlapping explanations for the trend should also be considered. Possible explanations of a declining proportion of drug offenders include:

Reporting and/or Recording Changes. The Federal Bureau of Prisons may have changed how it categorizes inmates.

Diversion of Drug Offenders. Drug courts mushroomed in the mid-1990s, so it is possible to hypothesize that the trend is due to non-incarcerative treatment options or more lenient sentencing for drug-related offenses.

Community Re-entry. If larger numbers of drug offenders rather than other types of offenders left the prison system, then the proportion of drug offenders could decline.

Stabilization of the Global Illicit Drug Market. During the late 1980s and early 1990s, the global illicit drug market expanded significantly, particularly in relation to the illicit production of opiates, cocaine and amphetamine-type stimulants. If the expansion of the global drug market accounts for some of the increase in drug-related incarcerations, perhaps its more recent stabilization (particularly for opiates and cocaine) reduced the input of drug offenders.

Sentence Lengths. The number of prison inmates is a function of the number of new incoming inmates (the incidence rate) and outgoing inmates (the release rate), measured via sentence lengths. Perhaps drug offense sentence lengths were short compared with those of other offenses. This could produce a huge throughput of drug offenders, but little change in the total number of drug offenders when measured at any one point in time.

Presidential Terms. Although President Richard Nixon declared the war on drugs in the early 1970s, the main drug war effect coincides with the terms of Ronald Reagan and George Bush Sr. in the 1980s and early 1990s. Allowing for a lag of two or three years to reflect processing and change, perhaps the 1990s trends reflect Bill Clinton's presidency. This is speculation and probably coincidence (although the fit with presidential terms is even better when only federal inmates are considered). If it is true, then a George Bush Jr. effect might (like father, like son) produce an increase in the proportion of drug offenders around 2004 or 2005.

Change Relating to Non-Drug-Offense Inmates. Drug offenders have only declined in recent years when compared with non-drug-offense inmates. Perhaps the war on drugs has continued apace, but the war on other types of offenses has expanded. This could reflect changes either in law, law enforcement practice and priorities, prosecution, court or sentencing practices, or the overall makeup of crime (such as the possibility of increased organized crime).

Discussion

The first hypothesis—that reporting or recording practices changed—cannot be eliminated but seems unlikely to be a valid explanation since it would probably manifest itself as a sudden or one-off statistical change. The diversion, release, fewer drug crimes and reduced sentence severity hypotheses all seek explanations in terms of a decline in the number of drug offenders. Yet, since there has been no decline in the absolute number of drug offenders (see Figure 1), these hypotheses can be dismissed altogether. The presidential term hypothesis is probably spurious: It would manifest itself via more local mechanisms, such as changes in law, law enforcement and sentencing. Further, while it cannot necessarily be wholly ruled out at this stage, it also seems to be a drug offense-based explanation.

The most compelling explanation seems to be that the declining proportion of drug offenders is due to the more marked increase in non-drug-offense inmates. As a preliminary explanation, this fits with the evidence: A more explosive increase in non-drug-offense inmates began to overshadow the increase in drug offenders. The nature of this change, and how and why it occurred, however, are beyond the scope of this article. Additional research would be required to thoroughly investigate the relevant issues. Such research would require lower-level data relating to offense types, as well as, perhaps, extensive information on various aspects of the criminal justice system. Identifying a need for additional research is not unusual. Further research is still required to explore issues relating to the fact that

even when the proportion of U.S. drug offenders was at its highest in the early 1990s, it was still below the levels of several European countries (Van Horne and Farrell, 1999).

Is the drug war over? Has it been over for a decade? Almost certainly not: It may be premature to herald the end of an era. Drug offenders have stabilized, and even decreased, as a proportion of total inmates. However, the most compelling explanation is that the volume of sentenced non-drug-offense inmates has surged to the extent that they even outweigh the continuing increase in drug offenders resulting from an ongoing war on drugs. Perhaps this reflects a new war on violence and on organized and transnational crime rather than a reduction of the war on drugs. Increased attention on non-drug offenders could itself be linked to the illicit drug trade, perhaps reflecting increased sentencing for racketeering, money laundering or other linked charges, some of which may not be classified as drug offenses in prison statistics. It is worth noting that the first of the rival hypotheses, relating to classification, and the reporting and recording of inmates, could not be entirely eliminated and warrants further examination. The volume of drug offenders continues to increase so there does not seem to have been a reversal in a national trend in incarceration that has dominated prison discourse and much of criminal justice discourse for a generation.

The analysis presented herein is elementary. The intention was to document the markedly different tale of events that emerges when relative rather than absolute numbers of inmates are considered. The findings are not necessarily in contradiction with Blumstein and Beck's interpretation that drug offenders were the dominant factor in the 200 percent increase in prison inmates between 1980 and 1996. However, between 1980 and 1996, the increase in drug offenders accounted for 33 percent of the increase in the U.S. prison population.[3] Between 1980 and 2000, drug offenders accounted for 29 percent of the increase in the U.S. prison population.[4] Consequently, while the degree of "dominance" of drug offending depends on the level of disaggregation of the data, the present analysis sheds a different light on the situation. At a minimum, the decreasing proportion of drug offenders, which may well reflect the rise in non-drug-offense inmates, may warrant further examination.

ENDNOTES

[1] All federal inmate numbers are from: Federal Bureau of Prisons. 2002. *Quick facts, May 2002.* Available at www.bop.gov/fact0598.html.

State inmate numbers for 1980, 1985, 1990, 1991, 1992, 1993 and 1994 are from: Beck, A. J., and D. K. Gillard. 1995. *Prisoners in 1994.* Washington, D.C.: Bureau of Justice Statistics.

State inmate numbers for 1981, 1982, 1983, 1984, 1986, 1987, 1988 and 1989 are from: Snell, T. L. 1995. *Correctional populations in the United States, 1993.* Washington, D.C.: Bureau of Justice Statistics.

State inmate numbers for 1995, 1996 and 1997 are from: Chaiken, J. M. 2000. *Correctional populations in the United States, 1997.* Washington, D.C.: Bureau of Justice Statistics.

State inmate numbers for 1998, 1999 and 2000 are from: Harrison, P. M. and A. J. Beck, 2003. *Prisoners in 2001*. Washington, D.C.: Bureau of Justice Statistics.

[2] As our convenience sample of experts, we are grateful to professors Francis T. Cullen, John Eck, Edward J. Latessa, Patricia Van Voorhis and John Wooldredge for comments and advice on previous drafts.

[3] Between 1980 and 1996, the total prison population increased by 798,740 inmates, of whom 262,947—or 32.9 percent—were drug offenders (see Table 1).

[4] Between 1980 and 2000, the total prison population increased by 1,003,887 inmates, of whom 291,249—or 29 percent—were drug offenders (see Table 1).

REFERENCES

Blumstein, A. and A. J. Beck. 1999. Population growth in U.S. prisons, 1980–1996. In *Crime and justice: A review of research,* eds. M. Tonry and J. Petersilia, 17–62. Chicago: University of Chicago Press.

Brown, J. M., D. K. Gillard, T. L. Snell, J. J. Stephan and D. J. Wilson. 1996. *Correctional populations in the United States, 1994.* Washington, D.C.: Bureau of Justice Statistics.

Gillard, D. K. and A. J. Beck. 1996. *Prison and jail inmates, 1995.* Washington, D.C.: Bureau of Justice Statistics.

Gillard, D. K. and A. J. Beck. 1998. *Prisoners in 1997.* Washington, D.C.: Bureau of Justice Statistics.

Van Horne, S. and G. Farrell. 1999. *Drug offenders in the global criminal justice system.* HEUNI Paper series, paper 13. Helsinki, Finland: European Institute for Crime Prevention and control. Available at www.vn.fi/om/suomi/heuni/news/hp13.pdf.

Graham Farrell, Ph.D., is an associate professor in the Division of Criminal Justice at the University of Cincinnati. He was previously deputy research director at the Police Foundation in Washington, D.C., prior to which he researched international drug policy at the United Nations. David E. Carter is a doctoral candidate in the Division of Criminal Justice at the University of Cincinnati and assistant administrator for the master's degree in criminal justice with a focus in addiction studies. He holds an M.A. from East Tennessee State University.

From *Corrections Compendium*, February 2003, pp. 1-4, 28. © 2003 by the American Correctional Association, Lanham, MD 20706-4322. Reprinted by permission.

So here's to privatizing the public costs of alcohol abuse

By Konrad Moore

As matters of economic analysis, alcohol and tobacco carry high societal price tags. While recent litigation and settlements have succeeded in shifting some of the costs associated with tobacco use to cigarette companies, the alcohol industry has essentially managed to avoid similar liability.

Given the increasing need to reduce public spending, it is time to extend the same liability to the alcohol industry and for shareholders to replace taxpayers as the group principally responsible for payment of expenses underlying the alcohol industry's profits.

The potential savings from privatizing alcohol's costs are enormous, and in large measure stem from the fact that alcoholism is an astonishingly prevalent and costly disease. According to the National Institute on Alcohol Abuse and Alcoholism, alcoholism affects some 8 percent to 14 percent of the population. Chronic liver disease and cirrhosis are the 12th leading cause of death in the United States, and the third leading cause of preventable mortality.

In economic terms, these statistics translate into staggering sums. From 1985 to 1992, the costs of alcoholism and alcohol-related problems rose by more than 40 percent to $148 billion, according to the National Institutes of Health. Moreover, untreated alcoholics incur health-care costs at least 100 percent higher than those of nonalcoholics. Ironically, the profits of the alcohol industry remain largely undisturbed by these burgeoning expenses.

Comparing the costs of alcohol to those associated with tobacco reveals striking parallels. In 2002, the California Supreme Court, commenting on tobacco wrote,"Tobacco-related illnesses are a leading cause of death in this state and worldwide, and these debilitating illnesses have imposed enormous costs on tobacco users, their families and society." Replace the word "tobacco" with "alcohol" and the sentence loses nothing in its meaning or accuracy.

Indeed, the parallels extend to indirect victims. Scores of non-smokers die from second-hand smoke, and so too thousands pay the wages of others' alcohol usage. Alcohol drives a substantial amount of crime. It is typically found in the offender, victim or both in about half of all homicides and serious assaults. Alcohol abuse is likewise involved in a high percentage of rapes, robberies and incidents of domestic violence. While perhaps more difficult to quantify, these costs are clearly significant.

When the discussion turns to liability, however, the similarities end. Under California law, the alcohol industry enjoys a peculiarly sheltered status. California Civil Code Section 1714.45 (dubbed the "Immunity Statute") presently shields alcohol manufacturers from product liability actions. Incomprehensibly, under this 1978 statute, alcohol is lumped with sugar, castor oil and butter as commodities whose manufacturers are largely immune from product liability lawsuits.

Until 1998, the tobacco industry was a member of the same exclusive club, benefiting from what one California Court of Appeals described as a ride on "the coattails of a legislative compromise." The ride ended when tobacco was effectively delisted through an amendment which repealed the protection for cigarette companies and manufacturers of other tobacco products.

Since then, the public has substantially benefited by shifting many tobacco-related costs to companies earning revenue from its sale. In time, the opportunity to recoup taxpayers' money may motivate a similar amendment to place the alcohol and tobacco industries on equal footing.

Outside the legislative arena, some pioneering groups are already seeking to impose a measure of accountability. In early February 2004, a California couple whose 20-year-old daughter was killed by an underage drunk driver filed suit against Anheuser-Busch and Miller Brewing, claiming their advertising targets minors. In part, the suit alleges that as recently as 2001, Anheuser-Busch advertised on television shows where the youth audience exceeded 50 percent of the viewership.

Suits like these may well be stymied by the Immunity Statute, although Business and Professions Code 17200, which prohibits unfair and fraudulent business acts, including misleading advertising, may provide a vehicle for limited recovery.

Further, there is a separate and apparently untested basis for challenging the exemption Civil Code Section 1714.45 purports to create. One of the requirements for immunity is that the inherently unsafe nature of the product is known to the consumer "who consumes the product with the ordinary knowledge common to the community." It would seem a compelling argument may be made that alcohol producers, through television and print advertising, have effectively worked to assuage the public's appreciation for the dangers of alcohol.

Anyone with children who watches television, reads magazines or drives past billboards is aware that the inculcation of children into the fun alcohol promises begins well before they reach drinking age. Pretty girls, popular guys and beer bottles playing football all deliver the message the alcohol is an innocuous and seemingly essential ingredient to a good time.

Of course, critics of corporate accountability may contend that alcohol, unlike tar and nicotine, offers some redeeming benefits. For some, moderate alcohol use may even provide a marginal health benefit. It arguably helps people relax and for a large majority of the population presents no direct health threat. Under this line of reasoning, all that is needed is for persons with an alcohol problem to stop drinking. The alcohol industry has even coined a helpful phrase to guide behavior, "Enjoy responsibly."

The problem with a self-responsibility argument is that it ignores the status of alcoholism as a heritable trait. A predisposition to alcohol addiction is programmed into many of us, and lies silently in the genes of many of our children. While choice, no doubt, will play an important role in abusing the drug, a significant number of victims nonetheless will inexorably fall victim to the ravaging effects of alcoholism. Moreover, it is essential to distinguish between the debate over the moral responsibility of alcoholics and alcohol's undeniable economic costs.

Advocating increased liability for the makers of Coors or Budweiser is a far cry from lobbying for prohibition. Rather, a call for corporate responsibility seeks only to more closely align the real costs of alcohol with its profits. Both as a matter of fiscal analysis and fairness, if producers can pay millions of dollars for advertising the popularity and fun alcohol promises, they surely can pay a more substantial share when that promise goes horribly awry.

More to the point, whether by negotiation or litigation, just as with the tobacco industry before it, taxpayers should no longer be required to so substantially underwrite corporate profits.

Konrad Moore is a deputy public defender in Bakersfield.

A Prescription For Abuse

BY RUSSELL SCHANLAUB

The abuse of prescription drugs is certainly not a new crime in the law enforcement arena. However, with drug technology improving by leaps and bounds and newer and more potent drugs hitting the streets, this is a good time to take another look at an ever-changing drug scene.

Most people who are prescribed drugs take them in a responsible, safe and legal manner. Most doctors who prescribe scheduled drugs do so with the best interest of their patients in mind. The exceptions to the rules are those adding to a constantly growing problem that has reached near epidemic proportions in some areas.

If a drug is used by any person other than the one to whom it was prescribed, or if it is used for any purpose other than what it was prescribed for, it is deemed as "non-medical use." The prescription drugs become abused when they are used for the purpose of getting high, sold or given to others, taken with alcohol or other drugs, taken in a larger dose than prescribed, etc.

Law enforcement training over the years has focused on drugs that are produced illegally and many jurisdictions may have lacked training specific to the diversion of legal drugs. Additionally, the large variety and identification process for the drugs make it an area that requires more training and reference materials than identifying what we generally considered street level drugs.

A relaxed approach to prescription drug abuse may be taking its toll. Robberies, thefts and burglaries associated with prescription drugs are on the rise nationwide. Pharmacies have been robbed of their more potent drugs in a strong-armed fashion by crooks who didn't even ask for money, just the drugs.

The Numbers

According to the National Institute on Drug Abuse, in 1999, more than nine million Americans used prescription drugs for non-medical reasons. Among adolescents, prescription drugs rank second in overall abuse among 12- to 14- year-old kids and the improper use of medication kills more than 125,000 Americans each year.

The sheer number of people who are prescribed drugs is awe-inspiring. One study reports that in 2000, Americans bought 2,587,575,000 prescriptions—that's over 2.5 billion, which equals nine prescriptions for every man, woman and child. A recent study though, indicates that children using prescription drugs are on a sharper rise than adults.

Medco Health Solutions, a pharmacy benefits management company and subsidiary of Merck released a study that indicates that prescription drug use is growing faster among children than among the elderly and baby boomers, according to a new study that says spending on prescription medicines for pediatric patients has increased by 85% over the past five years.

Medco points out however, that although there is a dramatic increase in the number of children receiving prescription drugs, the children still make up only about five percent of the drug market. Dr. Robert Epstein, Medco Health's chief medical officer, found that 48.9% of children took one or more prescription medications within the past year compared with 45.7% five years ago.

Another dramatic study showed that an estimated two to four million children and one million adults nationwide are prescribed Ritalin legally. Ritalin is a stimulant and typically is prescribed for children diagnosed with attention deficit/hyperactivity disorder. This kind of availability is making Ritalin an ideal candidate for abuse among young people. Children who have a legitimate prescription for the tablets may sell them to others, or the pills are stolen from book bags and lockers.

The reality is prescription drugs are legal. They are easy to obtain and often, people misuse and abuse what they find in their own medicine cabinets. Many experts report that some people tell themselves they "aren't using something old Joe cooked up in a garage somewhere," they may figure a legitimate manufacturer made the drug, "so what could be the harm?"

The Basics Of Prescription Drugs

The prescription drugs of abuse can be basically broken down into three categories: Opioids, CNS Depressants and CNS Stimulants (CNS stands for Central Nervous Stimulant). The accompanying table published by the National Institute On Drug Abuse helps illustrate what conditions

Drug Type	Common Brand Names	Prescribed For	Physiological Effects	Adverse Effects
Opioids/ Pain relievers	Dilaudid, Lorcet, Lortab, OxyContin, Percocet, Percodan, Tylox, Vicodin	Pain, cough, diarrhea	Affects brain refion that mediates pleasure resulting euphoria	Life-threatening respiratory depression
Depressants (benodiazepines, tranquilizers, barbiturates, sedatives)	Valium, Xanax	Anciety, sleep disorders	Slows down brain activity resulting in a drowsy or calming effect	Seizures, respiratory depressions, decreased heart rate
Stimulants	Adderall, Concerta, Ritalin	Narcolepsy, attention deficit/hyperactivity disorder, obesity	Enhances brain activity resulting in an increase in alertness, attention and energy	High body temperature, irregular heart rate, cardiovascular system failure, fatal seizures, hostility or feeling of paranoia

the drugs are likely to be prescribed for and relates some of the name brands that you may have heard of.

The establishment of the Controlled Substances Act brought about a system of classifying drugs for law enforcement purposes. The DEA lists controlled drugs into "Schedules." Schedule I: Controlled substances which have no approved medical use in the United States, and have a high potential for abuse. Schedule II: Controlled substances, including OxyContin®, which are approved for medical use, and have the highest abuse potential among controlled substances approved for medical use. Schedules III, IV and V: Controlled substances that have a currently accepted medical use, and diminishing potential for abuse.

It's important to keep in mind that there are many prescription drugs that are controlled but not "Scheduled." They require a prescription to possess, however, in many states the offense for illegally possessing or dealing in a schedule drug is a felony, whereas the offense for illegally possessing or dealing in a controlled drug which is not a "scheduled" drug, is only a misdemeanor.

One To Watch

Although there are hundreds of schedule drugs on the market, there may be one that deserves special mention, and that would be OxyContin®.

In 1995 Purdue Pharma introduced a controlled release formulation of OxyCodone, which was intended as treatment for chronic moderate to severe pain. The tablet is marketed as OxyContin® and almost immediately began being abused. A controlled release mechanism was developed into the pill. That mechanism causes the product to be dissipated at a slower rate into the body to provide a longer period of pain relief.

However, abusers soon found that the time release mechanism could be circumvented if they crushed the pill and then swallowed, snorted or injected the drug. This provided a more rapid and intense high for the abuser. Law enforcement reporting indicates that OxyContin, which has heroin-like effects that last up to 12 hours when crushed as described, is the fastest growing threat among oxycodone products. (Oxycodone also is sold under the trade names Percocet, Percodan and Tylox.)

Since 1996, the number of OxyContin® prescriptions has risen to approximately 5.8 million prescriptions in 2000, becoming the number-one prescribed Schedule II narcotic in the United States.

What To Do

Police agencies may consider adding training specific to identifying prescription drugs and investigating prescription drug diversion crimes. The DEA offers training for local and state agencies. Also, information is available in the form of booklets and handout materials through various government sources.

Patrol officers already alert during any occasion that places them inside of a person's residence or vehicle should train themselves to look for evidence of prescription drug abuse with the same diligence as they would look for evidence of marijuana, cocaine or any other controlled substance. While scanning for evidence in plain view or while conducting searches, officers should be aware of the rise in prescription-based drug crimes. With the exception of marijuana, no other drug is abused more than prescription medication.

Officers should be alert for any prescription bottles or more so for any pills they observe that are not in a prescription bottle. A person in possession of a prescription bottle belonging to someone else, pill bottles containing more than one type of drug, or bottles with the label removed are certainly indicators that would warrant further investigation.

The National Drug Information Center is an excellent resource for information and training materials. The Food and Drug Administration also hosts an excellent Web site offering training references and resources. The Drug Enforcement Administration offers training and information on a wide variety of drug topics to local and state police agencies.

Identifying Pills

As far as identifying pills in question, there are many sources available. *The Drug Identification Bible* has been a very popular resource for law enforcement for many years now. The book contains color photographs as well as an identification section where a tablet may be identified based on its design, color and markings. The *Drug Identification Bible* is available from Amera-Chem, P.O. Box 518, Grand junction, CO 81502, Phone: (800) 772-2539, Fax: (800) 852-7870.

Most local pharmacists are able to offer identification of pills as well as inform you of their intended use, schedule location and chemical make-up.

In many states, the Poison Control Center will offer identification over the telephone to law enforcement agencies. You should contact them ahead of time to confirm whether or not they provide this service, what non-emergency number you should dial, and what information they will require. You can locate your local poison control center in your local telephone book, through your local hospital, or online by your city and state or zip code.

An interesting note regarding those selling or dealing prescription drugs. More agencies are reporting that the suspects are over the age of 50, and quite frequently are women. This trend is prevalent to the point that the National Drug Information Center has listed "Pill Ladies" as a street term now used by drug users to describe senior citizen females who are selling their prescriptions.

Prescription drugs, which are widely available and easy to obtain, provide young and old alike with an easily accessible, inexpensive means of altering their mental and physical states. Prescription drugs, when taken as prescribed by a physician, successfully treat a variety of mental or physical conditions. However, when abused, these drugs can alter the brain's activity and lead to debilitating or life-threatening health problems and result in physical or psychological dependence.

Russell Schanlaub is a Special Agent with the Bi-State Drug Task Force in northeast Illinois and northwest Indiana. He is a former Captain with the Newton County, IN Sheriff's Department, a state-certified firearms instructor and charter member of ILEETA. He may be reached at russman@ffni.com.

From *LAW and ORDER* Magazine, November 2003, pp. 93-94, 96. Copyright © 2003 by Hendon Publishing Co. Reprinted with permission. www.lawandordermag.com.

UNIT 2

Understanding How Drugs Work—Use, Dependency, and Addiction

Unit Selections

8. **The Surprising Truth About Addiction**, Stanton Peele
9. **The Addicted Brain**, Eric J. Nestler and Robert C. Malenka
10. **The End of Craving**, Michael Abrams
11. **A New Treatment for Addiction**, Etienne Benson
12. **More Than a Kick**, Kendall Morgan
13. **The Down Side of Up**, Alexis Jetter
14. **Finding the Future Alcoholic**, Steven Stocker
15. **Research Finds Alcohol Tolerance Gene**, Carl Hall
16. **In the Grip of a Deeper Pain**, Jerry Adler

Key Points to Consider

- Why are some drugs so reinforcing?

- Why do some people become dependent upon certain drugs far sooner than other people?

- Is it possible to predict one's personal threshold for becoming drug dependent or addicted? Explain.

 **Links: www.dushkin.com/online/**
These sites are annotated in the World Wide Web pages.

Centre for Addiction and Mental Health (CAMH)
http://www.camh.net
The National Center on Addiction and Substance Abuse at Columbia University
http://www.casacolumbia.org
National Institute on Drug Abuse (NIDA)
http://www.nida.nih.gov

Understanding how drugs act upon the human mind and body is a critical component to the resolution of issues concerning drug use and abuse. An understanding of basic pharmacology is requisite for informed discussion on practically every drug-related issue and controversy. One does not have to look far to find misinformed debate, much of which surrounds the basic lack of knowledge of how drugs work.

Different drugs produce different bodily effects and consequences. All psycho-active drugs influence the central nervous system, which, in turn, sits at the center of how we physiologically and psychologically interpret and react to the world around us. Some drugs, such as methamphetamine and LSD, have great immediate influence on the nervous system, while others, such as tobacco and marijuana, elicit less-pronounced reactions. Almost all psychoactive drugs have their effects on the body mitigated by the dosage level of the drug taken, the manner in which it is ingested, and the physiological and emotional state of the user. Cocaine smoked in the form of crack versus snorted as powder produces profoundly different physical and emotional

effects on the user. However, even though illegal drugs often provide the most sensational perspective from which to view these relationships, the abuse of prescription drugs is being reported as an exploding new component of the addiction problem. Currently, the non-medical use of pain-relievers such as oxycodone and hydrocodone is occurring at rates not observed since the mid-70s. Forty percent of the 119,000 mentions of narcotic pain medications in emergency rooms involved either oxycodone or hydrocodone. This trend has been increasing steadily since 1994.

Molecular properties of certain drugs allow them to imitate and artificially reproduce certain naturally occurring brain chemicals that provide the basis for the drug's influence. The continued use of certain drugs and their repeated alteration of the body's biochemical structure provide one explanation for the physiological consequences of drug use. For example, heroin use replicates the natural brain chemical endorphin, which supports the body's biochemical defense to pain and stress. The continued use of heroin is believed to deplete natural endorphins, causing the nervous system to produce a painful physical and emotional reaction when heroin is withdrawn.

A word of caution is in order when proceeding through the various explanations for what drugs do and why they do it. Many people, because of an emotional and/or political relationship to the world of drugs, assert a subjective predisposition when interpreting certain drugs' effects and consequences. One person's alcoholic is another's social drinker. People often argue, rationalize, and explain the perceived nature of drugs' effects based upon an extremely superficial understanding of diverse pharmacological properties of different drugs. A detached and scientifically sophisticated awareness of drug pharmacology may help strengthen the platform from which to interpret the various consequences of drug use.

Drug dependence and addiction is usually a continuum comprised of experimentation, recreational use, regular use, and abuse. The process is influenced by a plethora of physiological, psychological, and environmental factors. Although some still argue that drug dependence is largely a matter of individual behavior, something to be chosen or rejected, most experts assert that new scientific discoveries clearly define the roots of addiction to live within molecular levels of the brain. Powerful drugs, upon repeated administration, easily compromise the brain's ability to make decisions about its best interests.

Largely, drugs are described as more addictive or less addictive due to a process described as "reinforcement." Simply explained, reinforcement results from a drug's physiological and psychological influence on behavior that causes repeated introduction of the drug to the body. Cocaine and the amphetamines are known as drugs with high reinforcement potential. Persons addicted to drugs known to be strongly reinforcing typically report that they care more about getting the drug than about anything else.

Reinforcement does not, however, provide 'the' basis for understanding addiction. Addiction is a cloudy term used to describe a multitude of pharmacological and environmental factors that produce a compulsive, non-negotiable need for a drug. A thorough understanding of addiction requires an awareness of these many factors. Additionally, the recent mapping of the human genome is providing a new understanding of the genetic influence on the process of addiction. With each passing year, discoveries related to genetics influence thinking on almost all processes related to addiction.

The articles in unit 2 illustrate some of the current research and viewpoints on the ways that drugs act upon the human body. An understanding of these pharmacological processes is critical to understanding the assorted consequences of drug use and abuse. Science has taken us closer to understanding that acute drug use changes brain function profoundly, and that these changes may remain with the user long after the drug has left the system. Subsequently, many new issues have emerged for drug and health-related public policy. Increasingly, drug abuse competes with other social maladies as public enemy number one. Further, the need for a combined biological, behavioral, and social response to this problem becomes more self-evident. Many health care professionals and health care educators, in addition to those from other diverse backgrounds, argue that research dollars spent on drug abuse and addiction should approach that spent on heart disease, cancer, and AIDS.

The Surprising Truth About Addiction

More people quit addictions than maintain them, and they do so on their own. That's not to say it happens overnight. People succeed when they recognize that the addiction interferes with something they value—and when they develop the confidence that they can change.

By Stanton Peele

Change is natural. You no doubt act very differently in many areas of your life now compared with how you did when you were a teenager. Likewise, over time you will probably overcome or ameliorate certain behaviors: a short temper, crippling insecurity.

For some reason, we exempt addiction from our beliefs about change. In both popular and scientific models, addiction is seen as locking you into an inescapable pattern of behavior. Both folk wisdom, as represented by Alcoholics Anonymous, and modern neuroscience regard addiction as a virtually permanent brain disease. No matter how many years ago your uncle Joe had his last drink, he is still considered an alcoholic. The very word *addict* confers an identity that admits no other possibilities. It incorporates the assumption that you can't, or won't, change.

But this fatalistic thinking about addiction doesn't jibe with the facts. More people overcome addictions than do not. And the vast majority do so without therapy. Quitting may take several tries, and people may not stop smoking, drinking or using drugs altogether. But eventually they succeed in shaking dependence.

Kicking these habits constitutes a dramatic change, but the change need not occur in a dramatic way. So when it comes to addiction treatment, the most effective approaches rely on the counterintuitive principle that less is often more. Successful treatment places the responsibility for change squarely on the individual and acknowledges that positive events in other realms may jump-start change.

Consider the experience of American soldiers returning from the war in Vietnam, where heroin use and addiction was widespread. In 90 percent of cases, when GIs left the pressure cooker of the battle zone, they also shed their addictions—in vivo proof that drug addiction can be just a matter of where in life you are.

Of course, it took more than a plane trip back from Asia for these men to overcome drug addiction. Most soldiers experienced dramatically altered lives when they returned. They left the anxiety, fear and boredom of the war arena and settled back into their home environments. They returned to their families, formed new relationships, developed work skills.

> *The very word "addict" confers an identity that admits no other possibilities. It incorporates the assumption that you can't or won't, change.*

Smoking is at the top of the charts in terms of difficulty of quitting. But the majority of ex-smokers quit without any aid—neither nicotine patches nor gum, Smokenders groups nor hypnotism. (Don't take my word for it; at your next social gathering, ask how many people have quit smoking on their own.) In fact, as many cigarette smokers quit on their own, an even higher percentage of heroin and cocaine addicts and alcoholics quit without treatment. It is simply more difficult to keep these habits going through adulthood. It's hard to go to Disney World with your family while you are shooting heroin. Addicts

Six Principles of Change

One The belief that you can change is the key to change. This is not the powerlessness message of the 12 steps but rather the message of self-efficacy. Addictions are really no different from other behaviors—believing you can change encourages commitment to the process and enhances the likelihood of success.

Two The type of treatment is less critical than the individual's commitment to change. People can select how they want to pursue change in line with their own values and preferences. They don't need to be told how to change.

Three Brief treatments can change longstanding habits. It is not the duration of the treatment that allows people to change but rather its ability to inspire continued efforts in that direction.

Four Life skills can be the key to licking addiction. All addictions may not be equal; the community-reinforcement approach, with its emphasis on developing life skills, might be needed for those more severely debilitated by drugs and alcohol.

Five Repeated efforts are critical to changing. People do not often get better instantly—it usually takes multiple efforts. Providing follow-up care allows people to maintain focus on their change goals. Eventually, they stand a good chance of achieving them.

Six Improvement, without abstinence, counts. People do not usually succeed all at once. But they can show significant improvements; and all improvement should be accepted and rewarded. It is counter-productive to kick people out of therapy for failing to abstain. The therapeutic approach of recognizing improvement in the absence of abstinence is called harm reduction.

who quit on their own typically report that they did so in order to achieve normalcy.

Every year, the National Survey on Drug Use and Health interviews Americans about their drug and alcohol habits. Ages 18 to 25 constitute the peak period of drug and alcohol use. In 2002, the latest year for which data are available, 22 percent of Americans between ages 18 and 25 were abusing or were dependent on a substance, versus only 3 percent of those aged 55 to 59. These data show that most people overcome their substance abuse, even though most of them do not enter treatment.

How do we know that the majority aren't seeking treatment? In 1992, the National Institute on Alcohol Abuse and Alcoholism conducted one of the largest surveys of substance use ever, sending Census Bureau workers to interview more than 42,000 Americans about their lifetime drug and alcohol use. Of the 4,500-plus respondents who had ever been dependent on alcohol, only 27 percent had gone to treatment of any kind, including Alcoholics Anonymous. In this group, one-third were still abusing alcohol.

Of those who never had any treatment, only about one-quarter were currently diagnosable as alcohol abusers. This study, known as the National Longitudinal Alcohol Epidemiologic Survey, indicates first that treatment is not a cure-all, and second that it is not necessary. The vast majority of Americans who were alcohol dependent, about three-quarters, never underwent treatment. And fewer of them were abusing alcohol than were those who were treated.

This is not to say that treatment can't be useful. But the most successful treatments are nonconfrontational approaches that allow self-propelled change. Psychologists at the University of New Mexico led by William Miller tabulated every controlled study of alcoholism treatment they could find. They concluded that the leading therapy was barely a therapy at all but a quick encounter between patient and health-care worker in an ordinary medical setting. The intervention is sometimes as brief as a doctor looking at the results of liver-function tests and telling a patient to cut down on his drinking. Many patients then decide to cut back—and do!

Smoking is at the top of the charts in terms of difficulty of quitting. What may be especially remarkable is that most ex-smokers quit without any type of therapy.

As brief interventions have evolved, they have become more structured. A physician may simply review the amount the patient drinks, or use a checklist to evaluate the extent of a drinking problem. The doctor then typically recommends and seeks agreement from the patient on a goal (usually reduced drinking rather than complete abstinence). More severe alcoholics would typically be referred out for specialized treatment. A range of options is discussed (such as attending AA, engaging in activities incompatible with drinking or using a self-help manual). A spouse or family member might be involved in the planning. The patient is then scheduled for a future visit, where progress can be checked. A case monitor might call every few weeks to see whether the person has any questions or problems.

The second most effective approach is motivational enhancement, also called motivational interviewing. This technique throws the decision to quit or reduce drinking—and to find the best methods for doing so—back on the individual. In this case, the therapist asks targeted questions that prompt the individual to reflect on his drinking in terms of his own values and goals. When patients resist, the therapist does not argue with the individual but explores the person's ambivalence about change so as to allow him or her to draw his own conclusions: "You say that you like to be in control of your behavior, yet you feel when you drink you are often not in charge. Could you just clarify that for me?"

Miller's team found that the list of most effective treatments for alcoholism included a few more surprises. Self-help manuals were highly successful. So was the community-reinforcement approach, which addresses the person's capacity to deal with life, notably marital relationships, work issues (such as simply getting a job), leisure planning and social-group formation (a buddy might be provided, as in AA, as a resource to encourage sobriety). The focus is on developing life skills, such as resisting pressures to drink,

coping with stress (at work and in relationships) and building communication skills.

These findings square with what we know about change in other areas of life: People change when they want it badly enough and when they feel strong enough to face the challenge, not when they're humiliated or coerced. An approach that empowers and offers positive reinforcement is preferable to one that strips the individual of agency. These techniques are most likely to elicit real changes, however short of perfect and hard-won they may be.

Psychologist Stanton Peele first wrote about addiction in the classic book Love and Addiction *(with Archie Brodsky) in 1975. This summer, his latest book,* 7 Tools to Beat Addiction, *will be published by Random House/Three Rivers Press.*

The *Addicted* BRAIN

Drug abuse produces long-term changes in the reward circuitry of the brain. Knowledge of the cellular and molecular details of these adaptations could lead to new treatments for the compulsive behaviors that underlie addiction.

By Eric J. Nestler and Robert C. Malenka

White lines on a mirror. A spoon. For many users, the sight of a drug or its associated paraphernalia can elicit shudders of anticipatory pleasure. Then, with the fix, comes the real rush: the warmth, the clarity, the vision, the relief, the sensation of being at the center of the universe. For a brief period, everything feels right. But something happens after repeated exposure to drugs of abuse—whether heroin or cocaine, whiskey or speed.

The amount that once produced euphoria doesn't work as well, and users come to need a shot or a snort just to feel normal; without it, they become depressed and, often, physically ill. Then they begin to use the drug compulsively. At this point, they are addicted, losing control over their use and suffering powerful cravings even after the thrill is gone and their habit begins to harm their health, finances and personal relationships.

Neurobiologists have long known that the euphoria induced by drugs of abuse arises because all these chemicals ultimately boost the activity of the brain's reward system: a complex circuit of nerve cells, or neurons, that evolved to make us feel flush after eating or sex—things we need to do to survive and pass along our genes. At least initially, goosing this system makes us feel good and encourages us to repeat whatever activity brought us such pleasure.

But new research indicates that chronic drug use induces changes in the structure and function of the system's neurons that last for weeks, months or years after the last fix. These adaptations, perversely, dampen the pleasurable effects of a chronically abused substance yet also increase the cravings that trap the addict in a destructive spiral of escalating, use and increased fallout at work and at home. Improved understanding of these neural alterations should help provide better interventions for addiction, so that people who have fallen prey to habit-forming drugs can reclaim their brains and their lives.

Overview/*The Evolution of Addiction*

- Drugs of abuse—cocaine, alcohol, opiates, amphetamine—all commandeer the brain's natural reward circuitry. Stimulation of this pathway reinforces behaviors, ensuring that whatever you just did, you'll want to do again.
- Repeated exposure to these drugs induces long-lasting adaptations in the brain's chemistry and architecture, altering how individual neurons in the brain's reward pathways process information and interact with one another.
- Understanding how chronic exposure to drugs of abuse reshapes an addict's brain could lead to novel, more broadly effective ways to correct the cellular and molecular aberrations that lie at the heart of all addiction.

Drugs to Die For

THE REALIZATION that various drugs of abuse ultimately lead to addiction through a common pathway emerged largely from studies of laboratory animals that began about 40 years ago. Given the opportunity, rats, mice and nonhuman primates will self-administer the same substances that humans abuse. In these experiments, the animals are connected to an intravenous line. They are then taught to press one lever to receive an infusion of drug through the IV, another lever to get a relatively uninteresting saline solution, and a third lever to request a food pellet. Within a few days, the animals are hooked: they readily self-administer cocaine, heroin, amphetamine and many other common habit-forming drugs.

What is more, they eventually display assorted behaviors of addiction. Individual animals will take drugs at the expense of normal activities such as eating and sleeping—some even to the point that they die of exhaustion or malnutrition. For the most addictive substances, such as cocaine, animals will spend most of their waking hours working to obtain more, even if it means pressing a lever hundreds of times for a single hit. And just as human addicts experience intense cravings when they encounter drug paraphernalia or places where they have scored, the animals, too, come to prefer an environment that they associate with the drug—an area in the cage in which lever pressing always provides chemical compensation.

When the substance is taken away, the animals soon cease to labor for chemical satisfaction. But the pleasure is not forgotten. A rat that has remained clean—even for months—will immediately return to its bar-pressing behavior when given just a taste of cocaine or placed in a cage it associates with a drug high. And certain psychological stresses, such as a periodic, unexpected foot shock, will send rats scurrying back to drugs. These same types of stimuli—exposure to low doses of drug, drug-associated cues or stress—trigger craving and relapse in human addicts.

Using this self-administration setup and related techniques, researchers mapped the regions of the brain that mediate addictive behaviors and discovered the central role of the brain's reward circuit. Drugs commandeer this circuit, stimulating its activity with a force and persistence greater than any natural reward.

A key component of the reward circuitry is the mesolimbic dopamine system: a set of nerve cells that originate in the ventral tegmental area (VTA), near the base of the brain, and send projections to target regions in the front of the brain—most notably to a structure deep beneath the frontal cortex called the nucleus accumbens. Those VTA neurons communicate by dispatching the chemical messenger (neurotransmitter) dopamine from the terminals, or tips, of their long projections to receptors on nucleus accumbens neurons. The dopamine pathway from the VTA to the nucleus accumbens is critical for addiction: animals with lesions in these brain regions no longer show interest in substances of abuse.

Rheostat of Reward

REWARD PATHWAYS are evolutionarily ancient. Even the simple, soil-dwelling worm *Caenorhabditis elegans* possesses a rudimentary version. In these worms, inactivation of four to eight key dopamine-containing neurons causes an animal to plow straight past a heap of bacteria, its favorite meal.

In mammals, the reward circuit is more complex, and it is integrated with several other brain regions that serve to color an experience with emotion and direct the individual's response to rewarding stimuli, including food, sex and social interaction. The amygdala, for instance, helps to assess whether an experience is pleasurable or aversive—and whether it should be repeated or avoided—and helps to forge connections between an ex-

perience and other cues; the hippocampus participates in recording the memories of an experience, including where and when and with whom it occurred; and the frontal regions of the cerebral cortex coordinate and process all this information and determine the ultimate behavior of the individual. The VTA-accumbens pathway, meanwhile, acts as a rheostat of reward: it "tells" the other brain centers how rewarding an activity is. The more rewarding an activity is deemed, the more likely the organism is to remember it well and repeat it.

Although most knowledge of the brain's reward circuitry has been derived from animals, brain-imaging studies conducted over the past 10 years have revealed that equivalent pathways control natural and drug rewards in humans. Using functional magnetic resonance imaging (fMRI) or positron emission tomography (PET) scans (techniques that measure changes in blood flow associated with neuronal activity), researchers have watched the nucleus accumbens in cocaine addicts light up when they are offered a snort. When the same addicts are shown a video of someone using cocaine or a photograph of white lines on a mirror, the accumbens responds similarly, along with the amygdala and some areas of the cortex. And the same regions react in compulsive gamblers who are. shown images of slot machines, suggesting that the VTA-accumbens pathway has a similarly critical role even in nondrug addictions.

Dopamine, Please

HOW IS IT POSSIBLE that diverse addictive substances—which have no common structural features and exert a variety of effects on the body—all elicit similar responses in the brain's reward circuitry? How can cocaine, a stimulant that causes the heart to race, and heroin, a pain-relieving sedative, be so opposite in some ways and yet alike in targeting the reward system? The answer is that all drugs of abuse, in addition to any other effects, cause the nucleus accumbens to receive a flood of dopamine and sometimes also dopamine-mimicking signals.

When a nerve cell in the VTA is excited, it sends an electrical message racing along its axon—the signal-carrying "highway" that extends into the nucleus accumbens. The signal causes dopamine to be released from the axon tip into the tiny space—the synaptic cleft—that separates the axon terminal from a neuron in the nucleus accumbens. From there, the dopamine latches onto its receptor on the accumbens neuron and transmits its signal into the cell. To later shut down the signal, the VTA neuron removes the dopamine from the synaptic cleft and repackages it to be used again as needed.

Cocaine and other stimulants temporarily disable the transporter protein that returns the neurotransmitter to the VTA neuron terminals, thereby leaving excess dopamine to act on the nucleus accumbens. Heroin and other opiates, on the other hand, bind to neurons in the VTA that normally shut down the dopamine-producing

VTA neurons. The opiates release this cellular clamp, thus freeing the dopamine-secreting cells to pour extra dopamine into the nucleus accumbens. Opiates can also generate a strong "reward" message by acting directly on the nucleus accumbens.

But drugs do more than provide the dopamine jolt that induces euphoria and mediates the initial reward and re-inforcement. Over time and with repeated exposure, they initiate the gradual adaptations in the reward circuitry that give rise to addiction.

An Addiction Is Born

THE EARLY STAGES of addiction are characterized by tolerance and dependence. After a drug binge, an addict needs more of the substance to get the same effect on mood or concentration and so on. This tolerance then pro-vokes an escalation of drug use that engenders depen-dence—a need that manifests itself as painful emotional and, at times, physical reactions if access to a drug is cut off. Both tolerance and dependence occur because fre-quent: drug use can, ironically, suppress parts of the brain's reward circuit.

At the heart of this cruel suppression lies a molecule known as CREB (cAMP response element-binding pro-tein). CREB is a transcription factor, a protein that regu-lates the expression, or activity, of genes and thus the overall behavior of nerve cells. When drugs of abuse are administered, dopamine concentrations in the nucleus accumbens rise, inducing dopamine-responsive cells to increase production of a small signaling molecule, cyclic AMP (cAMP), which in turn activates CREB. After CREB is switched on, it binds to a specific set of genes, trigger-ing production of the proteins those genes encode.

Chronic drug use causes sustained activation of CREB, which enhances expression of its target genes, some of which code for proteins that then dampen the reward cir-cuitry. For example, CREB controls the production of dynorphin, a natural molecule with opiumlike effects. Dynorphin is synthesized by a subset of neurons in the nucleus accumbens that loop back and inhibit neurons in the VTA. Induction of dynorphin by CREB thereby stifles the brain's reward circuitry, inducing tolerance by mak-ing the same-old dose of drug less rewarding. The in-crease in dynorphin also contributes to dependence, as its inhibition of the reward pathway leaves the individual, in the drug's absence, depressed and unable to take plea-sure in previously enjoyable activities.

But CREB is only a piece of the story. This transcription factor is switched off within days after drug use stops. So CREB cannot account for the longer-lasting grip that abused substances have on the brain—for the brain alter-ations that cause addicts to return to a substance even af-ter years or decades of abstinence. Such relapse is driven to a large extent by sensitization, a phenomenon whereby the effects of a drug are augmented.

Although it might sound counterintuitive, the same drug can evoke both tolerance and sensitization. Shortly after a hit, CREB activity is high and tolerance rules: for several days, the user would need increasing amounts of drug to goose the reward circuit. But if the addict ab-stains, CREB activity declines. At that point, tolerance wanes and sensitization sets in, kicking off the intense craving that underlies the compulsive drug-seeking be-havior of addiction. A mere taste or a memory can draw the addict back. This relentless yearning persists even af-ter long periods of abstention. To understand the roots of sensitization, we have to look for molecular changes that last longer than a few days. One candidate culprit is an-other transcription factor: delta FosB.

Road to Relapse

DELTA FOSB APPEARS to function very differently in addiction than CREB does. Studies of mice and rats indi-cate that in response to chronic drug abuse, delta FosB concentrations rise gradually and progressively in the nu-cleus accumbens and other brain regions. Moreover, be-cause the protein is extraordinarily stable, it remains active in these nerve cells for weeks to months after drug administration, a persistence that would enable it to maintain changes in gene expression long after drug tak-ing ceased.

Studies of mutant mice that produce excessive amounts of delta FosB in the nucleus accumbens show that prolonged induction of this molecule causes animals to become hypersensitive to drugs. These mice were highly prone to relapse after the drugs were withdrawn and later made available—a finding implying that delta FosB concentrations could well contribute to long-term increases in sensitivity in the reward pathways of hu-mans. Interestingly, delta FosB is also produced in the nu-cleus accumbens in mice in response to repetitious nondrug rewards, such as excessive wheel running and sugar consumption. Hence, it might have a more general role in. the development of compulsive behavior toward a wide range of rewarding stimuli.

Recent evidence hints at a mechanism for how sensi-tization could persist even after delta FosB concentra-tions return to normal. Chronic exposure to cocaine and other drugs of abuse is known to induce the signal-re-ceiving branches of nucleus accumbens neurons to sprout additional buds, termed dendritic spines, that bolster the cells' connections to other neurons. In ro-dents, this sprouting can continue for some months after drug taking ceases. This discovery suggests that delta FosB may be responsible for the added spines. Highly speculative extrapolation from these results raises the possibility that the extra connections generated by delta FosB activity amplify signaling between the linked cells for years and that such heightened signaling might cause the brain to overreact to drug-related cues. The dendritic changes may, in the end, be the key adaptation that accounts for the intransigence of addiction.

Learning Addiction

THUS FAR WE HAVE focused on drug-induced changes that relate to dopamine in the brain's reward system. Recall, however, that other brain regions—namely, the amygdala, hippocampus and frontal cortex—are involved in addiction and communicate back and forth with the VTA and the nucleus accumbens. All those regions talk to the reward pathway by releasing the neurotransmitter glutamate. When drugs of abuse increase dopamine release from the VTA into the nucleus accumbens, they also alter the responsiveness of the VTA and nucleus accumbens to glutamate for days. Animal experiments indicate that changes in sensitivity to glutamate in the reward pathway enhance both the release of dopamine from the VTA and responsiveness to dopamine in the nucleus accumbens, thereby promoting CREB and delta FosB activity and the unhappy effects of these molecules. Furthermore, it seems that this altered glutamate sensitivity strengthens the neuronal pathways that link memories of drug-taking experiences with high reward, thereby feeding the desire to seek the drug.

The mechanism by which drugs alter sensitivity to glutamate in neurons of the reward pathway is not yet known with certainty, but a working hypothesis can be formulated biased on how glutamate affects neurons in the hippocampus. There certain types of short-term stimuli can enhance a cell's response to glutamate over many hours. The phenomenon, dubbed long-term potentiation, helps memories to form and appears to be mediated by the shuttling of certain glutamate-binding receptor proteins from intracellular stores, where they are not functional, to the nerve cell membrane, where they can respond to glutamate released into a synapse. Drugs of abuse influence the shuttling of glutamate receptors in the reward pathway. Some findings suggest that they can also influence the synthesis of certain glutamate receptors.

Taken together, all the drug-induced changes in the reward circuit that we have discussed ultimately promote tolerance, dependence, craving, relapse and the complicated behaviors that accompany addiction. Many details remain mysterious, but we can say some things with assurance. During prolonged drug use, and shortly after use ceases, changes in the concentrations of cyclic AMP and the activity of CREB in neurons in the reward pathway predominate. These alterations cause tolerance and dependence, reducing sensitivity to the drug and rendering the addict depressed and lacking motivation. With more prolonged abstention, changes in delta FosB activity and glutamate signaling predominate. These actions seem to be the ones that draw an addict back for more—by increasing sensitivity to the drug's effects if it is used again after a lapse and by eliciting powerful responses to memories of past highs and to cues that bring those memories to mind.

The revisions in CREB, delta FosB and glutamate signaling are central to addiction, but they certainly are not the whole story. As research progresses, neuroscientists will surely uncover other important molecular and cellular adaptations in the reward circuit and in related brain areas that will illuminate the true nature of addiction.

A Common Cure?

BEYOND IMPROVING understanding of the biological basis of drug addiction, the discovery of these molecular alterations provides novel targets for the biochemical treatment of this disorder. And the need for fresh therapies is enormous. In addition to addiction's obvious physical and psychological damage, the condition is a leading cause of medical illness. Alcoholics are prone to cirrhosis of the liver, smokers are susceptible to lung cancer, and heroin addicts spread HIV when they share needles. Addiction's toll on health and productivity in the U.S. has been estimated at more than $300 billion a year, making it one of the most serious problems facing society. If the definition of addiction is broadened to encompass other forms of compulsive pathological behavior, such as overeating and gambling, the costs are far higher. Therapies that could correct aberrant, addictive reactions to rewarding stimuli—whether cocaine or cheesecake or the thrill of winning at blackjack—would provide an enormous benefit to society.

Today's treatments fail to cure most addicts. Some medications prevent the drug from getting to its target. These measures leave users with an "addicted brain" and intense drug craving. Other medical interventions mimic a drug's effects and thereby dampen craving long enough for an addict to kick the habit. These chemical substitutes, however, may merely replace one habit with another. And although nonmedical, rehabilitative treatments—such as the popular 12-step programs—help many people grapple with their addictions, participants still relapse at a high rate.

Armed with insight into the biology of addiction, researchers may one day be able to design medicines that counter or compensate for the long-term effects of drugs of abuse on reward regions in the brain. Compounds that interact specifically with the receptors that bind to glutamate or dopamine in the nucleus accumbens, or chemicals that prevent CREB or delta FosB from acting on their target genes in that area, could potentially loosen a drug's grip on an addict.

Furthermore, we need to learn to recognize those individuals who are most prone to addiction. Although psychological, social and environmental factors certainly are important, studies in susceptible families suggest that in humans about 50 percent of the risk for drug addiction is genetic. The particular genes involved have not yet been identified, but if susceptible individuals could be recognized early on, interventions could be targeted to this vulnerable population.

Because emotional and social factors operate in addiction, we cannot expect medications to fully treat the syndrome of addiction. But we can hope that future therapies will dampen the intense biological forces—the dependence, the cravings—that drive addiction and will thereby make psychosocial interventions more effective in helping to rebuild an addict's body and mind.

MORE TO EXPLORE

Incentive-Sensitization and Addiction. Terry E. Robinson and Kent C. Berridge in *Addiction*, Vol. 96, No. 1, pages 103–114; January 2001.

Molecular Basis of Long-Term Plasticity underlying Addiction. Eric J. Nestler in *Nature Reviews Neuroscience*, Vol. 2, No. 2, pages 119–128; February 2001.

Addiction: From Biology to Drug Policy. Second edition. A. Goldstein. Oxford University Press, 2001.

National Institute on Drug Abuse Information on Common Drugs of Abuse: **www.nida.nih.gov/DrugPages/**

ERIC J. NESTLER and ROBERT C. MALENKA study the molecular basis of drug addiction. Nestler, professor in and chair of the department of psychiatry at the University of Texas Southwestern Medical Center at Dallas, was elected to the Institute of Medicine in 1998. Malenka, professor of psychiatry and behavioral sciences at the Stanford University School of Medicine, joined the faculty there after serving as director of the Center for the Neurobiology of Addiction at the University of California, San Francisco. With Steven E. Hyman, now at Harvard University, Nestler and Malenka wrote the textbook *Molecular Basis of Neuropharmacology* (McGraw-Hill, 2001).

THE BIOLOGY OF... ADDICTION

The End of Craving

A controversial new drug seems to stop addiction cold

by michael abrams

THE RATS IN STANLEY GLICK'S LAB ARE junkies. They spend their days and nights lounging around in steel cages, twiddling their claws, waiting for the next hit. Each rat has a small plastic tube protruding from the base of its skull. Once a day, for an hour, each tube is connected to an infusion pump that controls a syringe containing a common addictive substance: morphine, cocaine, nicotine, or methamphetamine. The rats are trained to pull levers for water, but for one hour each day they can use the same system to mainline as much of the drugs as they want. And they want. "Just about any drug that humans abuse, animals will self-administer," Glick says.

Glick gets the rats addicted only to get them back on the wagon later with a substance called 18-methoxycoronaridine (18-MC, for short). The new drug may be the miracle pill that addicts have always needed: A single dose of it can remarkably diminish both withdrawal symptoms and craving. By revealing its mechanism, Glick, director of the Center for Neuropharmacology and Neuroscience at Albany Medical College in New York, offers a new understanding of the brain's pleasure zones.

On the Caribbean island of St. Kitts, neuro-pharmacologist Deborah Mash of the University of Miami has been running clinical trials of ibogaine on addicts. Of the 272 patients she has treated, none have had major side effects, and almost all have been drug-free at least a month.

Eighteen-MC is a synthesized derivative of ibogaine, an extract of the bark of the root of the African iboga shrub. For centuries the Bwiti tribe of West Africa has used the root for initiation ceremonies and, in smaller amounts, to stay awake during long hunts. The drug's story as an anti-addictive began in 1962, when college dropout and heroin addict Howard Lotsof obtained a dose from a chemist friend. "What happened is indelibly ingrained in my mind," Lotsof says. "I was living with my parents. I felt my feet hit the ground, and I realized I had no desire to use opiates."

In 1986 Lotsof created a company called NDA International and began to supply ibogaine to a clinic for addicts in Holland. The clinic found that ibogaine works in three stages. First the addict has about four hours of waking dreams in which he seems to confront inner demons. This is followed by an eight-to 10-hour "cognitive evaluation period," during which the user analyzes the waking dream. Then comes a sleepless day or two, which Lotsof calls the "residual stimulation phase."

The clinic treated about 30 addicts and reported impressive results: After a single dose, a majority stayed off drugs for several months or more. But Lotsof was unable to find funding for follow-up studies—and they were needed: One of the patients died of unknown causes, and a study at Johns Hopkins University showed that high doses of ibogaine cause brain damage in rats. Lotsof's lack of scientific degrees, as well as his history of drug use, also raised questions.

"The personalities involved are, for lack of a better word, peculiar," says Glick. He is lanky, has a closely trimmed beard, and wears a white lab coat over black pants as if to match his Holstein-style rats. The closest he has ever gotten to drug culture is playing trumpet in a jazz band called SwingDocs. "Certainly in the beginning everybody thought that Lotsof was an absolute lunatic, and I was included. But when you hear the same things enough times from enough people who have taken ibogaine, you've got to believe that there is at least something there that is worth investigating."

'What happened is indelibly ingrained in my mind. I felt my feet hit the ground, and I realized I had no desire to use opiates'

In 1991 Glick and his colleagues began to look for a synthetic derivative of ibogaine without the drug's side effects. The search eventually led to Martin Kuehne, a chemist at the University of Vermont who is an expert on the anticancer drug vincristine. Vincristine is structurally similar to ibogaine, and Kuehne knew how to tinker with the compound to produce derivatives. Glick tested 15 or so of the derivatives on rats before zeroing in on 18-MC.

"Withdrawal is related to the rapidity with which the drug disappears from the nervous system," Glick says. "It really reflects the change from the drug state to the nondrug state." To test 18-MC's effect on withdrawal, Glick gave the rats a continuous supply of morphine. He then administered an opiate antagonist that removes morphine from the neurons in the brain and causes immediate withdrawal symptoms. The rats given 18-MC suffered few if any withdrawal symptoms. Unlike people who take ibogaine, who may tremble as well as hallucinate, the animals seemed normal.

Hallucinogens like ibogaine raise serotonin levels in the brain; 18-MC doesn't. At the same time, 18-MC counteracts the increase in dopamine levels that opiates create. When Glick's addicted rats received 18-MC, their dopamine levels plummeted. The next time the rats were offered their daily hour of fun, they just said no. "Here's a drug that supposedly decreases craving, that supposedly decreases self-administration, and it also appears to block a key neurochemical correlate," Glick says. "But the real question is how exactly it is doing this. And this question plagued us for several years."

Activities in the brain occur at synapses, where neurons and receptors almost touch. Neurons fire off chemicals known as neurotransmitters (of which serotonin and dopamine are two), and neurotransmitters find their way to particular receptors. By using a technique that isolates receptors, called patch-clamp electrophysiology, Glick's colleague Mark Fleck discovered that 18-MC blocks only one kind of recep-

tor effectively (ibogaine blocks several, which accounts for its many side effects). Receptors of this kind are clustered in two very specific parts of the brain, which are connected by a channel called the habenulo-interpeduncular pathway.

Since the 1960s, scientists have known that the brain's primary reward circuit is the mesolimbic dopamine pathway. When rats are rigged with electrodes that allow them to stimulate this pathway by pressing a lever, they develop an instant and insatiable craving. "It's an amazing phenomenon," Glick says. "The rats wake up and as soon as they find the lever, they just go nuts pressing it. They'll do it to the exclusion of food and water." When Glick went back and examined similar studies done in the 1980s, he discovered that rats would behave the same way if they were allowed to stimulate another area of the brain—the medial habenula. As it happens, the medial habenula is also part of the habenulo-interpeduncular pathway. "What we believe is that we've found an alternate reward system that has been ignored for 15 years," Glick says.

The two pathways are tightly connected, and the secondary reward system seems able to modulate the activity of the primary pathway. When 18-MC binds to a receptor in the alternate circuit, it sends a signal to the main circuit that dampens its

responsiveness. When the rats in a later study had 18-MC injected directly into this secondary pathway, they all but stopped administering morphine to themselves—at least for a day, and sometimes for a few weeks.

Despite the mounting evidence that 18-MC is a simple and clean way to end addiction, Glick, like Lotsof, has had trouble raising funds to test the drug on humans. The problem, he says, is guilt by association. In 1995 the National Institute on Drug Abuse hired a panel of nine academics and nine members of the pharmaceutical industry to review all the existing ibogaine research. After hearing presentations from Lotsof and others, 16 of the panel members reportedly voted to end trials of ibogaine in humans. Unfortunately, Glick says, 18-MC was tarred by the same brush. "I keep fighting the same battles over and over again," he says. "People lump 18-MC with ibogaine, and I'm constantly making the same point—that we've got something that is a hell of a lot better."

In the meantime, Glick gets about three calls a month from addicts and their families. "They're desperate for anything that will help," he says. "They've tried everything. They always want to know when can I give them 18-MC, and it's really hopeless. I'm just not in the position to do that yet."

A new treatment for addiction

The FDA recently approved buprenorphine for the treatment of opiate addiction. Psychologists helped develop the drug and will provide key services to patients treated with it.

BY ETIENNE BENSON
Monitor **staff**

Approximately one million Americans are dependent on heroin, prescription painkillers and other opioids, but the vast majority of them—as many as 800,000—aren't receiving any treatment.

Opiate substitutes that prevent withdrawal are among the most effective treatments for such addictions, when combined with psychological counseling, researchers say. But until recently, only two such drugs—methadone and levo-alpha-acetyl methadol (LAAM)—were available, and only licensed treatment clinics were authorized to dispense them. Many addicts avoid opiate treatment programs (OTPs) because of their inconvenience or perceived stigma, and even those who would like to enroll sometimes can't because of limited treatment slots.

The approval of a new medication by the Food and Drug Administration (FDA) last fall, however, could reshape the landscape of opiate addiction treatment in the United States, making pharmacotherapy available and attractive to patients who previously shunned it, say researchers.

Psychologists have played a key role in developing the medication—buprenorphine—by conducting the basic and clinical research that defined its unusual pharmacology. They are continuing to shape its use by influencing training programs for physicians. And they are developing the behavioral and psychosocial treatments that are a critical part of any effective substance abuse treatment program.

And as the network of physicians who are certified to prescribe buprenorphine grows, it should also provide new opportunities for psychologists to get involved in pharmacotherapy-based substance abuse treatment by making such treatments available in a wide variety of settings and increasing the number of patients who use pharmacotherapies—and who therefore need the counseling and behavioral treatments that psychologists can provide.

"It's a very, very exciting time to be involved with buprenorphine work," says psychologist Leslie Amass, PhD, of the Friends Research Institute in Santa Monica, Calif., who has been studying the use of buprenorphine as a treatment for opiate addiction since the early 1990s.

"For those of us who have been involved with the medication from very early on, it's rewarding to see it get to this point and be offered to patients."

Unique pharmacology

Buprenorphine has been under development for several decades, during which time psychologists have discovered a great deal about its unusual pharmacology, says Amass.

Their discoveries have been made possible, in large part, by support from the National Institute on Drug Abuse (NIDA) and other government agencies concerned with substance abuse. NIDA's Division of Treatment Research and Development, headed by Frank Vocci, PhD, has played an especially important leadership role, says Geoff Mumford, PhD, APA's science policy director.

Like heroin, methadone and many prescription painkillers, buprenorphine acts on the brain's mu-opioid receptors to cause analgesia, euphoria and other effects. But unlike them, it is a partial agonist—a drug that has mechanisms of action that are similar to pure agonists, such as heroin, but with less potency. Even when it occupies almost all of the brain's mu-opioid receptors, buprenorphine has only about 40 percent of heroin's effect, says psychologist Mark Greenwald, PhD, of Wayne State University's Addiction Research Institute in Detroit.

Another pharmacological factor that makes buprenorphine well-suited to addiction treatment is its high affinity for the mu-opioid receptor, says psychologist James Woods, PhD, of the University of Michigan, who has studied buprenorphine's pharmacology in animals.

"It has an absolutely fascinating course of action," says Woods. Even after it's been removed from the blood by elimination and metabolism, he says, buprenorphine stays firmly attached to the brain's receptors, blocking the effect of other drugs with lower affinities. That means that opiate-dependent individuals who take buprenorphine won't get any additional kick from using other opiates, such as heroin.

Buprenorphine's stickiness has another advantage, says Greenwald. Because it clings to the receptor long after it has been administered, it can make the detoxification process gentler—more like sliding down a hill than falling off a cliff. "You get a softer landing, if you will, as you detoxify someone from buprenorphine," he says. It also means that buprenorphine doesn't have to be administered every day to be effective.

But while buprenorphine's stickiness and partial-agonist effects make it ideal for many addiction treatment applications, they also limit its effectiveness with the most heavily dependent individuals, researchers say. In such individuals, buprenorphine's insistent weakness—its ability to monopolize mu-opioid receptors while providing only a fraction of the effect of drugs such as heroin—can actually trigger withdrawal symptoms.

Although buprenorphine has been tested extensively in humans and nonhuman animals, there is still much to learn, researchers say. "There are very elemental things about the way it interacts with the receptor that we don't understand yet," notes Woods.

In ongoing efforts to resolve those uncertainties, psychologists' scientific training has been and will be critical, says Greenwald. "Their ability to design controlled studies—using valid and sensitive models that are relevant to drug dependence—gives them a unique opportunity to contribute," he notes.

Translation to practice

Psychologists have also played a key role in determining how buprenorphine can best be used clinically. The consensus is that, as with other medications used to treat addiction, buprenorphine will be most effective when paired with psychological treatments.

"No one feels that buprenorphine alone is going to be that successful in the treatment of a complex disorder such as addiction without appropriate counseling, psychotherapy, etc.," says psychologist Charles Schuster, PhD, of Wayne State University, who has been involved in both the research and regulatory aspects of buprenorphine's development.

"Now that the medication has been approved, psychologists trained in substance abuse treatment will be essential partners in this important new treatment paradigm," agrees H. Westley Clark, MD, JD, director of the Center for Substance Abuse Treatment (CSAT) at the Substance Abuse and Mental Health Services Administration (SAMHSA).

Clark notes that the legislation that authorized office-based prescription of buprenorphine—the Drug Abuse Treatment Act of 2000 (DATA)—explicitly acknowledges the importance of behavioral treatments. The law requires certified physicians to have the capacity to refer patients to qualified behavioral health treatment providers.

One of the psychologists who has studied buprenorphine the longest is Warren Bickel, PhD, of the University of Vermont. Bickel and his colleagues have shown that buprenorphine can still be effective when given on alternate days or even every third, fourth or fifth day. That, Bickel notes, could make a huge difference in states such as Vermont, where patients sometimes have to drive for hours to get to the nearest certified doctor or OTP.

The availability of buprenorphine in physicians' offices offers great opportunities, but it also raises new challenges, says Bickel. For instance, OTPs provide integrated pharmacotherapy and psychotherapy in a single setting—something that many patients who go to their physicians for buprenorphine won't find, he says.

"It's imperative that these patients not only receive medication, but also receive the additional services that they really need to do well," he says. "But getting that to happen, I think, is the challenge that faces us in this new era."

As buprenorphine use spreads, there is also the risk that the drug might be diverted from patients to abusers. Rickitt Benckiser Pharmaceuticals offers two formulations of the drug: Subutex, which contains just buprenorphine, and Suboxone, which contains a combination of buprenorphine and naloxone, an opiate antagonist. Neither formulation appears to have a large potential for abuse relative to other opioids. (Suboxone, which is expected to be the standard formulation, is an effective opiate substitute when taken under the tongue, but can trigger withdrawal if injected.)

But the FDA isn't taking any chances. Wayne State psychologist Schuster has been picked to lead a large-scale surveillance effort that includes ethnographic reports, surveys of physicians, monitoring of chat rooms, news groups and other Internet resources, and interviews with patients—all in the hopes of catching signs of buprenorphine abuse before it spreads.

The surveillance effort is slated to run for five years, with Schuster's research team providing quarterly reports to an advisory group. "If a problem is emerging, we want to catch it early," he says.

Building a network

Buprenorphine's transition from a promising experimental drug to a prescription medication was made possible by two events: the enactment of DATA and the FDA's approval, both of which were the culmination of many years of research and lobbying. But turning it into an effective treatment will require building a network of certified physicians and psychologists prepared to offer the kinds of therapy that are essential to the medication's success.

> **"Buprenorphine offers yet another opportunity to demonstrate the important contribution that psychologists can make in partnership with our physician colleagues."**
>
> *Norman B. Anderson*
> *APA CEO*

To aid patients and treatment providers in finding local physicians who can prescribe buprenorphine, CSAT offers on online Buprenorphine Physician Locator at http://buprenorphine.samhsa.gov/bwns_locator. Meanwhile, progress in training physicians—using curricula that have been shaped by psychologists—has been rapid.

For its part, APA has been trying to help build the buprenorphine network by encouraging appropriately trained psychologists to make themselves available to referral resources. In a recent letter to state psychological associations, APA CEO Norman B. Anderson, PhD, emphasized the importance of collaboration in realizing buprenorphine's potential. "Buprenorphine offers yet another opportunity to demonstrate the important contribution that psychologists can make in partnership with our physician colleagues," he wrote.

ON THE WEB

- **Substance Abuse and Mental Health Services Administrations:** http://buprenorphine.samhsa.gov
- **Food and Drug Administration:** www.fda.gov/cder/drug/infopage/subutex_suboxone
- **American Society for Addiction Medicine:** www.asam.org/conf/Buprenorphineconferences.htm
- **Reckitt Benckiser Pharmaceuticals:** www.suboxone.com

From *Monitor on Psychology*, June 2003, pp. 18-20. © 2003 by the American Psychological Association. Reprinted by permission.

MORE THAN A KICK

On its own, nicotine might promote tumors and wrinkles

BY KENDALL MORGAN

Nicotine shifts the body into high gear. Whether from a puff on a cigarette or a patch stuck to the skin, the drug enters the bloodstream and bathes the internal organs. But scientists generally attribute nicotine's power solely to the activity it sparks in the brain. That stimulation makes smokers feel good, even euphoric. It's also what makes them crave more. Physicians, however, generally finger tobacco's thousands of other chemical constituents, including known carcinogens—not nicotine—for cigarettes' nastiest side effects. Each year, tobacco accounts for 400,000 deaths among 48 million smokers in the United States alone.

TROUBLE MAKER— Nicotine, cigarettes' chemical lure, might also be an accomplice in many of the ailments spawned of tobacco.

Beyond its addictive appeal, nicotine itself might have devastating consequences throughout the body, some scientists now say. Acetylcholine—the natural nerve-signal carrier that nicotine mimics—is a jack-of-all-trades. The chemical acts on many cells, including those in the lungs and skin. Therefore, nicotine may goad many tissues into hyperactivity—a possibility that raises scientists' suspicions about its role in disease.

"It's an eye opener. Nicotine isn't just a drug that stimulates neurons. It does the exact same thing to cells outside of the nervous system," says dermatologist Sergei A. Grando of the University of California, Davis, who studies nicotine's effects on skin.

A handful of recent studies has suggested a link between nicotine and ailments ranging from sudden infant death syndrome (*SN: 9/14/02, p. 163*) to cancer. Scientists have found that the stimulant spurs the formation of blood vessels that could feed tumors and promote plaque buildup in arteries (*SN: 7/7/01, p. 6*). The body may also convert nicotine into the

chemical precursors of the carcinogen that scientists call NNK (*SN: 10/28/00, p. 278*).

The latest experimental work strengthens the connection between nicotine and disease and highlights additional ways that the chemical might promote tumors, age skin, and stall wound healing. Researchers say the drug may also literally cook proteins in the blood.

DEATH CAN BE GOOD Nicotine probably doesn't cause cancer, but new research suggests it might keep cancer cells alive. And it apparently does so in two different ways.

First, the drug prevents a cellular form of suicide, called apoptosis, that normally eliminates nascent cancer and other damaged cells, says clinical oncologist Phillip A. Dennis of the National Cancer Institute in Bethesda, Md.

In many cancers—including those of the breast, ovaries, prostate, and brain—a protein that normally keeps apoptosis under control gets stuck in its active form and thus shuts down the suicide sequence. More recently, Dennis' team discovered that the same molecule, called either Akt or protein kinase B, jams in the on-position in most lung cancer cells. The finding led the team to wonder whether constituents of tobacco activate Akt in the lung.

To find out, they tested the effect of nicotine and its derivative NNK on normal lung cells in lab dishes. Nicotine activated Akt at concentrations comparable to those that have been measured in smokers' blood, and the cell-suicide rate fell by 60 percent, the team reports in the January *Journal of Clinical Investigation*. It took more stress—ultraviolet radiation exposure, for example—to kill nicotine-activated cells than normal cells required, Dennis says.

Nicotine-treated cells acted abnormal in other ways, too. In lab dishes, lung cells usually stop growing when they become crowded, Dennis explains. "When treated with nicotine, lung

Not all bad

A once-good-for-nothing drug improves its reputation

The properties that make nicotine a health hazard might also make it a useful therapy for more than smoking cessation. "Nicotine is a drug—not a poison or carcinogen—but a drug," says Sergei A. Grando of the University of California, Davis. "Nicotine is often a bad guy," he adds, "but it can also be a good guy."

For one, nicotine can help alleviate the mind-numbing symptoms of Alzheimer's disease. Alzheimer's patients lack the normal number of one type of receptor that binds acetylcholine in the brain, making them less responsive to that nerve signal. The deficit leads to learning and memory problems, says neurobiologist Alfred Maelicke at Johannes-Gutenberg University in Mainz, Germany.

A similar shortfall plagues people with schizophrenia and epilepsy, among other disorders, he adds. In such cases, intermittent nicotine boosts to the brain can help, Maelicke says. Nicotine patches may also fight depression (SN: 5/11/02, p. 302). And there's more good news. Although regular nicotine use can delay wound healing, a new study finds that the stimulant speeds healing in mice with diabetes—a disease that normally impairs wound healing.

Prompted by his earlier discovery that nicotine spurs blood vessel growth, John P. Cooke of Stanford University wondered whether the drug might help close wounds. His team injured diabetic and nondiabetic mice and then applied a solution containing nicotine to some of the animals in each group.

After 5 days, diabetic mice receiving the nicotine treatment had healed substantially more than diabetic mice not getting the drug had, the team reported in the July 2002 American Journal of Pathology. Nondiabetic mice didn't benefit from the treatment with nicotine.

That result makes sense to Grando. "Like any drug, the dose is important," he explains. "At low doses, nicotine can favor faster wound healing, while in larger doses it has the opposite effect."

The challenge in all nicotine's possible uses is to identify people for whom the drug's benefits outweigh its risks and to develop targeted delivery methods, says Phillip A. Dennis of the National Cancer Institute in Bethesda, Md.—K.M.

versity. "They don't continue to grow and become malignant unless they can call blood vessels into themselves," he says.

Cooke's team has found that nicotine increases the speed at which human blood vessel cells grow in lab dishes. What's more, lung-tumor cells in mice given nicotine-laced water expanded faster than those in mice not given the drug (SN: 7/7/01, p. 6).

Nicotine may encourage blood vessel formation by stimulating the production of vascular endothelial growth factor, or VEGF, a second team of researchers has found. Vascular-system researcher Brian S. Conklin, now at Baylor College of Medicine in Houston, and his colleagues knew that VEGF shows up in the majority of cancerous tumors. It's also a player in plaque formation along blood vessel walls. Because vascular disease and cancer are both linked to smoking, Conklin and his colleagues wondered whether nicotine might ramp up blood concentrations of the growth factor.

The team tested the effects of nicotine and cotinine—the primary product of nicotine breakdown in the liver—on blood concentrations of VEGF in a pig artery. Both compounds hiked concentrations of the growth factor, the researchers reported in the February 2002 American Journal of Pathology.

FULL SPEED AHEAD Just as nicotine sparks activity in nerve and tumor cells, it speeds up normal cellular activity in the skin. For example, some cells exposed to nicotine might go through the same life stages in 10 days that would normally take 10 weeks, says dermatologist Grando.

Such hyperactivity occurs in cells called dermal fibroblasts that control the skin's texture by regulating the production of support proteins including collagen and elastin. When skin gets wounded, these fibroblasts send out proteins that clean the site. The cleanup crew acts like "biological scissors," Grando says, clearing the way for healing to begin.

In the February Laboratory Investigation, the team reports that nicotine sends fibroblasts into inappropriate activity. In the laboratory, the researchers exposed human fibroblast cells to the drug. Enzymes normally unleashed to clean wound sites were deployed in the absence of injury. Those proteins then chewed up the scaffolding that keeps skin flexible and strong. That effect would leave skin sagging and wrinkled, Grando explains.

On the other hand, in regular users of tobacco, another mechanism of skin healing slows down as a result of nicotine's ability to speed cells up. Normally at a cut, skin cells called keratinocytes crawl out from the edge of a wound and cover the broken surface. Acetylcholine sets those cellular healers in motion. That led Grando and his colleagues to ask whether nicotine interferes with keratinocyte migration.

The researchers grew human skin cells in lab dishes and treated some cells with growth factors and others with growth factors in combination with nicotine. Nicotine-treated cells started to move as if on a healing mission but stopped short of the distance that cells not given nicotine traveled, the team reported 2 years ago. The span traveled by keratinocytes declined further as more nicotine was added to the lab dishes.

The fast-paced lifestyle that nicotine induces in cells might explain why, Grando says. Nicotine cuts skin cells' active life

cells kept growing to the point of coming right out of the plastic," he says.

NNK also enhanced cell survival by stimulating Akt. Therefore, NNK might exacerbate nicotine's cancer-promoting ability, Dennis suggests.

Nicotine's boost to cell survival could be important to other cancers associated with tobacco, including those of the head, neck, kidney, and bladder, he says.

Nicotine has a second talent for enhancing tumor growth, two lines of research suggest. The drug makes tumor-nurturing blood vessels sprout. Tumors can only grow to a certain point before they must be fed, says John P. Cooke of Stanford Uni-

short, leaving them with too little time to seal a wound before they conk out, he hypothesizes.

NOW WE'RE COOKING Nicotine's widespread effects result primarily from its imitating the natural stimulant acetylcholine. But a new study suggests that a derivative of the drug might also interact with the blood to literally fry proteins.

While poring over the chemical structure of nornicotine—a minor metabolite of nicotine—chemist Kim D. Janda of Scripps Research Institute in La Jolla, Calif., recognized that the compound has the potential to mangle proteins. The metabolite could spur the same chemical transformation that occurs when potatoes are fried, he suspected, a reaction familiar to food scientists as the browning effect. A similar reaction can occur without the high temperatures, Janda explains. Proteins altered in this way have been implicated in diabetes, cancer, and normal aging.

In the laboratory, Janda and his colleagues added nornicotine to solutions of blood proteins. Nornicotine attached to the proteins, so that at the molecular level, the product looked like "Christmas trees with nornicotine lightbulbs on them," Janda says. when food browns, similar structures result.

In separate experiments on whole blood from smokers and nonsmokers, the team found that smokers' blood contains more such nornicotine-altered proteins than nonsmokers' blood does. The researchers reported their findings in the Nov. 12, 2002 *Proceedings of the National Academy of Sciences.*

"It's pretty shocking," says Janda. "Nornicotine can be involved in a chemical reaction no one had thought about." The team is now conducting studies to find out how common the nornicotine-blood reaction is in animals and people.

For people trying to kick the cigarette habit, gums, patches, lollipops, and lip balms that contain nicotine are often useful. High-dose nicotine replacements can deliver the stimulant at concentrations comparable to those in cigarettes while giving a person a more constant blood-nicotine concentration than smoking does and avoiding many of cigarettes' harmful components.

"It's still most important that people stop smoking—if they need [nicotine-replacement therapy] to do that, fine," says oncologist Dennis. "But nicotine itself might be harmful in the long term," he adds.

Some people use quitting aids for longer than the recommended few months. Ann N. Dapice, an educator at the addiction treatment center T. K. Wolf in Tulsa, Okla., says she's worked with people who have used nicotine patches and gums for years.

Although scientists don't know all of nicotine's long-term effects in people, emerging evidence makes a "whole new case" for the drug's potential to cause problems outside the nervous system, says oncologist John D. Minna of the University of Texas Southwestern Medical Center in Dallas.

And once scientists look closer, he adds, they might find disease connections to nicotine that haven't been considered yet.

THE DOWN SIDE OF UP

**Paxil has made life worth living for people around the world.
But for those who want off, the wonder drug can turn scary.**

By Alexis Jetter

IT ALL STARTED with a nervous stomach. Janelle Leonard, a third-grade teacher in Bradford, Massachusetts, just wanted to get through her morning commute without having to make a restroom stop. So 3 years ago she mentioned the problem to her doctor, who said, "Try this," handing Leonard a prescription for Paxil. "It may help."

The doctor didn't tell her that Paxil was an antidepressant, or that there were any potential problems associated with it. "I looked at it almost like an antibiotic," Leonard says sheepishly. "You know, whatever helps."

The little pink pill did help—for a while. But after 2 years, Leonard's stomach jitters returned, so she quit the drug. "Within 24 hours I went into severe vertigo," says Leonard, now 31. "I was absolutely spinning. I couldn't move." Her husband had to carry her from room to room, and violent nausea reduced her to a helpless mess. Over the next several months, her physician alternately diagnosed Leonard with flu, strep throat, a sinus infection, and an ulcer. Leonard's mother had a simpler theory. "You know, you stopped taking that medication," she told her daughter. "Maybe it's that." So Leonard stumbled into her bathroom and gulped down a single Paxil tablet. Twelve hours later, she says, "I was absolutely fine."

On her doctor's advice, Leonard resumed taking Paxil, then gradually lowered her 20-milligram dose (a commonly prescribed amount) by 5 milligrams every 3 weeks. But each cutback brought a new wave of symptoms: tremors, weeping, sweating, diarrhea, insomnia, a strange tingling sensation under her skin, and a sickening taste in her mouth. Down to only 2.5 milligrams a day, Leonard could no longer work, leave the house, even stand upright. For the first time in her life, she contemplated suicide. "My mother and husband wouldn't leave me alone, because they were afraid of what I might do," Leonard says.

Paxil (a.k.a. paroxetine) is known for its power to change lives for the better. Introduced in the United States in 1993 by Britain-based GlaxoSmithKline (GSK), it has eased depression and anxiety for tens of millions of people around the world. Like Prozac and Zoloft, it's a selective serotonin-reuptake inhibitor (SSRI), which elevates mood by increasing the brain's supply of serotonin. And Paxil, the second-best-selling antidepressant in America, does more than just lift spirits. More than 30 million prescriptions for the drug were written in 2002 in the United States alone, in part because it has been approved by the U.S. Food and Drug Administration (FDA) to treat more conditions—including panic attacks, post-traumatic stress disorder, and acute shyness—than any other SSRI. Many clinicians expect the number of women taking Paxil to jump, because a recent study found it can diminish the severity and frequency of menopausal hot flashes.

But across the United States and Europe, thousands of people have described harrowing physical ordeals when they stopped taking Paxil. According to the World Health Organization, there have been at least 2,380 reports from physicians of problems in patients who go off the drug. And in the United States, more than 2,000 people in more than 30 states have filed suit against GSK, charging that they should have been alerted to the possibility of developing a dependence on Paxil. Despite television commercials that until recently said "Paxil is non-habit-forming," researchers at Massachusetts General Hospital in 1998 found that more than half of patients who take this SSRI may experience moderate to severe side effects if they quit taking it abruptly. In most cases, the disturbing symptoms clear up in a week or two. But as the stories of Leonard and others indicate, for some people those symptoms linger.

"Paxil is notorious for this withdrawal syndrome," says Lalith Tissera, M.D., a Boston-area psychiatrist and psychopharmacologist who treats at least a dozen patients a year who run into trouble when they try to stop taking the drug. "One has to be very, very cautious with it. And we have to alert our patients."

Some scientific reports suggest that even tapering off doesn't always work. "I've had patients who went off cigarettes cold turkey who couldn't get off Paxil," says Joseph Glenmullen, M.D., a psychiatrist and clinical instructor at Harvard Medical School who wrote *Prozac Backlash: Overcoming the Dangers of Prozac, Zoloft, Paxil, and Other Antidepressants With Safe, Effective Alternatives*. "I've had patients who took 6 months to taper off. And I've talked to others who have not been able to get off it at all."

"It felt like bust-your-butt electric shock. I remodeled an apartment once, and I got shocked. That's exactly what it felt like."

Jane Lawrence (not her real name), 41, a Houston area lawyer who took Paxil for anxiety, says quitting triggered a sensation akin to sticking her finger in an electrical outlet. "It felt like bust-your-butt electric shock," she says. "I remodeled an apartment once, and I got shocked. That's exactly what it felt like."

In lawsuits and online, other women with no history of mood or sensory disorders describe rage, suicidal thoughts, visual disturbances such as flashing lights, and migraine headaches when they tried to go off of Paxil. According to Britain's Medicines and Healthcare Products Regulatory Agency, the U.K. equivalent of the U.S. FDA, Paxil causes 10 times as many withdrawal complaints as Zoloft and 150 times as many as Prozac. A 2000 study of 107 patients at Massachusetts General Hospital found that those who abruptly quit Paxil experienced a 76 percent spike in dizziness, nausea, agitation, and other side effects after just 4 days. Patients who quit Zoloft reported an 18 percent increase; those who stopped Prozac reported none.

It took only two missed Paxil doses for that sick feeling to kick in, according to Maurizio Fava, M.D., a Harvard Medical School psychiatrist who co-authored the study and directs Massachusetts General's Depression Clinical and Research Program. How long a patient has been taking the antidepressant seems to be key.

"You can stop the drug abruptly after a few weeks if you're not tolerating it, and it's very unlikely you'll have a reaction," Fava says. "But if you've been on it for 3 months or more, you're more likely to have a reaction."

GSK says the problem is being overstated. According to company spokeswoman Mary Anne Rhyne, only 7 percent of patients who gradually quit Paxil feel dizzy, a sensation that can signal withdrawal. But she says the company is up front about the possibility of what it calls discontinuation effects. "Consumers need to know that they may experience certain side effects when they stop taking the drug," Rhyne says.

GSK says that the withdrawl problem is overstated, but also that consumers need to know they may experience side effects when they stop taking Paxil.

Paxil's packaging insert—the small-print dosing guide inside each box—has included a brief reference to withdrawal symptoms since 1994, when GSK began using a tapered regimen in its own clinical trials of the medication. (A sentence about discontinuation appeared toward the end of the roughly 15,000-word insert.) It was partly those clinical trials, started in 1994 and submitted to the FDA in 2000, that prompted the agency in 2001 to require GSK to provide explicit warnings about the possibility of problems when a patient attempts to get off the drug. Quitting, the insert now says, has been associated with "dizziness, sensory disturbances such as ... electric shock sensations, agitation, anxiety, nausea, and sweating."

The instructions add: "If intolerable symptoms occur following a decrease in the dose or upon discontinuation of treatment, then resuming the previously prescribed dose may be considered. Subsequently, the physician may continue decreasing the dose but at a more gradual rate."

People like Janelle Leonard might put that a little differently: You may be on Paxil for a lot longer than you expected, because it might be too tough to stop.

UNFORTUNATELY, many doctors don't appear to be getting the word. A 1997 study conducted in England found that 70 percent of primary care providers—who prescribe the bulk of antidepressants—were unaware of the withdrawal syndrome associated with Paxil and, to a lesser extent, other SSRIs. Even among psychiatrists, nearly 30 percent didn't know about it. The situation was similar on this side of the Atlantic, says Michael Craig Miller, M.D., assistant professor of psychiatry at Harvard and editor-in-chief of the Harvard Mental Health Letter. Doctors have become more aware of the potential for difficulty in getting off Paxil in recent years, he says, "but many still aren't alert to the problem or don't know how to deal with it."

Lalith Tissera, the psychiatrist who weaned Janelle Leonard off the drug using other medications, finds that inexcusable. "Psychiatry is not rocket science," he says. "There are only about 30 drugs to learn. But too many psychiatrists like to practice in a cocoon, disregarding the effects of these drugs on other systems in the body. They don't bother to learn about the pharmacology of these drugs."

As a result, Tissera and others say, many physicians mistake withdrawal—which can include crying spells, insomnia, and irritability—for the return of their patients' original symptoms. Instead of helping these patients get off Paxil, the doctors renew the prescription.

"Everyone concludes it's relapse, and the patients go back on the drug for literally years," Harvard's Glenmullen says. "They're medicating withdrawal, chasing their tail."

Why is it so hard for some people to quit Paxil? The answer is unclear, but it may lie in the drug's potency and in the complex behavior of serotonin, which is only partially understood.

Serotonin is a messenger chemical in the brain; it passes its signal by traveling from one brain cell to another. SSRI antidepressants work by blocking the absorption of serotonin after it's done its job. That leaves more of the chemical around to elevate mood.

But only 5 percent of serotonin is stored in the brain; the rest of it is distributed throughout the body, especially to the stomach and cardiovascular system. So a change in levels can affect everything from mood and memory to libido, appetite, sleep, and digestion.

Paxil's prowess in boosting serotonin, researchers say, may also be behind some of the withdrawal troubles. The drug is faster-acting than Prozac, for instance, quickly reaching high concentrations in the bloodstream. Conversely, once it's stopped, Paxil leaves the body so rapidly—in just 21 hours—that serotonin levels plummet quickly as well. Prozac, by contrast, lingers in the body for 2 weeks after patients quit; Zoloft, with a half-life of 26 hours, falls in between. Effexor, an antidepressant closely related to the SSRIs, is even faster-acting than Paxil.

For each drug, the likelihood of withdrawal symptoms appears to be related to the speed with which it's processed: Prozac triggers far fewer withdrawal side effects than Paxil, Zoloft causes more than Prozac but fewer than Paxil, and studies show that Effexor may be most prone to causing problems when a patient stops taking it.

In addition, Paxil has some distinctive properties that in theory could contribute to withdrawal, experts say. One is called nonlinear kinetics, which means that a twofold increase in dose—from 10 milligrams to 20 milligrams—can trigger a sevenfold increase of Paxil in the bloodstream. That's because once the drug reaches high concentrations in the body, Paxil interferes with the action of the enzyme that breaks it down. The flip side is that as blood levels of the drug fall, the enzyme chews up Paxil at an increasing rate. So as people whittle their Paxil intake, the medication leaves their systems faster than the dose alone may indicate.

Paxil's prowess in boosting serotonin, researchers say, may also be behind some of the drug's withdrawal troubles.

Whatever the reasons, it's clear that some people experience substantial difficulties when they stop taking Paxil. GSK says those problems don't mean that the drug is addictive. "When you talk about addiction, what comes to mind is heroin and cocaine," says Philip Perera, M.D., medical director for the company's psychiatry research and development group. "Addiction causes craving and abnormal behavior, and it affects your social and occupational functioning. Those things don't happen with SSRI antidepressants."

Glenmullen says it is true that people taking Paxil don't crave it or find illicit ways to hoard it. "But you must deal with what these words mean to the public. When you say it's nonaddicting and non-habit-forming, that means if they decide on Friday morning that they want to get off it, they can," he says. "If it's aspirin, that's true. If it's Paxil, it's not necessarily true."

PAXIL ALLOWS Elizabeth Cooke to walk down the streets of New York without scanning the sky nervously. Cooke, 45, an advertising copywriter who lives five blocks away from Ground Zero, started taking the antidepressant not long after she and her then-2-year-old daughter witnessed the second plane smash into the World Trade Center on September 11, 2001.

The fast-talking New Yorker is not easily cowed. But, she says, "when I'm off Paxil, the sound of any plane in the sky—I can feel it in my chest. I start to panic. That's how I know whether I've taken the pill or not."

A few months ago, Cooke misplaced her Paxil bottle and went on a family vacation without her 20-milligram daily supply. "No problem," she thought. "I don't need to take it for 4 days."

But Cooke says she grew so furious, so unapproachable, that for the first time in her marriage, she and her husband had a spate of bitter arguments.

"A wonderful relationship got troubled," Cooke says. "Now, believe me, I take that pill. The simple act of spacing it out can have disastrous consequences."

Not all people are content to stay on a pill for the rest of their lives, of course, particularly if their original problem wasn't terribly nettlesome. And particularly if they're pregnant.

Jane Lawrence, the Texas lawyer, wanted to get off the drug when she became pregnant 3 years ago. But every time she tried to cut back, "it was like chewing bullets," she says. "My entire system was so agitated. And the baby was agitated inside of me." On medical advice, Lawrence continued on Paxil.

Lawrence's daughter was born with respiratory distress, a problem that may be more common in newborns whose mothers used the drug during late-stage pregnancy, according to a recent study in the Archives of Pediatric & Adolescent Medicine. Her baby was in intensive care for a week. "I can't say that she definitely had withdrawal," Lawrence says. "But I harbored guilt for having that medication in my system."

Ultimately, Lawrence went off her 50-milligram dose cold turkey, but it wasn't easy.

"It goes through your whole body," she says. "When my husband left for work, I lay in the bed all day and let it fire." It took 4 months, but she finally got through.

"Paxil helped me through a really hard time," Lawrence says. "But getting off it was hell. Patients should be told about that before they take their first tablet."

Harvard's Michael Craig Miller agrees. Every medication has its advantages and disadvantages, he says. "Paxil is a perfectly good drug for treating depression. And it's useful to keep as many of these drugs as we can in our medicine bag, because we don't ever know which is going to be the best one for any given individual.

Still, Miller says, "doctors and patients plainly need to be aware of the problems that can occur when Paxil is stopped."

How to Quit—Smartly and Safely

DOCTORS OFTEN MISS signs of Paxil withdrawal, say Boston-area psychiatrist Lalith Tissera, M.D., and others, mistakenly attributing symptoms to a return of the depression or anxiety disorder for which the patient was on the drug in the first place. Relapse is a possibility, of course, but experts say there are good ways to tell the difference.

"If you're having symptoms you didn't have when you were depressed, that's a clue," says Jerrold Rosenbaum, M.D., chairman of the psychiatry department at Massachusetts General Hospital. "The classic symptom of discontinuation is dizziness. That's a good marker, because it doesn't easily get confused with depression."

Timing is another giveaway, says Joseph Glenmullen, M.D., a psychiatrist and clinical instructor at Harvard Medical School. Symptoms that appear within a week of stopping a drug are signals of withdrawal. "Relapse is typically much later, from weeks to months," Glenmullen says.

The simplest test: Resume taking the drug. If agitation or newly emergent flulike symptoms disappear, those side effects were likely due to withdrawal.

Symptoms of withdrawal are disturbing but not dangerous, says Michael Craig Miller, M.D., assistant professor of psychiatry at Harvard and editor of the *Harvard Mental Health Letter*.

Here are suggestions from patients and researchers for quitting Paxil or similar antidepressants.

- **Don't stop** taking it without consulting your primary care doctor or psychiatrist. He or she may suggest reducing the dose gradually and may also prescribe some medications to help wean you off the drug. (Benadryl may help you sleep; motion sickness medicines such as Dramamine may ease nausea.)
- **Exercise** as much as you can.
- **Eat healthy** foods; drink lots of water.
- **Take** a multivitamin.
- **Don't tough out** severe withdrawal problems; make smaller reductions instead. (A prescription for liquid Paxil allows you to decrease the dose by small amounts.)
- **Remember** that even tapering off the drug may cause severe mood swings. Watch out for suicidal thoughts.
- **Steer clear** of stressful situations when possible if withdrawal is making you anxious.
- **Keep in mind** that quitting gradually may take several months. The last 10 milligrams may be the hardest.
- **Chart your course** in a daily journal so that you can more accurately describe symptoms to your doctor

---

PAXIL WAS APPROVED 12 years ago, so why is the withdrawal issue gaining attention now? FDA spokeswoman Susan Cruzan says the studies GSK submitted in 2000, along with what the agency calls an excess of patient complaints, have shed new light on the problem.

And recent FDA warnings that Paxil may increase suicidal behavior in children, adolescents, and adults have raised safety issues about SSRIs that many doctors and patients believed had long been resolved (see "Antidepressants and Suicide: Is There a Link?").

But psychiatrists have been researching Paxil withdrawal since the early 1990s. David Healy, M.D., a British psychiatrist, author, and former researcher for SmithKline Beecham (now GSK), says he has seen a number of large studies in the company's private archives in Harlow, England, that indicate the firm has known since the late 1980s that Paxil can cause severe withdrawal symptoms.

"So many times I thought, 'Oh my God, if I just took a Paxil, this would all be over.' My doctor suggested that."

Healy was given access to those files in March 2001 while serving as an expert witness in a lawsuit against GSK. He reviewed 34 studies the company conducted on "healthy volunteers"—people with no prior history of mental illness—before Paxil was approved in the United States. "There's withdrawal

syndrome from Paxil that comes through in spades in these healthy-volunteer studies," Healy says. But few scientists have ever seen those reports, because most have never appeared in a medical journal. "Inconvenient data for pharmaceutical companies is left unpublished," Healy says. "And there is a vast amount of inconvenient data that is unpublished."

FDA officials, though, say they are satisfied with the information about withdrawal that GSK has provided them. Beyond asking the company to include warnings in its insert, the FDA has not alerted U.S. physicians to possible side effects of quitting Paxil—although Russell Katz, M.D., director of the FDA's Division of Neuropharmacological Drugs, acknowledges that patients frequently don't read or even see package inserts anymore. (Pharmacists, who receive the drug in its original box, often substitute a drugstore printout after portioning out the pills into individual prescriptions.)

In contrast, European medical authorities have been warning patients about the possibility of withdrawal problems for years. Italian and Swiss labels for Seroxat, the trade name for Paxil in most of Europe, state explicitly that symptoms appearing within a few days after quitting ought not be confused with relapse. Irish officials last year ordered GSK to remove the phrase "Remember, you cannot become addicted to Seroxat" from patient leaflets (the company complied).

And the British government is investigating SSRI withdrawal, including the reasons Seroxat seems to trigger a disproportionate number of cases.

The more muted FDA response leaves some former patients like Janelle Leonard upset, and pretty much on their own. "There were so many times when I thought, 'Oh my God, if I just took a Paxil, this would all be over,'" Leonard says. "My doctor suggested that. But I said, 'Absolutely not. This does something to you, and I don't want it.'"

Leonard has returned to teaching and is expecting her first child this spring. But she says she's still not back to her old self—not completely, anyway. The nausea never fully went away. And sometimes, as she lies in bed at night, she's gripped by anxiety as well.

"Occasionally, I'll wake up in the middle of the night and I'll have to calm myself down," Leonard says. "I never had that before the Paxil. The best way I can put it is, it caused for me everything the commercials say it cures."

Contributing Editor Asexis Jetter has also written for Mother Jones, The New York Times Magazine, *and* Vogue.

FINDING THE FUTURE ALCOHOLIC

Scientists may soon be able to identify children who are likely to become alcoholics. But will society be able to prevent their addiction?

By Steven Stocker

Many alcoholics tell the same story: Before they took their first drink they felt constantly anxious, irritable, or depressed. Afterwards, they felt normal for the first time in their lives.

The first time Judy drank alcohol, she knew it was for her. "It was a sort of 'Eureka!' experience. It wasn't so much that I felt good, it was just that I suddenly felt right," she says.

Judy had been a shy, depressed teenager in high school, but in college she blossomed, largely under the influence of alcohol. Drinking helped her socialize, dance, and even write. But eventually alcohol began to show its downside, contributing to the breakup of her first marriage and causing problems at work. After 13 years of heavy drinking, Judy quit and is now in her twentieth year of recovery.

Researchers speculate that people who abuse alcohol are trying to self-medicate some type of brain abnormality. Alcohol temporarily quells the symptoms of this abnormality, but when its effects wear off the symptoms return, worse than ever. To keep them under control, people continue to drink—greater amounts and more frequently—until they become dependent on alcohol.

People from families of alcoholics respond differently on certain blood and electroencephalogram (EEG) tests, raising the possibility that either these tests, or perhaps tests for genes associated with these abnormal responses, might be able to identify children who are more likely to become alcoholics. Once identified, they

could be treated with medications and/or behavioral therapies to prevent them from becoming dependent on alcohol.

The Personality of the Alcoholic

C. Robert Cloninger, a psychiatrist at Washington University in St. Louis, has proposed that there are two fundamental personality types among alcoholics. The first, like Judy, is anxious, inhibited, eager to please others, and rigid. The second resembles an action hero: confident, impulsive, socially detached, and constantly seeking new experiences. The second type is also aggressive, getting into bar fights when drunk and often crossing the line into criminal behavior.

> Research suggests that the anxious, inhibited type of alcholic may have a brain that is hypersensitive to stress.

The two personality types were first identified in studies of adopted men and women in Sweden, where careful records are kept on alcoholics. Because the alcohol-related behaviors of these people were more similar to their biological parents than to their adopted parents, researchers suspected that distinct genes were contrib-

uting to the development of the two alcoholism personality types.

More recent studies indicate that the two types of alcoholic personalities—inhibited and impulsive—respond differently on biological tests, supporting the notion that their differences are associated with distinct genes. For example, research at the Johns Hopkins University School of Medicine suggests that the anxious, inhibited type of alcoholic may have a brain that is hypersensitive to stress. This hypersensitivity can be detected by measuring the blood level of the hormone cortisol that is secreted in response to a chemical stressor.

Hypersensitivity to stress might be caused by a deficiency in the brain of *endogenous opioids*, compounds similar to morphine and heroin that occur naturally in the brain and the body and slow the release of stress hormones such as cortisol, according to neuroendocrinologist Gary Wand, who is conducting the Johns Hopkins research.

These natural opioids provide people with a sense of well-being. When the effects of the opioids are blocked, people feel depressed, tense, tired, and confused, and they have a hard time concentrating, performing poorly on reasoning and memory tasks.

Theoretically, people with opioid deficiency would feel tense all the time, as if they were in the middle of final exams week every second of their lives.

Wand believes that the high cortisol producers may be using alcohol to self-medicate their underlying opioid deficiency. Alcohol releases opioids in the brain, which would bring the opioid levels up to where they should be, at least temporarily.

Monkeys reared without adults, with only same-aged peers, show prolonged immaturity, including fearfulness and emotional instability. Such experiences have long-term effects on the brain and behavior, increasing risk for alcohol abuse during adolescence and impaired neurotransmission in some systems of the adult brain.

Another reason that high cortisol producers would like alcohol better than normal cortisol producers is that high cortisol levels produced by chronic stress make the brain's reward system more responsive to potentially addictive substances such as alcohol. As a result, high cortisol producers get more "bang for the buck" from an alcoholic drink.

Although Wand thinks that opioid deficiency is genetic, he leaves open the possibility that it is acquired during childhood. "Households with alcoholics are generally dysfunctional, where there's a lot more stress, so we may be looking at the adverse effects of chronic stress on the development of brain opioid activity," he says.

Anxiety and Alcoholism In Monkeys

In a recent study conducted by psychologist James Dee Higley and others at the National Institutes of Health Animal Center in Poolesville, Maryland, researchers induced stress in six-month-old rhesus monkeys by separating them from other monkeys to which they were emotionally attached. The monkeys' blood cortisol levels were measured during the separation. When the monkeys were four years old, the scientists gave them access to alcohol and found that the monkeys who drank the most alcohol were also the ones who had produced the highest levels of cortisol when stressed as infants. The monkeys

continued to produce high levels of cortisol throughout their life span.

The researchers call these high cortisol-producing animals their "uptight" monkeys. They cower in their cages, hugging themselves and sucking their thumbs. They seldom approach other monkeys or rise to a high social rank. Higley notes that when uptight monkeys drink alcohol they seem to be self-medicating, because alcohol causes them to stop exhibiting anxious behaviors and to interact better with the other monkeys.

Let's assume that high cortisol levels in response to stress during development can help to produce uptight humans who self-medicate their chronic anxiety with alcohol, just like the uptight monkeys. Theoretically, if we could identify these at-risk children, perhaps using a genetic test, we could find ways to prevent them from becoming alcoholics.

Substance abusers may turn to drink and drugs because their brains are hyperactive and they are trying to calm themselves down.

One possibility, Wand speculates, is to treat them with antidepressants, such as Prozac or Zoloft, that have been shown to be effective in treating anxiety disorders. Another possibility is to treat them with a new class of medications being developed that blocks the action of CRH, the hormone that triggers the release of stress hormones. CRH also acts as a neurotransmitter in the brain, where it mediates that tense, aversive feeling you get when you're unpleasantly stressed. Higley and his colleagues will be administering one of these new CRH blockers on a long-term basis to a group of their uptight monkeys starting in infancy to see if it can prevent them from developing their passion for alcohol.

Understanding the Hyperexcitable Brain

Unlike the shy and depressed Judy, Eric represents the impulsive, antisocial type of substance abuser who generally starts drinking and taking drugs earlier than the anxious type. Eric smoked his first joint at age 10, started drinking alcohol at 14, and began using cocaine at 17.

Even if we don't force every child to take alcoholism vulnerability tests, controversy is still inevitable when we start medicating those who score positive on the tests.

"I was always hyper. I lived for excitement—fighting, chasing girls," says Eric. "I was always seeking attention. I felt that, if I didn't get enough attention, I was going to do something to get it." He remembers that when he was five or six years old he broke a fish tank in his elementary school because he felt that his teacher wasn't paying enough attention to him.

Substance abusers such as Eric may turn to drink and drugs because their brains are hyperactive and they are trying to calm themselves down. This theory, proposed by neuroscientists Henri Begleiter and Bernice Porjesz at the State University of New York Health Science Center in Brooklyn, is derived from EEG studies of alcoholics and their offspring. They found similar brain-wave responses to stimuli between alcoholics and their sons.

EEGs will probably never be used to screen all children for potential alcoholism because it is too time-consuming and cumbersome, according to Begleiter. Studying brain-wave responses in children at risk for alcoholism is principally a step toward identifying genes that confer a vulnerability to alcoholism, since genes that contribute to a reduced brainwave response to stimuli should also contribute to this vulnerability. Once the genes are identified, tests for these genes could be conducted using blood samples taken from children, and medications could be given to the children who test positive for the genes. The medications would reduce the overexcitation in their brains, thereby theoretically reducing their inclination to drink alcohol when they get older.

Preempting Alcoholism: A Scenario

Let's assume that scientists eventually develop genetic or other tests that reliably identify children at risk for alcoholism. And let's say further that we start giving these tests to every 10-year-old in the country. One day, a child will refuse to take the genetic test. How should society react?

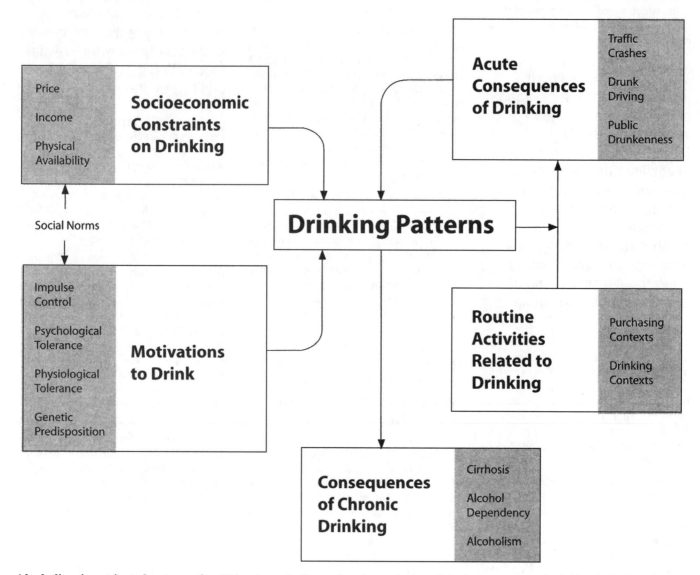

Alcoholism is not just about genetics. This schematic illustration shows the interlinked components of drinking behavior: the motivations to drink, socioeconomic constraints on drinking, health and other consequences of drinking, and routine activities.
Source: *Alcohol Health and Research World*/NIAAA

"Society has yet to compel anyone to take a genetic test or even a test for an infectious disease such as AIDS no matter how damaging their future behavior may be," notes Gary Wand. He points to court cases in which rape victims wanted to know the HIV status of their perpetrators, but the courts ruled that rapists could not be forced to take HIV tests.

Even if we don't force every child to take alcoholism vulnerability tests, controversy is still inevitable when we start medicating those who score positive on the tests. Given that the biological forces

contributing to alcoholism are probably complex, it will be a long time before clinicians agree on which medications are best. And inevitably, many parents will not want to give their children psychoactive medications.

James Dee Higley of the National Institutes of Health sees a situation developing that is similar to what we have now with Ritalin and attention deficit disorder (ADD). Ritalin and other mild stimulants have been shown to help children with ADD pay attention, but many parents are reluctant to give these drugs to their children.

However, giving medications to children is probably not the only way to prevent alcoholism. "I suspect that we could prevent much of the alcoholism that occurs simply by altering rearing conditions and teaching good parenting skills," says Higley. This is because environmental factors—such as interactions in the family, school, or neighborhood—contribute as much to the development of alcoholism as bad genes do.

Higley argues that he can produce a monkey that consumes vast quantities of alcohol no matter what its genetic makeup is simply by taking it away from its mother at birth and raising it in a cage with three other monkeys of the same age. "Monkey mothers do two things extraordinarily well," he explains. "First, they reduce arousal in their infants by comforting them so that, in time, the infants learn how to reduce their own arousal. And second, they react negatively when the infants behave inappropriately."

In the absence of its mother, the infant monkey develops into an anxious adult, because it has never learned how to reduce its own arousal, and also into an impulsive adult, because it has never learned how to limit its behavior. It drinks alcohol when given the opportunity because it constantly feels bad—a sort of monkey form of existential nausea—and has learned that alcohol can make it feel better. In other words, the motherless monkey is like a hybrid of the two types of human alcoholics: the anxious type and the impulsive type.

In the future, both medications and behavioral treatments will have roles to play in preventing these two types of alcoholism. In some instances, medications will be useful, like Ritalin in the more severe cases of ADD. In other cases, we must teach parents how to be better parents.

About the Author

Steven Stocker is a science writer who has published articles in *The Washington Post* and *Baltimore City Paper*. He has also written for magazines published by the National Institute on Drug Abuse and the National Center for Research Resources, both of which are components of the National Institutes of Health. His address is 18712 Curry Powder Lane, Germantown, Maryland 20874. Telephone 1-301-216-2071; e-mail sstockerl@earthlink.net.

Originally published in the May/June 2002 issue of *The Futurist.*, pp. 41-46. Used with permission from the World Future Society, 7910 Woodmont Avenue, Suite 450, Bethesda, MD 20814. Telephone: 301/656-8274; Fax: 301/951-0394; http://www.wfs.org. © 2002.

Research finds alcohol tolerance gene

UCSF worm study may lead to benefits for human drinkers

Carl T. Hall

After a six-year study of intoxication in laboratory roundworms, scientists at UCSF's Gallo Clinic and Research Center have found a gene that may explain why some people can handle their liquor better than others.

The findings shed new light on the mysterious workings of humankind's favorite drug of abuse and social elixir. Researchers hope the findings lay groundwork for new medical treatments for recovering alcoholics, perhaps even a fast-acting pill to help someone sober up.

That's only speculation, and it may take years just to confirm the relevance of the latest findings to people. At the very least, however, the findings suggest alcohol has more complex effects on brain cells than previously imagined.

The experiments, reported today in the journal Cell, were led by Dr. Steven McIntire, a UCSF assistant professor of neurology and principal investigator at the Gallo Clinic, a 20-year-old Emeryville affiliate of the UCSF neurology department initially financed by wine magnate Ernest Gallo.

McIntire screened thousands of the fast-breeding lab worms known as C. elegans in search of genes that could explain why some worms seem all but immune to the effects of alcohol—even when given doses sufficient to put an ordinary worm under the table.

Results showed that strong resistance to alcohol intoxication could be explained entirely by mutation of a single gene, called slo-1.

Ordinarily, the slo-1 gene produces a special protein, known as the BK channel, which sits like a gate in the outer membrane of nerve cells, allowing potassium ions to flow out of cells. Potassium ions are charged particles whose flow has big effects on the activity of neurons. When the BK channels become overactive, too much potassium flows out of nerve cells, weighing down their ability to fire normally.

Alcohol, McIntire discovered, homes in on the BK channels, causing them to open more often than they should. When he put the worms on an alcohol-soaked surface, allowing them to absorb it into their systems, the ordinary worms became markedly sluggish and uncoordinated—as if they had just downed two or three martinis. The mutant worms without the normal slo-1 gene wiggled about normally.

Similar molecular machinery is known to exist in humans and many other creatures. Ray White, a genetics specialist who serves as director of the Gallo Center, has already begun studying a population of human drinkers to determine if slo-1 gene mutations might help explain alcohol resistance in people.

So far, the strongest conclusion that can be drawn is that the newfound pathway is a central mechanism for alcohol variability—if you happen to be a worm.

"I think it's likely playing a similar role in humans," McIntire said, pointing to earlier laboratory studies involving cultured mammalian cells. "It could be that this gene, or other genes that interact with this gene, could account for some of the variability in the way humans respond to alcohol."

This is not simply a matter of clearing up ancient barroom debates as to why certain people handle their booze much better than others. Research has long showed that alcohol resistance is closely related to alcohol problems: the more someone can drink without getting drunk, the more likely he or she is to become hooked on the bottle.

But independent experts said the new experiments, although provocative, offer little practical help to the 16 million Americans now classified as heavy drinkers.

"The circuits in mammalian brains affected by alcohol are fairly complicated, and there are numerous neurotransmitters and receptors involved," said Dr. David Crabb, chairman of the department of medicine at Indiana University and director of the Indiana Alcohol Research Center.

The newfound links between alcohol resistance and potassium channels deserve a closer look, Crabb said, but it will take some careful studies in mice, and eventually people, to prove real-world significance. "It's a good hypothesis until we do that work, and nothing more really," he said.

Keith Trujillo, a psychopharmacologist at California State University San Marcos who studies drugs of abuse, said the new study is "a really thorough piece of work."

The problem, he said, is that alcohol is a relatively tiny molecule that acts in many ways, on many systems—a "dirty drug" whose myriad effects are difficult to pin down. "It's hard to bring out the signals from the noise," Trujillo noted. "It's a needle-in-a-haystack situation. What these researchers have been able to do is simplify the haystack by studying these simple roundworms."

The same potassium channels found in human nerve cells also are scattered throughout the body, playing vital roles in basic cell function. Ways might be found to tailor a drug to act only to counter alcohol, but it would be "very difficult" to be sure such a drug would not have serious side effects, Trujillo said.

"It's premature to say we've got a target for a drug here," he added.

But McIntire said the new findings at least raise the possibility that alcohol is not such a "dirty drug" after all, if it turns out that the potassium channels are as central to alcohol's workings in the human brain as they seem to be in explaining the squiggles of C. elegans.

E-mail Carl Hall at chall@sfchronicle.com

OPIOIDS For people with chronic suffering, these powerful pills are a godsend.
For others, they're a prescription for abuse and misery.

IN THE GRIP OF
A DEEPER PAIN

BY JERRY ADLER

THEY WERE INVENTED TO STOP PAIN, THE KIND THAT TRAVELS up the spinal cord, and they're remarkably effective at it: the synthetic opioids developed since the 1970s can mute the agony of slipped disks, deteriorating joints, tooth decay and even terminal cancer. If that was all they did, then it wouldn't be much of a problem; most people acquire the drugs innocently enough by prescription and take them only as long as they need to, and even the risk of dependence may be worth running, if the alternative is lifelong pain. The problem with painkillers is they also work on existential pain, the kind that originates in the mind— such as might be experienced by a right-wing radio host who doesn't have Bill Clinton to torture anymore. Cindy McCain, the wife of the Arizona senator, took Vicodin, a common opioid, for back pain, but she found it also helped her get through the "Keating Five" investigation involving her husband. "The newspaper articles didn't hurt as much, and I didn't hurt as much," she wrote in NEWSWEEK in 2001. "I've had clients describe Vicodin as 'a four-hour vacation'" from daily stress, says Robert Weathers, clinical director at Passages, a Malibu, Calif., super-deluxe rehab facility catering to clients who can afford monthly charges north of $30,000.

And more and more people are making that unfortunate discovery, it seems. Illegitimate use of OxyContin (a trade name for oxycodone), one of the drugs to which Rush Limbaugh was allegedly linked, has skyrocketed in recent years. At least 1.9 million Americans have admitted taking it illegitimately at least once, the Drug Enforcement Administration recently reported. "Right now it's

one of the most abused prescription drugs," says one DEA official. "It's certainly the most dangerous."

Limbaugh's other narcotic of choice, according to news reports, was hydrocodone, the generic name for a family of drugs including Vicodin, Lorcet and Lortab. These drugs also have a high potential for abuse—although the DEA lists them on Schedule III, a lower level of control than OxyContin, a Schedule II drug—and they accounted for slightly more emergency-room visits than oxycodone last year. Both classes of drugs work the same way, by locking on to a chemical receptor called *mu*, which blocks the transmission of pain in the spinal cord. Taken quickly and in large doses, the drugs also stimulate the production of dopamine in the brain, which can produce effects that mimic street narcotics. Long-term use of Vicodin has been linked, in very rare cases, to hearing loss; there's no published data yet on OxyContin. There's one other big difference, which helps explain why OxyContin has such a high profile in the DEA's view. Its great virtue is that it can be formulated in time-release tablets, packing as much as 12 hours worth of medication in one dose; hydrocodone pills, by contrast, usually last only about four hours. But that also opens the door to abuse; if you can defeat OxyContin's time-release function by pulverizing the pills and then swallowing, snorting or dissolving and injecting the powder, you can get seriously high. People can and do become addicted to hydrocodone, which is more widely prescribed than OxyContin. But Vicodin and its relatives also contain acetaminophen (Tylenol), creating a built-in disincentive to overdose: winding up in the hospital with liver failure.

HOW PAINKILLERS WORK

Millions rely on them for legitimate medical relief. But the illegal use of these drugs has jumped in recent years, as have related visits to the emergency room. Here's how opioids function in the body, and how they can lead to addiction.

1 TARGET SITES: Opioids travel through the bloodstream to the brain, where they interrupt incoming pain signals.

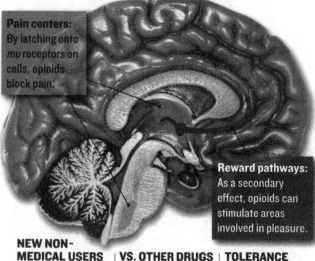

Pain centers: By latching onto *mu* receptors on cells, opioids block pain.

Reward pathways: As a secondary effect, opioids can stimulate areas involved in pleasure.

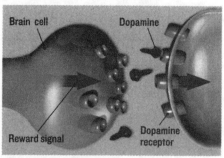

2 NORMAL BRAIN: The chemical dopamine jumps between brain cells in the reward pathway, producing pleasurable feelings.

Increased signal

3 BRAIN ON OPIOIDS: Painkillers can stimulate the release of extra dopamine, strengthening reward signals and pleasurable sensations.

NEW NON-MEDICAL USERS

(Graph showing growth from 1965 to 2001, scale 2 million, 1)

VS. OTHER DRUGS Millions of users in 2002, 12 yrs old+	
Marijuana	25.7
Painkillers	**11.0**
Cocaine	5.9
Ecstasy	3.2
Heroin	0.4

TOLERANCE When users take these drugs excessively, their brains become accustomed to an overstimulated reward pathway.

SOURCES: NATIONAL INSTITUTE OF DRUG ABUSE, SUBSTANCE ABUSE AND MENTAL HEALTH SERVICES ADMINISTRATION. WRITTEN BY JOSH ULICK. GRAPHIC BY KARL GUDE AND TONIA COWAN—NEWSWEEK

Purdue Pharma, acutely aware of the negative publicity around OxyContin, is working furiously to protect its $1.5 billion brand. It has committed $150 million to measures including public-service ads and the distribution of fraud-resistant prescription pads to physicians (try to photocopy it, and the word "void" miraculously appears). The company is also researching ways to make OxyContin less addictive, by adding a compound such as naltrexone that binds to the same receptors in the brain and blocks the action of oxycodone. The trick is to formulate the naltrexone so that it gets into the bloodstream in large amounts *only when the pill is crushed in order to get high*. Purdue's goal—probably five or so years off—"is to make it less desirable enough that abusers won't be interested in it," says Dr. Paul D. Goldenheim, the company's chief scientist.

The company obviously can't talk about individual patients, even famous ones. Goldenheim says, though, that it's extremely rare for a person with no history of substance abuse to become addicted to OxyContin after using it correctly. Outside authorities agree with that assessment. Goldenheim is drawing an important distinction between "dependence" and "addiction." Most people who take a powerful drug like OxyContin long enough will become physically dependent on it and suffer withdrawal symptoms (including pain, restlessness and nausea) if it's taken away; doctors deal with this by tapering down the dosage to zero and then, if all goes well, it's over. Or, if the pain is chronic, the patient stays on the drug indefinitely. In principle there's no more shame or harm in being dependent on painkillers than on, say, beta blockers for high blood pressure.

BY CONTRAST, A DRUG ADDICT has a psychological craving as well, which returns even when the physical dependence is overcome. That is what makes addiction so notoriously hard to treat; Limbaugh, who headed straight for rehab after signing off last week, has admitted attempting to kick his habit at least twice before. The state of the art, for people who can afford it, is a monthlong stay in a residential facility that offers both medically supervised withdrawal and psychological and spiritual counseling, usually based on the 12-step program. The best-known treatment center is Hazelden, based in Minnesota but with centers in four other states as well. For all forms of addiction, Hazelden claims that 53 percent of its patients stay clean for a year—in other words, after spending four weeks and $19,000, almost half its clients relapse within months. Nationwide, 12-step programs do poorly in treating painkiller abuse: relapse rates after a year approach 80 percent.

The other route to getting clean is a protocol developed in the past decade sometimes known as "rapid detox." It involves delivering a large intravenous dose of naltrex-one to a patient under anesthesia—a dose so large it would be intolerable if the patient were conscious. The Waismann Institute in Beverly Hills, which pioneered the technique, says its program—which takes three to four days and costs around $10,000—has a 65 percent one-year success rate. "Our patients don't want to go to a 30-day program and 'talk about it' with a bunch of drug addicts," Dr. Cliff Bernstein says dismissively. "They just want to be off the drugs." Either way, it's not an easy thing to do. As long as there is pain, people will try to escape it—and sometimes wind up with something worse.

With CLAUDIA KALB, DEBRA ROSENBERG, MARY CARMICHAEL and ANNE UNDERWOOD

UNIT 3

The Major Drugs of Use and Abuse

Unit Selections

17. **Alcohol's Deadly Triple Threat**, Karen Springen and Barbara Kantrowitz
18. **When Drinking Helps**, Janet Raloff
19. **Binge Drinking Holds Steady: College Students Continue to Drink Despite Programs**, Alvin Powell
20. **Dangerous Supplements Still at Large**, Consumer Reports
21. **Addicted to Anti-Depressants?**, Stephen Fried
22. **Stronger Pot, Bigger Worries**, David Wahlberg
23. **Inside Dope**, Quentin Hardy
24. **Heroin Hits Small-Town America**, Tim Jones
25. **What You Need to Know About Club Drugs: Rave On**, Kerri Wachter

Key Points to Consider

• How is it that specific drugs evolve, develop use patterns, and lose or gain popularity over time?

• How does the manner in which a drug is ingested help define its respective user population?

• How does the manner in which a drug is used influence the severity of consequences related to that drug? Or does it?

 **Links: www.dushkin.com/online/**
These sites are annotated in the World Wide Web pages.

QuitNet
   http://www.quitnet.org

The following articles discuss those drugs that have evolved to become the most popular drugs of choice. Although pharmacological modifications emerge periodically to enhance or alter the effects produced by certain drugs or the manner in which various drugs are used, basic pharmacological properties of the drugs remain unchanged. Crack is still cocaine, ice is still methamphetamine, and black tar is still heroin. In addition, tobacco products all supply the drug nicotine, coffee and a plethora of energy drinks provide caffeine, and alcoholic beverages provide the drug ethyl alcohol. These drugs all influence how we act, think, and feel about ourselves and the world around us. They also produce markedly different effects within the body and within the mind.

To understand why certain drugs remain popular over time, and why new drugs become popular, one must be knowledgeable about the effects produced by individual drugs. Why people use drugs is a bigger question than why people use tobacco. However, understanding why certain people use tobacco, or cocaine, or marijuana, or alcohol is one way to construct a framework from which to tackle the larger question of why people use drugs in general. One of the most complex relationships is the one between Americans and their use of alcohol. More than 76 million Americans have experienced alcoholism in their families.

The most recent surveys of alcohol use estimate that 120 million Americans currently use alcohol. The use of alcohol is a powerful influence that serves to shape our national consciousness about drugs. The relationship between the use of alcohol and the use of tobacco, and the use of alcohol and illicit drugs provides long-standing statistical relationships. The majority of Americans, however, believe that alcohol is used responsibly by most people who use it, even though approximately 10 percent of users are believed to be suffering from various stages of alcoholism.

Understanding why people initially turn to the non-medical use of drugs is a huge question that is debated and discussed in a voluminous body of literature. One important reason why the major drugs of use and abuse, such as alcohol, nicotine, cocaine, heroin, marijuana, amphetamines, and a variety of prescription, designer, over-the-counter, and herbal drugs retain their popularity is because they produce certain physical and psychological effects that humans crave. They temporarily restrain our inhibitions; reduce our fears; alleviate mental and physical suffering; produce energy, confidence, and exhilaration; and allow us to relax. Tired, take a pill; have a headache, take a pill; need to lose weight, take a pill; need to increase athletic performance, the options seem almost limitless. There is a drug for everything. Some drugs even, albeit artificially, suggest a greater capacity to transcend, redefine, and seek out new levels of consciousness. And they do it upon demand. People initially use a specific drug, or class of drugs, to obtain the desirable effects historically associated with the use of that drug. Heroin and opiate-related drugs such as Oxycontin and Vicodin produce, in most people, a euphoric, dreamy state of well-being. The abuse of these prescription painkillers is one of the fastest growing, and alarming, drug trends. Cocaine and related stimulant drugs produce euphoria, energy, confidence, and exhilaration. Alcohol produces a loss of inhibitions and a state of well-being. Nicotine and marijuana typically serve as relaxants. Ecstasy and other "club drugs" produce stimulant as well as relaxant effects. Various over-the-counter and herbal drugs all attempt to replicate the effects of more potent and often prohibited or prescribed drugs. Although effects and side effects may vary from user to user, a general pattern of effects is predictable from most major drugs of use and their analogs. Varying the dosage and altering the manner of ingestion is one way to alter the drug's effects. Some drugs, such as LSD and some types of designer drugs, produce effects on the user that are less predictable and more sensitive to variations in dosage level and to the user's physical and psychological makeup.

Although all major drugs of use and abuse have specific reinforcing properties perpetuating their continued use, they also produce undesirable side effects that regular drug users attempt to mitigate. Most often, users attempt to mitigate these effects with the use of other drugs. Cocaine, methamphetamine, heroin, and alcohol have long been used to mitigate each other's side effects. A good example is the classic "speedball" of heroin and cocaine. When they are combined, cocaine accelerates and intensifies the euphoric state of the heroin, while the heroin softens the comedown from cocaine. One present popular trend is to mix energy drinks with alcoholic beverages to mitigate the drowsiness associated with drinking alcohol. Some alcoholic beverage companies are producing recipes to capitalize on this trend. Other related drug trends, availability, price, and the public's perception of the drug's safety often influence the degree to which some drugs remain popular.

Drug abuse in America spans the spectrum of legality. To associate only illegal drugs with abuse and criminality is short-sighted. In terms of drug-related social impacts, any discussion of major drugs could begin and end with the topics of alcohol and nicotine. The pursuit of drugs and the effects they produce may be influenced by, but not bound by, legal status. For the student of drug-related phenomena, an attachment to the concepts of legality or illegality for purposes of comprehensively rationalizing drug-related reality is inappropriate. For example, annual alcohol-related deaths far outnumber deaths from all illegal drugs combined. And the current rates or the non-medical abuse of prescription narcotic pain killers is unprecedented.

Alcohol's Deadly Triple Threat

*Women get addicted faster, seek help less often
and are more likely to die from the bottle*

By Karen Springen and Barbara Kantrowitz

Pat Staples's childhood gave birth to the demons that nearly killed her. Her father was a volatile alcoholic. "I was physically, verbally and emotionally abused," she says. "Nose broken, head into the walls." In kindergarten she started dreaming about running away; she finally escaped in 1959, at the age of 20, when she married young to get out of the alcoholic house. But she couldn't flee her past. Over the years she gradually became an addict herself first with pills and then with alcohol. Still, her life seemed good on the surface. The marriage endured, defying the odds, and she and her husband had two healthy daughters. "Our house was on the home tour," she says. "Our kids were perfect."

The reality was far more bleak. She felt constantly under stress, anxious and terrified. "I was taking pills and drinking to keep it up," she says. Her husband started marking the bottles in the bar area, but she would just add water so he couldn't tell how much she had drunk. He checked the trash, too, and when she could no longer hide the empty bottles under newspapers, she started stashing them on the hill behind their house. Finally, one day in 1985, Staples went into the kitchen to get more ice for her vodka and saw her younger daughter, Tracy, then a high-school senior, making soup. The sweet smile on Tracy's face triggered something in Staples. "I looked at her, and I walked over, and I put my arms around her, and I said, 'Tracy, I need help'." Tracy replied, "I'm so proud of you." A few weeks later, when Staples entered the Betty Ford Center in Rancho Mirage, Calif., she was hemorrhaging rectally. "The alcohol had stripped the veins in my stomach," says Staples, now 64. "I would be dead today if I hadn't gotten sober."

Staples's grim assessment echoes new research about the devastating effects of alcohol on women. "Women get ad-dicted faster with less alcohol, and then suffer the consequences more profoundly than men do," says Susan Foster, director of policy research and analysis at the National Center on Addiction and Substance Abuse at Columbia University. A single drink for a woman has the impact of two drinks for a man. One reason: women's bodies contain proportionately less water than men's, and a given amount of alcohol produces a higher concentration in the bloodstream. For women, anything more than one drink a day (five ounces of wine or a 12-ounce bottle of beer) is considered risky. The limit for men is two. Women who start drinking young and become heavy drinkers as they get older are more vulnerable to a range of major health problems, from infertility to osteoporosis to cancer. At the same level of consumption, controlling for body size, women seem more likely than men to develop alcohol-related liver disease.

But new evidence about the dangers of alcohol hasn't stopped women from drinking. Researchers say that about 60 percent of American women consume alcohol on a regular basis and about 5 percent average two or more drinks a day. Many female alcoholics keep their drinking secret for years. "Our culture is still more critical of women who are intoxicated than of men who are intoxicated," says psychologist Nancy Waite-O'Brien of the Betty Ford Center. Women who drink heavily are denigrated as sluts, while a man may be praised for his hollow leg. That bias means many women drink in secret and don't seek help until major health problems make denial impossible.

Most experts say the best way to spare women from alcoholism is to get them when they're young. People who drink before they're 15 are four times as likely to be alcohol-dependent or have alcohol problems when they're adults. Drinking can also damage the still-developing teen-age brain, according to the American Medical Association. Unfortunately, that message isn't getting out. Even though drinking under the age of 21 is illegal in all 50 states, 41 percent of ninth graders reported drinking in the past month, according to National Institutes of Health literature. Other studies have shown that more teen girls are getting drunk, and they're trying to keep up with the boys, drink for drink. "It puts them at risk of sexual assault, of physical violence," says Foster.

Many teen girls see drinking as cool, a way to be social. Elizabeth Anderson, now 26, started drinking with her friends when she was a 15-year-old high-school student in suburban Boulder, Colo. A year later she had her first blackout. Still, she did well in school, graduating in the top 10 percent of her class. She continued drinking at the University of Colorado, where she graduated with degrees in French and advertising. At 22 she crashed her car after drinking. At 23 she got a DUI. She doesn't remember much of the next year—there were more blackouts, and eventually she was fired. At 24 she was deep in debt and finally called her father for help. He got her into rehab, and she says she's been sober ever since. She avoids drinking parties and begs off when friends go to bars. Instead, she cherishes the friends she has made through a 12-step program—people who can understand what she's been through. "More than anything, what keeps me sober is looking at my life today," she says.

As women get older, their drinking threatens their children's health as well. During pregnancy especially, doctors say, women should abstain completely. "We haven't established that there's any safe level of drinking during pregnancy or lactation," says Foster. Fetal alcohol syndrome is the leading preventable cause of mental retardation in the United States. And it's not the only risk children face when pregnant women drink. Fetal alcohol spectrum disorders, which affect as many as 40,000 infants a year, can include a range of physical, mental, behavioral and learning problems.

Some studies indicate that women in unhappy or stressful relationships are the most likely to turn to alcohol for comfort. Women who have never been married or who are divorced are more likely to drink heavily than married women. And women who were sexually abused as children are more than three times as likely to suffer from alcohol problems, according to Sharon Wilsnack of the University of North Dakota School of Medicine and Health Sciences, who has conducted a 20-year study of women and alcohol. Depression is a common trigger for drinking in women. What women should watch for, doctors say, is a pattern of using alcohol to be less stressed or angry. "Alcohol is pretty good in the early stages at dealing with bad feelings," says Wilsnack. But ultimately drinking becomes as big a problem as depression and can even exacerbate negative feelings.

Wilsnack and her colleagues found that women are less likely to drink as they age—which is a good thing, because older women who drink heavily are at much higher risk for diseases of aging. Heavy alcohol use irreversibly weakens bones, and while there's some evidence that one drink a day may decrease the risk of heart disease, there's also research suggesting that the same amount of alcohol can increase the risk of breast cancer. A woman with a family history of heart disease but no family history of alcoholism or breast cancer could have a drink a day, but a woman with a family history of those diseases might want to abstain.

If you drink at all, drink sensibly—aim for no more than one drink a day. Don't drink alone. And don't drink to medicate your moods. If you think you have a problem, seek help. "It's not a moral issue," says Staples. "It's a disease. It needs to be treated by professionals who understand the disease. If a person wants it, there is help and there is hope." That's a message you can't get in a bottle.

WHEN DRINKING HELPS

Sorting out for whom a nip might prove therapeutic

BY JANET RALOFF

Downing a cocktail or other alcoholic drink at least three to four times a week appears to substantially cut a man's risk of heart attack, Boston-area researchers reported in early January. Less than a week later, a U.S.-Canadian team of epidemiologists focusing on African Americans announced it had found no clear benefit to people drinking the same amount of alcohol per week. These reports joined other seemingly conflicting studies on the health impacts of alcohol that have emerged in the past few years.

Some research found that regular, moderate drinking not only helps preserve mental clarity in both young and elderly people but also increases blood-sugar control in people with diabetes. Other studies linked low but regular consumption of alcohol with an increased risk of certain cancers and a stunting of children exposed to alcohol in the womb. These subtle detrimental effects, of course, add onto the potentially catastrophic acute events caused by alcohol-impaired judgment.

With dozens of conflicting reports spilling out each year, is it any wonder that the public is confused about alcohol and health?

Yet, in probing the scores of published papers on alcohol's impacts, researchers have begun to discern a few trends. Chief among them: Alcoholic beverages can offer large pharmacological benefits, especially to people at elevated risk of heart disease. Various studies have begun unveiling why (*SN: 1/5/02, p. 8*).

In fact, argues Jurgen Rehm of the Centre for Addiction and Mental Health in Toronto, because alcohol's benefits appear primarily from slowing the progression of chronic diseases that usually emerge in or after middle age, there seems to be little health justification for drinking alcohol before age 40.

Among older adults, however, benefits of moderate drinking "appear to be huge," notes Tim Stockwell, director of the National Centre for Research into the Prevention of Drug Abuse at Curtin University of Technology in Perth, Australia. Data in his country indicate that among people who regularly down a few

drinks a day, "there are approximately 6,500 lives saved each year by alcohol's protective effects on cardiovascular disease." Even factoring in alcohol-associated deaths from breast cancer and other malignancies, he says, "the net benefit for [moderate] drinking here appears to be about 5,000 lives a year."

"Although I think alcohol can be part of a healthy lifestyle, it's not a necessity," says Eric B. Rimm of the Harvard School of Public Health in Boston. Moreover, he adds, one wouldn't want to push abstainers to start drinking if they have cultural, religious, or other prohibitions against it—or an inability to hold their drinking to a few glasses per day. And drinking should never, he says, be portrayed as a substitute for exercise, eating a healthy diet, or giving up cigarettes as the best ways to stave off heart disease.

> "There are probably many cases where some people should be told to drink a little more."
>
> —ERIC B. RIMM

But among people who now drink occasionally, Rimm says, the accumulating evidence of alcohol's potential benefits is "so overwhelming that there are probably many cases where some people should be told to drink a little more."

RISKS IN ABSTAINING Alcohol is without question a poison. People die from binging, and many children enter the world with a retardation that traces to prenatal alcohol exposure. In fact, Rehm says, more than 60 diseases have been linked to excessive consumption of alcohol.

Although one might expect those risks to increase linearly with consumption, they don't. Stockwell points to hundreds of studies showing that a little daily drinking is more healthful than either abstaining or drinking to excess.

Epidemiologists refer to this as alcohol's "J-shape curve, for the contour that the risk data take when plotted on a graph. That provocative contour emerged strongly in a new review of 35 studies on stroke performed by researchers at Tulane University in New Orleans. In the Feb. 5 *Journal of the American Medical Association*, Kristi Reynolds and her colleagues confirm "a J-shaped association between alcohol consumption and the relative risk of… ischemic stroke," a disorder that traces to blockages in the brain's blood vessels.

Two years ago, Rehm and his colleagues reported a J-shape curve for alcohol consumption and premature deaths from all causes in their 11-year study of 5,200 U.S. men and women.

Economists at Duke University in Durham, N.C., published data 2 years ago showing a J contour in alcohol's impacts on disability claims. For 6 years, Jan Ostermann and Frank A. Sloan followed 12,650 people initially in their 50s or 60s. People drinking one or two drinks a day were least likely to report a disabling event, such as stroke or arthritis, "whereas abstainers generally were most likely to be disabled."

No matter how many possibly confounding factors they investigated, Sloan says, "we could not make the effect go away."

Rimm's team also observed a disadvantage for abstainers in a new 12-year study of heart-disease risks in 38,000 male health professionals. Overall, the researchers report in the Jan. 9 *New England Journal of Medicine*, disease risk fell as the volume of regularly consumed alcohol rose.

SWEET NEWS A J-shape curve has emerged in alcohol's effects on diabetes and also on cognition. Last spring, federal scientists at the Beltsville (Md.) Agricultural Research Center linked alcohol consumption directly to blood sugar and insulin benefits in a trial with 63 healthy postmenopausal women.

In one 8-week phase, the women drank orange juice laced with 15 grams of alcohol each night before bed; in another, they drank juice containing 30 grams a night, the equivalent of two drinks. To keep other aspects of the diet from affecting the parameters being measured, the scientists administered carefully controlled meals to every woman throughout the trial. Such costly, controlled-feeding trials represent the gold standard of nutritional studies.

In the May 15, 2002 *Journal of the American Medical Association*, David J. Baer and his colleagues report that the women's insulin values, blood sugar, and cholesterol were healthiest during the two-drink-per-day regimen.

Although this trial used straight ethanol in juice, other studies have shown that certain pigmented compounds, called phenolics, that show up in beer and red wine can have their own healthful effects on people's hearts and blood sugar.

Pierre-Louis Teissedre and his colleagues at the University of Montpellier, France, gave diabetic rats phenolics-enriched white wine for 6 weeks in amounts equivalent to a person's intake of a half-liter per day. Afterward, the rats' blood quashed oxidative reactions—a major cause of diabetes complications—as well as the blood of healthy rats did. The treated animals also showed slightly improved control of blood-sugar concentra-

tions. The findings appear in the Jan. 1 *Journal of Agricultural and Food Chemistry*.

The researchers then further enriched the wine with phenolics to achieve what Teissedre describes as pharmacological doses. In just-completed tests, this doctored wine "corrected the diabetes" by bringing control of the animals' blood sugar into a normal range, Teissedre reports.

One interesting observation: The antidiabetes effect diminished when the animals received phenolics without alcohol.

A clear J-shape curve is also showing up in studies of alcohol's effects on cognition. For instance, a year ago, Dutch researchers found that moderate drinkers have a lower risk of Alzheimer's disease and dementias than do abstainers or heavy drinkers (*SN: 2/2/02, p. 67*).

While that study was in the works, Constantine G. Lyketsos and his colleagues at Johns Hopkins University in Baltimore investigated effects of long-term drinking on reasoning, memory, decision making, and psychomotor speed in nearly 1,500 people. Scores on the test used in the study typically drop about 1 point per decade during early adulthood and 2 to 3 points per decade for people in their 60s. But in the new 13-year study, both young and old adults who regularly drank outperformed abstainers of the same age.

The finding was particularly robust for women, the Johns Hopkins team reported in the Oct. 15, 2002 *American Journal of Epidemiology*. Nondrinking women declined a point more on the test during the study than did moderate, habitual drinkers. For perspective, Lyketsos notes, "people with Alzheimer's disease tend to decline an average of 3 to 4 points on this scale every year, so a 1-point drop is not negligible." In fact, he concludes, because even heavy drinkers outperformed teetotalers, "the findings suggest that maybe the worst thing you can do is not drink."

TROUBLING TESTIMONY Such statements trouble Nancy L. Day of the Western Psychiatric Institute and Clinic in Pittsburgh. Many women don't know they're carrying a child until well into their pregnancy, she notes, and her data indicate that "no amount of alcohol is healthy during pregnancy"—at least for the child.

Over the past couple decades, she and her colleagues have been measuring the growth and development since birth of 565 children from low-income, inner-city families. In the October 2002 *Alcoholism: Experimental and Clinical Research*, Day's group reported that 14-year-old children who had been exposed in the womb to alcohol were—as they had been at birth—shorter and leaner than the offspring of women who eschewed alcohol during pregnancy. The finding was true even for the women who downed just one or two drinks per month during their first trimester—a finding that "blew us away," Day told *Science News*.

By age 14, children of the lightest drinkers averaged 3 pounds less than nondrinkers' children; offspring of the heaviest drinkers, 16 pounds less. Though smoking during pregnancy also yields smaller babies, those kids "usually catch up within the first year or so," Day notes.

What concerns her most is that teenage children of drinkers had a smaller average head circumference—"a very crude measure of brain size"—than nondrinkers' teens had. Indeed, her latest findings show that fetal-alcohol exposure correlated with subtle changes in information processing that could impair learning.

For adults, drinking alcohol has also been tied to cancer. Many analyses show a steadily increasing risk of breast cancer as the average daily consumption of alcohol increases. For example, one 1998 study found that alcohol equivalent to one drink a day increases the risk of breast cancer by about 9 percent.

Characteristics of drinking can have an effect, too. People who down a significant share of their alcohol outside of meals, for instance, face at least a 50 percent higher risk of cancer in the oral cavity, pharynx and esophagus than do people who drink only at meals (*http://www.sciencenews.org/20030215/food.asp*).

BINGEING BACKFIRES A growing number of studies are finding new risks from binge drinking, which is usually defined as downing five or more servings of alcohol in one day. Lyketsos and his colleagues found in their study that people who typically binged had more cognitive decline than did heavy, frequent drinkers consuming comparable volumes of alcohol.

Indeed, Rehm and Christopher T. Sempos of the University of Buffalo's Department of Social and Preventive Medicine suspect that bingeing may account for the results of their team's analysis of drinking and health in 2,000 African Americans.

They analyzed 19 years' of dietary data for blacks in the National Health and Nutrition Examination Survey (NHANES). The epidemiologists compared alcohol consumption per week with death from any cause. In the January *Alcoholism: Experimental and Clinical Research*, they report that the data for the African-Americans didn't follow the J curve, but risk of death "increased with increasing average consumption."

FORTIFIED WHITE—Domaine Virginie of Bezier, France, has begun marketing Paradoxe Blanc as "the first white wine offering the same health benefits as red wine." The chardonnay, developed at the University of Montpellier, is enriched with phenolics that are good for the heart.

Rehm and Sempos note that the survey asked only how many servings of alcohol people typically down in a week. If the answer was 10 to 14, for example, but that amount was consumed only over the weekend, that's bingeing, Sempos says.

In fact, the researchers cite three studies since 1995 indicating that the African-American community has a higher proportion of abstainers and bingers than the white population does. Moreover, says Thomas K. Greenfield of the Alcohol Research Group in Berkeley, Calif., some studies have reported "that because of larger containers and higher-alcohol-content products marketed to African-Americans, surveys [like NHANES] may even underestimate the heavy quantities consumed by ethnic minorities."

Fuzzy reporting of consumption patterns compromises data from most alcohol surveys, Rehm observes. That's why many researchers would prefer data from experiments in which people drink alcohol only under researchers' supervision.

Shela Gorinstein of the Hebrew University-Hadassah Medical School in Jerusalem says her team expects to begin just such a clinical trial soon. Some lucky recruits will get free beer for 10 years.

From *Science News*, March 8, 2003, pp. 155-156 by Janet Raloff. © 2003 by Science Service Inc. Reprinted by permission via the Copyright Clearance Center.

Binge drinking holds steady:

College students continue to drink despite programs

By Alvin Powell
Gazette Staff

College students have continued binge drinking at about the same rate over the past 10 years, despite increases in alcohol education programs and substance-free on-campus housing, and a decrease in high school binge drinking, according to a Harvard School of Public Health study.

The positive trends have been offset by an increase in heavy drinking by students who do drink, with an increase in the percentage of frequent binge drinkers to 22.8 percent from 19.7 percent in 1993.

"This to us indicates very strong forces are continuing to support drinking on campus," said Henry Wechsler, director of College Alcohol Studies and a lecturer on social psychology at the Harvard School of Public Health. "The drinking style on campus is still one of excess."

About 44 percent of college undergraduates reported binge drinking at least once in the two weeks prior to being surveyed, according to findings in the 2001 College Alcohol Study, whose results were released March 25. The study, which was also conducted in 1993, 1997, and 1999, also indicated that, of students who drink, 70 percent engage in bingeing. The study defines binge drinking as having five or more drinks on one occasion for men and four or more drinks on one occasion for women. Frequent binge drinkers binged on at least three occasions in the previous two weeks.

The survey includes responses from more than 10,000 full-time students at 119 four-year colleges located in 38 states. Wechsler declined to identify individual schools, saying it's a problem of all colleges, not just those involved in the survey. He did say that selective schools such as those in the Ivy League had results similar to other institutions. Results were published in two articles in the Journal of American College Health's March issue.

The surprising thing in this year's study was the steady 44 percent rate despite other positive changes, Wechsler said. That indicates not that those changes were failures, Wechsler said, but that they alone can't fix the problem.

"I think what colleges need to do is go beyond the kinds of programs in place at most schools aimed at educating students to a restructuring of the whole environment, both campus and the community," Wechsler said.

Counterbalancing the positive changes are entrenched forces that promote drinking, Wechsler said. Fraternities and sororities continue to be centers of campus drinking, he said, with 75 percent of those living in frat or sorority houses reporting binge drinking in the survey. While that number is actually down from 83 percent in 1993, it's still indicative of a problem, Wechsler said.

Another problem area is college athletics, Wechsler said, with drinking commonly being associated with athletic events and, outside those events, athletes often involved in heavy drinking.

Economics are also working against a downward trend in heavy drinking, Wechsler said. Typical college campuses are ringed by bars and liquor stores that market heavily on campus, offering low prices and easy access.

While the overall bingeing rate held steady, the overall picture of college drinking hasn't been completely static, Wechsler said. There has been a trend of polarization, with more students abstaining and heavier drinking by those who drink. More students are living in substance-free housing on campus, rising from 17 percent in 1993 to 28 percent in 2001. Rates of bingeing at all-women colleges have risen, from 24 percent in 1993 to 32 percent in 2001. Despite that increase, bingeing rates at all-women colleges are still lower than for women at coed institutions.

While fewer high school students are bingeing, underage drinking at college campuses continues to be a problem. Underage students accounted for about half—48 percent—of the drinking on campus.

Student housing was a major factor in the level of drinking, Wechsler said, with 75 percent of those living in frat or sorority houses reporting bingeing, 51 percent living in dormitories, 50 percent in off-campus housing without their parents, 36 percent living in substance-free housing, and 25 percent living at home with their parents.

The study did provide cause for hope. Wechsler said that states with tough underage drinking laws reported lower rates of underage drinking, showing that those laws are working.

Colleges and universities need help from the surrounding communities to tackle this problem, Wechsler said, with tougher laws, limits on on-campus alcohol marketing, and higher prices for alcohol. Colleges, for their part, he said, should look into the connection between drinking and athletics and fulfill their longstanding promises to crack down on fraternity- and sorority-related drinking.

Finally, Wechsler said, parents should take an active role, talking to their children about alcohol use and—at a minimum—refrain from bringing alcohol to their underage children in the dormitories, as some students reported.

"I think parents should take the problem of drinking alcohol seriously for their underage students," Wechsler said. "I think the one thing we need to do is get real about this. It's a serious problem and people are groping for quick and easy solutions. And there aren't any."

___

alvin_powell@harvard.edu

___

Dangerous Supplements Still At Large

If you can buy it at a clean, well-lighted store, if it's "all natural," it's not going to do you serious harm, right? That's what many Americans assume about dietary supplements. But while most supplements are probably fairly benign, CONSUMER REPORTS has identified a dozen that according to government warnings, adverse-event reports, and top experts are too dangerous to be on the market.Yet they are. We easily purchased all 12 in February in a few days of shopping online and in retail stores.

These unsafe supplements include Aristolochia, an herb conclusively linked to kidney failure and cancer in China, Europe, Japan, and the U.S.; yohimbe, a sexual stimulant linked to heart and respiratory problems; bitter orange, whose ingredients have effects similar to those of the banned weight-loss stimulant ephedra; and chaparral, comfrey, germander, and kava, all known or likely causes of liver failure. (For a complete list of the "dirty dozen," see the table: Twelve supplements you should avoid.)

U.S. consumers shelled out some $76 million in 2002 for just three of these supplements: androstenedione, kava, and yohimbe, the only ones for which sales figures were available, according to the Nutrition Business Journal, which tracks the supplement industry.

The potentially dangerous effects of most of these products have been known for more than a decade, and at least five of them are banned in Asia, Europe, or Canada. Yet until very recently, the U.S. Food and Drug Administration had not managed to remove a single dietary supplement from the market for safety reasons.

After seven years of trying, the agency announced a ban on the weight-loss aid ephedra in December 2003. And in March 2004 it warned 23 companies to stop marketing the body-building supplement androstenedione (andro).

Despite these actions against high-profile supplements, whose dangers were so well known that even industry trade groups had stopped defending them, the agency continues to be hamstrung by the 1994 Dietary Supplement Health and Education Act (DSHEA, pronounced de-*shay*).While drug manufacturers are required to prove that their products are safe before being marketed, DSHEA makes the FDA prove that supplements on the market are *unsafe* and denies the agency all but the sketchiest information about the safety record of most of them.

CR Quick Take

A CR investigation found that many dangerous supplements can easily be purchased in stores and online. Many of these supplements have been banned in other countries. Why can't the U.S. Food and Drug Administration ban these products now?

We found that regulatory barriers created by Congress, supplement industry pressure, and a lack of resources at the FDA have resulted in major risks for consumers.

- These widely available dietary supplements (see table) may cause cancer, severe kidney or liver damage, heart problems, or even death. They should be avoided by consumers.

- These supplements are sold under a profusion of names, making it difficult for consumers to know what they're purchasing.

- Most also appear in combination products marketed for a broad array of uses, such as asphrodisiacs, athletic-performance boosters, and treatments for anxiety, arthritis, menstrual problems, ulcers, and weight loss.

"The standards for demonstrating a supplement is hazardous are so high that it can take the FDA years to build a case," said Bruce Silverglade, legal director of the Center for Science in the Public Interest, a Washington, D.C., consumer advocacy group.

At the same time, the FDA's supplement division is understaffed and underfunded, with about 60 people and a budget of only $10 million to police a $19.4 billion-a-year industry.To regulate drugs, annual sales of which are 12 times the amount of supplement sales, the FDA has almost 43 times as much money and almost 48 times as many people.

"The law has never been fully funded," said William Hubbard, FDA associate commissioner for policy and planning. "There's never been the resources to do all the things the law would command us to do."

Twelve supplements you should avoid

The 12 supplements ingredients in this table have been linked to serious adverse events or, in the case of glandular supplements, to strong theoretical risks. They're all readily available on the Web, where our shoppers bought them both individually and in multi-ingredient "combination products." We think it's wise to avoid all of them. But the strength of that warning varies with the strength of the evidence and the size of the risk. So we've divided the dirty dozen into three categories: definitely hazardous, very likely hazardous, and likely hazardous.

NAME (ALSO KNOWN AS)	DANGERS	REGULATORY ACTIONS
DEFINITELY HAZARDOUS *Documented organ failure and known carcinogenic properties*		
Aristolochic acid (*Aristolochia*, birthwort, snakeweed, sangree root, snagrel, serpentary, serpentaria; asarum candense, wild ginger)	Potent human carcinogen; kidney failure, sometimes requiring transplant; deaths reported.	FDA warning to consumers and industry and import alert, in April 2001. Banned in 7 European countries and Egypt, Japan, and Venezuela.
VERY LIKELY HAZARDOUS *Banned in other countries, FDA warning, or adverse effects in studies*		
Comfrey (*Symphytum officinale*, ass ear, black root, blackwort, bruisewort, consolidae radix, consound, gum plant, healing herb, knitback, knitbone, salsify, slippery root, symphytum radix, wallwort)	Abnormal liver function or damage, often irreversible; deaths reported.	FDA advised industry to remove from market in July 2001.
Androstenedione (*4-androstene-3, 17-dione*, andro, androstene)	Increased cancer risk, decrease in HDL cholesterol.	FDA warned 23 companies to stop manufacturing, marketing, and distributing in March 2004. Banned by athletic associations.
Chaparral (*Larrea divaricata*, creosote bush, greasewood, hediodilla, jarilla, larreastat)	Abnormal liver function or damage, often irreversible; deaths reported.	FDA warning to consumers in December 1992.
Germander (*Teucrium chamaedrys*, wall germander, wild germander)	Abnormal liver function or damage, often irreversible; deaths reported.	Banned in France and Germany.
Kava (*Piper methysticum*, ava, awa, gea, gi, intoxicating pepper, kao, kavain, kawa-pfeffer, kew, long pepper, malohu, maluk, meruk, milik, rauschpfeffer, sakau, tonga, wurzelstock, yagona, yangona)	Abnormal liver functin or damage, occasionally irreversible; deaths reported.	FDA warning to consumers in March 2002. Banned in Canada, Germany, Singapaore, South Africa, and Switzerland.
LIKELY HAZADOUS *Adverse-event reports or theoretical risks*		
Bitter orange (*Citrus aurantium*, green orange, kijitsu, neroli oil, Seville orange, shangzhou zhiqiao, sour orange, zhi oiao, zhi zhi)	High blood pressure; increased risk of heart arrythmias, heart attack, stroke.	None
Organ/glandular extracts (brain/adrenal/pituitary/placenta/other gland "substance" or "concentrate")	Theoretical risk of mad cow disease, particularly from brain extracts.	FDA banned high-risk bovine materials from older cows in foods and supplements in January 2004. (High-risk parts from cows under 30 months still permitted.) Banned in France and Switzerland.
Lobelia (*Lobelia inflata*, asthma weed, bladderpod, emetic herb, gagroot, lobelie, indian tobacco, pukeweed, vomit wort, wild tobacco)	Breathing difficulty, rapid heartbeat, low blood pressure, diarrhea, dizziness, tremors; possible deaths reported.	Banned in Bangladesh and Italy.
Pennyroyal oil (*Hedeoma pulegioides*, lurk-in-the-ditch, mosquito plant, piliolerial, pudding grass, pulegium, run-by-the-ground, squaw balm, squawmint, stinking balm, tickweed)	Liver and kidney failure, nerve damage, convulsions, abdominal tenderness, burning of the throat; deaths reported.	None
Scullcap (*Scutellaria lateriflora*, blue pimpernel, helmet flower, hoodwort, mad weed, mad-dog herb, quaker bonnet, scutelluria, skullcap)	Abnormal liver function or damage.	None
Yohimbe (*Pausinystalia yohimbe*, johimbi, yohimbehe, yohimbine)	Change in blood pressure, heart arrythmias, respiratory depression, heart attack; deaths reported.	None

Sources: Natural Medicines Comprehensive Database 2004 and Consumers Union's medical and research consultants.

The agency has learned that it must tread carefully when regulating supplements. The first time it tried to regulate the dangerous stimulant ephedra, in 1997, overwhelming opposition from Congress and industry forced it to back down.

As a result, the FDA is sometimes left practicing what Silverglade calls "regulation by press release"—issuing warnings about dangerous supplements and hoping that consumers and health practitioners read them.

There are signs of hope. The FDA has said that if the ban on ephedra holds up against likely legal challenges, it plans to go after other harmful supplements. Legislation has been introduced to strengthen the FDA's authority under DSHEA and give the agency more money to enforce the act.

But the supplement marketplace still holds hidden hazards for consumers, especially among products that aren't in the headlines. "Consumers are provided with more information about the composition and nutritional value of a loaf of bread than about the ingredients and potential hazards of botanical medicines," said Arthur Grollman, M.D., professor of pharmacological sciences at the State University of New York, Stony Brook, and a critic of DSHEA.

A QUESTION OF SAFETY

Supplement-industry advocates say the ephedra ban demonstrates that DSHEA gives the FDA enough power to protect consumers from unsafe products. "I don't think there's anything wrong except that FDA has only recently begun vigorous and active enforcement of the law," said Annette Dickinson, Ph.D., president of the Council for Responsible Nutrition, a major trade association for the supplement industry.

But critics of DSHEA think the ban illustrates the extremes to which the FDA must go to outlaw a hazardous product.

When the agency initially tried to rein in ephedra use in 1997, after receiving hundreds of reports of adverse events, it sought not an outright ban but dosage restrictions and sterner warning labels. The industry mounted a furious counterattack, including the creation of a public-relations group called the Ephedra Education Council and a scientific review from a private consulting firm, commissioned by Dickinson's trade group, that concluded ephedra was safe. After the U.S. General Accounting Office said the FDA "did not establish a causal link" between taking ephedra and deaths or injuries, the agency was forced to drop its proposal.

The industry continued to vigorously market and defend ephedra. Metabolife International, a leading ephedra manufacturer, did not let the FDA know that it had received 14,684 complaints of adverse events associated with its ephedra product, Metabolife 356, in the previous five years, including 18 heart attacks, 26 strokes, 43 seizures, and 5 deaths. It took the pressure of congressional and Justice Department investigations to get the com-

pany to turn over the complaints in 2002. Then Steve Bechler, a pitcher for the Baltimore Orioles, died unexpectedly in 2003 while taking another ephedra supplement, Xenadrine RFA-1. With sales suffering from the bad publicity, manufacturers began to replace ephedra with other stimulants such as bitter orange, which mimics ephedra in chemical composition and function.

"All of a sudden Congress dropped objections to an ephedra ban and started demanding the FDA act," said Silverglade.

To amass the necessary scientific evidence that it hoped would satisfy the demanding standard set by DSHEA, the FDA took aggressive action: It commissioned an outside review from the RAND Corporation, analyzed adverse-event reports, and pored over every available shred of scientific evidence.

"We've gone the whole nine yards to collect and evaluate all the possible evidence," Mark McClellan, commissioner of the FDA, said in announcing the ban. "We will be doing our best to defend this in court, and if that's not sufficient, it may be time to re-examine the act."

DRUGS VS. SUPPLEMENTS

In an October 2002 nationwide Harris Poll of 1,010 adults, 59 percent of respondents said they believed that supplements must be approved by a government agency before they can be sold to the public. Sixty-eight percent said the government requires warning labels on supplements' potential side effects or dangers. Fifty-five percent said supplement manufacturers can't make safety claims without solid scientific support.

SUFFERED SIEZURE

**Gretchen Fitzgerald, age 21,
Fort Collins, Colo.**

PROBLEM She took Xenadrine EFX "thermogenic" diet pills to boost her energy while studying for final exams, believing they were safe because they were labeled ephedra-free. After three weeks of taking the product she had a seizure. The neurologist consulted told her the bitter orange in the Xenadrine was the probable cause. Xenadrine's manufacturer did not return our phone calls. Since going off the Xenadrine, Fitzgerald has had no further problems.

They were wrong. None of those protections exist for supplements—only for prescription and over-the-counter medicines. Here are the major differences in the safety regulations:

Testing for hazards. Before approval, drugs must be proved effective, with an acceptable safety profile, by means of lab research and rigorous human clinical trials

KIDNEYS FAILED

**Beverly Hames, age 59,
Beaverton, Ore.**

PROBLEM Hames went to an acupuncturist in 1992 seeking a "safe, natural" treatment for an aching back. She got a selection of Chinese herbal products, at least five of which were later found to contain aristolochic acid. By mid-1994, she had symptoms of kidney failure, and in 1996 she underwent a kidney transplant. She must take anti-rejection drugs for life. The herbs' distributor said his Chinese suppliers had substituted Aristolochia for another herb without his knowledge.

involving a minimum of several thousand people, many millions of dollars, and several years.

In contrast, supplement manufacturers can introduce new products without any testing for safety and efficacy. The maker's only obligation is to send the FDA a copy of the language on the label (see Names & Claims).

"Products regulated by DSHEA were presumed to be safe because of their long history of use, often in other countries," said Jane E. Henney, M.D., commissioner of the FDA from 1998 to 2001. "As their use dramatically increased in this country after the passage of DSHEA, the presumption of safety may have been misplaced, particularly for products other than traditional vitamins and minerals. Some, like ephedra, act like drugs and thus have similar risks."

The only exceptions to this "presumption of safety" are supplement ingredients that weren't being sold in the U.S. when DSHEA took effect. Makers of such "new dietary ingredients" must show the FDA evidence of the products' safety before marketing them. The FDA invoked that rarely used provision in its action against androstenedione. After years of allowing andro to be marketed without restriction, the agency declared that it was "not aware" that the supplement was used before DSHEA, so it couldn't be sold without evidence of safety.

Disclosing the risks. Drug labels and package inserts must mention all possible adverse effects and interactions. But supplement makers don't have to put safety warnings on the labels, even for products with known serious hazards.

We bought a product called Relaxit whose label had no warning about the kava it contained, even though the American Herbal Products Association, an industry trade group, recommends a detailed, though voluntary warning label about potential liver toxicity on all kava products.

Ensuring product quality. Drugs must conform to "good manufacturing practices" that guarantee that their contents are pure and in the quantities stated on the label. While DSHEA gave the FDA authority to impose similar standards on supplements, it took until 2003 for the

agency to propose regulations—as yet not final—to implement that part of the law.

Contaminants, too, regularly turn up in supplements. In 1998 Richard Ko, Ph.D., of the California Department of Health Services reported that 32 percent of the Asian patent medicines he tested contained pharmaceuticals or heavy metals that weren't on the label. The FDA has seized supplements adulterated with prescription drugs, including, in 2002, an herbal "prostate health" supplement called PC SPES that turned out to contain a powerful prescription blood thinner, warfarin.

Reporting the problems. By law, drug companies are required to tell the FDA about any reports of product-related adverse events that they receive from any source. Almost every year, drugs are removed from the market based on safety risks that first surfaced in those reports.

In contrast, supplement makers don't have to report adverse events. Indeed, in the five years after DSHEA took effect, 1994 to 1999, fewer than 10 of the more than 2,500 reports that the FDA received came from manufacturers, according to a 2001 estimate from the inspector general of the U.S. Department of Health and Human Services. (Other sources of reports included consumers, health practitioners, and poison-control centers.) Overall, the FDA estimates that it learns of less than 1 percent of adverse events involving dietary supplements.

THE 'NATURAL' MYSTIQUE

Many makers market their supplements as "natural," exploiting assumptions that such products can't harm you. That's a dangerous assumption, said Lois Swirsky Gold, Ph.D., director of the Carcinogenic Potency Project at the University of California, Berkeley, and an expert on chemical carcinogens. "Natural is hemlock, natural is arsenic, natural is poisonous mushrooms," she said.

A cautionary example is aristolochic acid, which occurs naturally in species of Aristolochia vines that grow wild in many parts of the world. In addition to being a powerful kidney toxin, it is on the World Health Organization's list of human carcinogens. "It's one of the most potent chemicals of 1,400 in my Carcinogenic Potency Database," Gold said. "People have taken high doses similar to the doses that animals are given in tests, and they both get tumors very quickly."

The dangers of aristolochic acid have been known since at least 1993, when medical-journal articles began appearing about 105 patrons of a Belgian weightloss clinic who had suffered kidney failure after consuming Chinese herbs adulterated with Aristolochia. At least 18 of the women also subsequently developed cancer near the kidney.

These findings prompted the FDA to issue a nationwide warning against Aristolochia in 2001 and to impose a ban on further imports of the herb. But in early 2004, more than two years after the import ban went into effect, CONSUMER REPORTS was able to purchase products online that were labeled as containing Aristolochia. In

names&claims

THE ART AND LAW OF SUPPLEMENT LABELS

- "New 21st century 'designer' D-Bol is so potent it turns genetically average guys into supernatural studs no one messes with!"

- Xenadrine EFX "provides the most effective approach to losing weight ever developed!"

- "Thousands of testimonials" credit chaparral "for tumor remission and complete cures. Other medical evidence indicates it is an anti-inflammatory and antimicrobial agent and a possible treatment for asthma."

Does the government really allow supplement companies to make extravagant promises like those, which we found on Web sites promoting products we purchased? The answer is murky at best.

Under the 1994 Dietary Supplement Health and Education Act, manufacturers can't claim that a product prevents or treats a disease or disorder. But they can say it affects the "structure and function" of the body—"supports healthy prostate function," for example—or shows a "link" to a disease or disorder, and allow consumers to draw their own, often erroneous, conclusions. The FDA can require that a manufacturer change a label that it decides is making an unauthorized claim.

DSHEA does say, confusingly, that supplement makers must be able to "substantiate" their claims. But it does not specify what that means, nor does it require that the evidence be shown to anybody, not even the FDA.

The Federal Trade Commission has the authority to punish companies whose ads are intentionally misleading. Unlike the FDA, it can force companies to give it documents substantiating suspect claims and order the products off the market if it decides that the substantiation isn't sufficient. But it can't move against a category of products, such as those containing ephedra, nor can it act against dangerous products that aren't advertising to the public.

Since DSHEA's passage, the FTC has brought more then 100 cases against supplement marketers for deceptive advertising. But "there are literally hundreds, perhaps thousands, of companies out there that probably deserve scrutiny," said Richard Cleland, assistant director of the FTC's division of advertising practices, "We don't have the resources to look at every one."

2003, Gold identified more than 100 products for sale on known or suspected to contain aristolochic acid.

Donna Andrade-Wheaton, a former aerobics instructor in Rhode Island, learned those facts too late to save her kidneys. After taking Chinese herbs containing Aristolochia for more than two years, she suffered severe kidney damage; her kidney tissues were found to contain aristolochic acid. In late 2002, at age 39, she underwent a kidney transplant.

Andrade-Wheaton is suing both the acupuncturist who gave her the herbs and several companies that manufactured them. The acupuncturist declined to discuss the case on the record, and the manufacturer did not return our phone calls.

There's another widespread and false assumption about natural supplements: that they're always pure, unprocessed products of the earth. Because DSHEA permits the marketing of concentrates and extracts, supplement makers can and do manipulate ingredients to increase the concentrations of pharmacologically active compounds.

That's especially true of the many weight-loss supplements designed for "thermogenic" stimulant effects-boosting calorie expenditure by revving the metabolic rate.

On one Internet shopping tour, for instance, we bought a product called Thermorexin—"the Hottest new Ther-

mogenic on the market!" Its label says it contains, among its 22 ingredients, 30 milligrams of theophylline derived from a black tea extract and the stimulant bitter orange. Sold as Theo-Dur and other brands, theophylline is a prescription drug and an effective asthma treatment, but most doctors seldom prescribe it because it can cause seizures and irregular heartbeats at relatively low doses.

Larry Berube, president of Anafit, Thermorexin's manufacturer, based in Orlando, Fla., described how the product's combination of ingredients was developed: "Once we find out that the FDA says it's OK, we put them together in the lab, run our tests, and do our trials, and if it comes up good, we capsulate it, put it online and in the stores and sell it," he said.

Those tests involved asking fitness professionals to use the supplement, and measuring their heart rate and blood pressure, Berube said. The company doesn't use a control group, he said.Then "we go to the fitness discussion boards and let trainers and people know we have a new product and do they want to try it," he said."And then they try it, and they report back." Berube said he has not heard of any bad reactions to Thermorexin.

WHAT YOU CAN DO

Sen. Richard Durbin, Democrat of Illinois, and Rep. Susan Davis, Democrat of California, have each intro-

KIDNEYS FAILED

**Donna Andrade-Wheaton, age 40,
Cranston, R.I.**

PROBLEM Andrade-Wheaton's acupuncturist pre-scribed more than a half dozen Chinese herbal supple-ments to treat health conditions, including endometriosis. At least one of the products listed Aris-tolochia as an ingredient, even after the FDA issued a nationwide Aristolochia safety warning in 2001. She underwent a kidney transplant in September 2002 and must take anti-rejection drugs for life.

duced legislation that for the first time would require supplement manufacturers to disclose reports they re-ceive of "serious" adverse events. Durbin's bill also sets up a separate category for stimulants,which would have to receive FDA safety approval before being marketed, and reclassifies androstenedione and similar "steroid precursors" as controlled drugs. The Davis bill also strengthens the FDA's powers to investigate emerging supplement safety problems. Davis's bill exempts vita-mins and minerals from its provisions. (Consumers Union, publisher of CONSUMER REPORTS, supports both bills.)

Though the bills are still in committee, the supplement industry has mobilized in opposition. On its Web site and in flyers handed out at supplement stores, the National Nutritional Foods Association, a supplement retailers' trade group, says the legislation "would significantly un-dermine many of the freedoms that American consumers of dietary supplements like you hold dear."

The industry is supporting a more limited bill intro-duced by Sen. Orrin Hatch, Republican of Utah, and Sen. Tom Harkin, Democrat of Iowa, that would give the FDA an extra $20 million this year, and more in subsequent years, to enforce DSHEA and would reclassify andros-tenedione and other steroid precursors as controlled drugs. Unlike the Durbin bill, however, this measure would exempt the steroid dehydroepiandrosterone, or DHEA, allowing it to continue to be marketed as an anti-aging product. Some $47 million worth was sold in 2002, according to the Nutrition Business Journal.

Until the law is substantially changed and the FDA is adequately funded, you cannot rely on the federal gov-ernment to ensure that dietary supplements are safe and effective. Here are some steps you can take to minimize your risk from any supplements you decide to take:

Stay away from the dirty dozen. All carry risks that in our view are unacceptable (see table). In combination products, you need to read the detailed ingredient list in the tiny print on the back.Who could otherwise guess, for instance, that Gaia Herbs' PMS Day 14-28 capsules con-tain kava? (To the company's credit, the label includes a warning about liver toxicity.)

Do not take daily doses of vitamins and minerals that exceed the safe upper limits. While vitamins and minerals are by far the safest and best-studied of supple-ments, it's possible to overdose on some of them. For more information, see "Fortified Foods: Too Much of a Good Thing?,"CONSUMER REPORTS, October 2003. Recommended allowances and safe upper limits can be found online at www.ific.org/publications/other/driupdateom.cfm.

Limit your intake of other supplements. Over the years, our medical and nutritional consultants have iden-tified and tested a few products, other than standard mul-tivitamins, with possible benefits and sufficiently low risks to recommend for general use: saw palmetto for be-nign enlarged prostate in men, glucosamine and chon-droitin for arthritis, and fish-oil capsules (omega-3 fatty acids) for heart disease. (We plan to test additional sup-plements with potential benefits, such as probiotics.)

Tell your doctor about your supplements. "The Achil-les' heel of unregulated supplements is the risk created by herb-prescription drug interactions," said Grollman, the pharmacologist at the State University of New York. "St. John's wort, used to treat depression, for instance, may reduce the effectiveness of prescription drugs used by millions of Americans for hypertension, AIDS, heart fail-ure, asthma, and other chronic diseases."

Stay away from supplements for weight control. These products frequently contain several stimulants that have never been adequately tested separately, let alone in combinations. "I'd just as soon experiment with rats first rather than using the U.S. population as guinea pigs," said Bill Gurley, Ph.D., professor of pharmaceutical sci-ences at the University of Arkansas.

Do your own research. Health-foodstore clerks and mar-keters, alternative medicine practitioners, herbal company Web sites, and even physicians are not necessarily knowl-edgeable about the scientific evidence regarding dietary sup-plements. These two Web sites contain reliable information: the National Institutes of Health site at ods.od.nih.gov/databases/ibids.html and Memorial Sloan-Kettering Cancer Center's site at www.mskcc.org/mskcc/html/11570.cfm.

Watch for adverse events. Let your doctor know if you experience anything worrisome after starting a supple-ment. If your doctor concludes that the side effect may be related to the supplement, be sure to report it to the FDA, by calling 800-332-1088 or by visiting www.fda.gov/medwatch.

Addicted to anti-depressants?

The controversy over a pill millions of us are taking

*Scores of patients call Paxil, a top-selling antidepressant, their emotional lifesaver.
But some say that getting off the drug has been physically torturous.
Now they're asking, Why weren't we warned?*

By Stephen Fried

It wasn't until she felt the zaps—sharp, electrifying jolts causing sizzles of pain behind her green eyes—that Adrienne Bransky knew she was in trouble. "It was the worst pain I'd ever had in my life," she says.

She'd felt flu-ish all day during the conference she was attending, but her Chicago firm had flown the 29-year-old strategic management consultant to New York to troll for new contacts in the world of corporate mergers, so she tried to tough it out. The dizziness, nausea and vertigo got so bad, though, that she finally retreated to her hotel room.

She changed from her tailored suit into her old, comfy sweatpants and lay down on the king-size bed. Nothing helped—she couldn't stop the world from spinning. And then she felt that first zap. "Oh, my God," she said aloud as she burst into tears. "What was that?"

"If I moved my head," she recalls now, "it was like I was seeing in slow motion and the rest of my brain had to catch up. And when it caught up, I got the jolts, which just killed!"

Lying in the darkness, she wished she could talk to her husband, Aaron, a medical student, but he was unreachable at the hospital. Eventually, she contacted her personal physician and reported the symptoms, but the internist was baffled.

Then Bransky mentioned that her psychiatrist was weaning her off her antidepressant. She had been taking Paxil (paroxetine), among the most popular of the selective serotonin reuptake inhibitors (SSRIs), the class of psychiatric medicines that also includes Prozac and Zoloft. Bransky had been on Paxil ever since suffering what she refers to as a "breakdown" in her midtwenties, when she says she was "severely depressed and obsessed with running away from my life or killing myself." Paxil helped her in a matter of weeks, and she had been taking it successfully for four years, maintaining a moderate dosage of 30 mg per day. She'd asked her doctor to help wean her off the drug because she wanted to try to get pregnant.

Mysteriously—and violently—ill

Virtually all drugs may trigger side effects, and Bransky knew firsthand that Paxil can make your weight go up and your libido go down, something the drug's manufacturer, GlaxoSmithKline (GSK), acknowledges. But no one had ever told her that *quitting* the drug could cause problems. So she hadn't anticipated any.

Bransky's internist had a gut feeling that the Paxil was somehow to blame for her symptoms and told her to page the psychiatrist who'd prescribed the drug. The psychiatrist, however, assured her

that as long as she had gradually reduced her dosage as instructed, Paxil could not be the culprit, Bransky says.

Mystified and violently ill, Bransky booked a flight home for the following morning. Then she curled up in a fetal position and cried herself to sleep.

> **"** *I thought that if I ever had to go through that hell again, I would kill myself.* **"**

At the emergency room back in Chicago, doctors ran tests for everything from vertigo to serious neurological conditions; all were inconclusive. Bransky's internist continued to suspect Paxil, but she rarely prescribed the drug and didn't know its safety profile well. So she checked with the psychiatrist and ultimately deferred to her expert opinion that Bransky's discontinuation of her antidepressant wasn't to blame. Bransky was eventually sent home, where she lay in bed with no answers, still waiting for the shocks and the dizziness to stop.

"It was like I was drunk on an out-of-control cruise ship," she remembers.

Finally, about three weeks after the symptoms first appeared, they began to dissipate. At the one-month mark, she still felt drunk, but at least the cruise ship had docked in calm harbor. Eventually, Bransky was able to return to the office.

Don't take any drug until you read this!

Adverse drug reactions, commonly known as side effects, can occur when you start or stop taking a new medication, or at any time in between. You can minimize your risks by following these simple steps, developed in consultation with Brian L. Strom, M.D., director of the Center for Clinical Epidemiology and Biostatistics at the University of Pennsylvania School of Medicine.

Before you take a new medication, tell your doctor about all your old ones—prescription, over-the-counter and naturopathic. Also mention any drugs that have caused you problems in the past.

Ask your doctor if the drug she is prescribing is new to the market. If it's been available for less than a year, its potential side effects can't possibly be well-known yet. If you're being switched to a new drug for a condition your doctor has treated successfully in the past with something else, be especially curious. Doctors sometimes suggest swapping your old drug for another simply because your health insurer made a deal to buy the new one for less.

Never stop taking a prescribed medication—even for just a few days—without approval from your doctor.

Still, the memory of her world spinning out of control remained vivid.

"I thought that if I ever had to go through that hell again, I would kill myself," she says.

An army of angry patients

That episode occurred in 1998, and it would take more than a year for Bransky to feel sure that Paxil had, in fact, triggered her medical crisis. Yet even today—after experiencing a second episode of what she refers to as "Paxil withdrawal" and switching to another drug—she admits that Paxil "worked amazingly well. It saved me." The drug gets similarly ecstatic reviews from legions of other patients—most of them female, since the majority of those taking Paxil, and all antidepressants, are women. But an estimated one in 10 patients will experience problems if the drug is abruptly discontinued, and one in 20 may develop

more serious symptoms, similar to Bransky's, according to a leading expert on SSRI discontinuation, Jerrold F. Rosenbaum, M.D., chair of psychiatry at Massachusetts General Hospital in Boston. With approximately 25 million prescriptions written for Paxil last year, it's likely that hundreds of thousands of patients are affected.

A growing number of these patients assert that they they weren't adequately warned about how hard it can be to stop taking Paxil. Some have joined a major lawsuit in California that charges GSK with deliberately withholding information about "withdrawal." (Similar suits have been filed in at least 14 other states.) The firm handling that suit has heard from more than 6,000 prospective clients, and of the 35 named plaintiffs in the suit—those with the most typical symptoms and strongest cases—two thirds are women. Bransky is one them. "I'm not looking to get anything out of this financially," she says, "but these pharmaceutical companies are not educating doctors and patients!"

There is no question that Paxil and the other SSRI medications have revolutionized the treatment of depression. They have relieved symptoms for millions of patients worldwide, becoming one of the pharmaceutical industry's blockbuster categories in the process. For the past several years, Paxil has been the top-selling drug for GSK, with some $2.67 billion in global sales last year (second only to Zoloft among the SSRIs).

But ever since the first SSRI, Prozac, came on the market in 1987, there have been questions about the potential for significant side effects. For years, the SSRI manufacturers and the Food and Drug Administration only glancingly acknowledged the fact that the drugs can cause sexual problems—everything from dampening of libido to complete inability to have an orgasm—affecting perhaps as many as half of all patients; they can also cause weight gain. Such problems are among the reasons that many patients have a love-hate relationship with their psychiatric drugs and often look forward to a day when they can manage without them.

Given this yearning to stop taking antidepressants, it is bitterly ironic that

some of the worst side effects can hit when patients least expect them: The moment they try to get *off* the drugs. Many patients suffer nothing more than flulike symptoms. But the more extreme cases, frequently involving Paxil, include symptoms like severe nausea, dizziness, disorientation and "zaps"—the feeling of a lightning jolt in the brain. Studies report that these patients often miss days or weeks of work and still don't feel *right* even after they return to their normal routines. Many find that the only thing that makes them feel better is going back on their medication. Talk to them and you find that most knew nothing about the risk of withdrawal when they were put on antidepressants: They received no warnings from their doctors and read no prominent advisories in GSK's package insert; FDA regulation did not protect them. The message to the rest of us? When your doctor starts you on a prescription drug, particularly one that's relatively new to the market, you may not get the whole story on its side effects. And the whole story, argue women like Bransky, is exactly what you need to stay safe.

Drug company denials

While these side effects can occur with all SSRIs, they occur more frequently with Paxil, according to sources such as *The Journal of Clinical Psychiatry*. This is especially troubling because Paxil is FDA-approved to treat more symptoms than any other SSRI, including anxiety, panic disorder, social phobia (clinical shyness) and, most recently, post-traumatic stress disorder. Physicians also favor Paxil because it's thought to be the fastest-acting SSRI.

The Paxil discontinuation syndrome and the reasons for it were explored anecdotally in reports throughout the mid-nineties. Then in 1997, papers by Dr. Rosenbaum and others cited studies that proved the symptoms existed and could be serious. Why might Paxil cause more problems when halted than other SSRIs? Dr. Rosenbaum and his colleagues explained that the drug stops working as quickly as it starts, exiting the body in four days. (Prozac, by contrast, can linger up to four weeks.) Apparently, this abruptness causes a sudden chemical imbalance and in some cases makes patients physically ill.

Those who have had the most difficult experiences getting off Paxil, along with some vocal physicians and health care advocates, claim that patients are becoming "addicted" to their antidepressants and are experiencing true withdrawal. They are harshly critical of GSK's actions—and inaction—over the years. "What shocks me, to be quite honest, is not the existence of this very nasty side effect but the way [GSK has] denied it," says British pharmaceutical safety activist Charles Medawar, whose lobbying helped persuade his government to change the drug's label warnings in the United Kingdom. "There is clear evidence of withdrawal, and a risk of dependence exists for a minority of users."

GSK refutes such charges and says the symptoms critics call "withdrawal" are, in most cases, little more than a rapid relapse of the psychiatric illness the drug was prescribed for. "Many of these discontinuation symptoms overlap with the symptoms of anxiety and depression," says Alan Metz, M.D., GSK's vice president, psychiatry, clinical research and medical affairs. "It may be difficult to distinguish discontinuation symptoms from a relapse of the underlying illness." According to prescribing materials for Paxil, these symptoms are usually "mild" and "may have no causal relationship to the drug," "did not require medical intervention" and, in any case, "have been reported for other selective serotonin reuptake inhibitors." In other words, the symptoms are minor and common to all SSRIs. Dr. Metz strongly denies the harshest accusation, that Paxil is addictive, pointing out: "With addictive medications, it's very clear that the longer you take them, the more likely you are to become dependent. If this were to occur with Paxil, it should get worse when the patient takes the drug for long periods. But we found that the symptoms were less frequent in the longer-term studies."

Dr. Metz does admit, however, that the company discovered long ago that tapering the dose, rather than stopping the drug cold turkey, appeared to prevent many patients from suffering discontinuation symptoms. (Tapering doesn't help everyone, though, as Bransky's case illus-

trates.) In fact, all GSK clinical trials with Paxil since 1994 have included a tapered regimen. But it took the company nearly eight more years, until December 2001, to directly acknowledge the problems of discontinuation symptoms and suggest tapering to patients and physicians in Paxil's FDA-approved prescribing information. Because of that delay, advocates say, hundreds of thousands of patients may have needlessly suffered when they stopped taking the drug suddenly.

> "We all hope that we won't have to take these pills forever. That's why drug companies need to be more responsible."

Martha Folmsbee, a 40-year-old microbiology graduate student at the University of Oklahoma, says she is one of those patients. Her Paxil "withdrawal" experience began when her fanny pack, which had her medication, was stolen while she was at a scientific conference in Los Angeles. Folmsbee had been on Paxil for a year, and while it effectively controlled her depression, she was uncomfortable with the idea of taking the drug indefinitely. She decided to use the pilfering of her pills to see how she felt without Paxil. Several days later, she had her answer: She was in agony. "I was vomiting and had horrible diarrhea, constant nausea, migraines and extreme weakness," she recalls. Her doctors, like Bransky's, could determine nothing from numerous tests. But when she started taking Paxil again and all the symptoms miraculously disappeared, she felt certain that she had experienced Paxil "withdrawal."

"I was told by a doctor that I had just relapsed, but these weren't symptoms of my depression, which I know well," Folmsbee says. "When Paxil was abruptly withdrawn, I was *physically* sick, with awful vomiting, diarrhea, disorientation and confusion." She tried to wean herself off the drug, but the "withdrawal" symptoms returned whenever she got down to 5 mg. It took a year of lowering her dose by minute increments to finally wean herself completely. "The hardest part is that you don't have an organized support network like the ones people rely on to

get over many other addictions," she says. "My family helped pull me through. Even so, it took all my determination."

The question of addiction

So what truly goes on in patients' bodies when they try to go off Paxil? Many experts believe they are experiencing neither relapse of psychiatric symptoms nor true withdrawal. "It's a classic rebound effect," says John Urquhart, M.D., professor of pharmaco-epidemiology at Maastricht University in the Netherlands. Rebound effects occur when a body system that has been artificially regulated by medication is suddenly left to its own devices again—and temporarily over-regulates before finding a new happy medium. The harsh post-Paxil symptoms might just be the serotonin system sputtering as it readjusts. Other commonly used drugs can cause rebound effects when stopped—for example, getting off some beta blocker medication can cause anything from severe anxiety to a full-blown heart attack. Many patients don't know about rebound effects, says Dr. Urquhart, because "what happens to patients when they stop taking drugs turns out to be a major blind spot in drug development. Companies invariably invest major efforts in studying the onset of drug action but hardly ever study the 'offset' of drug action."

The big difference between beta blockers and Paxil, however, is that the rebound effects of heart drugs are well-known by physicians and pharmacists, and the warnings on their labels are far more prominent than those on Paxil's. In a 1997 study, 70 percent of general practitioners surveyed and 28 percent of psychiatrists didn't know that SSRIs could cause discontinuation symptoms; only 17 percent of general practitioners and only 20 percent of psychiatrists were consistently cautioning their patients about how to slowly taper off the drugs. And for years, the FDA allowed GSK to describe Paxil as "non-habit-forming" in its print and TV ads, even though critics say this scientific claim is false.

In a California federal court hearing last August, U.S. district judge Mariana Pfaelzer banned, in the name of "public interest in health and safety," all ads making the claim that Paxil wasn't habit-forming. The court order was quickly reversed, but last October GSK voluntarily dropped the troublesome language. And new ads running this winter included a warning that patients should consult their doctors before discontinuing the drug.

For Monica Keller, a 40-year-old accountant for Ticketmaster who is a member of the California suit, those concessions are too little, too late. "For years, they claimed it wasn't habit-forming. That was the biggest lie!" she fumes. Keller originally took Paxil for panic attacks and was incapacitated for more than a month with "withdrawal" symptoms; they vanished the day after she resumed taking the drug. It took her more than two years of repeated attempts before she finally quit Paxil for good. "It *is* habit-forming," she says. "And I was a drug addict."

An online underground

For quite a while, Adrienne Bransky didn't believe her physical breakdown at the conference had anything to do with her antidepressant. When the episode ended, she was happy not to think about it. She got pregnant in 1999, several weeks after her worst symptoms abated, and her mood remained fairly stable during her first and second trimesters. In the middle of the third trimester, however, she became depressed and even entertained what her husband describes as suicidal thoughts—"although I don't think she would have done anything to herself," he says. Finally, her condition seemed too dangerous to leave untreated. Her doctors decided she had to go back

on Paxil. Once again, her depression quickly lifted. If anything, she experienced postpartum elation after giving birth to her son.

Life went on. Soon Bransky was back at work, the baby was doing fine and Paxil was, once again, her wonder drug. Then about a year later, she began having "breakthrough symptoms," signs of depression indicating that her current dosage of medication was no longer adequate to control her illness. Bransky had switched psychiatrists when she and Aaron moved to Milwaukee for his residency; her new doctor suggested an increase in her dosage of Paxil. That seemed logical, but Bransky wanted to do some research on the Internet first. There she discovered the growing controversy over "Paxil withdrawal."

She quickly tapped into a cluster of Web sites that constitute the "Paxil withdrawal" underground—a community of advocates and patients trying to inform the public about the syndrome and help one another break free of the drug. That's when Bransky told her doctor she "just wanted off Paxil," no matter how bad quitting might make her feel. After reading countless discontinuation accounts that sounded strikingly similar to her own, she simply couldn't bring herself to give one more penny of her money to GSK. So she endured a second wave of flulike symptoms and disorientation. This time, however, she was better prepared: At the suggestion of her new psychiatrist, Bransky added Prozac to her pharmacological cocktail during the weaning process. With the longest half-life of all the SSRIs, Prozac keeps

regulating serotonin long after Paxil has left the building. The combo technique is now recommended by sources like *Prescriber's Letter* and *Harvard Mental Health Letter.*

Eventually, Bransky got pregnant again, and in her second trimester the depression returned, full force. She and her doctor decided to try a lesser-known antidepressant called Celexa, marketed by Forest Laboratories, in the hopes that it would cause fewer side effects and discontinuation problems. So far, so good: Bransky says she has had "no issues" with the drug, and her depression is currently in check.

She remains a member of the California suit, however, and follows the case closely. While she was relived when GSK dropped the "non-habit-forming" lines and added a warning to its new ads, she continues to worry that patients will start taking the drug without any knowledge of the complications they could encounter while getting off it. "Most people don't want to rely on antidepressants all their lives," she says. "We all hold out the hope that we don't have to take these pills forever. That's why pharmaceutical companies need to be more forthright and responsible and need to put more money into educating doctors about the risks of withdrawal. Maybe then you'll have fewer patients going through the hell I went through."

Stephen Fried is the author of Bitter Pills: Inside the Hazardous World of Legal Drugs. *His latest book is* The New Rabbi: A Congregation Searches for Its Leader.

Stronger pot, **bigger** worries

BY DAVID WAHLBERG

ATLANTA—Problems with marijuana abuse and addiction have increased over the past decade, even though the percentage of people using pot has remained roughly the same, a new study says.

The reason: It's not your parents' marijuana.

A 25 percent increase in serious problems with marijuana from 1992 to 2002 is likely explained by a 66 percent increase in the potency of the drug, researchers from the National Institute of Drug Abuse report in today's Journal of the American Medical Association.

Marijuana today has nearly five times the level of THC, the drug's most active ingredient than was in the pot of the 1970s, government figures suggest. Marijuana has become so strong that the liberal government of the Netherlands is considering classifying it as a "hard" drug to be banned from the "coffee shops" of Amsterdam, where it has been sold openly for years.

Hydroponic growing techniques and the selective use of seeds from powerful strains contribute to the higher levels of THC, researchers say. Superstrong "BC Bud" from British Columbia can easily be obtained, especially in the northwest United States.

"People still have a naive approach to marijuana and think of it as a harmless substance," said Dr. William Compton,

lead author of the new study and an epidemiologist with the National Institute of Drug Abuse, one of the National Institutes of Health. "It's not as innocent as they might expect."

"People still have a naive approach to marijuana and think of it as a harmless substance. It's not as innocent as they might expect."

Dr. William Compton

lead author of the new study and an epidemiologist with the National Institute of Drug Abuse

About 4 percent of Americans age 18 and older say they smoked marijuana in the past year, the same as a decade ago, the study found. But use of the drug among African-Americans and Hispanics increased significantly, with use among blacks now surpassing that by whites.

Rates of abuse and addiction increased the most among racial and ethnic minorities, with serious marijuana problems now more common among blacks and Hispanics than in whites. Overall, more than a third of marijuana users report signs of abuse or addiction.

The study is based on two sets of information gathered in interviews by the U.S. Census Bureau. Marijuana users who acknowledged at least one of four

criteria for abuse, such as pot-related legal problems or interference with job performance, were considered abusers.

Those who noted at least three of six other criteria—including the need to use more pot to achieve the same effect and unsuccessful attempts to cut back—were categorized as dependent, or addicted.

"This study shows that there is a certain propensity to addiction for marijuana," Compton said. "That may surprise people, that marijuana can be addictive."

Another report, released last month by the National Center on Addiction and Substance Abuse at Columbia University, said that among people ages 12 to 17, marijuana use appears to have stabilized in recent years.

But emergency room visits implicating marijuana use among that age group jumped 48 percent from 1999 to 2002, the report said. The proportion of children and teenagers in treatment for marijuana use soared 142 percent from 1992 to 2001.

"We think potency is probably the explanation," said Joseph Califano, president of the drug research center at Columbia and former secretary of the U.S. Department of Health, Education and Welfare, now known as Health and Human Services.

Califano directed the U.S. government's campaign against smoking tobacco in the late 1970s, after he quit smoking it himself. He said he had no problem telling younger people not to do something he had once done, because a better understanding of the dangers had emerged.

The message is the same today for parents who smoked marijuana in their youth and who may be unsure how to talk to their children about pot, he said.

"There's nothing hypocritical about it," Califano said. "This stuff is much stronger today."

David Wahlberg writes for The Atlanta Journal-Constitution. E-mail: dwahlberg(at)ajc.com

Inside Dope

Canada's dirty, well-lit marijuana trade is rich, expanding ... and unstoppable

By Quentin Hardy

IN THE QUIET COUNTRYSIDE JUST OUTSIDE VAN-COUVER, B.C. an ambitious young entrepreneur surveys a blindingly bright room filled with lovely plants—dozens of stalks of high-power marijuana. Almost ready for harvest, they hold threadlike, resin-frosted pot flowers, rust-and-white "buds" thickening in a base of green-and-purple leaves. The room reeks of citrus and menthol, a drug-rich musk lingering on fingertips and clothes.

"There's no way I won't make a million dollars," says the entrepreneur, David (one-name sources throughout this story are pseudonymous). He runs several other sites like this one, reaping upwards of $80,000 in a ten-week cycle. Says he: "Even if they bust me for one, I'm covered."

So, it seems, is much of Canada—covered with thousands of small, high-tech marijuana "grows," as the indoor farms are known. Small-time marijuana growing is already a big business in Canada. It is likely to get bigger, despite all the efforts of the antidrug crowd in Washington, D.C. On Oct. 14 the U.S. Supreme Court, by refusing to disturb an appeals court ruling, gave its stamp of approval to doctors who want to recommend weed to ease their patients' pain or nausea. In the U.S. nine states have enacted laws permitting marijuana use by people with cancer, AIDS and other wasting diseases. The Canadians are even more cannabis-tolerant; although they have not legalized the drug, they are loath to stomp out the growers. This illicit industry has emerged as Canada's most valuable agricultural product—bigger than wheat, cattle or timber.

Canadian dope, boosted by custom nutrients, high-intensity metal halide lights and 20 years of breeding, is five times as potent as what America smoked in the 1970s. With prices reaching $2,700 a pound wholesale, the trade takes in somewhere between $4 billion (in U.S. dollars) nationwide and $7 billion just in the province of British Columbia, depending on which side of the law you believe.

In the U.S. the never-ending war on drugs endures, to modest discernible effect. In a largely symbolic act the

U.S. Justice Department has just imprisoned an icon of the pot-happy 1970s—Tommy Chong of the old Cheech & Chong comedy team—for selling bongs on the Internet. But in Canada the trade in pot, or cannabis (as many Canadians call it), is an almost welcome offset at a time when British Columbia's economy is in the doldrums.

Tourism here is down, and thousands of jobs got axed when the U.S. slapped tariffs on exports of softwood and then banned Canadian beef after an outbreak of mad cow disease. The marijuana business, by contrast, is thriving, not least because Canada shares a thinly guarded 5,000-mile border with the U.S., a big market. Ultimately much of the revenue flows into the coffers of hundreds of legitimate businesses selling supplies, electricity and everything else to the growers and smugglers.

And who are these growers? Not a small coterie of drug lords who could be decimated with a few well-targeted prosecutions, but an army of ordinary folks. "I know at least a hundred [of them], 20 years old to 70," says Robert Smith, who isn't part of the trade but indirectly profits from it at the furniture store he owns in Grand Forks, B.C., 110 miles north of Spokane, Wash. "Of the money coming through my door, 15% to 20% comes from cannabis—we'd be on welfare without it."

Mexico remains the biggest supplier of foreign pot for U.S. consumers, growing valleys of lower-grade grass and sending it north; some 500 tons of pot were seized at the Mexican border in 2001, more than 100 times the volume confiscated at the Canadian boundary. California is a prodigious supplier, as well. But Canada's industry is notable for its dispersion. The scattered and all but undetectable production may well herald a modus operandi for other regions.

Small growers like David bring in $900 a pound at the low end, with net margins of 55% to 90%, depending on quality, depreciation and labor costs. They produce half a pound to 30 pounds every ten weeks, selling their product to local users or peddling it to "accumulators," who then smuggle it over the border or sell it up the chain to larger brokers. Accumulators and brokers typically add $80 a pound to the cost, as do the high-volume smugglers who buy from them. Smugglers returning money to Canada for other dealers skim a 2% laundering fee.

"The first time somebody gives you a bag of money so heavy that you can't lift it, it's surreal. Pretty soon, it's just dirty paper," says Jeff, who recently retired from smuggling up to a ton of weed a week.

Jeff started out a few years ago by growing just 8 pounds of pot with his friends. Within a year they were brokering hundreds of pounds from other small growers to someone with connections to large U.S. distributors. When that person's buyer retired, Jeff paid him $250,000 for the buyer's client list. "Sounds astronomical," he says, "but at the time it looked free."

Once in the U.S. the bud usually stays on the West Coast. In Seattle a pound of top-quality pot sells for $4,000, and by the time it hits Los Angeles it runs up to $6,000. High-grade cannabis then sells at smaller weights, eventually burning up at $600 to $800 an ounce.

Back in British Columbia the business of pot encompasses wholesaling different strains of seeds for 95 cents to $1.90 apiece, the prices depending, among other things, on how well a strain's buds rank at annual (and very public) "breeders' cup" competitions in Amsterdam and Vancouver. Plants can also be propagated from cuttings, sold for $3 to $10 each, wholesale.

This is a job-creating industry. Trimming the dried flowers to maximize look and taste of the top product pays about $15 an hour for a skilled laborer; it takes ten hours for an experienced trimmer to turn out a pound of buds. Consultants get $40 an hour for helping junior growers.

Marijuana underwrites other businesses, too. Vancouver tour guides brag of quality "B.C. bud," and "smokeasies" near the Canadian border cater to Canadian and U.S. customers. Local authorities wink at the offense. The owners of these smokeshops resemble camp followers of a particularly tough Grateful Dead tour. Customers include clean-cut men in golf shirts, grannies and women cradling babies.

Advice magazines offer tips on growing; lighting shops are spread across the country to serve novice farmers; and fertilizer companies target their marketing to pot growers (see box). In the wake of a federal crackdown on makers of marijuana pipes in the U.S., those businesses are relocating north of the border.

In the Kootenay mountains of B.C., Gary Bergvall sold lights from a 15-by-15-foot space in 1996. Now he employs 28 people and runs a factory that ships, each week, lighting systems as well as two tractor-trailers full of air filters. Could the activated charcoal filters be useful for absorbing the telltale odor of certain plants? Maybe. The lights? Bergvall is circumspect. They are used "for a special purpose, whatever that may be," he says.

Marc Emery started a mail-order marijuana-seed business in Vancouver in 1994, moving 100,000 seeds a year at

Cannabits

THE ESTIMATED VALUE OF Canada's marijuana production—up to $7 billion—exceeds its farm receipts of both cattle ($5.63 billion) and wheat ($1.73 billion), or the $4.3 billion taken in by forestry and logging. Only oil and gas extraction, worth $15.8 billion, is worth more.

CANADA'S LEGAL farm operators have net margins of 5.5%. An economist in Vancouver's Simon Fraser University figures pot growers have a 72% annual rate of return, after discounting for costs, labor, thefts and arrests.

an average $3.75 each. Today the tax-paying entrepreneur sells 350,000 seeds a year, even though he has more than 20 Canadian competitors (plus rivals in Holland, Spain and the U.K.). Selling seeds in Canada is illegal, but just about no one is busted for it.

Web sites from Vancouver to Montreal sell pot to medical patients in Canada; one site requires only a doctor's letter testifying you have one of 192 afflictions (including writer's cramp and hiccups). Barbara St. Jean, a financial planner, got a pot prescription to treat pain associated with lupus. She and her husband, Brian Taylor, a former mayor of Grand Forks who later ran for national office on the Canadian Marijuana Party ticket, have taught college courses on how to grow cannabis indoors. St. Jean once gave a speech to some 40 city planners from across B.C., extolling the potential benefits of cannabis to their local economies.

All of this action owes much to the U.S. and an inflow of draft-dodging pot smokers during the Vietnam War. The marijuana growers among them introduced sinsemilla (Spanish for "without seeds"), the unpollinated female plant, which is far more potent than its male counterpart. In the 1980s refugees from a northern California war on pot also headed to B.C., just as 1,000-watt lights made possible year-round production of top-grade strains. Locals learned to grow for their climate.

The market is now mature enough for precise segmentation. Dealers grade buds like bonds, starting at BB, worth just $800 a pound because of its chemical taste and black ash when burnt. A-quality cannabis tends to be well-grown outdoor product, at $1,300 because of its somewhat loose buds. AAA, the type David grows and Jeff smuggled, is characterized by tight clusters of flowers, a pleasant smell of eucalyptus and enough drug-rich resin to coat the sides of a plastic bag. Even on a carefully grown plant only 50% of the buds are the right size and shape for AAA. The best stuff has odd varietal names—Mango and Blueberry for the fruity-smelling strains, and F---ing Incredible and Romulan (a nod to the warriors with dented heads on *Star Trek*), a testimony to the euphoric, incapacitating effects.

Except for a few hundred medical users, who are permitted to grow for personal use, and some firms like Prairie Plant Systems, a Saskatoon, Sask. firm with a $4.3 million contract to grow for the Canadian government, cultivators of weed in Canada are operating outside the law. You wouldn't know it, though, from a trip to Advanced Nutrients' fertilizer factory.

"We've got 86 different products, eight labs, 65 employees, and we'll gross $12 million (Canadian) this year, $20 million in 2004," says Michael Straumietis, who with partners Robert Higgins and Eugene Yordanov owns this firm. "I'd say 85% of this is related to the marijuana industry. We hope it's all for medical, but we can't control that." The Advanced factory, 50 miles outside of Vancouver, can product up to 1.5 million liters of nutrients a month. Products like Dr. Hornby's Big Bud and Sensipro [as in "sinsemilla"] are distributed to some 380 stores in the U.S. and Canada, plus another 260 in Australia.

By supplying medical patients with their products for free (and shipping Voodoo Juice to the University of Mississippi, where scientists grow marijuana for the U.S. government), they have generated testimonials and "studies" showing their products produce bigger, stronger pot plants than the competition.

"Look at this—2.13 pounds per light!" says Yordanov, brandishing a paper. "We beat them in THC [tetrahydrocannabinol], too. A pound per light used to be good—we'll do 3."

For the beginner, there is a $375 kit of seven nutrient boxes, one for each week of a quick grow. "Totally idiot-proof," says Straumietis, a 43-year-old American who fled to Canada from a since-dismissed marijuana charge. "We've revolutionized marketing a packaging."

The trio began business in 1996 with a hydroponic shop, later moving into lighting and electrical supplies. In 2001 they were charged by Canadian authorities with conspiracy to export and conspiracy to traffic in cannabis, stemming from a 200-pound smuggling bust in Washington State. Last March the Canadian government halted prosecution, for reasons unknown, but could start again.

The three deny the charges but also figure increasing liberalization of the law in Canada makes the nutrients more of a promising line, anyway. "There's more money in this than in growing," Straumietis says. "In five to seven years we could gross $100 million. If cannabis is legal[ized], we'll probably charge less, make it up on volume."   —Q.H.

Producing the seeds of such strains is up to guys like Daniel, a third-year apprentice breeder along western B.C.'s coast. He helps produce about 60 varieties, starting with a dark green bud called "Mighty Mite," a plant for urban window boxes that grows to the size and shape of a corn dog. At the other end are 14-foot-high monsters that reflect their origins in the Brazilian jungle.

Daniel's newest creation is a straight-stemmed plant that stands 8 feet high and has thick, well-spaced clumps of flowers. "This is a good prairie strain," says the Alberta native. "You could harvest it with a combine or a sunflower cutter. I'd like to produce seeds in 50-pound bags." Like many people in the Canadian cannabis trade, he expects marijuana cultivation will be fully legal before long.

For Daniel, thieves, not the police, are the big worry. And with good reason: The Royal Canadian Mounted Police, which opposes many of Canada's pro-pot steps, concedes that in B.C. only one-fifth of marijuana busts result in incarceration and the average sentence is only four months. "Maybe the police can take these plants," Daniel says, nodding to a packed greenhouse. "Maybe they'll even take me downtown, maybe arrest me. Maybe. But we have clones and copies of every one of our plants in three more locations."

With seeds or clones an indoor grower can spend just $1,600 to set up a 9-square-foot indoor plot capable of hosting 72 small plants that produce 3½ pounds of mixed-quality buds in seven weeks. A well-wired operation with 20 lights costs $20,000 to set up. Most growers stop at 10 lights lest they attract attention with a steep electricity bill.

A good rule of thumb in figuring yield is 1 to 1½ pounds of bud per light. By using cuttings and closely regulating how much light the plants get, indoor gardeners crush a normal five-month growing cycle into ten weeks. Like high-end winemakers, these producers obsess about methods, singing the virtues of organic gardening, hydroponics (soilless agriculture), even aeroponics (with nutrient misted on the plants). Some pot farmers pump carbon dioxide into the room. Growing AAA is labor intensive: The plants need daily watering, spraying and cutting back, producing a trash bag full of unwanted leaves each week for a small grow.

David, the western B.C. grower who dreams of making a million, has hired caretakers to oversee three additional rooms of 20 lights each; the employees include a retired mining executive and a middle-aged American fugitive, he says. They get 25% of the crop, and David splits the rest with his financier, a retired grower/smuggler. His landlords get an extra $1,500 a month on top of the rent, and he pays for repairs from any water or soil damage when production ceases. He lives in a neat house on a quiet cul-de-sac, rigged with radio-controlled motion detectors. Full of kids, dogs and golf clubs, it is prosperous and unremarkable, except for details like the beat-up cracker box brimming with the household pot stash and

Building the Perfect Bud

Want dope? Plant seeds. Want high-end dope? Pay attention.

LIGHTS: With 1,000-watt metal halide lights first blasting clones for 24 hours a day, followed by 12-hour intervals of dark to force budding, a half-year grow cycle is cut to ten weeks.

GENETICS: Breeding stock is critical to top-quality pot. Branches of the best female plants are cut and potted. The genetically identical offspring are also cloned.

AIR: Temperatures in the 70s. Added carbon dioxide boosts production, quality.

DIRT: Or hydroponics or aeroponics. Nitrogen for growth, phosphorous and potassium for resinous flowers. Beneficial fungi and bacteria to boost THC.

Source: Ed Rosenthal; Advanced Nutrients.

Cannabits

"CANVAS" IS DERIVED FROM the word "cannabis." Many of the great paintings are on marijuana fibers.

MARIJUANA HAS BEEN CULTIVATED FOR ITS fiber since at least 8000 B.C. and used as a drug since about 2000 B.C. In Europe it was cultivated for rope, paper and cloth for centuries, with no broad understanding of the plant's psychoactive properties until the 19th century, after Napoleon Bonaparte invaded Egypt.

HENRY VIII, AND many New World governors, mandated the growing of hemp (marijuana) for rope. Many farmers resisted because the crop paid poorly and smelled bad as it was curing.

THC IS CONCENTRATED in marijuana's trichomes, which are tiny stalked glands with a stem and a ball-like tip, clustered around the flowers of an unfertilized female plant.

ACCORDING TO A 1999 study by the Institute of Medicine, marijuana addicts 9% of its users. Alcohol addicts 15% of users, heroin, 23% of users, and tobacco, 32% of users.

ONE MARIJUANA cigarette deposits four to five times more tar in the lungs than a tobacco cigarette. Thus, smoking three or four joints is like smoking up to a pack of cigarettes.

MARIJUANA WAS EFFECTIVELY OUTLAWED in the U.S. with the passage of the 1937 Marijuana Tax Act. There are now an estimated 500,000 marijuana arrests in the U.S. each year.

THE MOST RIGOROUS SCIENTIFIC EVIDENCE of medical benefits from marijuana use centers on ameliorating the negative effects of cancer chemotherapy, appetite loss associated with AIDS, and to a lesser extent, pain management, multiple sclerosis and glaucoma. As a medicine it is considered limited by the side effect of intoxication.

POT SEEDS ARE nutritious and are often used in bird food.

Sources: Statistics Canada, Professor Stephen Easton; "The Science of Marijuana" by Leslie L. Iverson, Oxford University Press, 2000; "The Big Book of Buds" by Ed Rosenthal, Quick American Archives, 2001.

the note on the fridge that reads: "Gretchen called: Probation!" It seems almost like a game, until Anne, his wife, voices the underlying stress.

"When someone goes down, we all feel really bad, but you can't get too close to someone who's involved with the law," she says as she prepares the kids' breakfast. "You try to keep them away from it as much as possible." A helicopter cuts through the morning fog, and she tenses momentarily. "You do a lot of yoga; you try to pretend it isn't real."

Prepared product is packed in half-pound lots. Forty bags fit into a typical carry-on suitcase. Small-scale marijuana smugglers, or "rabbits," run dope to the U.S in car rides, marathon jogs, three-hour kayak trips or floating hollowed-out logs on the tide. The Mounties, with a patrol fleet of just four boats, are not a big worry on the water.

"You can get 80 pounds into a backpack, and you get big legs running over the mountain," says Paul de Felice, co-owner of the Holy Smoke smokeasy in the eastern B.C. town of Nelson. "I've seen them so nervous they vomit before they take off—but I never see them stop."

As in all business, it is important to manage risk. Jeff would first try a smuggling method with 50 pounds; if it worked, he would try 100, then 300. He moved pot in the fiberglass hulls of yachts and in the false floors of long horse trailers. "No border agent wants to unload all those horses, shovel out that manure," he says.

One method: Drag a shipment underwater behind a fishing boat. A zinc strip fastens a buoy and a length of line to the package. If the boat is stopped, the crew cuts loose the shipment, which sinks, buoy and all. The zinc dissolves in the seawater within 12 to 18 hours, and the buoy surfaces with its line tied to the pot, letting Jeff recover the dope. Another method involves bisecting a pro-

pane truck, inserting 500 pounds of bud below a false floor and setting the gas pressure in the truck to read as if it were full.

Eventually "you use a lot of planes," he says. "They're faster, they give you more control and you get better prices if you can deliver 40 miles over the border, past the hot zone." Pilots fly low, hugging mountains on the lee side of fire towers.

Jeff has retired in the face of exhaustion, a fear of snitches in the network and rumors that the U.S. government has planted an agent in the system, who over time is rising high enough to decapitate a big smuggling operation. When asked how many people in the big operations really leave, however, he says, "Maybe 5%. I've got pilots I made millionaires, and they still fly."

Jeff's fear of a mole may be well grounded, for the Mounties hope to strike a blow to Canada's cannabis business with a string of big, high-profile busts over the next several years. But the pot business, with a structure less like typical crime rings and closer to that of the Internet—lots of little nodes (in this case, producers) feeding a loosely organized hierarchy—will be difficult to shut down.

The Mounties are not happy about legal marijuana for medical patients—they say the drug needs more study before it is dispensed—but they worry more about the effect of the marijuana-rich gangs on the Canadian economy. It is not just the possible violence (U.S. guns have been traded for Canadian pot), but the business considerations. "There are many millions of dollars here, wrecking the legitimate business," says Rafik Souccar, director general of drugs and organized crime enforcement for the Mounties. The contraband dealers launder money through unprofitable concerns, which then charge artificially low prices for legit goods.

Police also worry about the hazards of poor electrical wiring, hazardous molds and excessive chemical use at grow houses—and a public too blasé about the dangers of drug use. "Part of the problem is a laissez-faire attitude on the part of the public," says Charlie Doucette, a Mountie in charge of drug enforcement in Vancouver. "We don't have an appetite in Canada to say 'This isn't right.'"

Some police think the battle may well be over. Rollie Woods, head of vice and narcotics enforcement for the Vancouver police department, noticed indoor growers throwing out unwanted leaves and dirt at a site the city uses for refuse collection. He told the staff there to note the license plate numbers of every such farmer but called off his plan a few months later. "There were hundreds [of cars]. No way we could track them all." At this point he supports legalization, if only so he can concentrate on Vancouver's growing crack problem.

"If it wasn't for pressure from the U.S., we'd just regulate this," says Woods, who has all of six agents pursuing the pot trade. Investing millions more in a crackdown may be of little consequence, he adds. "You could give me a hundred people, and it wouldn't make a difference."

Heroin Hits Small Town America

'We're up to our eyeballs in it'

Chris Thomas, 52, rattles off the specific dates, seared in her memory, of devastating events in the family's war with heroin. The car accidents, multiple DUI charges, the credit card spending binges, the relapses into drug use, the days they threw their sons out, and last New Year's Eve—when they were arrested for possession of heroin—are recounted, sometimes by the time of day. The question "Is he alive?" has worked its way into the daily vernacular.

Tim Jones

A costly struggle against heroin rages in the comfy, cedar-paneled home on West Hanley Road, and everyone inside is losing.

The adult sons of Steve and Chris Thomas have stolen more than $50,000 from their parents' business to support their heroin addictions. The Thomas home is in a lockdown state, with money and other valuables that could be traded for drugs kept away from the boys. A bolt lock protects the master bedroom.

The Thomases now finance their vending machine business on low-interest introductory credit card offers, switching to new cards every 6 months.

Last week a Richland County judge arraigned Mark, 22, and Matt, 18, on felony drug possession charges. The next day Mark Thomas was caught by his parents using heroin again and, as has happened before, was thrown out of the house. It's a war with no victory in sight.

"I don't know what we're going to do," Chris Thomas said.

This is but one snapshot of a rising tide of small-town heroin abuse in the Midwest, occurring in tidy little communities with town squares, bicycles on front lawns and American flags flapping in the breeze. Hospitals and drug counselors note an alarming spike in overdoses, and overmatched police agencies are scrambling to address a drug onslaught once deemed the exclusive purview of big cities and longtime addicts.

In the northern Ohio railroad town of Willard, population 6,800, police are investigating five fatal heroin overdoses since December, two of them on a recent weekend.

"All of a sudden it blossomed," is how Capt. Robert McLaughlin of the Huron County Sheriff's Department described the arrival of heroin. "We're up to our eyeballs in it."

Although marijuana, sheltered among the tall stalks of cornfields, and crack cocaine, brought in from Detroit, had long been the mainstays in the tightly defined universe of illegal drug users, police officials and treatment experts say the heroin market has expanded beyond the predictable clientele.

More troubling, the price of heroin is dropping, the availability is increasing and the purity of the drug is rising. "It is much stronger than what abusers are used to," said Mansfield Police Chief Phil Messer, who leads a 10-county drug task force called METRICH.

This region of Ohio, described ruefully by one undercover police officer as "conveniently located" amid the inverted urban triangle of Detroit, Cleveland and Columbus, is especially susceptible to drug trafficking because of easy access to several major highways. Formerly isolated and exclusively rural communities are now primarily bedroom communities. It was often considered the "Crossroads of America," but many of Ohio's small towns have lost their insularity and are now part of interstate drug traffic.

Deb Kline, a nurse in rural Crestline, said the number of intravenous heroin addicts treated at Freedom Hall Treatment Center, about an hour north of Columbus, has quadrupled. Worse, Kline said, the universe of drug abusers is expanding from hardened addicts in their 40s and 50s to people in their early 20s.

"Kids who come from upper-middle class families, kids who had pretty decent high school careers," she said. "I wish I knew why."

Few people wonder more than the Thomases, who built their home 15 years ago amid the tall pines in rural Lexington, population 4,200. As Steve Thomas put it, they came to raise their boys "away from the bull-crap of the city." He was building what would become a thriving vending machine business.

"We're first-generation success," the 54-year-old Thomas likes to say, pointing to the 61-inch Sony TV in the living room. The TV is a symbol of achievement, he said. Leading by the example of hard work was the best teacher for his boys, Thomas believes.

Early signs of trouble

There were early signs of drug trouble with Mark, who started smoking marijuana at 14. Steve Thomas said he would occasionally smoke marijuana in front of his boys. "I knew when to stop and I expected the boys to be just as responsible with drugs as I was," he said.

They weren't.

Then teenagers, Mark and Matt would help their parents empty the coin trays from pop, cigarette, candy, pinball and other machines. Every night the Thomases would bring bags of coins home. They said they wanted to be home for their boys.

The skimming began at least two years ago—a few hundred here and there that would soon end up in the eager hands of heroin dealers on the east side of Columbus, about an hour away. Both boys had cars and every other day would make the run to Columbus.

"Steve would come home and wonder where the money was going," Chris Thomas said. "We never dreamed our kids would take it."

Their sons had stolen at least $50,000, but Round 2, the in-house war, had only begun. More thefts followed—money, alcohol, prescription drugs, keys to vending machines. After throwing the kids out of the house, they changed the locks. Mark and Matt crawled through the attic and dropped in through a ceiling entry.

"We don't keep any money here, and what we do have we hide. We don't keep keys to anything here," Steve Thomas said. "It's like the enemy living right beside you, right under your nose."

Chris Thomas, 52, rattles off the specific dates, seared in her memory, of devastating events in the family's war with heroin. The car accidents, multiple DUI charges, the credit card spending binges, the relapses into drug use, the days they threw their sons out, and last New Year's Eve—when they were arrested for possession of heroin—are recounted, sometimes by the time of day. The question "Is he alive?" has worked its way into the daily vernacular.

'I feel very betrayed'

Steve Thomas said he could shoot the person who turned Mark onto drugs, but he won't.

"I feel very betrayed, especially by my oldest son. They should give loyalty to their parents. They deceived me," he said. "I don't understand why my son doesn't have this hunger for knowledge and growth and achievement."

And he doesn't understand how anyone could take heroin.

"And you never will because you're not an addict," Chris Thomas said.

Their anger is mixed with guilt and second thoughts about all the long hours spent building a business. Chris Thomas clings to hope, however frail, and pulls the lyrics of music that Mark recently wrote, expressing remorse for his addiction:

"I was so numb and had no feeling to feel,
I was so dumb because I never realized this was real.
I still didn't care when you gave all you could give,
I just got around and got high with no reason to live."

That hope withered last week when she found a bag of heroin in Mark's room. Once again, Mark is out of the house. He is living temporarily in a family-owned apartment in nearby Mansfield, paying $20 a day to his parents. "I told him that was the last kind gesture," Chris Thomas said. "That was hard for me."

For now, Matt stays at home with his parents. He passed a milestone Friday. He has been drug-free for 90 days. That gives his mom cause for hope.

But neither parent expressed much confidence about their sons' future. They've been through too much to be optimistic. "I really get the feeling that Mark's never gonna quit," Steve Thomas said. "With Matt it can go either way.

"We just want the boys to get on with their lives so we can get on with ours," he said.

The nightmare for the Thomases reflects, in part, the new availability of illegal drugs. The reasons for the surge in heroin use vary—a poor economy, proximity to big cities and increased competition among dealers.

Sgt. Rick Sexton of the Willard Police Department said the annual influx into the region of migrant workers from Mexico, a country that is a major source of illegal drugs, is also a factor. Some police officials point to the post-9/11 obsession with terrorism, saying it has diverted attention from the drug fight.

Availability increasing

"The feds are claiming there are more drugs being seized at the border. But we haven't seen the effects of that locally. We haven't seen a spike in prices that would occur if interdiction efforts were working," Messer said.

"The availability is increasing. We're seeing a lot of young people—high school kids—using heroin," Messer said.

That analysis is confirmed by addicts, who were accustomed to dealing with older adults and driving an hour to get their fix.

"When I first started, I had to go to Cleveland or Columbus to get it," said a heroin addict who now does undercover drug buys for METRICH in Mansfield. "It's much easier to get now. I don't have to run all over the place to find it. Now it's just down the street.

"People figure they can deal drugs because of terrorism and the war. They figure everybody's got their minds on that," the addict said.

An old industrial city of 50,000, Mansfield offers a grim reminder of possible consequences of drug trafficking—three state penitentiaries and the now-abandoned gothic prison used in the movie "The Shawshank Redemption." At SCCI Hospital, emergency room doctors have a ringside seat to the effects of the drug trade.

"We see a ton of prescription drug abuse, and I've seen more heroin in the last two years than I've seen in the previous 10," said Dr. Anthony Midkiff.

To be sure, heroin is not the only drug threat in the region. In some rural counties, crystal meth is a bigger problem. In Richland County, it's crack cocaine.

Paul Jones, an investigator with the Richland County Coroner's Office, said drug users are mixing prescription drugs. When combined with heroin, the powerful pain reliever Oxy-Contin or methamphetamine, an addictive stimulant, "it can be just enough to push them over the edge, and they don't realize it," Jones said.

What You Need to Know About Club Drugs: Rave On

Kerri Wachter

NEW ORLEANS—The club drugs methylenedioxymethamphetamine, ketamine, flunitrazepam, and [Gamma]-hydroxybutyrate top the hit list on the rave scene these days, Dr. Mark B. Stephens said at the annual meeting of the American Academy of Family Physicians.

"In supposedly drug-free zones, 40% of high school seniors say it's relatively easy to get drugs and about 5% of eighth graders say they have used Ecstasy once. About 15% of high school seniors say they have. It's definitely an issue," said Dr. Stephens of the Naval Hospital at Sigonella, Italy.

Once known for warehouse-size venues, today's raves are smaller, themed, underground parties featuring electronica music, laser light shows, and an abundance of drugs. Dr. Stephens outlined the most popular:

- **Methylenedioxymethamphetamine.** Better known as Ecstasy, Methylenedioxymethamphetamine (MDMA) was initially used as an appetite suppressant, then as a psychiatric drug, before becoming the star of the rave scene. "It's a stimulant and a hallucinogen, so it's kind of an intriguing chemical product because it crosses traditional boundaries in terms of effect," said Dr. Stephens.

MDMA acts on dopaminergic centers in the brain producing feeling-related changes, and it also produces more amphetamine-like stimulatory changes. Users are seeking a euphoric, hypermotor state.

Often rave-goers will wear a surgical mask with vapor rub dabbed on the inside because they believe it heightens the sensory experience.

Street names for MDMA include X, Adam, XTC, love drug, clarity, 007, and others.

Patients who present to the emergency department on MDMA appear wired, with psychomotor agitation and sometimes hallucinations, making it hard to pinpoint.

Look for hypertension, tachycardia, changes in mental status, and most importantly changes in core tempera-

ture. "Some of these folks have problems with malignant hyperthermic state," said Dr. Stephens.

A urine test can be used to confirm diagnosis. Care comes down to managing the patient's ABCs (airway, breathing, and circulation) and keeping the patient quiet.

MDMA is a schedule I drug. Its use accounts for 5,000-6,000 emergency department episodes yearly, according to the federal Drug Abuse Warning Network (DAWN), a federal effort which allows physicians to report different toxicities to a national database.

- **Ketamine.** Developed to replace phencyclidine (PCP) as a dissociative anesthetic, ketamine is used most commonly in veterinary medicine. Most ketamine used at raves is diverted from veterinary sources, said Dr. Stephens.

Ketamine is available as a clear liquid or a white powder.

Ketamine users are trying to get to "k-land" and avoid going to "k-hole." K-land refers to the dissociative experience that accompanies ketamine use. "'Folks will tell you that they can see a sound or hear a color in this bizarre synesthetic state," he said.

K-hole refers to the frightening, out-of-body experience associated with ketamine overdose.

Large doses can produce vomiting and convulsions and may lead to oxygen starvation to the brain and muscles.

Street names for ketamine include cat valium, special k, jet, and others.

The effects of a ketamine 'high' are short-lived, usually lasting an hour, but sometimes 4-6 hours. Ketamine users who present to the emergency department exhibit increased blood pressure and heart rate. Ketamine overdose is associated with severe dissociation, vomiting, restlessness, and tiredness. Ketamine is not detectable on a routine urine screen.

Emergency treatment of patients with ketamine toxicity is primarily supportive, said Dr. Stephens. Maintain the ABCs and fluid status.

Ketamine is a schedule III drug.

- **Flunitrazepam.** Flunitrazepam (Rohypnol) is 10 times more potent than Valium.

Today it is manufactured as 1-mg tablets that are legally available in Europe, Mexico, and Colombia for the treatment of severe sleep disorders. It is not manufactured or approved in the United States. Historically it has come over the borders from Mexico.

Until 1999 it was colorless but a colorimetric compound is now added that turns the drug blue when added to a liquid-making it obvious that a drink has been tampered with. Flunitrazepam has earned a reputation as a date-rape drug. Use has fallen in part due to the color change and in part due to the Drug-Induced Rape Prevention and Punishment Act of 1996, which made it punishable to commit a violent crime using a controlled substance such as flunitrazepam.

This benzodiazepine begins to work in a short period of time, producing muscle relaxation, sleepiness, mental and physical paralysis, and anterograde amnesia that is especially pronounced when combined with alcohol. In short, it's perfect for sexual predators.

Street names for flunitrazepam include roofies, roapies, la roacha, roach-2, Mexican valium, and others.

Flunitrazepam can be identified in a urine sample up to 72 hours after ingestion.

"If there is concern about assault, you need to send off for the 7-amino metabolite of flunitrazepam for forensic evidence to hold up," said Dr. Stephens. Care for patients is primarily supportive.

Flunitrazepam is currently classified as schedule IV, but the U.S. Drug Enforcement Administration is considering reclassifying it as schedule I.

- **[Gamma]-Hydroxybutyrate.** The rise in popularity of [Gamma]-hydroxybutyrate (GHB) is another reason why flunitrazepam use has fallen.

GHB first garnered use among body builders, who used the drug's euphoric effects to help with marathon weight-lifting sessions. GHB was originally marketed as a compound that increased growth hormone release.

It can be a clear, odorless liquid or a white powder that is easily slipped into drinks. It has since found a niche in the club scene as a predatory drug. The Food and Drug Administration approved GHB (Xyrem) for the treatment of narcolepsy last year.

GHB is a quick-acting sedative that can produce coma at higher doses. It's often mixed with alcohol, which increases the sedative effect.

Street names for GHB include liquid X, Georgia home boy, verve, grievous bodily harm, and others.

It is difficult to detect in someone's system. A standard urine drug screen does not test for GHB. The best chance of identifying it is to request a specific gas chromatograph analysis.

"This is where communication with your lab is important," said Dr. Stephens. GHB has a quick clearance time—6 hours—making it difficult to determine if it was used for date rape after that window has passed.

A patient who is toxic with GHB presents to the emergency department completely obtunded. The typical approach is to maintain ABCs, run a routine urinalysis, and check some major serochemistries.

"You come up totally empty and eventually they sleep it off. In retrospect, you'll ask them what was that and you hear blue thunder or jolt—street names for GBH," said Dr. Stephens.

The Hillory J. Farias and Samantha Reid Date-Rape Drug Prohibition Act of 2000 reclassified GBH as a schedule I substance. While GHB falls under the controlled substances act, it is still easy to obtain, he commented.

Two cousins—[Gamma]-butyrolactone and 1,4-butanediol—are easily obtained on the Internet and converted to GHB with a little bathtub chemistry. Recipes abound on the Internet.

For more information, go to `http://dawninfo.sam-hsa.gov` or visit the club drug Web page of the National Institute on Drug Abuse at `www.clubdrugs.gov`.

From *Family Practice News*, Vol. 33, No. 2, November 15, 2003, pp. 18. Copyright © 2003 by Family Practice News/International Medical News Group (IMNG), an Elsevier company. Reprinted by permission from Elsevier.

UNIT 4
Other Trends in Drug Use

Unit Selections

26. **Blowing the Whistle on Drugs**, Mark Starr
27. **Baseball Takes a Hit**, Richard Corliss
28. **Designer Steroids: Ugly, Dangerous Things**, Ken Mannie
29. **Ever Farther, Ever Faster, Ever Higher?**, The Economist
30. **Life or Meth?**, Outword Magazine
31. **Teens Tell Truth About Drugs**, Michael Shaw
32. **Prescription Drug Abuse: FDA and SAMHSA Join Forces**, Michelle Meadows
33. **Adolescent OxyContin Abuse**, Debra A. Katz, M.D. and Lon R. Hays, M.D.
34. **Warning Label: Teens Find a Dangerous, Cheap High in Over-the-Counter Cough Medicine**, Will Evans

Key Points to Consider

- How have the drug use increases of the 1990s suggested valid new worries about drug use by the young?

- What factors cause drug-related trends and patterns to change?

- How are drug-related patterns and trends related to specific subpopulations of Americans?

- How significant is socioeconomic class in influencing drug trends? Defend your answer.

 **Links: www.dushkin.com/online/**
These sites are annotated in the World Wide Web pages.

Marijuana as a Medicine
http://mojo.calyx.net/~olsen/

Rarely do drug-related patterns and trends lend themselves to precise definition. Identifying, measuring, and predicting the consequences of these trends is an inexact science, to say the least. It is, nevertheless, a very important process.

Some of the most valuable data produced by drug-related trend analysis is the identification of subpopulations whose vulnerability to certain drug phenomena is greater than that of the wider population. These identifications may forewarn of the implications for the general population. Trend analysis may produce specific information that may otherwise be lost or obscured by general statistical indications. For example, tobacco is probably the most prominent of gateway drugs, with repeated findings pointing to the correlation between the initial use of tobacco and the use of other drugs.

The analysis of specific trends related to drug use is very important, as it provides a threshold from which educators, health care professionals, parents, and policy makers may respond to significant drug-related health threats and issues. Currently, more than 19 million Americans report the use of illegal drugs, Marijuana remaining the most commonly reported. Alarmingly, the number of admissions to substance abuse treatment for adolescents ages 12 to 17 increased again this past year, continuing a ten-year trend. This increase was largely due to the increase in the number of adolescents who reported marijuana as their primary drug of abuse. Over the past ten-year period of study the number of adolescent treatment admissions for primary marijuana abuse increased 350 percent. Alcohol was involved as a secondary drug in 48 percent of these admissions.

Historically, popular depressant and stimulant drugs, such as alcohol, tobacco, heroin, and cocaine, produce statistics that identify the most visible and sometimes the most constant use patterns. Other drugs such as marijuana, LSD, Ecstasy and other 'club drugs' often produce patterns widely interpreted to be associated with cultural phenomena such as youth attitudes, popular music trends, and political climate. Still other drugs, such as methamphetamine, suggest use patterns of cocaine-like proportions.

One of two emerging drug trends that are expressing consistent and alarming concerns the use of club drugs such as MDMA (ecstasy), GHB (grievous bodily harm), Rohypnol (roofies, r-2, forget me drug), Ketamine (jet, special k, honey oil), PMA (death, mitsubishi double-stack), Nexus (venus, bromo, toonies), and PCP (angel dust, rocket fuel). Often, these drugs are perceived as less dangerous and less addictive as some mainstream drugs such as heroin and cocaine. Unfortunately, however, the quality of these drugs varies significantly and often substitute drugs are sold in their place. Since distribution networks associated with club drugs are unpredictable, users are subject to a constant menu of "look-alikes" or analogs. Rohypnol exists as one good example, as supplies are limited as a result of a significant government effort to curtail its availability. The government's Drug Abuse Warning Network (DAWN) that tracks drug-related emergency room visits is reporting drastic increases in emergency room treatment for overdoses of Ecstasy and GHB.

Two other continuing trends are those that involve the abuse of prescription drugs and those that involve the use of designer

steroid-type drugs used to enhance athletic performance. Americans are abusing prescription drugs more than ever before with the most frequently mentioned offenders being oxycodone and hydrocodone. Forty percent of the 119,000 mentions of narcotic pain medications in emergency rooms involve these two drugs. Substance Abuse and Mental Health Services Administration Administrator Charles Curie states that, "the abuse of narcotic pain relievers is a serious and growing public health problem."

The trends concerning the pervasive use of performance enhancing drugs in sports is an additional controversy addressed significantly in Unit 4. From baseball, to track and field, to cycling, to the Olympics in Athens, conversations concerning drugs and well-known sports figures were ever-present. Many commentators suggested that the scrutiny given to doping by Olympic athletes was visible in the decrease in medals won by some athletes from former Eastern Bloc countries with long histories of suspected doping of its Olympic athletes.

Information concerning drug use patterns and trends obtained from a number of different investigative methods is available from a variety of sources. On the national level, the more prominent sources are the Substance Abuse and Mental Health Services Administration, the National Institute on Drug Abuse, the Drug Abuse Warning Network, the National Centers for Disease Control, the Justice Department, the Office of National Drug Control Policy, and the surgeon general. On the state level, various justice departments, including attorney generals' offices, the courts, state departments of social services, state universities and colleges, and public health offices maintain data and conduct research. On local levels, criminal justice agencies, social service departments, public hospitals, and health departments provide information. On a private level, various research institutes and universities, professional organizations such as the American Medical Association and the American Cancer Society, hospitals, and treatment centers, as well as private corporations, are tracking drug-related trends. Surveys abound with no apparent lack of available data. As a result, the need for examination of research methods and findings for reliability and accuracy is self-evident. The articles in this unit provide information about some drug-related trends occurring within certain subpopulations of Americans. While reading the articles, it is interesting to contemplate whether the trends and patterns described are confined to specific geographical areas.

Blowing the Whistle on Drugs

A raid on a California laboratory threatens to blemish America's atheletes—again

BY MARK STARR

It is America's dirty little secret (actually not so very secret): there is an epidemic of performance-enhancing drugs at the heart of our sports culture. Fans know it intuitively, from the bulked-up athletes whose heft dwarfs those of prior generations to the obliteration of longstanding records. Insiders make a compelling case that illegal substances—steroids, human growth hormone and others—have propelled many of the historic achievements of this era, from our most popular pro sports to virtually every Olympic venue.

Now a burgeoning scandal involving a small "high-tech nutrition" company that boasts a large roster of big-name athletes as clients may provide a window into the problem. Last month in California, multiple federal agencies raided the facilities of Bay Area Laboratory Co-Operative (BALCO) and went on to confiscate containers of steroids, human growth hormone and synthetic testosterone from an off-site storage facility. As a result, a grand jury in San Francisco has subpoenaed some 40 athletes—reportedly including baseball superstars Barry Bonds and Jason Giambi, several NFL players and Olympic queen Marion Jones—to testify about what BALCO has to offer. "This has the potential to explode into the biggest doping scandal ever to hit our shores," says Charles Yesalis, coeditor of "Performance-Enhancing Substances in Sport and Exercise."

None of the athletes appears to be a target of the current investigation, and the handful who have acknowledged receiving a subpoena have denied any wrongdoing. But all are reportedly BALCO customers. Bonds has sung the praises of its program to a fitness magazine, an endorsement the company featured on its Web site. The home of Bonds's personal trainer was raided at the same time as the police action against BALCO.

The federal investigation was launched after a track coach sent a used syringe containing what he said was a new "designer steroid" to the United States Anti-Doping Agency (USADA), an independent body formed three years ago to police this country's Olympic sports. The anonymous whistle-blower indicated that the compound—tetrahydrogestrinone (THG)—was similar to other banned steroids, but altered to make it undetectable with existing tests. And he pinpointed BALCO as its source. An attorney for BALCO's owner, Victor Conte, denied that the company provided steroids to athletes. In an e-mail to the San Francisco Chronicle, Conte, a former bass player with the '70s rock group Tower of Power, blamed the investigation on "jealous competitive coaches and athletes."

The USADA sent the syringe to the International Olympic Committee's accredited testing laboratory at UCLA. Lab chief Dr. Don Caitlin confirmed that the compound was THG and developed a test that could detect the steroid in urine samples. The lab then retested 350 stored samples from this summer's U.S. Track & Field Championships, resulting in a handful of positives for THG. No

---

> ### Chemistry for Jocks
>
> Here are some of the more effective —but banned—ways to boost performance.
>
> - **Anabolic steroids:** Synthetic versions of testosterone that increase strength and muscle mass.
> - **THG:** An anabolic steroid chemically altered to elude drug tests.
> - **Human growth hormone:** A muscle-building aid, hGH is tough to test for because it also occurs naturally in the body.
> - **Blood doping:** A way to increase stamina by injecting oxygen-carrying red blood cells.
> - **Modafinil:** An alertness-enhancing stimulant that may increase competitiveness.

The Magic of Mushrooms

Holy shiitake! That—is short, unscientific terms—is the reaction of researchers hunting for potential new medicines in mushrooms. Tests in lab dishes indicate that fabulous fungi with names like lion's mane and turkey tail harbor novel antiviral and antibacterial compounds. Even the NIH is interested, funding the screening of mushrooms for agents to fight SARS and West Nile virus. "It's completely irrational that we haven't looked here before," says Dr. Andrew Weil, the nation's leading proponent of integrative medicine. "The greatest success of the pharmaceutical industry in the 20th century—antibiotics—came from molds, which are closely related." No new drugs have emerged yet from the research. But use of supplements is, excuse us, mushrooming, with sales of general immune-boosters like maitake, shiitake, reishi and cordyceps up as much as 300 percent since last year. Better yet, says Weil, try a blend like Host Defense from New Chapter. With flue season at hand, it couldn't hurt.

—ANNE UNDERWOOD

offenders will be named publicly until a test of a second sample duplicates the result. But USADA chief Terry Madden was not withholding judgment: "What we have uncovered appears to be intentional doping of the worst sort. This is a conspiracy involving chemists, coaches and certain athletes."

Track and field and other Olympic sports are bracing for an onslaught of bad news and a public backlash. (The NFL has said it will consider retesting, but Major League Baseball's anti-steroids plan doesn't even include testing.) The UCLA lab has shared its new test protocol with all IOC-accredited labs around the world, and a retesting of recent samples has begun. Last week one prominent British sprinter, Dwain Chambers, said he has been informed that he tested positive for THG. While Chambers denies he took a steroid intentionally, he says he did acquire a nutritional supplement from BALCO. Meanwhile, sprinter Kelli White, who won the 100 and 200 meters at the World Championships in August, could be stripped of her medals after testing positive for the stimulant modafinil. White, a BALCO client, claimed she took the medication because of a family history of narcolepsy. The UCLA lab also retested its samples for modafinil and, according to a knowledgeable source, found "a lot of narcolepsy going around track and field."

Last week USA Track's top executive, Craig Masback, urged more whistle-blowers to come forward, as well as "former cheats ... to tell us how they did it." Yesalis believes the cheaters will simply move on to a new drug. He notes that practically every major drug scandal over the past decade has resulted not from testing, but rather from police action. "If we really wanted to go after it, we'd have undercover sting operations aimed at our elite athletes," he says. "And that ain't going to happen." Still, the anti-doping community was cheered by what it regards as the biggest breakthrough since Canada's Ben Johnson was stripped of his 100-meter gold medal at the 1988 Olympics in Seoul. "The noose is tightening," says Dick Pound, the Canadian attorney who heads the World Anti-Doping Agency. "We're getting to the point where you can run, but you can't hide." Stephen Ungerleider, author of "Faust's Gold: Inside the East German Doping Machine," hopes that by warning athletes about these newer, more sophisticated tests, this scandal will produce "a sea change"—or, at the very least, a start at cleaning up athletics. True sports fans can only hope it's not a false start.

Baseball Takes a Hit

A steroid probe involving top players threatens to blight the game, anger fans and alter record books

By Richard Corliss

When Roger Maris broke Babe Ruth's home-run record in 1961, commissioner Ford Frick ruled that because Maris' season was eight games longer than Ruth's had been, the new record deserved an asterisk. Today fans wonder whether the slugging records of recent years will require similar caveats because of charges that top players have used anabolic steroids to help them turn fly balls into moon shots.

A steroid asterisk? Call it an asteroid.

And it could soon strike Earth, ruining what should be baseball's blithest month. Spring training is a time for hope, not dread; every team is tied for first, and each nonroster player can dream of starring in the majors. But in February, three weeks after President Bush made the war on steroids a priority in his State of the Union address, Attorney General John Ashcroft announced the indictments of four men—two executives of the Bay Area Laboratory Co-Operative (BALCO), track coach Remy Korchemny and Greg Anderson, a personal weight trainer whose clients include San Francisco Giants home-run king Barry Bonds—charging that they distributed steroids to top athletes.

Last week the San Francisco *Chronicle* cited unnamed sources who alleged that Bonds and New York Yankees stars Jason Giambi and Gary Sheffield, among others, had received illegal performance-enhancing drugs from BALCO. The four indictees proclaim their innocence, and all three players deny having taken steroids.

Reporters, smelling doped blood, bombarded players and managers with questions and accusations. "There's no need to address anything other than baseball," Bonds said at the Giants' Scottsdale, Ariz., training camp. Commissioner Bud Selig slapped a gag order on all major-league personnel. And Gene Orza, chief operating officer of the players' union, said it would continue to fight any expansion of testing procedures because steroids "are not worse than cigarettes." To which some major leaguers must have thought, show me a cigarette that can help me hit 73 homers a season, and I'll buy a carton.

Powerful forces are marshaled on both sides of the debate (and in the middle). The union is fighting to limit the number of players whose steroid tests the government can subpoena. The owners—grateful for the home-run explosion that helped put fans back in the seats after the bitter 1994 strike but worried that fans will cry foul over steroid use—have assumed their familiar duck-and-cover stance. And Bush, a former co-owner of the Texas Rangers, is reportedly trying to organize a steroids summit. Tony Serra, Anderson's lawyer, argues Bonds is a "trophy martyr." Says Serra: "It's part of the Bush-Ashcroft platform. Knock off the celebrities, get total obedience to a federal mandate at the cost of the reputation of people." A pall has been draped over the Grapefruit League, as if Florida were Mordor.

So far, the primary evidence that stars are taking steroids is ocular. "I look around the league, and I see guys a lot bigger," notes Andy Van Slyke, who in the 1980s roamed the Pittsburgh outfield with Bonds and who last week said he believed Bonds took steroids. "When I played, I worked out with weights, I ate right, and I could never gain 25 lbs. in the off-season. I just couldn't do it." Of course, with steroidophobia in the air, bulking up is suddenly not so chic. Giambi, who claims he lost only 4 lbs. over the winter, looks as if he's shrunk a few shirt, shorts and shoe sizes. "Spring training used to be an annual game of who got bigger," says Josh Suchon, an Oakland *Tribune* sportswriter who wrote a book on Bonds. "This year it's the game of who got smaller."

But it's in the nature of competition for baseball athletes to scrounge for an advantage. "Historically, they'll scuff a ball, cork a bat, steal signs," says NBC sportscaster Bob Costas. "If everyone is looking for any edge, it's foolish to think that some won't go the chemical route."

Chemistry and history intersect in this steroid story. "Most of the drugs of abuse came to the marketplace as great advances in medicine," says Dr. Gary Wadler, a New York University professor of medicine and member of the World Anti-Doping Agency. Jocks may even have been among the first users of the hormone EPO, which some athletes have been taking to improve endurance.

The newest performance enhancer to emerge is the designer drug THG, a previously undetectable steroid for which five track athletes and four Oakland Raiders football players tested positive last year. "It's clear that THG was made for no medical purpose," says Charles Yesalis, professor of health policy at Penn State. "It was clearly made to circumvent the testing process. And to create something like this, you don't have to possess the Nobel Prize in chemistry."

And history? Baseball is all history: comparing today's players with yesteryear's is among the great pleasures of the sport. That makes

baseball fans more fervent lovers of tradition than Tevye. They can cite, as Scripture, the career home-run totals of Ruth (714) and Hank Aaron (755). And they're not always eager to see records broken. So old-time fans are skeptical of modern-era players, who have had as many 50-homer seasons in the past decade as occurred in the previous century. Bonds, 39, set the all-time season home-run record in 2001 and, at 658 homers, is aiming to wrest the all-time career title.

Fans should consider this possibility: some players are great. In 1927, when Ruth became the first player to wallop 60 home runs, only one other major leaguer, Ruth's Yankee teammate Lou Gehrig, hit more than 30. Indeed, the Babe connected more times that year than 11 of the 15 other *teams*. (And what illegal substance was he on? Prohibition-era booze.) Bonds could be playing at that level. When he walks to the plate, he's not really facing the pitcher on the mound; he's facing down the legends of the game. That quest is motivation enough for him to pamper and punish his body legally. Or perhaps illegally.

Costas believes it's time for players to clean their own locker rooms. He imagines this revisionist pep talk: "We've got to have some comprehensive drug testing for three reasons. 1) It's an unlevel playing field; 2) you're forcing some of us to make the decision to either fall behind competitively or place our own health at risk; and 3) many of us have achieved great things legitimately—why should these cheating bums cast doubts on our achievements?"

There's a fourth reason: steroids can kill. Athletes in any sport might consider football's Lyle Alzado, an all-pro defensive lineman who took anabolic steroids throughout his career and later believed they were linked to the brain cancer that killed him. "Now I'm sick, and I'm scared," he said just before his death, at 43, in 1992. "Look at me. My hair's gone, I wobble when I walk and have to hold on to someone for support, and I have trouble remembering things. My last wish? That no one else ever dies this way."

Don't ask a ballplayer whether steroids are good for sports. Ask Lyle Alzado's widow.

DESIGNER STEROIDS:
UGLY, DANGEROUS THinGs

By Ken Mannie
STRENGTH/CONDITIONING COACH, MICHIGAN STATE UNIVERSITY

The word is out. The media are pointing fingers. Subpoenas have been issued, and many athletes are running for cover.

"Designer" steroids are in the news and circulating in the bloodstreams of some very successful, unethical, and unintelligent athletes—and the situation appears to be getting uglier by the minute.

Exactly what is a designer steroid? Simply put, it is an anabolic drug that has been structurally manipulated to mimic the muscle-building effects of testosterone, while sidestepping a positive test result. The drug "designers" are very well-versed on the mechanisms of the current testing technology and have the bioengineering expertise necessary to fool the system.

Those of us who hold sacred the integrity of athletics at all levels must understand that we are not dealing with some college kids delving in bathtub chemistry.

Individuals with serious scientific acumen are on a mission to produce the perfect performance-enhancing drugs—ones that build muscle and are invisible.

WELCOME TO THE AGE OF STEALTH STEROIDS

ESPN recently reported that more than 40 track athletes were subpoenaed to testify before a federal grand jury that is investigating a prominent sports "nutritionist' on what is being called "an international doping conspiracy." Several track and field performers have tested positive for Tetrahydrogestrinone, or THG, which is the most talked about designer steroid.

Even more frightening is that many experts contend that THG may be only one of a bevy of other chemicals that unscrupulous biochemists have feverishly produced to fly under the testing radar.

Now that THG is detectable, the questions remain: How long have athletes been using this stuff and what else is out there that we still can't detect? Could there be a multitude of these undetectable compounds in the illegal, performance-enhancing drug pipeline?

Terry Madden, Director of the U.S. Anti-Doping Agency, indicated that what appears to have been uncovered is "intentional doping of the worst kind." People who are one step ahead of the system have taken the cat-and-mouse game of circumventing the testing technology to another level.

And while track and field is being indicted as a major offender of THG abuse, other sports—including the NFL, NHL, and Major League Baseball—are being scrutinized for having potential participants in this dangerous game of hormonal roulette.

The International Olympic Committee (IOC) and the NFL are considering retroactive testing of urine samples to examine the extent of THG abuse. This could result in medals being stripped and suspensions being imposed.

For some inexplicable reason, MLB and the NHL are still dragging their prehistoric knuckles on implementing year-round, random, unannounced steroid testing. This "hear no evil, see no evil, speak no evil" mentality continues to erode the credibility of these sports and victimizes the clean players through guilt by association.

The ugly possibilities presented by these recent revelations make corked bats and spitballs seem relatively insignificant.

THE SCOPE OF THE PROBLEM

The scourge of illicit anabolic steroid abuse in athletics is nothing new. They were formulated back in the 1930's for treating a host of muscle wasting diseases and sexual dysfunctions. However, the reported dosages used for performance-enhancement and/or increased muscular size are 10-100 times the medical indications.

Unprincipled doctors, coaches, and athletes have channeled them into sports. Their motive is simple: Bigger, stronger muscles can equate to more strength and speed, and steroids offer a potential shortcut to that end.

That assumption can be debated to a degree, but most experts seem to agree that steroids—when combined with aggressive training protocols—can achieve those intended goals at a faster rate and to a higher level in most cases.

The majority of people who abuse steroids are not athletes. They are everyday Joes and Janes who have either self-esteem issues about their bodies or are simply looking for a cosmetic quick fix.

Whatever we're doing in our schools from an educational standpoint doesn't appear to be having an impact…
More kids are using steroids, and, for some unknown reason, they erroneously believe that the health risks have mysteriously diminished.

Evidence from a survey conducted by The National Institute on Drug Abuse (NIDA) revealed there was a significant increase in steroid use in 8th-12th graders from 1991-1999. Among seniors, there is also a noted decrease in the perceived harmful effects of the drugs.

Whatever we're doing in our schools from an educational standpoint doesn't appear to be having an impact.

The bottom line: More kids are using steroids, and, for some unknown reason, they erroneously believe that the health risks have mysteriously diminished.

Kids are taking steroids in a variety of ways: orally, through intramuscular injection, and even in gels or creams that are rubbed on the skin. Contrary to the reports in underground publications, there is no scientifically substantiated "safe" way to put this poison into your body.

Some abusers believe that you can avoid the negative side-effects by "cycling" or "pyramiding" the doses from low to high for 6-12 weeks, then backing-off for a few weeks before resuming the process. The efficacy of these techniques is strictly anecdotal, with no sound science to support any one method for all individuals.

Your odds of choosing a safe steroid cycle are about as good as winning the lottery.

OVER-THE-COUNTER DEATH PILLS

The Anabolic Steroid Control Act of 1990 banned the illicit distribution of all then known steroids. However, Congress could not forsee the new wave of over-the-counter (OTC) anabolic drugs known as "pro-steroids" and "precursor steroids."

Two such compounds in the pro-steroid classification are 1-testosterone and 4-hydroxy-testosterone, which escaped mention in the legislation because they were virtually unknown. The drug manufacturers claim that these are "natural" substances and market them as dietary supplements that increase strength and build muscle.

These anabolic compounds have surfaced on nutrition store shelves in alarming numbers. It must be understood

---

PARTIAL LIST OF POSSIBLE HAZARDOUS
SIDE-EFFECTS OF ANABOLIC STEROID ABUSE

- Negative effect on blood lipid profile (increase in LDL, the "bad cholesterol," and decrease in HDL, the "good" cholesterol) which is a leading contributor to heart disease
- Liver tumors and/or dysfunction
- Testicular atrophy
- Infertility
- Premature closure of growth plates in bones, resulting in diminished stature.
- Increase in connective tissue (e.g., tendon) injuries
- Enlargement of the heart's left ventricle, which can lead to serious malfunctions of the heart muscle.
- Strokes
- Disruption of endogenous (normal) hormonal production and functions, which can lead to a host of serious sexual and growth dysfunctions in both males and females.

---

that these compounds have all the markings of full-blown anabolic steroids. How did these chemicals slip through the legal barriers and proliferate as OTC dietary supplements?

Here are the loopholes: The steroid precursors convert to illegal drugs only after they have been ingested.

The pro-steroids—which are much more potent than the precursors because they don't require conversion in the body—are either difficult to detect, or are undetectable by current testing procedures.

The deleterious effects of using these so-called supplements, however, is considered by many experts to just as serious as any other class of anabolic steroids.

Athletes, coaches, and administrators must be cognizant of these OTC products and thoroughly examine the labels on any purchased supplements for potentially dangerous steroidal compounds. Someone who is qualified to identify these chemicals on the list of ingredients should be called on before any supplement distribution takes place.

FINAL REP

The sports community must realize that fortune and fame—rather than ethics and fair play—are the motivational fuel for many athletes. And there will always be plenty of chemists, whose sole motivation is money, willing to satisfy those needs through any means necessary, as their motivation is strictly monetary.

Those of us who have the power and resources to curb this problem must attack it aggressively on several fronts:

1. Stay ahead of the testing tit-for-tat game so that our technology is up to snuff with the clandestine labs that are hard at work hoodwinking the system.
2. Incorporate the very best testing procedures at the collegiate, professional, and international levels on a year-round, random and unannounced basis.
3. Institute strict penalties for athletes who test positive for anabolic drugs.
4. Encourage the Food and Drug Administration (FDA) to take more of a pro-active role in regulating the OTC supplement industry, especially with the advent of pro-steroids and precursor steroids.
5. Intensify and update the educational programs at the junior and senior high school levels on a yearly basis.

The exposure of the designer steroid conspiracy should be a wake-up to all coaches, administrators, parents, the governing bodies of high school associations, the NCAA, professional sports, and state and federal lawmakers. There are athletes out there searching for external growth at the risk of internal death, and they are getting plenty of help from people who really don't care about them.

To all athletes, both young and old, I remind you that *dying is not winning*!

Ken Mannie, Michigan State University Duffy Daugherty Building, East Lansing, MI 48824 or via email at mannie@ath.msu.edu

Ever Farther, Ever Faster, Ever Higher?

The Athens Olympics will be a crucial battle in sport's war on drugs

"OLYMPISM seeks to create a way of life based on the joy found in effort, the educational value of a good example and respect for universal fundamental ethical principles." So said Baron Pierre de Coubertin, the founder of the modern Olympic games. Alas, there is every chance the 28th summer Olympiad, which opens in Athens on August 13th, will make headlines less for the joy of effort—and still less for good example or respect for universal ethics—than for athletes caught cheating with performance-enhancing drugs.

The past year has brought plenty of evidence that "doping" is rife. In June 2003, a syringe containing a hitherto unknown and undetectable steroid, tetrahydrogestrinone (THG), was sent to America's Anti-Doping Agency (USADA), apparently by a disaffected coach. Speedily designed tests, some applied retrospectively to old urine samples, showed that use of THG had been widespread among top athletes. The drug was allegedly made by BALCO (the Bay Area Laboratory Co-operative), in California, as a "nutritional supplement". BALCO's clients included many top sports stars, such as Tim Montgomery, world champion in the 100m sprint; his partner, Marion Jones, the reigning women's Olympic 100m champion; Shane Mosley, a former boxing world champion; several members of the Oakland Raiders American football team; and Barry Bonds, who holds baseball's record for the most home runs in a season.

Although some of these athletes deny using THG, others have already been banned from their sport for doing so, including Dwain Chambers, a top British sprinter. The USADA is seeking a lifetime ban for Mr Montgomery. After wide investigations, criminal charges have been brought against several people connected with BALCO—though no athletes, as yet—including its boss, Victor Conte, who has been indicted for allegedly supplying illegal drugs and laundering money. A lawyer for Mr Conte has hinted that other well-known athletes, due to compete in the Olympics, have yet to be identified as THG users, and that his client may be prepared to name them as part of a plea-bargain.

But the litany of recent illegal drug use stretches far beyond BALCO. Even cricket, the sport of gentlemen, has been tainted. Shane Warne, an Australian spin bowler, was banned for a year for taking a drug that can be used to mask steroids; on his return, he rivalled the record for the highest number of wickets taken in a Test (a record he shares, ironically, with a Sri Lankan who has been accused of cheating in a more old-fashioned way, by using an illegal bowling action). In soccer, England's top defender, Rio Ferdinand, was banned for eight months for failing to take a mandatory drug test.

Another Briton, Greg Rusedski, escaped a ban this year despite testing positive for nandrolone. The tennis star argued that he had been given the steroid without his knowledge by officials of the sport's governing body, the Association of Tennis Professionals (ATP). In 2003, the ATP let off seven unnamed players who failed drug tests, apparently for the same reason. Drug scandals have erupted in rugby league, ice hockey, orienteering, the triathlon and so on and on.

Cycling has provided many milestones in the history of doping in sport, including the first sportsman allegedly to die as a result of taking drugs, Arthur Linton, in 1896, and the first drug-related death during a televised event, of Tom Simpson, in the 1967 Tour de France. It continues to be rife with drug-taking. David Millar, a British world champion, has admitted taking steroids. Several top cyclists were recently accused of using a room at the Australian Institute of Sport as a "shooting gallery" in which they injected drugs. Even Lance Armstrong, the American cyclist who (inspirationally) recovered from cancer to become a multiple winner of the Tour de France, entered this year's race—the sixth he has won—embroiled in a court battle with the authors of "L.A. Confidential", a book alleging that his achievements were not wholly above board. Mr Armstrong strenuously denies the allegations, and in 2000 even joked about them in a Nike commercial: "What am I on? I'm on my bike, six hours a day."

Recent drug scandals have led to much rewriting of the record books, as well as the return of unfairly won medals and trophies. Mr Millar will have to give back his world-champion's rainbow jersey. Michael Johnson, an American runner, may have to return a gold medal because a fellow member of his 4x400m relay team was found guilty of drug-taking. Tragicomically, Anastasiya Kapachinskaya, a Russian runner, had to give back her world indoor 200m gold after failing a drug test, but at the same time was handed the previous year's outdoor 200m gold after the woman who beat her, Kelli White, was banned for taking performance-enhancing drugs.

In such a climate, the validity of almost any outstanding sporting achievement is likely to be questioned. And politicians have got interested. George Bush even referred to the problem in this year's state-of-the-union address, calling on those in charge of sport to "get tough and to get rid of steroids now". Stopping doping is now at the forefront of Mr Bush's broader war on illegal drugs—not least, cynics say, because it is probably easier to notch up a big success in tackling steroids in sport than to stop cocaine crossing the Mexican border. The BALCO indictments were announced not quietly, by some local prosecutor, but in a blaze of publicity by John Ashcroft, Mr Bush's attorney-general.

Congress has also jumped in. The Senate Commerce, Science and Transportation Committee—sport being commerce—issued a subpoena to obtain documents from the BALCO investigation, which it then handed over to the USADA. In July, a committee of British MPs produced a report that criticised the inconsistent treatment of drug offences by the governing bodies of different sports.

Victorian values

Faced with so much evidence of doping, and with the fact that the discovery of THG was a lucky break and not the result of new detection techniques, you might expect the chief crusaders against drugs in sport to be thoroughly depressed. Yet Dick Pound, a Canadian former Olympic swimmer who now runs the World Anti-Doping Agency (WADA), could hardly be more upbeat. He regards the Athens Olympics as a potential turning point in the war against doping and, though he does not proclaim certain victory, he thinks he has the drug cheats on the run.

Mr Pound is an idealist in the Victorian mould. It was the Victorians who formalised the rules of many of the sports played today, imposing order on what was then anarchy. They saw in sport a way to educate the populace in the importance of the rule of law, and to deepen character by teaching how to play hard but fair: to, as Rudyard Kipling put it, "meet with Triumph and Disaster/And treat those two impostors just the same". De Coubertin's Olympism was the summit of that Victorian idealism.

In a similar spirit, Mr Pound, as he explains in his new book, "Inside the Olympics" (Wiley), sees sport, and in particular the Olympic movement, as providing young

people with the "ethical platform" they need to guide them in a "world that has lost its ethical path". Sport, he says, "can provide an extraordinary value system for today's and tomorrow's youth". But only if it can end the "moral decay" in sport itself, of which doping is a big, though not the only, part: Mr Pound also headed an investigation into corruption in Olympic bidding after a scandal before the opening of the Salt Lake City Winter Olympics in 2002.

His old-fashioned idealism, and his readiness to criticise those who do not share his enthusiasm for WADA—created by the International Olympic Committee (IOC) and various member governments in 1999, but very much his baby—has made him a controversial figure. Sepp Blatter, head of FIFA, the governing body of soccer, once described WADA as a "kind of monster." The saintly cyclist Mr Armstrong even criticised Mr Pound in an open letter in March, after he said that Tour de France cyclists were known to be taking banned substances. "Athletes need to be confident that WADA's programmes are run by fair and straightforward people," said Mr Armstrong.

None of this seems to worry Mr Pound. WADA today is no longer the six-stone weakling it seemed to be at the 2000 Olympics in Sydney, the first at which the Olympic oath sworn by the athletes included the phrase, "committing ourselves to a sport without doping and without drugs". It has come up with many new tests. For instance, samples collected in Athens are expected to be subject to new tests for human growth hormone, either at the games or later.

More crucially, in order to take part in Athens, the world governing body of each sport in the games has had to sign up to the world anti-doping code, agreed in 2003. This created, among other things, a single list of banned substances, a standard set of sanctions for offenders and a dispute-resolution mechanism through the Court of Arbitration for Sport. All the governing bodies have now signed up, though some have attached caveats that WADA may not agree to at future Olympics. FIFA, for example, has won an exemption from the code's blanket two-year ban for offenders.

Cold war temptations

Drugs have been part of sport since at least the 1860s, when swimmers in Amsterdam's canal races were doped in various ways, and long before then if alcohol is counted. In the 19th century, alcohol and strychnine were commonly used to ease pain during boxing bouts. The technology of doping has clearly advanced in leaps and bounds since then. But Mr Pound reckons that the failure, at least until now, to tackle the problem owes less to inability to keep pace with science than to lack of will. WADA is the first systematic attempt to test thoroughly for doping, and to punish offenders severely.

Why has it taken so long? One "excusable" factor, says Mr Pound, was that until the "Olympic economic model" changed, sometime in the 1980s, many sports did not have the money to carry out proper tests. Less excusably, he says, many simply turned a blind eye to the health risks of doping. And during the cold war, many communist countries did not hesitate to dope in order to win. Eastern Germany and, more recently, China at times systematically doped their athletes, often without telling them; who can forget the then female, now male, East German shot-putter nicknamed "Hormone Heidi"? Western countries, desperate to hold their own, often ignored drug-taking by their own athletes if it brought them success.

Some of that cold-war mentality still persists, says Mr Pound. Some governments, including America's, have been slow to make promised payments to WADA's budget. Arguably, it took the BALCO scandal to shock America's Olympic Committee into getting serious about doping. This spring Michele Verroken, until this year the head of anti-doping at UK Sport, told a committee of MPs that she may have lost her job because her strong stance on cheating could have damaged Britain's bid to hold the 2012 Olympics in London. Mr Pound thinks that governments will take the problem far more seriously in future, not least because public anger—combined with governments' full adoption of the WADA code, probably in 2005 in the form of a United Nations convention—will force them to do so.

Public outrage about drug-taking, and the widespread consensus that certain substances must be banned from sport, is unlikely to change. As Mr Pound points out in his book, the catalyst for the creation of WADA was the public fury that greeted remarks made in 1998 by the then head of the IOC, Juan Antonio Samaranch. Watching reports of the arrest of cyclists in the Tour de France after police had discovered doping substances, Mr Samaranch commented to a journalist that prohibited drugs, whether performance-enhancing or not, should be limited to those that are dangerous to health, and that the (then) current list of banned substances was too long. At the emergency meeting of the IOC board soon afterwards, WADA was born, with a philosophy of banning that was a long way from Mr Samaranch's.

To be banned by WADA, a drug has to meet at least two of three criteria: it must enhance performance, be harmful to health and (a very Victorian touch) be against the spirit of sport. Clearly, this would allow a drug to be banned if it had no adverse health effects but was, even so, ruled contrary to whatever is deemed to be the spirit of sport. Mr Pound, for one, seems to regard any use of a drug to enhance performance as against that spirit: it is, quite simply, cheating.

A fierce critic of this approach to drugs in sport is Norman Fost, director of the medical-ethics programme at the University of Wisconsin. He calls the claims made about the harmful effects of steroids "incoherent and flat-out wrong". Mostly, they have small, temporary side-effects, he says, not life-threatening ones. Indeed, the risks are much smaller than those routinely taken by athletes. A man who plays American football professionally for three years has a 90% chance of suffering a permanent physical injury.

If health is the chief concern, surely certain sports should be banned entirely-and athletes should not be allowed to smoke or drink, activities that do far more harm than taking steroids. As for enhancing performance, that is not seen as cheating if it is done by, say, training at high altitude or in a sealed space that simulates high altitude, says Dr Fost, though such training would have exactly the same effect-an increase in oxygen-carrying red blood cells—as the banned steroid EPO, which is especially popular with cyclists.

Gary Wadler of the New York University School of Medicine, who is a member of WADA, dismisses such arguments as "university debating points", and notes that athletes may have no idea of the risks they are running when they take drugs. He blames the 1994 legal change that exempted many dietary supplements from approval by America's Food and Drug Administration, spawning an $18 billion vitamins industry that is now a powerful lobby against re-regulation.

Setting their own rules

In principle, the best way to decide how much performance-enhancement and health risk is acceptable would be by a vote of those who play the particular sport. Yet Mr Pound directs some of his strongest criticism at so-called "professional sports" (aren't all sports professional nowadays?) that are self-regulated, such as tennis and baseball. WADA currently has no authority over these sports. In major league baseball, with its powerful players' union, the drug-testing regime is part of contract negotiations and is extremely relaxed—last year, 5-7% of drug tests showed positive, but offenders were hardly punished.

Arguably, if all the players agree that using performance-enhancers is not cheating, then it isn't really cheating. But Mr Pound reckons that baseball players are badly led, by people who care more about making money than about the true values of sport. He maintains that baseball's top officials are much more upset by players caught using recreational drugs, such as cannabis, which hurt their brand, than about performance-enhancing drugs, which, after all, may make the game more exciting.

The biggest challenge to WADA is to devise tests to keep up with advances in doping. None will be trickier than the expected emergence of gene therapy, starting with treatments for, say, muscular dystrophy. Hoping to anticipate future doping strategies, WADA held a conference with leading genetic scientists in 2002. Unfortunately, it seems that the likeliest way to detect gene therapy is a muscle biopsy, which, Mr Pound mercifully concedes, is "too invasive". Instead, WADA is calling for research, to be funded by itself and governments, into how to identify whether gene therapy has been used. Mr Pound hopes that governments will make creating such a test a condition of winning regulatory approval. Alas, this strategy is rather unlikely to work.

And will the public endorse Mr Pound's Olympian idealism? Certainly, parents seem to be warming to his message that "children shouldn't have to become chemical stockpiles to succeed in sport, or be cheated by those who are"—though will they still do so when they think that, with a little help, Junior might become the next Barry Bonds? Surveys suggest that 2.5% of eighth-graders (13-14-year-olds) have used steroids. UK Sport recently launched "Start Clean", a programme to stop sporty 12-17-year-olds resorting to performance-enhancing drugs. Yet it is hard to see the trend reversing when, outside sport, performance-enhancement seems ever more central to modern life—thanks to Viagra, Prozac, Ritalin and the rest. And, if doping were defeated, would sports fans really be content with the lack of record-breaking feats?

It would be nice to think so. Yet much of this debate may be academic if WADA fails to create tests to spot the use of gene therapy. Watch out for a surge in world-record breaking in the 2012 Olympics. In the meantime, may the best man or woman win (and we don't mean you, Heidi—sorry, Andreas).

Life or Meth?

It's being dubbed "Satan's drug." It's as addictive and destructive as heroin and crack cocaine. It's already destroyed the lives of thousands of Americans. It's called crystal meth, and its use is growing in the gay scene.

Imagine a dance club where the air is dark and sinister. A noise not unlike a cacophony of cement trucks blasts away at your eardrums as the aloof, detached crowd avoids eye contact, glancing at each other only to glare with empty, cold eyes and clenched jaws. There is no love, no laughter, no uplifting dance vibe; just grinding, dense negativity. This is the disturbing state of much of today's gay dance and circuit scene in America.

Methamphetamine (a.k.a. crystal meth, tina, ice, shabu, base, yaba, glass, crazy medicine) is a powerful highly noxious form of speed that ultimately wreaks havoc on the central nervous system, impairing the functioning of the brain and spinal cord. The drug was discovered in Japan in 1919 and developed by Nazi chemists during World War II to enable German soldiers to stay awake, alert and compulsively focused, while also rendering them emotionally sterile and quasi-psychotically aggressive.

These days 'crystal meth' is mostly mass-manufactured in illegal labs from an array of toxic substances including drain cleaner, lithium from camera batteries, antifreeze, ephedrine, red phosphorous and hydrochloric acid. Produced in concentrated crystal form and liquid, it is chemically concocted to artificially stimulate the brain's reward center inducing feelings of alertness and elation, giving the user a false sense of superhuman invincibility, control and power. Snorted, smoked or ingested, the effect is stronger than amphetamines like speed or cocaine, and the comedown—'crash'—significantly more intense.

Like heroin and crack cocaine, the first crystal meth hit delivers an almost instantaneous, euphoric high which locks seductively into the user's subconscious memory, enticing him to repeat the experience. Crystal meth preys on the addictive personality: the more the abuser consumes—chasing the high while delaying the onset of the crash—the less pleasurable the effect due to methamphetamine's ability to erode the brain's production of dopamine, the 'pleasure neurotransmitter' responsible for positive feelings. Job satisfaction, enjoyable social interactions, feelings of contentment, that life is meaningful and counts for something… all rely on dopamine transmission. Driven by his craving, crystal meth cynically zaps the abuser's dopamine and takes control, sucking him into a downward spiral of abuse and dependency.

Literally detached from all positive feelings, the abuser cannot experience or express love, happiness, joy or pleasure. Instead, crystal meth feeds on his fears and insecurities, turning him inward and causing him to react negatively to his environment. Unresolved painful issues from childhood may resurface to torment him and significantly intensify his growing psychological turmoil. Hitler himself was said to receive daily injections of methamphetamine from 1942, corrupting his judgment, undermining his health and, possibly, changing the course of World War II.

Physical symptoms—dry skin, sores, sweating, numbness, dilating pupils, dizziness, grinding of the teeth, impaired but incessant speech, ulcers, sleeplessness, nausea, exhaustion, vomiting, diarrhea, hypothermia, convulsions—manifest, and interest in the normal rewards of life fade as people, places and activities associated with using crystal meth take precedence. It also induces chronic loss of appetite and weight loss, satisfying the abuser in the early stages as fat is stripped away. But as crystal meth takes control his starved body starts feeding away at is own muscle tissue, resulting in a wasted, pallid appearance and ravaged facial features.

Crystal meth's toll is a tragically dehumanizing one. The abuser's deterioration into an 'empty shell' of his former self is likened to an internal light being snuffed out. He no longer even seems to be the same person, appearing 'wired'—nervous, depressed, irritable, fearful, anxious, compulsive, agitated, unpredictable, paranoid—and exhibiting signs of schizophrenia (panic, anger, repetitive behavior patterns, auditory and visual hallucinations). The abuser remains unaware or in denial of his erratic actions, believing himself to still be focused and in control and convinced that it is his external world that is going crazy.

The abuser's constant flow of anti-social behavior puts his career and financial security at risk, while love-based relationships and friendships are destroyed by his need to plug into, and drain any external sources of energy available to him. Relationships that persist become unhealthy co-dependent, fraught and abusive:

"Tina totally ruined a relationship I had with someone I loved very much," recalls Gary, a 37 year old New Yorker who was in a relationship of 13 years. "I can't tell you how I anguished over my lover and his addiction. It was as if I was watching someone drown. I tried so many times to throw him a lifeline, but he was unable or unwilling to grab it. In the end it was too much for me to bear and I had no choice but to leave. The simple face was that he was in love with someone else. Someone named Tina. And she was more important than me."

The abuser can't look others in the eye or at his own, gaunt reflection, and will resent anyone and anything that does not fit in with his addiction. If circumstances allow, he will isolate himself at home with the lights low and curtains drawn, sometimes too paranoid even to answer the phone or switch on the television or computer. Persistent denial and continued use will inevitably lead to destitution, poverty, despair and constant thoughts of suicide. Recorded suicide rates of gay male crystal meth abusers in America are rising dramatically and threaten to eventually outstrip deaths from AIDS, while murders triggered by acute paranoia have been directly attributed to the drug.

If he is lucky, the abuser's circumstances will force him to awaken to his problem and seek help medically or via a recovery and support program like Crystal Meth Anonymous (CMA). Methamphetamine abusers are among the hardest to treat of all drug users, often extremely resistant to any form of intervention, but acknowledging that they have a problem is a major first step toward recovery. The severe effects of withdrawal—drug craving, irritability, loss of energy, depression, fearfulness, insomnia, palpitations, sweating, hyperventilation—can last up to several weeks, but the 'wall' (craving) period continues six to

eight months for casual users and two to three years for addicts. The temptation to relapse is always strong, and there is growing concern in the medical field that some former abusers may never recover from irreversible damage to the brain, remaining dissatisfied with life and its rewards.

Significantly compounding the threat of crystal meth's influence on gay men is a heightened and compulsive desire to indulge in sex which, combined with sleeplessness—often lasting up to several days—and impaired judgement is often unsafe (the availability of protease inhibitors is typically cited as an excuse to engage in such activity). Although methamphetamine has been used as a 'dirty' recreational drug in the U.S. since the 80's, its use by gay men during most of that time was confined mainly to the AIDS-inflicted 'gay suburb' of West Hollywood in Los Angeles, and was largely non-sexual due to its constrictive effect on blood vessels, making erections difficult to sustain.

Crystal meth's use as a sexual aid was inadvertently popularized by the arrival, in 1998, of Viagra, which provided the solution to 'crystal dick'. Gay men, particularly on the 'party circuit', quickly discovered that crystal meth taken with Viagra simultaneously boosted sexual prowess and longevity. Like a time bomb waiting to explode, Viagra has fuelled crystal meth's use throughout other major U.S. cities; no longer was crystal meth just a drug for 'lost souls'. Alarmingly, this union also accelerated the risk of HIV transmission due to higher levels of unsafe sex induced by false feelings of invincibility. Even practiced safely there is a compounded risk of friction tears on the protective shield due to the significantly prolonged sexual duration crystal meth and Viagra together allow.

Viagra's arrival has coincided with the arrival of internet sex sites like 'Men-Men', specifically designed to make sex a commodity as easily available as home-delivered pizza. Today, a sizeable core group of users of these sites have emerged who remain online 24 hours a day in search of crystal-induced sex with fellow 'teachers', and who are upfront in their preference for unprotected 'bareback action'. 'Binge partying', where the abuser is typically awake for four straight days, crashes the following three and starts again, is driven by his compulsive desire for sex, which in turn is driven by his constant craving for crystal meth. Because crystal meth desensitizes, sex between abusers is rendered coldly 'mechanical', devoid of the usual free-flowing exchange of feelings and emotions. Where only one participant is an abuser he will, effectively, 'feed' off the other's higher energy levels, leaving the non-abuser feeling drained and listless.

Crystal meth is a very long-acting sympathomimetic and far more immunosuppressive than HIV, leaving someone immunosuppressed for days on end. This, combined with superhuman feelings of immunity to HIV, has triggered an epidemic of seroconversions in the USA. In Los Angeles alone over 75% of new HIV infections are now crystal meth related. Its ravaging of the body's immune system also hastens the onslaught of AIDS in HIV positive people, yet a recent U.S. study revealed that 47% of gay male crystal meth abusers were knowingly HIV-positive, with HIV rates high for casual users too. And in a report just published, a third of gay men surveyed in San Francisco reported using Viagra despite it being a prescription-only drug.

Crystal meth is ecstasy's complete antithesis, spawning an ugly new breed of insecure, sexually intense clubber, and transforming once uplifting dance environments into battlegrounds.

Combined with the alarming rise in crystal-induced HIV and syphilis infection over the last couple of years, much of the tireless work of America's safe sex campaigners since the start of the AIDS pandemic has been undone, with new rates of infection now higher than at any time since the early 90's. Little wonder that the marriage of crystal meth and Viagra is being referred to as 'the new gay plague'.

It is in some of the large dance clubs of major American cities and on the party circuit—lavish, decadent all-male dance events held throughout the States—where crystal meth's insidious influence is most evident. With the arrival of Viagra, club-goers have increasingly flocked from 'fun drugs' like ecstasy to crystal meth, enabling them to start the night with a buzz and stay awake, alert and 'hungry' for sex. Crystal meth's infiltration into social environments popular with abusers over the last couple of years has wreaked a devastating toll on the direction they have taken.

Over the last year alone in one of New York City's premier gay nightclubs, swelling numbers of crystal meth users have become abusers. Once fresh, vibrant faces are now etched in anger and paranoia as their dopamine levels progressively deplete, turning the venue palpably darker and more aggressive by the week. Alarmingly, this particular club is not alone in having adapted to this increasingly negative mindset; 'darker' forms of music are known to induce negative emotional responses, which explains why its DJ starts the night with uplifting tracks but, as the 'teachers' start to crash en masse, rapidly descends into a disharmonious, bass-heavy, discordant sound dubbed 'pots and pans'.

Where, just 18 months ago, this club was alive with people dancing and raising their spirits to uplifting deep house grooves and tribal rhythms, today the same environment resembles a swirling, dense 'no-man's land' driven by this sinister new sound seemingly tailored specifically for the crystal-addicted market. The crowd sways to and fro to the mind-numbing, soulless noise in a detached, hollow-eyed, emotionless state. Even the occasional vocal track like 'I'm Addicted'—which provocatively repeats its title, mantra-like, over and over—seemingly serves to reinforce their dependency.

In just 18 months, an epidemic of crystal meth addiction has cut a vast, soul-destroying swathe through Manhattan's gay community, threatening to turn it in on itself as it did to the gay community of West Hollywood in the 90's. A walk along the Chelsea strip of 8th Avenue and in some of the more popular gay meeting places—including restaurants, cafes and gyms—indicate that the negative, hostile vibes that are the consequence of crystal meth addiction are not confined to the club scene. In just one year Manhattan's CMA meetings have exploded from one a week to almost daily, with attendance quadrupling from 15 to as many as 60 per class—a statistic that is all the harder to grasp in the wake of September 11, when New Yorker's generally united to rebuild their shattered city.

Circuit-goers, too, note with growing despair a palpably doom-laden vibe permeating their events, as Viagra and her twisted sister strengthen their destructive bond. Recalling a recent trip to Europe in the latest issue of the circuit bible, *Circuit Noize*, editor Steve Kammon lamented: "I felt like I'd been transported back to a happier time. People were really grooving on the music, dancing with abandon, and their faces were almost uniformly smiling—there was a really up, positive vibe... How different it seemed from so many of the all-night parties I'd been to this past year in Miami, Los Angeles and New York."

For all its negative press, in its 90's heyday, ecstasy connected people with their feelings, erased their barriers and, ultimately, brought them together in joy. Crystal meth is ecstasy's complete antithesis, spawning an ugly new breed of insecure, sexually intense clubber, and transforming once uplifting dance environments into battlegrounds of testosterone-fuelled masculinity. Ego and power play have always been an unfortunate aspect of gay club culture, not least in the U.S., but they are now becoming the dominant force. People just out for a fun time cannot express themselves in environments inflicted with crystal meth abuse. Their laughter and exchanges of affection are invariably met with bitter, resentful looks, even abuse, and the ensuing negativity forces them to leave earlier and earlier. Ultimately, they choose to stop clubbing altogether or are assimilated into the crystal herd, thereby perpetuating the cycle of abuse. People have been known to become addicted to meth while taking ecstasy because the pills can contain primarily methamphetamine.

American club and circuit promoters everywhere need to recognize their duty in placing the physical safety and mental well-being of their customers ahead of their profits, a responsibility they demonstrated with a widespread zero-tolerance policy towards GHB; a 'feel good' drug which, taken safely, has no lasting detrimental affect, but if overdosed rapidly sends a person into a deep sleep. If consumed in significant qualities with *any* amount of alcohol GHB can kill. Understandably, the unwholesome prospect of onsite paramedics tending to unconscious customers on their premises prompted this clampdown; yet agonizingly painful out-of-sight, out-of-mind crystal meth-induced deaths are significantly higher.

Many gay men drawn to the escapism of the gay dance scene have been playing Russian roulette with their lives for years now. Until we understand the impulses that drive us to indulge in self-destructive modes of behavior, and the reasons for our internalized homophobia which we project onto others, be it in the clubs, cafes, gyms, wherever, we will never shake free the shackles with which we allow mainstream society's narrow-minded, ignorant, views imprison us. Unless we say no now, then the horror that is crystal abuse will, like AIDS before it,

play into their hands, providing a weapon for them to attack us with, while we continue to tear ourselves apart. It is down to individual choice whether we allow crystal to control us, snuff out our light and provide our own weapon for fast-track self-annihilation. Or we can reject this cancer in favor of the very thing that crystal seeks to detach us from: love and respect, of ourselves and others.

Editor's Note

Again, I would like to remind our readers that we are offering this and other articles in [Outward Magazine, Volume 16, Issue 5, No. 236, March 13, 2003—March 27, 2003] as information. The views expressed are not necessarily those of this publication.

Teens tell truth about drugs

Cannabis before school and whisky during lessons—pupils reveal all in TV documentary.

Michael Shaw

A 15-year-old girl at a city academy in London has revealed how she smokes cannabis before school and used to drink whisky during lessons.

Research this week suggests that Natalie Mitchell's experiences with drink and drugs are typical for hundreds of teenagers.

The pupil, who lives in Hackney, east London, told *The TES* that she now smokes cannabis before school less often than in the past, only once every three weeks.

"It makes me think a bit more about my work, makes me concentrate more," she said. "I'm more chilled and less loud in class."

Her behaviour and attendance have improved significantly since last year, when she used to go on drinking binges on school nights, downing cider, brandy, vodka and Bacardi Breezers with a 17-year-old friend.

The teenager claims she never suffered hangovers but would often arrive at lessons tired and would occasionally fall asleep.

She would even bring alcohol into school on Fridays to give herself a "head start" for the weekend's heavy drinking.

"It was only in the last lesson, after three o'clock," she said. "It would be JD (Jack Daniel's bourbon) in a coke bottle. I would just have a little drop, then more later."

Natalie is one of 10 young people who agreed to be followed by a camera crew as part of a Channel 4 documentary on modern teenage life.

As part of their research, the producers surveyed more than 1,000 14 to 19-year-olds.

They found that more than half had come across people selling cannabis and alcohol in their school. Around 70 per cent said they regularly smoked cannabis and had seen pupils drinking in school grounds.

In addition, at least 60 of those surveyed said they had a friend who had lost their virginity at school.

Heather Rabbatts, managing director of 4Learning, Channel 4's education department, said the research showed that the rebellious teens of previous generations were being replaced by "teen adults" or "child carers".

The teenagers were often hedonistic, she said, but many had weighty responsibilities caring for family members, partly as a result of divorce and absent fathers.

Prescription Drug Abuse: FDA and SAMHSA Join Forces

By Michelle Meadows

Kyle Moores, 19, of Manassas, Va., says he knew he needed help when his abuse of the pain reliever OxyContin (oxycodone) left him drowning in debt and unable to hold a job. "It put me basically in a zombie mode for a year and a half," says Moores, who crushed and snorted the drug. "I finally realized I was losing my life."

Moores was successfully treated at an addiction facility in Richmond, Va. He spoke about his journey to recovery in January at a media event to kick off a joint public education program on the dangers of prescription drug abuse.

The program, sponsored by the Food and Drug Administration and the Substance Abuse and Mental Health Services Administration (SAMHSA) includes posters, public service announcements, and brochures featuring the slogans "The Buzz Takes Your Breath Away... Permanently" and "It's To Die For." The messages target people ages 14 to 25, but they are relevant to anyone who abuses prescription drugs.

John Jenkins, M.D., director of the FDA's Office of New Drugs, says the FDA is especially concerned about the misuse of single ingredient, controlled-release formulations of opiates, such as OxyContin. "Abuse and misuse of these products is particularly dangerous because they contain higher doses of the drug and are designed to release the drug slowly over a 12- or 24-hour, or longer, period of time for sustained relief of pain," Jenkins says. "Damaging the controlled-release mechanism for these products, such as crushing an OxyContin tablet, can result in immediate release of the high dose of drug, which can be fatal."

In 2001, almost 3 million youths ages 12 to 17 and almost 7 million young adults between 18 and 25 reported using prescription medications non-medically at least once in their lifetimes, according to the National Household Survey on Drug Abuse conducted by SAMHSA.

Data provided by SAMHSA's Drug Abuse Warning Network indicates that visits to hospital emergency departments related to narcotic prescription pain relievers increased significantly from 1994 to 2001. The highest increases were seen with oxycodone, methadone, morphine, and hydrocodone. Narcotic pain relievers, also known as opiates, are the most commonly abused prescription drugs.

The FDA is working with manufacturers of controlled-release opiates to implement risk-management plans aimed at minimizing abuse while still keeping the products available for people with a legitimate medical need. "In many cases, prescription opiate pain relievers are the most effective treatments available to help patients control their pain and lead productive lives," Jenkins says. But they also have potentially serious side effects,

the most serious of which is the risk of respiratory failure.

"While addiction occurs after repeated use, death can occur after a single dose," Jenkins says. "So the first time that someone decides to abuse or misuse a prescription opiate pain reliever may be their last decision."

H. Westley Clark, M.D., J.D., director of SAMHSA's Center for Substance Abuse Treatment, wants people who are abusing prescription drugs to know that effective addiction treatment is avail-

able. Clark says that primary care physicians play a critical role in screening, assessing, and referring people with potential substance abuse problems.

According to Clark, "The recent approval by the FDA of buprenorphine to treat prescription drug abuse, and the office-based use of other addiction medications likely to be approved in the years ahead, makes the role of primary care physicians more vital than ever." In October 2002, the FDA approved Subutex (buprenorphine) and Suboxone (bu-

prenorphine and naloxone)--the first narcotic drugs available to treat opiate dependence that can be prescribed in an office setting.

To contact SAMHSA's substance abuse treatment 24-hour helpline, call 1-800-662-HELP (1-800-662-4357) or visit www.findtreatment.samhsa.gov

---

From *FDA Consumer*, March/April 2003, p. 36. Published by the U.S. Food and Drug Administration.

Adolescent OxyContin Abuse

DEBRA A. KATZ, M.D., AND LON R. HAYS, M.D.

OxyContin, a prescription pain reliever, is a controlled-release form of oxycodone hydrochloride. The medication is supplied in 10-mg, 20-mg, 40-mg, and 80-mg tablets and provides delivery of oxycodone over a 12-hour period (Purdue Pharma LP, 2001). It is indicated for the management of moderate to severe pain. Although all prescription narcotics have the potential for abuse, some have called the recent surge in OxyContin abuse an epidemic in particular areas of the country (Baumrucker, 2001; Young, 2001). Since its introduction by Purdue Pharma in 1995, there have been news reports of overdose-related deaths among adolescents (CBSNews.com, 2002; Injuryboard.com, 2001; OxyABUSEkills.com, 2002; OxyContin Abuse News, 2002; Sunday Gazette-Mail Online, 2001) and more than 450 overdose-related deaths nationwide (U.S. Department of Justice, 2002). From 50% to 90% of new patients in methadone programs in Kentucky, Virginia, Pennsylvania, and West Virginia claim OxyContin as their primary drug of abuse (Hutchinson, 2002).

OxyContin has become a popular alternative to other street drugs such as heroin and has, in fact, been called "poor man's heroin" or "hillbilly heroin." Although it is available as an oral preparation, illicit users prefer to crush the tablet to disable the sustained-release coating and then swallow it, snort it, or dissolve it in water for injection. This results in an instant euphoria that is contributing to OxyContin's popularity and its comparison to the cocaine and heroin epidemics of the late 1980s. OxyContin is well absorbed orally and has high bioavailability due to low first-pass metabolism. It is metabolized to noroxycodone, oxymorphone, and their glucuronides and primarily excreted through urine.

Of the 7.2 million prescriptions written for single-entity oxycodone products in 2000, 5.8 million (81%) were for OxyContin, making it the number-one prescribed Schedule II narcotic in the United States (Hutchinson, 2002). At this time, little has been written about adolescents' abuse of this drug, despite the fact that adolescents are aware of OxyContin and abuse it. A recent survey at a rural Michigan high school showed that 98% of students had heard of OxyContin and 9.5% had tried it (Holstege et al., 2002). Of those who had tried OxyContin, 50% had taken it more than 20 times and over half had used it within the past month, mostly in the evenings and on weekends. Seventy-two percent of survey participants indicated that it was "not at all hard to get OxyContin."

These brief case reports of adolescents who were admitted for inpatient treatment emphasize the need for awareness of and further research on OxyContin abuse in adolescence.

Case 1

This 16-year-old girl with no history of substance use was admitted for treatment of OxyContin abuse. She had a history of depression and oppositional behavior. She first tried OxyContin at age 14 at the urging of a drug dealer, who then forced her into sexual activity. Within 6 months, she began stealing Percocet and then OxyContin from her mother, who took these medications for chronic pain. She intercepted a mail shipment of her mother's narcotic medication, then waited in the bathroom all night with a skillet, which she planned to use as a weapon on her mother if her mother tried to get the OxyContin from her. Despite a stay in a rehabilitation program, this patient's OxyContin use continued and she was hospitalized for two suicide attempts, one of which involved acetaminophen with codeine. The patient then began stealing needles from her pediatrician's office to use OxyContin intravenously. Abstinence was finally achieved after a "wilderness program" and a long-term residential treatment program. The patient still describes intense cravings and worries about how she will manage her abstinence in the face of her mother's opioid use for chronic pain.

Case 2

This 18-year-old single white girl with no known history of prior drug abuse reported using OxyContin for 2 years, on a daily basis for the previous year and a half. She snorted the OxyContin and had recently been leaving her infant son with her mother so she could spend her time using drugs. She reported selling all of her belongings and described not taking insulin for her diabetes because of her drug use, which escalated to 150 and then 200 mg of OxyContin per day. As a result of this, she dropped out of school and was spending most of her time crying, unable to sleep and unable to eat. She was finally admitted to an acute inpatient unit for detoxification from OxyContin.

Case 3

This 17-year-old single boy described using OxyContin for 1 month. His substance use had begun with cigarettes at age 11 and escalated to marijuana at age 12 and cocaine at age 16. He stole the OxyContin from his mother's supply and quickly escalated his use to 100 mg a day, which he snorted. The OxyContin use rapidly supplanted the use of all other substances and resulted in inpatient admission for detoxification 1 month after his use began.

DISCUSSION

These cases demonstrate that adolescents may quickly develop serious addictions to OxyContin. Patient 1 became addicted to OxyContin 6 months after her introduction to the drug, and patient 3 began using OxyContin exclusively after only 1 month. All three patients were desperate to obtain OxyContin and used this drug exclusively once the addiction developed. The stage model of substance abuse describes youths beginning their use of substances with legal and relatively less serious drugs and progressing to more serious drugs. Drugs used at earlier stages are generally not abandoned but are carried over into later stages, resulting in polysubstance abuse (Kandel, 1975; Kandel and Logan, 1984). Although patient 3 had a history of prior drug use, OxyContin quickly supplanted other drugs and became the sole focus of his use. Interestingly, patients 1 and 2 had no prior history of drug use and rapidly became dependent on OxyContin.

These adolescents, as well as several others we have followed, began using OxyContin in mid-adolescence, an age range at low risk for heroin or other opioid use (National Institute on Drug Abuse, 2002). The time from first exposure to abuse of or dependence on OxyContin may be more rapid due to (1) the wide availability of the drug in pharmacies and doctor's offices and on the street; (2) its aggressive marketing and promotion in an atmosphere of optimal pain management; (3) its positive image in comparison to heroin; (4) the ability to begin use with oral ingestion and to progress to snorting or intravenous use; and (5) the ease with which the tablet is crushed, thus destroying the controlled-release coating and making the active ingredient immediately available for a powerful heroin-like high. Behavior to obtain OxyContin often escalates quickly and can involve serious high-risk behaviors such as using stolen needles, neglecting medical care (e.g., insulin treatment), and stealing from doctors and family members. Involvement in crime to obtain OxyContin is characteristic of the addiction to this drug. For example, in October 2000, 90% of robberies in Pulaski, Virginia, were due to OxyContin

abuse, and half of the inmates in jail in Hazard, Kentucky, were incarcerated for OxyContin-related crimes (Suleman et al., 2002). The street value of 1 mg of OxyContin ranges from 50 cents to $1, and average doses are in the range of 180 mg per day (National Drug Intelligence Center, 2001). It is easy to see how quickly the funds needed to support this habit can escalate and how an illicit marketplace has rapidly developed for this drug. Other mechanisms for obtaining OxyContin include pharmacy diversion (the selling of OxyContin by pharmacy workers for personal gain), "doctor shopping" (visiting multiple doctors and obtaining multiple prescriptions), improper prescribing by physicians (ranging from "poor doctoring" to criminal conduct involving "OxyContin clinics"), and forged prescriptions and burglaries of pharmacies. The adolescents in this report stole primarily from their parents, used up all of their savings, and sold all of their belongings to obtain this drug. Information about illegal activities, including prostitution and violent crime, may be limited in the cases presented here since all patients were in active treatment.

Opioid dependence has been associated with a history of childhood sexual abuse and exposure to violence in approximately 25% of patients (Browne et al., 1998). In fact, those exposed to sexual abuse had an earlier age of onset of opiate injection (by approximately 3 years) and a longer duration of drug use. Sexual abuse may lead adolescents to block out painful emotions and memories through drug use as a form of "chemical dissociation." Themes of betrayal, lack of trust, and family disruption in response to childhood sexual abuse may further hinder an adolescent from accessing treatment and, instead, provide motivation for drug use. For example, patient 1 was introduced to OxyContin by the man who sexually abused her at age 14. It was not until she had made two suicide attempts and become heavily dependent on OxyContin that she revealed this abuse. The sequelae of sexual abuse, including increased risk-taking behaviors, social isolation, and academic decline, are particularly relevant in this population and in opioid-dependent patients in general. In addition to family disruption, involvement in crime, and school dropout, adolescents who abuse OxyContin are at a significantly increased risk for infection with hepatitis C and human immunodeficiency virus (HIV) and death as a result of drug overdose or drug-related accidents, homicides, or suicides.

At their time of treatment, all three patients were depressed, and patient 1 was hospitalized for two suicide attempts. Although she had a history of depression prior to her OxyContin use, she had never been hospitalized nor made a suicide attempt prior to her abuse of OxyContin. Earlier age of first substance use has been associated with more frequent and more severe comorbid psychiatric disorders (Deykin et al., 1992; Mezzich et al., 1992). Depression may precede or follow substance use, and an understanding of the relationship between the two may guide risk assessment and prevention (Bukstein et al., 1992; Deykin et al., 1992). Evaluation of depressive symptoms is therefore an important part of the overall treatment of substance abuse and appears significant in all three of the cases described here.

Prevention and Treatment

The rapid onset of OxyContin addiction and its potential for morbidity, mortality, and criminality point to the need for active efforts at prevention. Continuing medical education programs and drug education programs for teens, parents, teachers, and the law enforcement community to promote awareness for OxyContin abuse are critical. The use of tamper-resistant prescription pads, development of statewide or national prescription-monitoring programs for Schedule II drugs, and increased education of pharmacists to ensure security of scheduled drugs in pharmacies are some of the ways to reduce illegal access to opioids. Research and development of alternate pain medications with low abuse potential would reduce the availability of OxyContin.

Child and adolescent psychiatrists and other professionals who work with children need to be aware of risk factors, early symptoms of abuse, and methods of treatment for OxyContin abuse. Children who have family members using OxyContin for treatment of pain are particularly vulnerable. OxyContin abuse first developed in economically depressed areas with manual labor-based employment and associated disability. Living within a "pain culture," with the modeling of reliance on pain medications to "feel better," may make these medications more acceptable and available to adolescents. Addicted teens may engage in criminal activity to support their addiction or may steal the drug directly. Limited access to both education about the risks of OxyContin abuse and specialized services to treat it may exist in combination with the risk factors.

Because OxyContin addiction has been thought of as a problem only in rural areas and only in "hard-core" adult addicts, child and adolescent psychiatrists may neglect to ask about it. Adolescents should be asked directly about OxyContin use, which may also be known as "Oxy" and "Oxycotton." A complete substance abuse history should include inquiry about OxyContin use as well as parents' or other family members' use of pain medications and their attitudes toward them. In many of the patients we have seen, parental dependence on opioids was a significant risk factor for adolescent abuse.

In known OxyContin abusers, it is important to review all routes of drug administration (oral, intranasal, and intravenous) and any high-risk behavior used to obtain the drug (e.g., prostitution), with attention to associated medical problems (e.g., sexually transmitted diseases, hepatitis C, HIV). Comorbidity of opioid abuse with mood, anxiety, and conduct disorders as well as with sexual abuse and posttraumatic stress disorder needs to be evaluated. Adolescents need detoxification services in the acute period, along with thorough assessment of comorbid psychiatric conditions. All of the adolescents we have treated have required acute inpatient psychiatric hospitalization as well as close long-term follow-up. Long-term residential treatment and/or long-term medication-assisted (e.g., methadone) outpatient treatment may be indicated. Since OxyContin abuse is a new problem among adolescents, there are no research data on acute or long-term treatment outcomes. In our limited experience, this is a powerful addiction that has a high relapse rate. Adolescents, like adults, become rapidly dependent on OxyContin once they have tried it, and they need aggressive treatment. Because of the high relapse rate, these adolescents need close psychiatric follow-up with attention to depression, anxiety, and self-injurious behavior, family and school involvement in treatment, including evaluation of parental opioid use and availability of OxyContin within the home, and regular drug testing to ensure abstinence. Many patients need longer-term residential treatment to deal with urges to resume OxyContin use, to treat comorbid psychiatric symptoms and family disruption as a result of their addiction, and to fully understand the negative sequelae of OxyContin dependence.

REFERENCES

Baumrucker SJ (2001), OxyContin, the media and law enforcement. *Am J Hosp Palliat Care* 18:154-156

Browne R, Keating S, O'Connor J (1998), Sexual abuse in childhood and subsequent illicit drug abuse in adolescence and early adulthood. *Ir J Psychiatry Med* 15:123-126

Bukstein OG, Glancy LJ, Kaminer Y (1992), Patterns of affective comorbidity in a clinical population of dually diagnosed adolescent substance abusers. *J Am Acad Child Adolesc Psychiatry* 31:1041-1045

CBSNews.com: 48 Hours Investigates (2002), Addicted: an OxyContin tragedy; available at *http://www.cbsnews.com/stories/2001/12/12/48hours/main321066.shtml* (accessed October 28, 2002)

Deykin EY, Buka SL, Zeena TH (1992), Depressive illness among chemically dependent adolescents. *Am J Psychiatry* 149:1341-1347

Holstege CP, Kell S, Baer AB, Fatovitch T (2002), Prevalence of OxyContin abuse in high school students. *J Toxicol Clin Toxicol* 40:656

Hutchinson A (2002), Statement of Asa Hutchinson, Administrator, Drug Enforcement Administration, Before the House Committee on Appropriations, Subcommittee on Commerce, Justice, State, and Judiciary, National Clearinghouse for Alcohol and Drug Abuse Information; available at *http://www.dea.gov/pubs/cngrtest/ct121101.html* (accessed October 28, 2002)

Injuryboard.com (2002), Parents sue over OxyContin death-7/24/2001; available at *http://sundaygazettemail.com/display_story.php3?sid=200107156&format=prn* (accessed October 28, 2002)

Kandel DB (1975), Stages in adolescent involvement in drug use. *Science* 190:912-914

Kandel DB, Logan JA (1984), Patterns of drug use from adolescence to young adulthood, I: periods of risk for initiation, continued use, and discontinuation. *Am J Public Health* 74:660-666

Mezzich AC, Tarter RE, Hsieh Y, Fuhrman A (1992), Substance abuse severity in female adolescents. *Am J Addict* 1:217-221

National Drug Intelligence Center (2001), OxyContin diversion and abuse: available at *http://www.usdoj.gov/ndic/pubs/651/abuse.htm* (accessed January 5, 2002)

National Institute on Drug Abuse (NIDA) InfoFacts (2002), High school and youth trends; available at *http://www.drugabuse.gov/InfoFax/HSYouthtrends.html* (accessed January 5, 2002)

OxyABUSEkills.com (2002), Deaths related to Oxy; available at *http://www.oxyabusekills.com/victims.html* (accessed January 4, 2003)

OxyContin Abuse News (May 8, 2002), Available at *http://www.oxycontinabuse-news.com/html/news.html* (accessed January 4, 2003)

Purdue Pharma LP (2001), OxyContin (oxycodone HCl controlled-release) product information (brochure). Stamford, CT; available at *http://www.pharma.com/html/our_products/our_products.htm#Prescription_products*

Suleman R, Abourjaily H, Rosenberg M (2002), OxyContin—misuse and abuse. *J Mass Dent Soc* 51:56-58

Sunday Gazette-Mail Online (2001), OxyContin-related deaths up in metropolitan areas; available at *http://sundaygazette-mail.com/display_story.php3?sid=200107156&format=prn* (accessed January 4, 2003)

US Department of Justice Drug Enforcement Administration Diversion Control Program (2002), Drugs and chemicals of concern: summary of medical examiner reports on oxycodone-related deaths; available at *http://www.deadiversion.usdoj.gov/drugs_concern/oxycodone/oxycontin7.htm* (accessed October 28, 2002)

Young D (2001), Federal reports say oxycodone abuse is on the rise. *Am J Health-Syst Pharm* 58:1175-1191

From *Journal of American Academy of Child and Adolescent Psychiatry,* Vol. 43, No. 2, February 2004, pp. 231-234. Copyright © 2004 by Lippincott, Williams & Wilkins. Reprinted by permission.

Warning label

Teens find a dangerous, cheap high in over-the-counter cough medicine

By Will Evans

The first time Myles did "skittles" was at high school—and all the teachers were giving him strange looks. The curly haired sophomore couldn't control his forehead, couldn't put his eyebrows down.

His hands were quivering, his knees spasming. He couldn't walk straight.

Scary, this being his first time, and this was not expected, A told him it would be like smoking a joint. But cough medicine—especially these Coricidin HBP pills, called skittles on the street—was "way more intense."

At a party that night, Myles played the punching game bloody knuckles. He probably won, because he couldn't feel a thing, and he woke up later with bashed-up hands.

Slang terms: DXM, DEX, Skittles, Red Devils, Triple C, Robo

Not feeling any thing is a good feeling, says Myles, now 17, of Sacramento. But take it from him: "I actu-

---

Possible Symptoms and side effects

- Hallucinations
- Slurred speech, poor coordination and inability to move
- Drowsiness, sedation
- Dizziness, confusion, distorted perceptions
- Nausea, vomiting
- Rapid heart rate/dilated pupils
- Can become agitated, violent or psychotic
- Can become more susceptible to seizures, heart problems
- Death is possible, but rare
- Not addictive

---

ally don't recommend taking the whole package."

The use of cough medicine to get high is rising among teenagers nationwide and in the Sacramento region, according to poison-control centers.

The hallucination-inducing ingredient is the cough suppressant dextromethor phan (DXM). It's found in many over-the-counter medicines, from Robitussin DM to DayQuil,

---

Phone numbers for help:

California Poison Control System: **(800) 876-4766**

Center for Substance Abuse Treatment Referral helpline **(800) 662-4357 (HELP)**

Sutter Center for Psychiatry Call Center: **(916) 386-3077**

---

which are safe at the recommended dosage. Often, the medications contain other drugs harmful in the large quantities necessary to get the DXM fix.

In particular vogue are the red pills of Coricidin HBP Cough & Cold. The Sacramento division of the California Poison Control System has seen an increase in calls related to abuse of the readily available medicine.

"It has a pretty high concentration of the cough suppressant, and we believe that's why it is one of the drugs of choice for abuse," says Judith Alsop, division director.

A sampling of medications with DXM:

Coricidin HBP Cough & Cold, Robitussin DM, NyQuil, DayQuil, Tylenol Cold, Dimetapp Cold & Congestion Caplets, Sudafed Cold & Cough

Other ingredients to watch out for in cough medicine:

Chlorpheniramine: an antihistamine, which in high doses can cause increased heart rate, dilated pupils, uncoordination and lethargy, and even lead to seizures or a coma

Acetaminophen: pain reliever otherwise known as Tylenol, which in high doses can cause permanent liver damage

Pseudoephedrine: a decongestant which in high doses can cause increased heart rate and blood pressure, nervousness, agitation, irregular heartbeats and seizures

Street drugs similar to DXM:

PCP, Ketamine ("Special K")

Cough medicine is not one of the most dangerous or widespread abused substances among young people.

Calls about teenagers misusing DXM doubled nationwide from 2000 to 2003, according to the American Association of Poison Control Centers, but the 3,271 cases of 2003 represent a tiny fraction of some 2.3 million total calls. Locally, high school students say it happens, but it's not common.

"It's not something that's on our radar screen," says Drug Enforcement Administration spokeswoman Rogene Waite. Neither the Sacramento Police Department nor the Sacramento County Sheriff's Department has had to take action.

One of the biggest dangers of chugging syrup and popping cold tablets comes from the active ingredients other than DXM, says Steve Offerman, attending

emergency physician at UC Davis Medical Center.

But a few DXM-related deaths reported around the country and the upswing in popularity has caused doctors, educators and industry to take note.

This month, Walgreens nationwide began limiting the sale of Coricidin HBP Cough & Cold to three packages per person, and some stores now guard it behind the counter instead of putting it on the shelf. The maker of Coricidin HBP, New Jersey-based Schering-Plough, worked with the Partnership for a Drug-Free America to develop an online resource at **www.drugfreeamerica.org/dxm**.

Despite those efforts, Web sites aimed at abusers of the medication offer tips on what kind and how much cough medicine to down, "fun" things to do while high, how to distill DXM powder from medication and how to buy the powder in bulk.

But those finer points aside, much of the appeal, say teenagers, is that it's cheap and easily available—at the drugstore or at home in the medicine cabinet.

"If you didn't have any money to get stoned, basically you just drink a bottle," says Melissa Florez, a senior at McClatchy High School who guzzled cough syrup a few times when she was feeling depressed her sophomore year. "It seemed like the only thing to do was to get high however I could, and if it came down to a bottle of cough syrup, that's how it was."

But Florez, with pink bangs fringing her black hair and peace signs piercing her ears, describes the high as a woozy "sick feeling" and isn't a fan.

012345678ne of the biggest dangers of chugging syrup and popping cold tablets comes from the active ingredients other than DXM, says Steve Offerman, attending emergency physician at UC Davis Medical Center.

"These products, many of them are mixed with other stuff, and you can get poisoning from that stuff as well," he says.

In high doses, the antihistamine in Coricidin HBP Cough & Cold, for example, causes the heart to speed and symptoms of poor coordination on top of DXM's effects. In large enough quantities, it could even lead to a coma. Other preparations of Coricidin HBP and other cough medicines include acetaminophen, or Tylenol, which can ruin the liver in whopping doses.

Some cough medications, when taken to get high, could cause heart attacks among people with a family history of cardiac problems or seizures among people susceptible to attacks, says Alsop.

The heavy sedation of high doses could cause breathing problems or lead people to damage their body by lying out in the cold, Offerman says.

And sedation is sometimes blended with a "Hulk-ish" hyperstimulation. Some young people seen by James Margolis of Sutter Center for Psychiatry become violent and assault others when strung out on cough suppressants. Others come in with self-induced cuts, he says.

"They'll engage in dangerous behaviors," Margolis says. "They're not using good judgment (when high)."

Alsop is not aware of any fatalities in the region, but calls to the Sacramento center keep coming in, recently several a week:

- Two teenagers sent from school straight to the emergency room.
- A man who discovered two nieces watching a movie while tripping out.
- Freaked-out teenagers with raging heartbeats, afraid they took too much.

Mike Walsh, a toxicology specialist who fields calls, says the teens are usually sent to the hospital, given a nasty charcoal liquid, monitored till the effects wear off and sent home.

Most young people who do drugs in general have tried DXM, but most don't stick with it, in the experience of Jon Daily, an alcohol and drug abuse counselor with New Directions Counseling Associates in Fair Oaks.

He saw skittle abuse pop up last year and peak during the summer.

But it's still less than the popularity of other medicinal highs, like that from Vicodin, Valium and Oxycontin, he says.

"Everybody was worried about kids smoking marijuana, using crank and using alcohol," Margolis says. "What we're experiencing is that probably two-thirds of drug abuse is stuff in the home or stuff you can get in the drugstore."

The Bee's Will Evans can be reached at (916) 321-1987 or wevans@sacbee.com.

UNIT 5

Measuring the Social Cost of Drugs

Unit Selections

35. **Policing a Rural Plague**, Dirk Johnson
36. **About Face Program Turns Lives Around**, Mary Baldwin Kennedy
37. **Drug-Endangered Children**, Jerry Harris
38. **Fetal Exposure to Drugs**, Tina Hesman
39. **FDA Was Urged to Limit Kids' Antidepressants**, Rob Waters
40. **Date Rape Drugs**, John DePresca

Key Points to Consider

- What role does the media play in influencing drug-related crime?

- Explain why you believe that drug-related crime is either overrepresented or underrepresented.

- Survey your class to determine what percentage have been victims of crime. Determine what percentage of those were victims of drug-related crime.

- Consider the costs of drug-related crime on the criminal justice, health care, and educational systems in your community.

- How is the fear of crime continuing to change the way we live?

 **Links: www.dushkin.com/online/**
These sites are annotated in the World Wide Web pages.

Drug Enforcement Administration
http://www.usdoj.gov/dea/
The November Coalition
http://www.november.org
TRAC DEA Site
http://trac.syr.edu/tracdea/index.html

The most devastating effect of drug use in America is the magnitude with which it affects the way we live. Much of its influence is not measurable. What is the cost of a son or daughter lost, a parent imprisoned, a life lived in a constant state of fear? The emotional costs alone are incomprehensible.

The social legacy of this country's drug crisis could easily be the subject of this entire book. The purpose here, however, can only be a cursory portrayal of drugs' tremendous costs. More than one American president has stated that drug use threatens our national security and personal well-being. The financial costs of maintaining the federal apparatus devoted to drug interdiction, enforcement, and treatment are staggering. Although yearly expenditures vary due to changes in political influence, strategy, and tactics, examples of the tremendous effects of drugs on government and the economy abound. The federal budget for drug control exceeds 12.6 billion dollars and includes again, over 731 million dollars this year for the Andean Counter Drug initiative and 141 million dollars for Colombia alone. The Department of Justice commits over 2.7 billion dollars to antidrug efforts, and the Department of Health and Human Services commits over 3.6 billion dollars. Over 20 million dollars is committed to state and local authorities to clean up toxic methamphetamine labs. Drugs are the business of the criminal justice system. Approximately 80 percent of people behind bars in this country had a problem with drugs or alcohol prior to their arrest. The United States incarcerates more of its citizens than almost any other nation and the financial costs are staggering. Doing drugs and serving time produces an inescapable nexus and it doesn't end with prison. More than 36 percent of adults on parole or supervised release are classified with dependence on or abuse of a substance. Some argue that these numbers represent that Americans have come to rely on the criminal justice system as an unprecedented way of responding to social problems. Regardless of the way one chooses to view various relationships, the resulting picture is numbing.

In addition to the highly visible criminal justice related costs, numerous other institutions are affected. Housing, welfare, education, and health care provide excellent examples of critical institutions struggling to overcome the strain of drug-related impacts. In addition, annual loss of productivity in the workplace exceeds well over a 160 billion dollars per year. Alcoholism, alone, causes 500 million lost workdays each year. Add to this demographic shifts caused by people fleeing drug-impacted neighborhoods, schools, and businesses and one soon realizes that there are no victimless public or private institutions. Last year, 3.5 million Americans (1.5 percent of the population) received some kind of treatment related to the abuse of alcohol or other drugs. The number of persons needing treatment for an illicit drug problem was 7.7 million and the number of persons needing treatment for alcohol abuse was 18.6 million. Add 60,000 infants born each year who suffer from irreversible forms of fetal alcohol syndrome, and no amount of debating, arguing, or denying the specific cause and effect relationships really amounts to much in the face of reality. Add injured, drug-related accident and crime victims, along with demands produced by a growing population of intravenous-drug users infected with AIDS, and a failing health care system frighteningly appears. A universally affordable health care plan capable of addressing drug-related impacts of such vast medical consequences may not be possible. Health care costs from drug-related ills are overwhelming. Drug abuse costs the economy 13 billion dollars in health care costs alone.

It should be emphasized that the social costs exacted by drug use infiltrate every aspect of public and private life. The implications for thousands of families struggling with the adverse effects of drug-related woes may prove the greatest and most tragic of social costs. Children who lack emotional support, self-esteem, role models, a safe and secure environment, economic opportunity, and an education because of a parent on drugs suggest costs difficult to comprehend or measure.

As you read the following articles, consider the costs associated with legal and illegal drugs. However, before joining the debate on which is the greater harbinger of pain and suffering, consider the diversity of impacts to which legal and illegal drugs contribute. Combining pharmacological, environmental, legal, and the multitude of other factors influencing drug-related impacts with cause-and-effect propositions soon produces a quagmire of major proportions. Although it is tempting to generalize while considering and lamenting the impacts of drug use on our society, it seldom produces the most salient observations. An incremental approach to assessing drug-related impacts and costs may produce a greater understanding of how to measure social costs than an attempt to make a case for a combination of impacts generated because of issues such as the legal status of a drug.

Lastly, as you read and think about the different articles in this unit, keep in mind the pervasiveness of drug-related impacts affecting American families. Subsequent reflection reveals that we don't just "change schools," "move to a different town," or flee drug-related issues, and that the most critical component of defense against drug ills—the family—is the most mercilessly pursued target. Most people recognize that the world's most powerful institutions merely buy time in hopes that family institutions will come together, endure, and prevail against drugs.

Policing a Rural Plague

Meth is ravaging the Midwest. Why it's so hard to stop.

By Dirk Johnson

There is trouble on music Mountain Road. In the wooded hills at the edge of Hot Springs, Ark., a red pickup truck and a white SUV pull into a gravel driveway. Out of the vehicles jump six big men, moving like they mean business. One wears camouflage trousers and has a menacing tattoo on his neck: parental advisory. Another has a goatee, his stocking cap pulled low. They are clutching handguns. These are plainclothes detectives on a hunt for poison—methamphetamine.

Rapping on the front door, the cops are invited inside. Looking around, it doesn't take long for them to find telltale signs of a meth lab: household chemicals used to "cook" the drug. They also found three little kids—2, 3 and 5—sitting at a kitchen table eating oatmeal for breakfast. Police slapped the cuffs on Tony Tedeschi, 41, a bedraggled, rail-thin figure of a man with greasy hair and open sores on his arms, a familiar sign of a meth user—"tweakers," the cops call them.

The use of meth is soaring, with no end in sight. In the past year police busted more than 9,300 meth labs nationally, a nearly 500 percent increase since 1996. Meth is making its way to the East Coast, but the problem "has exploded" in the middle of the country, says Rusty Payne, a spokesman for the Drug Enforcement Administration. "Meth is now the No. 1 drug in rural America—absolutely, positively, end of question." In Tennessee, Missouri and

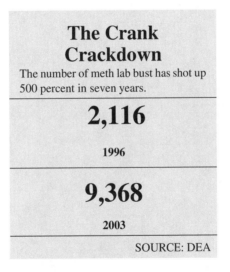

The Crank Crackdown

The number of meth lab bust has shot up 500 percent in seven years.

2,116

1996

9,368

2003

SOURCE: DEA

Arkansas—among the states with the worst problems—meth is overwhelming law-enforcement efforts to combat the homemade drug.

Meth can be smoked, snorted or injected. It produces a high that lasts for days. It also leads to delusions, sleeplessness and extreme paranoia. Once popular among outlaw biker gangs, police say meth nowadays is used by women and men, from teenagers to people in their 70s. Some shift workers sought the drug to keep them awake. Some women tried it for weight loss.

Feeling under siege, people in little towns are growing impatient: why can't the police stop this stuff? "The public is on

our butts, griping, 'You're not doing enough'," says Rick Norris, the coordinator of a drug task force in Garland County, Ark. "And they should gripe." The Garland County unit busted 100 labs last year. With more resources, Norris says, it could have doubled or tripled that number. The unit is spending nearly as much time and money on meth as it spends on every other drug combined.

If everybody knows about meth, why is it so hard to police? First, all the ingredients are legal and easy to find at a drugstore—camp fuel, iodine, drain cleaner and, most important, cold medicine. Remedies like Sudafed contain pseudoephedrine, the active ingredient used to concoct the drug. Big chains, including Wal-Mart and CVS, have enacted policies limiting quantities that can be sold per customer. Makers of meth tend to be mom-and-pop operations simply making enough for personal use, like the old booze stills, so cops can't simply choke off a major supply by targeting a big dealer. Covert operations in rural areas are difficult since everybody knows the cops in small towns. Busts are very time-consuming—typically six to eight hours—since police must wait for hazmat specialists to cart away the chemicals. To make a charge of meth-making stick, cops generally must find a meth lab in operation. "The courts say we've got to catch them red-handed," says Norris. For that reason, police were not able to charge Tedeschi with anything more than possession of drug paraphernalia with the intent to manufacture, a charge that often brings only probation. Tedeschi was taken to the Garland County Detention Center and released on $10,000 bond. He awaits trial.

Making meth can be deadly. Nationally, meth labs caused more than 200 fires and explosions last year, according to the DEA. Back on Music Mountain Road, Det. Cory BeArmon got that point across. "How can you do this with kids around?" he screamed at Tedeschi, the boyfriend of the kids' grandmother. "What if it'd blown up and killed one of them? I'd be here on a murder charge." For a cop waging war on meth, it was just one battle. So many more await.

About Face Program Turns Lives Around

By Mary Baldwin Kennedy

The About Face Program, operated by the Orleans Parish Criminal Sheriff's Office in New Orleans, provides an innovative approach toward helping the region's male inmates learn how to redirect their lives. Sheriff Charles C. Foti Jr. developed the program in 1986 as the nation's first regimented life-changing program operated at the parish/county level. "Although initially intrigued by the boot camp concept, we soon realized that to have a permanent impact on an individual, we would have to provide more than just short-term discipline," he explains. "As the name implies, the About Face Program seeks to turn lives around completely." Today, with more than 500 inmates in its various phases, the About Face Program has become one of the largest jail-based therapeutic communities in the country.

During the past 10 years, the program has changed to better meet the needs of its participants. At its inception, the About Face Program was primarily a boot camp designed to last six months. However, with the addition of a drug treatment component in the early 1990s, the term has been extended to nine to 12 months or longer, depending on the length of an inmate's sentence. Between 1996 and 2002, more than 2,500 inmates completed the program.

Currently, the About Face Program consists of three basic segments, each 12 weeks in length. A new class begins every 45 days. The initial phase operates within a strict boot camp environment that places heavy emphasis on self-discipline, responsibility for one's actions, education and some physical activity. All inmates are tested at entry to determine their educational level, the average of which for both reading and mathematics is fifth grade. Classes are divided into three levels: literacy (below the sixth-grade level), adult basic education or intermediate, and the GED preparation class (above the ninth-grade level). The goal for each inmate is that he attain his GED. While this is not realistic for some, in 2000, one out of every four GEDs earned in New Orleans was by a participant in this jail system. The figures for 2001 are consistent with those of 2000.

The second and third phases of the program operate according to a modified therapeutic community modality of substance abuse treatment. During these phases, individuals learn about addictions of all forms and are encouraged to confront the behaviors that led to their criminal activity. They are taught that alternatives exist and are urged to use these when faced with problematic situations that could lead them back into destructive behaviors. Emphasis on education, self-discipline and some

physical activity continues, and a work skills component is added when inmates approach the end of their sentence. After completion of the body of the program (the first three segments), inmates may first move to the re-entry phase, in which emphasis is on honing skills necessary for successful re-entry into society while maintaining the basic structure of the program. At the end of their incarceration, inmates may be eligible to move to a work tier in which they are taught a skill they can use to attain gainful employment such as various food service jobs, auto mechanics and body repair, horticulture, and electrical and plumbing repair. Inmates, however, must continue to work in their program and attend GED classes, if applicable.

Some of the men housed on the work tier are eligible for enrollment in a program sponsored by a local industrialist that attempts to train inmates about to be released in construction, home building/repair and related carpentry skills. These men go through an intensive training program, both in the classroom and on the job, and are guaranteed job placement in a related field after their release. The participants, with the direction and aid of professionals, have built new homes for low-income families in the New Orleans area. This program, which is supported by a grant from Louisiana, has been recognized as a model for its use of inmate skills in the redevelopment of housing in blighted areas.

Networks have been established in the community to ease offenders' transition back into life outside of the jail setting.

Networks have been established in the community to ease offenders' transition back into life outside of the jail setting. For some inmates with little or no support network, placement in a halfway house is recommended. Graduates are encouraged to return to the nightly group meetings held at the jail to continue their own recovery and give back to the therapeutic community their successes and struggles in remaining drug-free as they re-enter society.

In addition, the About Face Program also provides an aftercare program for its graduates in which they attend weekly drug and/or alcohol treatment meetings with a member of the counseling staff at a facility not affiliated with the jail system. This group has grown dramatically, and it is currently seeking a new home for its meetings as its numbers far exceed the space provided. Finally, the counseling staff welcome calls for assistance from graduates who have been released, and they are eager to provide whatever support is needed. "This long-term approach is what sets the About Face Program apart and makes it successful," Foti says.

Acceptance Process

Admission to the About Face Program begins with a referral. Judges may recommend that an individual be placed in the program at sentencing, inmates may self-refer at any time after conviction, family members or attorneys can request that an individual be evaluated or the jail administration may place an inmate in the program. Inmates are never removed from the program for misbehavior. After admission, there is a strict code of conduct to which inmates must adhere. Failure to comply with the rules in any phase of the program will result in immediate disciplinary action but will not be accepted as a mechanism to allow the inmate to avoid the rigors of the program. Both positive and negative reinforcement, when appropriate, are used to ensure that each individual receives everything the program has to offer. In certain cases, successful completion by offenders sentenced by the court may prompt the judge to re-evaluate and amend their sentence. The parole board also recognizes the value of this training for the inmates who come before it and often bases its decision for early release upon the inmate's successful program completion.

Upon referral, potential participants must meet certain screening criteria, the most important of which is a review of their criminal record for violent offenses. Charges or convictions for arson, kidnapping, armed robbery (more than one charge), sex offenses of any kind, homicide, escape, crimes against juveniles or any other charge that places the individual in a high-security category make applicants ineligible. In addition, applicants cannot have any out-of-parish or out-of-state warrants, or open state charges.

Most participants enter the program shortly after they are sentenced. Sentence length should allow for completion of the three main phases of the program, but not be so long that inmates grow frustrated with the daily routine of meetings and group sessions. However, individual attention is given by counseling staff to individuals who will be released from jail prior to the end of the third phase, but who actively seek the help. Inmates will stay in the About Face Program until they are released from custody, as a return to general population could cause them to revert and lose the focus developed during the course of their participation.

Following a criminal history review, potential participants are screened for any medical conditions that might preclude their being able to successfully complete the physical aspects of the program. An effort will be made by program staff to work with individuals who have limitations, but who are motivated and willing to make the effort necessary for completion. The primary focus of this program is in behavior modification for the individuals, not their physical fitness.

There are no age restrictions in the About Face Program, and it is the staff's belief that a cross-section of ages and backgrounds is preferable because it better-replicates free society. One About Face cohort of note had a 16-year-old (the age of majority in Louisiana is 17) who had been "waived up" and tried as an adult, as well as a 63-year-old. When young and old inmates go through the process together, they are generally better-equipped to deal with age-related issues after their release.

Core Curriculum

There is a strict code of discipline as well as many demands—mental, physical, intellectual and spiritual—made on the participants. After graduation from the boot camp phase, inmates move into the first of two drug treatment phases. Although some inmates have never used drugs or alcohol, they are addicted to the money that the sale of these substances provides; this addiction is just as powerful. In the first phase, the orientation, inmates learn to live in a therapeutic community setting and accept the responsibility placed on them for "their brothers'" recovery, as well as their own. The group, now known as the "family," moves through the program as a unit, much like the cohort effect seen in educational systems. There is a special language composed of terms such as learning experience, push up and pull up, which is used during group meetings and during the course of daily living in the therapeutic community. This modality emphasizes that the "family" must adopt a new set of standards to live by 24 hours a day, not just during group meetings. Using the tenets of Alcoholics Anonymous, Narcotics Anonymous and Cocaine Anonymous, intensive work is conducted on the effects of drug and alcohol use on the body, mind, spirit and community.

After completion of this phase, inmates move to the second drug treatment phase—main treatment—in which they work on their own personal addictions using the 12 steps of AA as their guide. All participants are required to change and to grow. Some, however, will be reluctant to take the risks and face the rigorous discipline and self-examination essential to this process—they will require more time and attention. Graduation from one phase to the next is not guaranteed, but must be earned based on successful completion of core curriculum in that phase.

While there is no structured input from the inmates' friends and families, they are encouraged to be supportive of the inmates' progress and be sympathetic to the pain they must endure to address their particular problems and situations and to make an honest commitment to change. The inmates are told that to be successful, they must change "their people, places and things"; families and other members of their support group have to work with them to make this possible.

In 2001, a female component was added that attempts to mirror the basic concepts of the male program. Because females represent less than 10 percent of the inmate population (rated capacity of 7,250 inmates), the actual structure of the female program had to be modified. Emphasis is placed on parenting and family management skills, preparation for work training, GED education, self-discipline, behavior modification and drug education/treatment. Group and individual counseling replaces the therapeutic community approach employed with the men.

Summary

With more than 500 inmates in the various phases, the About Face Program has become one of the largest jail-based therapeutic communities in the country. Its success can be attributed to the sheriff's foresight and his eagerness to have this program grow with the needs of his department and the community as a whole.

Last summer, a graduate of the program called and left the following message: "This is H. C. I was an inmate in the About Face Program about a year ago.... I was in the boot camp program. I want to thank you for allowing me to enter your program. It has changed my life a lot and I'm doing just fine. Tell Mr. M and the counselors that I say thank you.... God bless you and have a nice day, and remember—one day at a time. Peace."

In the 17 years since its inception, more than 2,500 men and 11 women have completed the About Face Program. It has shown them that they have options and choices in the lifestyles they choose. Some of them avail themselves of the options they have been shown in the About Face Program and many are successful in turning their lives around. A formal study of the program's recidivism rate is difficult due to problems with developing a control group to compare with its graduates. However, an informal study completed in the late 1990s showed that less than 10 percent of the program's participants returned to jail within the first six months after their release. For more information about this program, contact the Orleans Parish Criminal Sheriff's Office, 2800 Gravier St., New Orleans, LA 70119; (504) 827-8501; or visit www.opcso.org.

Mary Baldwin Kennedy is director of the About Face Program at the Orleans Parish Criminal Sheriff's Office in New Orleans.

From *Corrections Today*, April 2003, pp. 78, 80-81. © 2003 by the American Correctional Association, Lanham, MD. Reprinted by permission.

DRUG-ENDANGERED CHILDREN

By Jerry Harris, M.S.

The number of children in the United States exposed to the inherently hazardous processes used in the illicit manufacture of the controlled dangerous substance methamphetamine or meth has more than doubled in the past few years. Unfortunately, despite law enforcement efforts, these numbers continue to rise.

Just as alarming is the number of children negatively impacted by physical and emotional abuse, as well as neglect, by parents, guardians, or other adults who expose them to toxic meth lab operations, firearms, pornographic material, criminals and their unlawful activity, and domestic violence, just to name a few of the dangers. Methamphetamine abuse and production have become major factors in the increase of child abuse and neglect cases handled by the child welfare system.

THE GROWING MENACE

Estimates have indicated that children are found in approximately one-third of all seized meth labs. Of those children, about 35 percent test positive for toxic levels of chemicals in their bodies. In other areas, those numbers have proven even higher. More alarming, however, is the possibility that 90 percent of all meth labs go undetected, leaving many children to suffer needlessly.[1]

Although statistics are limited at present, an abundance of anecdotal evidence exists about the enormous physical, developmental, emotional, and psychosocial damage suffered by children exposed to illegal home-based drug production. The evidence comes from professionals in the fields of law enforcement, human services, medicine, education, and others who have first-hand experience with children living in homes where methamphetamine is illegally manufactured.

Children who inhabit homes where parents, guardians, or other adults undertake the illegal manufacturing of methamphetamine risk multiple exposures to many different chemicals and combinations of chemicals and their byproducts. They further risk toxic poisoning from the inhalation of chemical gases and vapors that damage their respiratory and circulatory systems; chemical bums; and the ingestion, absorption, or injection of drugs or chemicals. Such children also face the peril of injury or death from fires or explosions.

Often, these children live in poor conditions. Homes that house labs frequently are dirty, sometimes lacking water, heat, and electricity. The children typically have little to eat and do not receive adequate medical care, including immunizations, and dental services. The mothers rarely seek prenatal care for some of the same exposures. This constitutes not only child endangerment but, even worse, child abuse.

Exposure to these dangerous substances can cause serious short- and long-term health problems, including damage to the brain, liver, kidneys, lungs, eyes, and skin. The chaotic lifestyle of individuals involved in methamphetamine manufacturing and use places children at risk for physical and emotional trauma. To compound the problem, neglect or inconsistent parenting can interfere with children's cognitive, emotional, and social development. The children become exposed to drug-related violence and physical and sexual abuse at the hands of family members, neighbors, and an array of strangers who pass through the house to buy or sell drugs.

> " **The children found at these meth lab sites have suffered greatly and been denied access to social and health-related services.** "

Relatively few states have programs in place to deal with the problems associated with the manufacture of methamphetamine, especially when it comes to the children caught up in this illegal activity. The social and legal aspects of these types of cases are enormous. The parents, more often than not, have been getting away with the abuse and neglect of their children for along time. The children found at these meth lab sites have suffered greatly and been denied access to social and health-related services. What can be done to protect these drug-endangered children?

OKLAHOMA'S RESPONSE

In Oklahoma, a program began operating ad hoc after months of preparation and training. Meetings involved representatives from social, medical, law enforcement, and criminal justice agencies. These professionals saw the need and, thus, conjointly formed a state drug-endangered children (DEC) effort that, so far, has attempted to mirror the DEC program in California.[2]

The goal of the DEC effort is to intervene on behalf of children found living in horrific conditions produced by the unlawful and dangerous clandestine methamphetamine manufacturing processes and the environment associated with addiction. A further goal involves creating a collaborative multidisciplinary community response to identify and meet the short- and long-term needs of the children endangered by this exposure.

To accomplish this goal, the DEC program steering committee was set up to offer assistance to the multidisciplinary child abuse and neglect teams (CAN) that Oklahoma has mandated every county to establish. Currently, there are 50 functional teams, with more forming. The CAN teams, comprised of law enforcement officers, child protective service workers, mental health employees, medical personnel, prosecutors, and other professionals, address problems of child abuse and neglect and currently are the best suited to respond to the needs of drug-endangered children. Many teams, who have been called upon to do so, have worked in concert with other professionals to see that these children receive the kind of short- and long-term care needed and, when appropriate, ensure that the violators are prosecuted for child endangerment.

Only by working collaboratively can these professionals succeed in their endeavors. They must work toward a "win-win" situation in the best interest of the children. First responders must recognize that intervention on behalf of these children is of the utmost importance. This intervention, however, must take place without creating additional trauma to the children. Law enforcement officers take the children into protective custody, move them to a safe location, and attend to their immediate needs. Child protective services (CPS) personnel arrive on the scene as soon as possible to help the officers assess the needs of the children. Emergency medical technicians (EMTs), firefighters, and hazardous material professionals also stand by if needed.

Such coordinated efforts prove invaluable to the well-being of the children and must be worked out in advance and included in the operational protocols of the CAN team. For example, because removal of clothes and decontamination procedures according to federal instructions are certain to cause an increased sense of vulnerability and trauma to all but the smallest infants, this only should occur prior to CPS arrival in the most pressing and urgent circumstances.

The children should be transported to the appropriate medical screening facility for further evaluation as soon as possible after the intervention. If grossly contaminated children are discovered, they should be examined on the scene by trained EMTs. The children then should be transported by ambulance just in case complications arise en route. EMTs also should consider that they are traveling in a confined space and should allow for ventilation.

> **"**
> **Exposure to these dangerous substances can cause serious short- and long-term health problems....**
> **"**

Determining which member of the team should transport the children proves crucial to the CAN team's effectiveness. In the best interest of the children, team members must agree on the most appropriate method of transporting them. In some cases, a CPS worker may be the best choice. CAN members must consider the children's ages, as well as the safety of the person providing the transportation. While officers must maintain control of the situation, they may encounter difficulties in transporting the children to a medical screening facility out of their jurisdiction. The number of officers on duty may dictate whether they can leave their jurisdiction for that purpose. When officers provide the transportation, they cannot remain with the children at the medical screening facility for any length of time, no matter how much they would wish to, because they must return to their official duties. Similarly, the CAN team also must coordinate transportation to the receiving facility. The vast majority of the children taken into protective custody are eventually placed with relatives. While the remainder are sent to shelters.

Having a standing court order from the jurisdictional judge when children are found in meth labs expedites assuming temporary custody for the CPS worker. A standing court order regarding toxicology testing also helps in testing for ingested or assimilated chemicals and drugs. Based on the results of a urinalysis test, a blood test may be warranted and in the best interest of the children's health in terms of follow-up care. Although it is strongly recommended that children's urine/blood be obtained if possible within 2 hours as part of evidence collection, this is not absolutely necessary to conduct a thorough DEC investigation or prosecution. While the presence of toxins in the child's urine or blood will support child abuse charges, it is most important as a possible indicator of other chemical exposures and for identifying and treating any adverse health effects.[3]

CONCLUSION

Based on the California Drug-Endangered Children Program and what Oklahoma authorities have seen thus far, an effective comprehensive response to the needs of children endangered by the epidemic of methamphetamine use and production, as well as all substance abuse, must include prevention, intervention, enforcement, interdiction, and treatment. Multidisciplinary collaboration is key to ensuring that this comprehensive range of responses is activated.

In the state of Oklahoma, social, medical, law enforcement, and criminal justice agencies began working together to address this escalating problem. The team approach has become a valuable model of intervention for children and families endangered by the devastating intergenerational cycle, of alcohol and drug abuse of all kinds.

Participating agencies and elected representatives support this type of program. No better reason exists for this than the safety and health of innocent children. No one must add to the trauma and suffering these children have endured, and, more important, no one must fail to respond to their needs.

ENDNOTES

1. The author based these estimates on various reports that he has reviewed and on his personal experience as a narcotics agent for nearly 25 years.
2. For information on the California program, see Tom Manning, "Drug Labs and Endangered Children," *FBI Law Enforcement Bulletin*, July 1999, 10–14.
3. The state of California has established models of multidisciplinary protocols for intervening on behalf of children found in home-based meth labs. Their medical protocols for screening drug-endangered children will give medical professionals a starting point. While many physicians may find these protocols acceptable, most medical screening facilities will want to establish their own medical protocols. Medical professionals in any state should approach this situation with great care and establish medical protocols in the best interest of the child.

Agent Harris heads the Training and Education Section at the headquarters of the Oklahoma Bureau of Narcotics and Dangerous Drugs Control in Oklahoma City.

From *FBI Law Enforcement Bulletin*, February 2004, pp. 8-11, by Jerry Harris. Published in 2004 by the Federal Bureau of Investigation.

Fetal exposure to drugs, alcohol linked to later mental illness

Tina Hesman

SEATTLE—Prenatal exposure to alcohol, club drugs and environmental toxins, such as lead, may kill fetal brain cells and cause mental health problems, including schizophrenia, later in life, say researchers from Washington University and elsewhere.

Among the research results presented in a news conference Friday at the annual meeting of the American Association for the Advancement of Science, brain scientists found that: As few as two cocktails may kill fetal brain cells.

Women with high levels of delta-ALA, an indicator of lead exposure, in their blood were twice as likely to have a child with schizophrenia, as women with low levels of the substance.

An estimated 1 in 100 live births is affected by exposure to alcohol.

"We've known for 30 years that alcohol can have deleterious effects on the developing fetal nervous system. And for 30 years we've been trying to understand why," said Dr. John W. Olney, a neuroscientist at Washington University.

In humans, the brain goes through a growth spurt that starts toward the end of the second trimester of pregnancy and continues through the first three years of life.

During the growth spurt, new brain cells are added, connections form and dissolve between the brain cells, and some unnecessary cells are killed off.

Olney's research with infant mice indicates that brain cells called neurons are particularly vulnerable to committing suicide during the brain's growth spurt. Alcohol and drugs, such as anesthesia or anti-convulsants, interfere with neurotransmitters, including glutamate, which excites brain cells, and GABA, a brain chemical that inhibits neuron activity, Olney said. When those brain chemicals can't do their jobs, developing neurons shut down and die.

Olney and his colleagues have discovered that low levels of alcohol can accelerate brain cell suicide to two to four times the normal rate. A blood alcohol level of 0.07 percent—just below the legal intoxication limit—sustained for half an hour to an hour is enough to cause the brain damage. That blood alcohol level is about the equivalent of two cocktails, Olney said. The damage first appears in an area involved in controlling movement called the caudate nucleus, and in the cerebral cortex, the brain's "central intelligence agency," within four hours of alcohol exposure, Olney said.

Club drugs, such as the anesthetic ketamine—known as Special K—also can cause brain damage in developing fetuses, Olney said. Most people who use such drugs combine them with alcohol. The mixture is a recipe for brain cell suicide.

The brain damage caused by alcohol is not always readily apparent, said Ann P. Streissguth of the University of Washington. New brain imaging techniques may help researchers identify people who have damage associated with alcohol exposure in the womb, she said.

A study of 415 patients who had been diagnosed with fetal alcohol syndrome or fetal alcohol effects indicates that early brain damage can cause problems later in life.

More than 90 percent of the children, adolescents and adults in the study have mental health problems, Streissguth said. The problems range from attention deficit disorders in 60 percent of the children and adolescents, depression in 40 percent to 50 percent of the teenagers and adults, and psychotic behavior in about 30 percent of the adults. About 25 percent of adults with fetal alcohol problems had attempted suicide. And only 11 of the 90 adults in the study were able to live and work independently, Streissguth said.

The problems can extend into the next generation as well, she said

More than half of the 44 adults in the study who had become parents are no longer caring for their own children. Child protective services took children away from 36 percent of the mothers, and 45 percent of the fathers had given up raising their children, Streissguth said.

Alcohol and drugs are not the only substances that could damage the fetal brain and lead to lifelong mental problems.

A study by Columbia University epidemiologist Ezra S. Susser suggests that exposure to lead during pregnancy also may cause fetal brains to commit cell suicide and may be linked to the development of schizophrenia later in life. If the results of the study hold true when repeated, it would be the first time an environmental toxin has been linked to the mental illness, Susser said. The study will appear in the journal Environmental Health Perspectives.

FDA was urged to limit kids' antidepressants

Advice citing risk of suicide rejected

By Rob Waters

A medical reviewer at the Food and Drug Administration recommended earlier this year that the agency adopt a tough "risk management strategy" urging doctors to stop prescribing most antidepressants to children, but the FDA rejected his advice and instead asked drug companies only to warn patients and doctors about possible risks to young patients, The Chronicle has learned.

Dr. Andrew Mosholder, an epidemiologist in the FDA's Office of Drug Safety, analyzed 22 clinical trials of nine antidepressants and concluded that the drugs appeared to double the risk of suicidal behavior among children. A copy of his report, obtained by The Chronicle, shows that Mosholder recommended that the FDA adopt a "risk management strategy directed at discouraging off-label pediatric use of antidepressants" other than Prozac in the treatment of children with depression.

As reported by The Chronicle at the time, Mosholder's presentation to an FDA advisory committee in February was removed from the agenda by his superiors at the agency.

The FDA opted not to issue a recommendation to doctors that they stop prescribing the drugs to children, as British regulators did last year and as Mosholder had urged. Instead, the agency took a much milder step last month and called on drug companies to include warnings in the prescribing information provided to doctors about the risks of negative side effects among patients who start taking a drug or increase its dosage.

The agency also contracted with a group of doctors at Columbia University to reanalyze the clinical trial data provided by drug companies, the same data Mosholder reviewed, to see whether suicidal events were correctly classified. Agency officials have argued that the data from those trials are sometimes vague and that some behaviors—such as a child slapping herself in the head—may have been labeled wrongly as suicidal events by researchers conducting the drug company-funded studies.

Committees in both the House and Senate have opened investigations into the withholding of Mosholder's report and into efforts by the FDA's Office of Internal Affairs to identify the staff members who leaked information to The Chronicle.

> "There's no way to put a good face on this decision not to allow Dr. Mosholder to present his conclusions to the advisory committee."
>
> *a congressional source*

One congressional source predicted that the investigation was likely to trigger congressional hearings. "I think eventually there will be some hearings," the source said. "There's no way to put a good face on this decision not to allow Dr. Mosholder to present his conclusions to the advisory committee."

Despite repeated requests, senior FDA officials declined to comment for this story.

However, in a letter sent Wednesday to House Energy and Commerce Committee Chairman Joe Barton, R-Texas, an agency representative defended the agency's decision to keep Mosholder from presenting his report. Agency officials "decided that having Dr. Mosholder present his conclusion to the Advisory Committee, with the appearance that it was an agency determination, would be potentially harmful to public health as it might lead patients who were actually benefiting from the use of these drugs to inappropriately discontinue therapy," wrote Amit Sachdev, acting associate commissioner for legislation.

Critics of the FDA's handling of the antidepressant ruling reacted to details of the Mosholder report with outrage. "It's astounding that FDA officials actively blocked vital, possibly life-saving information about the suicide risks to children" of these drugs, said Vera Sharav, president of the Alliance for Human Research Protection, an advocacy group. "Every day that doctors and parents are not informed about the risks, children are at risk of dying."

In arguing that the agency should take strong action rather than wait for the reanalysis by the Columbia University group, Mosholder made much the same point in his report.

"Given the strength of the association shown by the present data, the clinical importance of the apparent effect, and the fact that the additional analyses are likely to take several more months to complete while considerable numbers of pediatric patients are being exposed to these drugs, I favor an interim risk management plan," he wrote.

Mosholder's report found that 74 children out of 2,298 who took antidepressants engaged in a "suicide-related event," compared to 34 of the 1,952 patients who took placebos, or fake pills. The drugs presenting the highest risk were Effexor and Paxil, which nearly tripled the risk of a suicidal event, and Zoloft, which more than doubled the risk, his research showed.

Prozac, which is now available in generic form, had the lowest risk among the major drugs, and is the only new-generation antidepressant specifically approved by the FDA for treating depressed children. For that reason, Mosholder recommended that Prozac alone continue to be prescribed to children.

But since drugs that have been cleared by the FDA for treatment of adults can be prescribed "off label" to children, other drugs—including Paxil, Zoloft, Effexor, Luvox, Remeron, Celexa, Serzone and Wellbutrin—are widely prescribed for children and teenagers. The FDA estimates that nearly 11 million antidepressant prescriptions were written for children in 2002, 2.7 million of them for children under 12.

Joseph Glenmullen, a clinical instructor in psychiatry at Harvard University, said the agency's withholding of the Mosholder report and its failure to take stronger action was an example of the FDA's failure to protect the public from the dangerous side effects of antidepressants.

"They have mishandled this issue for 15 years," he said. "They have not adequately protected American children."

Date Rape Drugs

John DePresca

Roofies, saltwater and Special K are not the ingredients to make a low fat, diet breakfast or the name of the next heavy metal band coming to town. They are terms you may very well hear when investigating your next sexual assault case. Because a rapist may not be able to take delight in a normal relationship, he uses these sinister tools to accomplish his goals.

Sometimes crime is easy to solve. Videotapes, latent prints, eyewitness accounts and good descriptions of a suspect all make the investigator's job, at times, not so difficult. However, there are those cases that will drive us to use every deductive fiber, training, skill and even luck to successfully bring a case to the prosecutor. How about a case where the victim tells you she knows a crime has been committed against her but can't tell you who did it, where it happened, when in happened, how it happened or why it happened? Every investigator will be called to task when looking into a date rape drug. Rapists now have in their lurid arsenal more than a couple of methods to render their victims helpless.

Rohypnol

This is the oldest drug used in this crime. It is the brand name for flunitrazepam. It is up to 10 times more powerful than valium and halcion and produces a slowing of physical and mental responses, muscle reflexes and amnesia in about 15 minutes. Rohypnol (pronounced ro-hip-nol) is manufactured by Hoffman-LaRoche pharmaceutical company and looks a lot like aspirin. When dropped in a drink, usually an alcoholic beverage, it is colorless and odorless. The drug usually takes full effect on the victim within 30 minutes to one hour of ingestion.

The initial effects on the victim may include confusion, a light-headed feeling or disorientation and have similar actions as one who is intoxicated by alcohol. As the drug progresses through the bloodstream, a feeling of lowered values and a loss of inhibitions occurs and eventually the victim is physically unable to resist the sexual attack.

Some victims may describe an almost "out of body experience" where they are aware of being undressed and assaulted but are not able to react. They may wake up in eight to 12 hours and only have minimum, if any, recall as

to what has taken place. If a high dosage is given, this blackout time can increase to 24 hours.

Rohypnol is not legally produced or dispensed anywhere in the United States. It is, however, legally used by doctors in almost 70 countries across South America, Latin America and Europe. In those countries it is administered in surgery where the patient may have to respond or cooperate during the procedure. In Mexico, one tablet can be bought for about 40 cents and sold here from anywhere between two and six dollars on the black market, thus making it a relatively affordable drug.

A simple and straightforward method of smuggling it into this country is wrapping it as a package and mailing it through the postal service or an overnight delivery service. Individuals, of course, transport it across borders by hiding it in their luggage or on their bodies.

One of the more popular street names for Rohpynol is "roofies." This term may have evolved after the devastating hurricane Andrew struck the southern part of Florida in 1992 and the drug was brought to the area by roofing workers. Other terms include: rope, R-2, rib, Roach-2 and Mexican valium. It is normally a white or off-white tablet about the size of an aspirin and has a cross or single-lined hash mark on one side and the word "Roche" with the number 1 or 2 on the other side. (Hence, the street term "Roach-2.")

Older tablets were produced in a 2 mg. dosage but now are produced in only 1 mg. The manufacturer, Hoffman-LaRoche, has gotten an enormous amount of negative press over the years and has tried to clean up its image by developing the drug so it will change colors when introduced in a liquid. This new variety of tablet will turn the liquid a bluish color in about 15 minutes. This may provide help to a potential victim who is drinking a clear drink in good lighting but may do little for one who is consuming a dark colored drink in a dimly lit nightclub.

Since they are packaged in clear blister or bubble packs, their looks may give an appearance of being legitimate. In their continued effort to reduce the illegal abuse of the drug, Hoffman-LaRoche has an information service to law enforcement and the public. The number is (800) 720-1076 or (800) 608-6540.

Gamma Hydroxy Butyrate

This date rape drug is strong, with potential deadly consequences. Grievous Bodily Harm, Liquid X, Saltwater and Easy Lay are some of the terms heard on the street. In the 1980s, GHB was actually available at health food and drug stores and advertised as a steroid that would enhance muscle tone and strength, and could be purchased without prescription.

In 1990, after a flood of overdoses and serious health problems, it was removed from the shelves. Now it is primarily made in home laboratories by people who have trouble controlling dosage and potency. If prepared in a non-controlled environment, such as a garage or a basement, the resulting mixture can have the same effects as lye, which is used in paint removal.

The most popular form of GHB will be a clear liquid. It is colorless and odorless and can easily be slipped into the drink of an unsuspecting victim. In rare instances it has been found as a white powder. Some victims have reported it had a mild salty taste. One of the reactions to this drug is a reduced respiratory capacity. Simply put, the body may forget to breathe. This symptom is greatly enhanced when the dosage is too strong for the victim's body weight and the drug is mixed with alcohol. Additionally, the drug produces a very thin line between intoxication (which the rapist wants the victim to feel) and coma.

One of the main reasons the drug is used prior to a sexual assault is its capacity to diminish memory. This amnesia effect is very powerful, allowing the victim to remember almost nothing about the assault. They may recall starting to feel euphoric, an increased feeling of sexual excitement, and then passing out. Although the coma effect of the drug lasts about three to four hours the intensity of the blackout is much more severe than Rohypnol. This coupled with the difficulty in breathing and the reduced heartbeat can very well lead to being fatal.

Because GHB is usually a clear liquid, it is carried and dispensed in seemingly innocent containers. In a bar or club situation the rapist may put a small plastic bottle of what appears to be eye drops or nasal spray on the bar or table. He may explain that the smoke in the room is bothering his sinuses but when the victim is distracted or momentarily leaves, he squirts the drug in her drink. An eye dropper filled with GHB, if carefully carried in a pocket, can be produced when the victim is not paying attention, and very quickly placed in a drink. Caps on plastic water bottles can be made to look as though they have never been opened and offered with the drug already in the water.

Officers responding to a call involving an incoherent or unconscious person, especially a female who appears to have been sexually assaulted, should seek medical attention for the victim immediately and advise the health care professionals of the possibility of GHB involvement.

Ketamine

A newer form of date rape drugs is called Ketamine (pronounced key-ta-mean). This drug was introduced in the early 1960s and its use helped many U.S. soldiers and Marines who were injured in battle during the Vietnam war. Its quick anesthetic effect also relieved the pain while the troops were being transported to a field hospital. Because of its difficulty to produce it does not lend itself to being manufactured in home laboratories.

It is formulated by the Parke-Davis drug corporation and has a legitimate use in the medical and veterinary profession. On occasion, doctors may use the drug to lessen the pain involved in changing dressings on burn victims and veterinarians use the drug when performing surgery on small domestic animals.

It is produced in a liquid form under the brand name of Ketajet, Ketaset or Ketelar, but its illegal use is usually seen as a white powder; however, the liquid form can be injected or placed in a beverage with a syringe. Some rapists inject the liquid into cigarettes and, when dried, the cigarette is offered to the potential victim.

Intentional users of the drug normally "snort" the powder and carry it in clear plastic bags, similar to heroin or cocaine. As Rohypnol is associated with valium, Ketamine is a cousin to PCP. It initially produces a hypnotic feeling but a larger dose can cause severe hallucinations, difficulty breathing, heart attack and, in extreme doses, it can be fatal.

The most common street name for Ketamine is "Special K" or "Vitamin K" and a single dose is called a "bump." Regional names have also emerged. In the Houston, TX, area it is called "Jet" and in southern California it may be referred to as "L.A. Coke." Like the other date rape drugs, Ketamine is used on the victim because of its effect on memory.

The initial "high" finally gives way to amnesia and the victim is unable to give details of the crime. Although the amnesia may last only one to two hours, as opposed to Rohypnol or GHB which last longer, the additional side effect with Ketamine is that flashbacks can occur up to two weeks after the encounter.

A major source of the drug is through burglaries of veterinary hospitals. Many vets have reported that the only item stolen in the burglary were injectable bottles of Ketamine. Dr. Wayne Kyle, DVM, a Texas veterinarian, added, "There is no situation where a veterinarian will give Ketamine to a pet owner for home treatment of the animal. It is only used in surgery and under strict supervision of the veterinarian." If you find a person with a bottle of this drug in his possession, do not believe he was giving it to his sick pet iguana.

In any case involving date rape drugs, the investigator will have to face a situation where the victim may not be able to give much information about the crime. In order to convince a prosecutor to present a case of this type, and a jury to convict, it will be necessary to dig for any type of evidence to connect the suspect, if any, with the victim. All the practices involved in investigating any sexual assault must be in place with the addition of informing emergency medical technicians and emergency room personnel that a date rape drug is suspected.

Ask for blood and urine tests that may show the presence of a specific date rape drug.

Obviously, the quicker the tests are conducted the better chance for detection. Rohypnol may be found in urine for up to 72 hours. Ketamine may be detected up to 24 hours while GHB traces may be lost in as soon as eight to 24 hours.

Along with the victim's clothes being tested, a "rape kit" test should be conducted at the hospital to detect the presence of semen, foreign pubic hairs and signs of forced penetration. If at all possible, try to recover the glass, cup or container, and the beverage in which the drug may have been dissolved. In the case of Rohypnol or Ketamine the drug manufacturer may also be consulted.

As in any crime prevention program, public awareness is vital. A department representative may ask to be invited to address a women's or civic group, or a high school or college. Participants may then be advised on how to reduce the possibility of becoming victims. Going to clubs with at least one other person she trusts can make it possible for a friend to watch the other's drink when she leaves the table to dance or use the restroom.

Also, she should avoid drinking anything from a common container, such as a punch bowl, unless she knows the person who prepared the beverage and the person giving it to her. In a bar setting, some rapists have paid a bartender to put the drug in a drink after the rapist strikes up a conversation with the victim and offers to buy her a drink. People should be advised to discard any beverage they have been given if it has an off-color or salty taste and, if offered a beverage that has a sealed cap, make sure they hear the sound of the breaking seal.

In the vast majority of these cases, the officer will encounter this type of crime where the victim is a female and the suspect is a male. Do not, however, think this will be the relationship in every case. Many agencies are reporting date rape drug crimes in the homosexual community are on the rise.

John DePresca is a former New York City officer and retired chief deputy with the Panola County, TX, Sheriff's Department. He may be reached at johndp@shreve.net.

From *LAW and ORDER* Magazine, Vol. 51, No. 10, October 2003, pp. 210. Copyright © 2003 by Hendon Publishing Co. Reprinted with permission. www.lawandordermag.com

UNIT 6

Creating and Sustaining Effective Drug Control Policy

Unit Selections

41. **Queen Victoria's Cannabis Use: Or, How History Does and Does Not Get Used in Drug Policy Making**, Virginia Berridge
42. **Social Consequences of the War on Drugs: The Legacy of Failed Policy**, Eric L. Jensen, Jurg Gerber, and Clayton Mosher
43. **How to Win the Drug War**, James Gray
44. **Tokin' Politics: Making Marijuana Law Reform An Election Issue**, Paul Armentano
45. **Drug Legalization**, Douglas Husak
46. **On the Decriminalization of Drugs**, George Sher
47. **Against the Legalization of Heroin**, Peter De Marneffe
48. **U.S., Canada Clash on Pot Laws**, Donna Leinwand

Key Points to Consider

- What do you believe to be the greatest drug-related threat facing our nation? Explain.

- How do drug-related threats and impacts differ from city to city and state to state? Why?

- It is often argued that Americans overreact and overemphasize the harm from illegal drugs while ignoring or underrepresenting the harm from legal drugs, namely alcohol and nicotine. Do you agree or disagree with this argument, and why?

- Has there been a significant shift in public concern over the abuse of legal drugs? Support your answer.

- Explain whether or not the harmful impacts from the abuse of drugs are greater today than they were a decade ago.

 **Links: www.dushkin.com/online/**
These sites are annotated in the World Wide Web pages.

DrugText
http://www.drugtext.org
The National Organization on Fetal Alcohol Syndrome (NOFAS)
http://www.nofas.org
National NORML Homepage
http://www.norml.org/

The drug problem consistently competes with all major public policy issues, including the economy, education, and foreign policy. Formulating and implementing effective drug control policy is a troublesome task. Some would argue that the consequences of policy failures have been worse than the problems they were attempting to address. Others would argue that although the world of shaping drug policy is an imperfect one, the process has worked generally as well as could be expected. Although the majority of Americans believe that failures and breakdowns in the fight against drug abuse have occurred in spite of various drug policies, not because of them, there is ever-increasing public pressure to rethink the get-tough, stay-tough enforcement-oriented ideas of the last two decades.

Policy formulation is not a process of aimless wandering. Various levels of government have responsibility for responding to problems of drug abuse. At the center of most policy debate is the premise that the manufacture, possession, use, and distribution of psychoactive drugs without government authorization is illegal. The federal posture of prohibition is an important emphasis on state and local policy making. Federal drug policy is, however, significantly linked to state-by-state data which suggest that illicit drug, alcohol, and tobacco use vary substantially among states and regions. Current federal drug policy continues to emphasize the reduction of drug use by 25 percent over five years. Core priorities of the overall plan are to stop drug use before it starts, heal America's drug users, and disrupt the illegal market. These three, core goals are re-enforced by specific objectives outlined in a policy statement produced by the White House Office of Drug Control Policy.

One exception to prevailing public views that generally support drug prohibition is the softening of attitudes regarding criminal sanctions historically applied to cases of simple possession and use of drugs. There is much public consensus that criminalizing use and addiction that is not related to other criminal misconduct is unjustified. The federal funding of drug court programs increased significantly to 70 million dollars in 2005. Drug courts provide alternatives to incarceration by using the coercive power of the court to force abstinence and alter behavior through a process of escalating sanctions, mandatory drug testing, and out-patient programs. One message delivered by drug courts to offenders is simple, successful rehabilitation accompanies the re-entry to society as a citizen, not a felon. The drug court program exists as one important example of policy directed at treating users and deterring them from further involvement in the criminal justice system.

The majority of Americans express the view that legalizing, and in some cases even decriminalizing, dangerous drugs is a bad idea. The fear of increased crime, increased drug use, and the potential threat to children are the most often stated reasons. Citing the devastating consequences of alcohol and tobacco use, most Americans question society's ability to use any addictive, mind-altering drug responsibly. Currently, the public favors both supply reduction, demand reduction, and an increased emphasis on prevention, treatment, and rehabilitation as effective strategies in combating the drug problem. Shaping public policy is a critical function that greatly relies upon public input. The policy making apparatus is influenced by public opinion, and public opinion is in turn influenced by public policy. When the president refers to drugs as threats to national security, the impact on public opinion is tremendous.

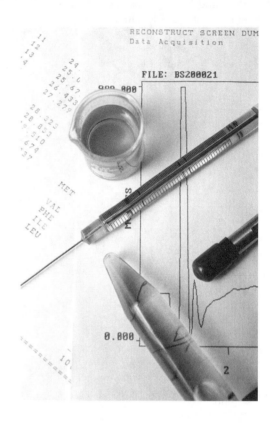

Although the prevailing characteristic of most current drug policy still reflects a punitive, "get tough" approach to control, an added emphasis on treating and rehabilitating offenders is visible in policy changes occurring over the past 10 years. Correctional systems are reflecting with greater consistency the view that drug treatment made available to inmates is a critical component of rehabilitation. A drug-abusing prisoner, initially committed to the prison system for drug offenses, who receives no drug treatment while in custody, is a virtual guarantee to reoffend. Nevertheless, the degree to which Americans are willing to support and sustain a less enforcement-oriented response to drug policy questions remains to be seen. There is concern that even with a shift in policy toward education, prevention, and treatment, an intense, enforcement-oriented perspective will continue to focus on the nation's poor, inner-urban, largely minority subpopulations.

Another complicated aspect of creating national as well as local drug policy is consideration of the growing body of research on the subject. The past twenty years have produced numerous public and private investigations, surveys, and conclusions relative to the dynamic of drug use in American society. Most literature reflects, however, an indirect influence of research on large-scale policy decisions. There is a saying that "policy makers use research like a drunk uses a lamppost—for support, rather than illumination." One exception to the continued enforcement-oriented nature of federal policy is the consistently increasing commitment to treatment. This commitment comes as a direct result of research related to progress achieved in treating and rehabilitating users. Treatment, in terms of dollars spent, can compete with all other components of drug control policy. Over 40 percent of the current federal budget is dedicated to drug education, prevention, research, and treatment—an unprecedented amount.

Further complicating the research/policy making relationship is that the policy making community is largely composed of persons of diverse backgrounds, professional capacities, and political interests. Some are elected officials, others are civil servants, and many are private citizens from the medical and educational communities. In some cases, such as with alcohol and tobacco, powerful industry players assert a tremendous influence on policy. As you read on, consider the new research-related implications for drug policy, such as those addressing the incarceration of drug offenders.

QUEEN VICTORIA'S CANNABIS USE: OR, HOW HISTORY DOES AND DOES NOT GET USED IN DRUG POLICY MAKING

Virginia Berridge

History is at an all time high as a popular public subject in the UK. Family history appeals to the expanding cohorts of the early retired; the series *The History of Britain* commanded large television audiences. Much popular programming relies on history for its staple diet. Historians too have dropped their earlier distaste for media history. Nowadays they are more willing to appear in docudramas, to speak animatedly in front of medieval cathedrals, or tell us all about the history of water, or the patient, on Radio Four. They have realised that it is in their interests to do so.

These activities see history engaging with the public, advancing understanding and adding to the richness of public experience. My view is that there is also a different, though related, role for history which needs more thought. This is the use of history as a tool of policy analysis, as a way of directly feeding into policy discussions. This is particularly so where drug policy is concerned. Here, I will reflect on where history has and has not come into some recent drug policy making—and what that tells us about the relationship between the two.

The current use of history in health policy making in general in the UK is problematic. At a recent seminar I attended, a senior Department of Health civil servant told us 'I found when I joined the department that history began in 1997' (the date the Labour government was elected). He was immediately taken to task by a senior health policy analyst, who commented that an awareness of some of the events in the health and social care arena in the 1970s, when Labour was last in power, might have saved this government from making very similar assumptions and mistakes.

But how has history been used, or not used, in the making of drug policy? If we go back to the formation of US drug policy in the 1960s and 70s, history did come into the debates. Researchers aiming at the reform of prohibitionist policy in the States used their interpretation of the history of drug policy in the UK in the 1920s to make an argument for a more liberal, not a punitive approach. American researchers who opposed the penal direction of US drug policy and the 'war on drugs' looked at Britain's apparent lack of a problem. They drew attention to the way in which, in their view, the medical profession and medical ways of dealing with addicts had won a victory over penal policies emanating from the Home Office in the 1920s. Doctors using maintenance policies had led, so it

was argued, to the lack of a British problem; and similar policies should be instituted in the States, with similar outcomes. Those arguments had their impact, although not without dispute.[1] But a few years later, the rise in heroin addiction in the UK made the apparently beneficial effects of the UK system of maintenance more controversial.

In more recent times, a different sort of history has emerged in the discussion of cannabis use in the UK and the moves towards greater liberalisation. Here we have had the strange saga of Queen Victoria's cannabis use. This 'historical fact' emerged sometime in the late 1990s as part of the rehabilitation of the medical use of cannabis, first officially promoted in the UK in the report of the House of Lords Science and Technology committee in 1998.[2] This was an international debate. In many countries, especially the US and the UK, arguments for the medical utility of cannabis have been a route for a possibly more liberal legal status for the drug. Opponents of cannabis restriction have argued that it is a preparation with benign medical uses, for example for MS and HIV/AIDS. Media articles on medicalising cannabis used a supposed history of cannabis. When Prince Charles asked an MS sufferer if she had tried cannabis, the *Guardian* commented, 'Prince Charles is not the first member of the royal family to support use of cannabis as a medicine. Queen Victoria is said to have used it to ease period pains.'[3] This 'fact' took on a life of its own, appearing three times in the *Guardian* alone in 1999, nine in 2000.[4] The connection with Queen Victoria made the requisite contemporary point. It seemed to argue that 'the Victorians', that respectable crew, used cannabis with no problems—so why not us, too?

But in other recent policy discussions, history is notable by its absence. The recent UK Home Affairs committee report on British drug policy makes no mention of historical forebears.[5] Yet two of its key recommendations—for a trial of injecting rooms and for a more widespread use of heroin prescribing— have direct historical precedents. Heroin prescribing was the norm until the 1960s; and injecting rooms made their appearance in some of the early Drug Dependence Units. Yet the report justifies these proposals by reference to recent European initiatives and the history is not mentioned. It uses the term 'British system' to mean Home Office licensing, not the general prescribing which operated until the late 1960s. The report is largely history free.

What do these examples tell us about the role of history in drug policy? Firstly, they tell us that having a marketable 'fact' or accessible interpretation is central. Queen Victoria used cannabis—everyone can remember that. Prescribing to addicts prevented a black market and criminalisation of drugs in the UK, so it could be applied to the US. But from the historians' perspective, there are a few problems here. For a start, there's the issue of historical interpretation and the evidence. British 'liberal' drug policy, so some analysts would argue, did not prevent a black market; there was no black market and no drug problem and so medical maintenance had no opponents. Cause and effect have been confused. And there is no evidence that Queen Victoria herself used cannabis. What the journalists have confused is the use of cannabis in the nineteenth century in a very limited way for dysmenorrhoea, a use advocated by Dr. Russell Reynolds, who was Queen Victoria's physician. Cannabis itself was recognised in the nineteenth century as a drug of variable effect and limited utility in European medicine. Those who did advocate its use, as for example in the treatment of insanity, were really out of the ordinary. The Victorians as a society didn't use cannabis.[6]

The Home Affairs committee report provides the clue to the relationship between history and policy. Here the historical dog didn't bark—because policy directions didn't justify it doing so. Better justify learning from 'best practice' in Europe now rather than reintroduce a policy or practice tried thirty years ago, and long before that too. History here might not give such a straightforward message.

Science policy analysts long ago recognised that the relationship between science (research) and policy is complex and reciprocal. Likewise the relationship between history and policy; historical analysis or 'facts' tend to emerge out of the needs of policy agendas rather than in any rational relationship. Historians have in any field, let alone drugs, rarely been in control of the policy uses to which their historical analysis is put. Yet, for all that, policy making in drugs is badly in need of some historical context. History is a potentially powerful tool of analysis, not just a cynical way of saying there is nothing new under the sun. An historical evaluation of heroin maintenance in the UK, or the operation of injecting rooms in the 60s and 70s is evidence which is as valid as the latest Dutch or Swiss trials. We need historians to rescue policy making from the saga of Queen Victoria's cannabis use.

Notes

1. For a survey of this use of history in policy making, see V. Berridge AIDS, drugs and history. In: R. Porter and M. Teich, *Drugs and Narcotics in History* (Cambridge, 1995), 187–198.

2. House of Lords, Science and Technology Committee, *Cannabis: The Scientific and Medical Evidence*, Ninth Report (London, 1998). See also House of Lords, Science and Technology Committee, *Therapeutic Uses of Cannabis*, Second Report (London, 2001).

3. A. Gentleman, 'Ever tried cannabis? Prince asks MS sufferer.' *Guardian*, 24 December 1998.

4. This was sometimes for use in childbirth and sometimes for period pains. One drugs report had her using cannabis for period pains in 1890, occasioning ribald comment in a reader's letter. Was this, he asked, the late Victorian period?

5. House of Commons. Home Affairs Committee. *The Government's Drugs Policy: Is It Working?* Third Report of Session 2001–2, Vol. I (London, 2002).

6. I discuss the nineteenth century uses of cannabis in England, including Russell Reynolds' recommendation, in my *Opium and the People. Opiate Use in Nineteeth Century England*, first published, with Griffith Edwards in 1981. Could the 1998 reports be a 'Chinese whispers' reinterpretation perhaps via the House of Lords report?

Social Consequences of the War on Drugs: The Legacy of Failed Policy

Eric L. Jensen
University of Idaho

Jurg Gerber
Sam Houston State University

Clayton Mosher
Washington State University–Vancouver

The current war on drugs has radically transformed the criminal justice system. Although criminologists are aware of the multitudes of problematic justice system outcomes associated with this war, the widespread social, economic, health, political, and human costs of the current antidrug crusade have not been studied extensively by criminologists. The objective of this study is to bring attention to these broader societal costs of the drug war.

In a previous article, we argued that "the 1986 War on Drugs has resulted in some of the most extensive changes in criminal justice policy and the operations of the justice system in the United States since the due process revolution of the 1960s" (Jensen & Gerber, 1996, p. 421). This most recent in a series of drug wars in the United States has now lasted almost 17 years. Although huge amounts of economic resources, $18.8 billion by the federal government in fiscal year 2002 alone, personnel, and massive prison construction have been hurled at the problem, the drug war has failed to eliminate illegal drug use. In fact, the Household Survey of Drug Abuse shows that illegal drug use was declining substantially in the 6 to 7 years before the drug war was declared by President Reagan and continued this downturn for the next 6 years with fluctuations occurring since the early 1990s (Jensen & Gerber, 1998; *Sourcebook of Criminal Justice Statistics*, 2001). Given this seemingly natural downturn—which was occurring in Canada also—the drug war seems to have had no effect on illegal drug use.

The war on drugs and its influences on the criminal justice system have received a great deal of attention from criminologists and other social scientists. Prison populations have exploded with persons convicted of drug offenses. Between 1980 and 2001, the number of persons in state and federal prisons for drug offenses increased by approximately 1,300% (`www.ojp.usdoj.gov/bjs/prisons.htm`). Incarceration and prison construction have become major industries; in part replacing the old

rust belt industries that were the economic backbone of America for decades (Christie, 2000). Law enforcement personnel are being redirected away from handling other types of crimes in favor of drug offenses (Mast, Benson, & Rasmussen, 2000). Criminal courts are so overloaded with drug cases that special drug courts have been created to more speedily handle the burdensome caseloads (Inciardi, McBride, & Rivers, 1996). For the first time in American history much harsher sentences are required for one form of an illegal drug (crack) than another form of the same substance (powder cocaine) (Belenko, 1993). Attempts have been made to criminalize the behavior of pregnant women by charging them with delivery of drugs to a minor (Beckett, 1995; Sagatun-Edwards, 1998). If these charges fail—as they most often do—child protection services have been used to remove the baby from its mother.

The drug war has also spread over into the civil arena. This pandemic spillover of state intrusion into the civil arena in the name of controlling crime represents a rapid and drastic slide down the slippery slope of reducing what heretofore were considered the due process rights of Americans. The most pervasive example of crime control absent due process is the civil forfeiture of assets in drug-related cases (Blumenson & Nilsen, 1998; Jensen, 2000). Law enforcement agencies seized nearly $7 billion in allegedly drug-related assets from fiscal year 1985 through 1999 (Jensen, 2000; *Sourcebook of Criminal Justice Statistics*, 2001). When law enforcement is partially self-financed, it becomes less accountable to the public.

Public school students are required to take drug tests in an increasing number of schools even when drugs have not been shown to be a serious problem in the school (see Crowley, 1998). Drug-sniffing dogs are frequently used in schools and school parking lots to uncover illegal drugs without search warrants.

The U.S. drug war is becoming global. The federal government is attempting to influence the governments of other nations throughout the world to deal with drug issues as the U.S. government sees fit. This international arm twisting and cajoling interferes with the sovereignty of foreign governments (Bouley, 2001; Bullington, Krebs & Rasmussen, 2000; del Olmo, 1993; Denq & Wang, 2001; Garcia, 1997; Ryan, 1998).

Although criminologists are aware of this multitude of problematic justice system outcomes associated with the War on Drugs, we must now begin to consider the widespread social, economic, health, political, and human costs of the current antidrug crusade. The objective of this article is to bring attention to these broader societal costs of the drug war. Drug policy has become a major force in the lives of millions of persons caught in the justice system; the same holds true for millions of their family members, relatives, and friends; and the inner-city communities that suffer as a result of the policies emanating from this state-constructed moral panic.

What does the future hold for the millions of young men—disproportionately African American—who will come out of prison to face a new life stigmatized as exconvicts and drug addicts? Will they find living-wage jobs and form stable families or return to the destructive lifestyles of their youth? How is the legitimate political influence of African Americans being influenced by the loss of the right to vote of millions of young, Black men who are convicted felons? How have repressive policies regarding syringes led to the spread of HIV/AIDS? The prison construction boom of the 1980s and 1990s may lead to the need for continued, expanded wars on crime when the cohorts of young men are smaller in the future—capacity causes utilization. Crime control is now a basic industry in the United States. The benefits of medical cannabis use for the chronically ill may not be realized due to the active federal intervention to stop state initiatives that allow it. These are the broader issues that we will begin to draw attention to in this article.

PRISON CAPACITY: IF YOU BUILD IT, THEY MUST COME

It has been argued by some criminologists that the creation of prison capacity generates the prisoners to fill this capacity (see Coates, Miller, & Ohlin, 1978); others assert that limited prison capacity acts as a constraint on prison populations. In the late 1960s, criminologists and other analysts of criminal justice system trends, perhaps deluded by the increased use of alternative sanctions such as probation, predicted a leveling-off, or even declines in the overall level of imprisonment in the United States (e.g., Blumstein & Cohen, 1973; Rothman, 1971). The President's Commission on Law Enforcement and Administration of Justice (1967, pp. 4–5) predicted that the increased use of community programs would curtail institutional growth: "the population projection for the prison system shows the smallest aggregate increase of any of the correctional activities." In addition to the impact of alternative sanctions on prison populations, some held that judicial decisions on prison overcrowding in the 1970s, which prevented corrections officials in some states from receiving new inmates and even ordered some facilities closed, presaged a decline in the use of incarceration (Zimring & Hawkins, 1991).

As early as 1971, however, the American Friends Service Committee (1971, p. 172) argued that the result of providing new cell space was "inevitable: the coercive net of the justice system will be spread over a larger number of people, trapping them for longer periods of time." Similarly, a 1980 study sponsored by the National Institute of Justice (1980), while indicating that the data were only "suggestive," asserted that

> as a matter of history, this study has found that state prison populations were more likely to increase in years immediately following construction than at any other time, and that increases in the numbers of inmates closely approximates the change in capacity. (pp. 138–139)

Between 1990 and 1999, the total number of inmates in state and federal prisons increased 75%. State prisoners increased by 71% and federal prisoners by 127%. States with the largest increases in prison populations during this time were Texas (173%), Idaho (147%), West Virginia (126%), and Hawaii (124%) (Bureau of Justice Statistics, 2000b). California has built 21 new prisons in the last 20 years and increased its inmate population eightfold. As Schlosser (1998) has noted, the number of drug offenders imprisoned in California in 1997 was more than twice the number imprisoned for *all* crimes in 1978.

During the mid-1990s, an average of three 500-bed prison facilities have opened *each week* in the United States (Schlosser, 1998). Christie (2000), in his provocatively titled book *Crime Control as Industry*, refers to low-level offenders as the "raw material" for prison expansion. He suggests that the prison industry needs inmates just as the paper industry needs trees—the key difference, however, is that trees may well turn out to be a finite resource.

And of course, the war on drugs has led to unprecedented racial disproportions in our prison population. Donzinger (1996) estimated that if current growth rates continue for the next 10 years, by the year 2020 more than 6 in 10 African American males between the ages of 18 and 34 will be incarcerated, with the total prison population topping 10 million. And once built at an average cost of $100,000 per cell, these prison beds must be occupied.

Significant developments in the 1980s and into the 1990s would appear to indicate that the incredible recent growth rates in incarcerated populations will not soon abate; although the rate of growth in prison populations slowed somewhat from 1999 through 2001 (Bureau of Justice Statistics, n.d.). Consider, in this context, the rising rates of juvenile incarceration and the continual calls for transferring more juveniles to adult court. There is also the issue of the increasing involvement of private companies in the imprisonment business (Quittner, 1998); the globalization of the economy, whereby companies that are unwilling or unable to obtain cheap labor in Third World countries are making increased use of prison labor (Overbeck, 1997; Robinson, 1998; Wright, 1998), and the growing interest of rural communities in securing prisons as a means of economic development (McDonald, 1997). As a prison liaison group chair in a rural Michigan jurisdiction noted, "this is going to mean more jobs and more money to the community … there's no possible way for those guys to get out, so we just reap the benefits" (as cited in Julien, 1998).

There is of course a very cruel irony in all these developments. As state governments take funds from education and social programs to expand their prison systems, citizens are less able to compete in an increasingly competitive marketplace. Skills will be low, employment opportunities limited, and more people will live in poverty. Such conditions are criminogenic, but instead of investing in programs to prevent criminal activity, "the government spends dollars on the final result of the poverty circle" (McDonald, 1997).

As Schlosser (1998) recently pointed out, there are several similarities between the emergent prison-industrial complex and the military-industrial complex that it appears to have superseded. Although crime has replaced communism as the external evil that can be exploited by politicians, the most striking similarity between the two is the need to create policies that are more concerned with the economic imperatives of the industry than the needs of the public it allegedly serves. In addition, the policies allegedly create significant employment opportunities in the communities where prisons locate, thereby tying the economic prosperity of literally millions of people to the growth of the crime control industry. Finally, both the military and prison industries have an internal logic that allows them to benefit regardless of whether their policies succeed or fail. As Donzinger (1998) notes,

> if we lose a war, we need more weapons to win the next one; if we win a war, we need more weapons so we can keep on winning; if crime is up, we need more prisons to lower crime, if crime is down, we need more prisons so it stays down.

The importance of labor market conditions was also emphasized by Sellin (1976, p. vii) who argued that "the demands of the labor market shape(d) the penal system and determined its transformation over the years, more or less unaffected by the theories of punishment in vogue." Similarly, Rusche and Kirchheimer (1939) in their classic historical-comparative study of prisons, noted that compared to European countries, the United States was characterized by a shortage of labor in the early industrial period, with the result that convict labor needed to be productive. However, this position has been critiqued for its tendency to economic reductionism (Greenberg, 1980; see also Zimring & Hawkins, 1991). In a recent comparative study of the influences on rates of imprisonment from 1955–1985, Sutton (2000) found that significant predictors of growth in prison populations in the United States were higher rates of unemployment, the right party (Republican) domination of the cabinet, and declines in welfare spending.

DIMINISHED LIFE CHANCES: INCARCERATION, JOBLESSNESS, AND WEAK SOCIAL BONDS

Between 1980 and 2001, the number of persons incarcerated in state prisons in the United States grew by 316% (Bureau of Justice Statistics, n.d.a.). Furthermore, the number of incarcerated persons per 100,000 population rose from 139 in 1980 to 470 in 2001 (Bureau of Justice Statistics, n.d.a.). Interestingly, "tough on crime" policies implemented during the Clinton administration resulted in the largest increases in federal and state prison populations of any president in American history (Feldman, Schiraldi, & Ziedenberg, 2001).

Incarceration is concentrated among young, uneducated males; particularly African Americans. In 1999, over 44% of the number of inmates in state and federal prisons and local jails were Black, and 11% of Black males in their 20s and early 30s were either in prison or jail in 1999 (Bureau of Justice Statistics, 2000a). In the mid-1990s, one out of every three young Black males was under some form of state supervision (Western & Beckett, 1999).

A growing proportion of prison inmates has been convicted of nonviolent drug offenses. In 1979, 6% of state prison inmates were convicted of nonviolent drug offenses, whereas in 1998 the proportion had increased to nearly 21%, nearly a fourfold increase (Bureau of Justice Statistics, n.d.b; Western & Beckett, 1999). In 1985, before the declaration of a new war on drugs and the passage of harsh federal antidrug legislation, 34% of federal prisoners were incarcerated for drug offenses. By 1998, 58% of federal prisoners had been sentenced for drug offenses (Bureau of Justice Statistics, 2000a).

Furthermore, sentences for drug offenses are long in comparison to other crimes. In 2000, mean times served for selected federal offenses were as follows: drug offenses 41 months, violent crimes 54 months, fraudulent property crimes 15 months, and other property crimes 19 months (*Sourcebook of Criminal Justice Statistics*, 2001). Thus, average times served for drug offenses were closer to those for violent crimes than for property offenses.

It has also been found that African Americans are more likely than Whites to be in prison for drug offenses (Irwin & Austin, 2001; Maguire & Pastore, 1998, p. 505). This disproportionality of incarceration by race is exacerbated by the infamous 100:1 sentencing ratio for crack offenses. In 1996, 86% of federal convictions for crack offenses were Black whereas only 5% were White (Maguire & Pastore, 1998, p. 415). In addition, the median sentence for Blacks convicted of a federal drug offense was 84 months—2 years longer than the average sentence for a violent crime—whereas it was 46 months for Whites (Maguire & Pastore, 1998, p. 396). Thus, Blacks experience the brunt of these extremely harsh crack sanctions.

In sum, the end result of these changes in penalties and prosecution of drug offenses is a large number of young, Black males in prison for such offenses. Additionally, they are serving long prison terms in comparison to many other inmates. Although the effects of this change in patterns of imprisonment for the criminal justice system are intuitively obvious, we must turn our attention to the long-term effects on society, specifically the unemployment and further marginalization of these men once they are released from prison.

Research has clearly shown that the likelihood of unemployment increases as a result of incarceration (Sampson & Laub, 1993; Western & Beckett, 1999). Western and Beckett (1999, pp. 1048–1051) found that incarceration has large negative effects on the employment of ex-prisoners, which decay 3 to 4 years after release. Changes in public policies since the Reagan Administration years have exacerbated this problem. As Petersilia (2003a, p. 4) has recently pointed out, "dozens of laws were passed restricting the kinds of jobs for which ex-prisoners can be hired, easing the requirements for their parental rights to be terminated, restricting their access to welfare benefits and public housing, disqualifying them from a host of job training programs" (see also Jensen, in press). In addition, the ability to find and retain employment are key factors in forming bonds to the conventional society and desistance from criminal behavior (Elliott & Voss, 1974; Sampson & Laub, 1993).

Employment, and the lack thereof, is related to marriage. Studies cited by Wilson (1996, p. 96) found that 20% to 25% of the decline in marriage rates of African Americans is due to the joblessness of Black males. This is particularly problematic for young Black males. In addition, these studies were of general samples of African Americans and not specific to the low income communities from which most drug prisoners are sentenced. The effect of the explosion in joblessness in inner cities combined with the obstacles faced by ex-prisoners finding employment can be expected to produce larger negative outcomes in these communities.

Research by Sampson (1995, p. 249) found that both the total sex ratios and the employment prospects of Black men had independent effects on the structure of Black families in cities in the United States: "this race-specific interaction clearly supports Wilson's (1987) hypothesis regarding the structural sources of black family disruption." In this earlier work, Wilson proposed that the ratio of employed men per 100 women of the same age and race influenced marital stability. With the decline in the number of economically stable Black men, Black female-headed households increased (Wilson, 1987). More specifically, Sampson (1995) also found strong independent effects of sex ratios and employment on family disruption among those families in poverty. That is, "the lower the sex ratio and the lower the male employment rate, the higher the rate of female-headed families with children in poverty" (Sampson, 1995, p. 250).

Furthermore, one of the strongest predictors of urban violence is family structure. With other factors controlled, "in cities where family disruption is high the rate of violence is also high" (Sampson, 1995, p. 249). Based on his earlier work, the author states that this causal connection appears to be based in patterns of community social ties and informal networks of social control (see Sampson & Groves, 1989; see also Hagan, 1994).

The causal chain between incarceration, joblessness, and weak social bonds is therefore long and complex. As stated by Sampson and Laub (1993),

> job stability and marital attachment in adulthood were significantly related to changes in adult crime—the stronger the adult ties to work and family, the less the crime … We even found that strong marital attachment inhibits crime and deviance regardless of the spouse's own deviant behavior, and that job instability fosters crime regardless of heavy drinking. Moreover, social bonds to employment were directly influenced by State sanctions—incarceration as a juvenile and as an adult had negative effects on later job stability, which in turn was negatively related to continued involvement in crime over the life course. (p. 248)

Thus, the binge of imprisonment for drug offenses has substantial negative outcomes for society and inner-city African American communities in particular. The incarceration of large numbers of young Black men for drug offenses has created an artificially low unemployment rate in the United States in recent years.

In 2002 alone, nearly 600,000 people were released from prison. This puts hundreds of thousands of young Black men with the stigma of ex-convict back into primarily low-income urban communities each year (see Petersilia, 2003a). The obstacles they face in finding employment that provides a living wage and related marital stability should be focal points of public concern and social policy in the immediate future. As they currently exist, the punitive justice policies so popular in the United States today simply continue to fuel the social disorganization and decline of the most disadvantaged segments of our society.

HIV/AIDS—"Invisible, Extrajudicial Executions?" (Green, 1996)

Two percent to 3% of state and federal prisoners are HIV-positive or have AIDS—a rate five times higher than that of the general population (Petersilia, 2003a). The number of confirmed AIDS cases among prisoners increased by nearly 400% between 1991 and 1997 (Bureau of Justice Statistics, 1999). Additionally, it is estimated that 22% of female and 13% of male inmates in New York City jails are HIV-positive (Aids in Prison Project, 1997). Marquart, Brewer, Mullings, and Crouch (1999) note that in the New York, California, and Texas prison systems, AIDS is now the leading cause of death. In 1997, about one in every five deaths of prisoners was attributable to AIDS-related causes (Bureau of Justice Statistics, 1999). The rate of mortality for HIV-infected prisoners is at least three times the rate of mortality of HIV-patients in non–prison communities (Center for HIV Information, 1997).

In addressing the issue of HIV in prisons, it is important to take into account the comparatively high rates of assault and sexual assault that can facilitate the spread of the virus. An earlier Federal Bureau of Prisons study reported that 30% of federal prison inmates engaged in homosexual activity while incarcerated (Nacci & Kane, 1984). Although no national studies of the extent of sexual assault in prisons have been conducted, based on projections from a number of studies, it is estimated that there were 530,000 male rape victims behind bars in the United States (Stop Prisoner Rape; www.igc.org/spr). A substantial proportion of these rapes occur in local and county jails, where over half the inmate population has not been convicted of an offense. There are, of course, other HIV-risk factors for prison inmates such as the frequent incidents of interpersonal violence in these settings involving lacerations and bites, which has been exacerbated by the double celling of inmates. The use of needles for tattooing and body piercing, and sharing of syringes for IV drug use in prisons are also of great concern.

Unfortunately, federal and state prison authorities have been slow to develop policies to deal with this crisis. In an international survey of 19 countries prepared for the World Health Organization, the United States was listed as one of four countries that did not have a national policy for HIV management in prison (Center for HIV Information, 1997). And although an increasing number of inmates in state and federal prisons are HIV-positive, the number of effective HIV prevention programs in these facilities is declining. In 1990, 96% of all state and federal prisons had AIDS education programs in at least one prison—by 1994, that rate had dropped to 75% ("HIV Prevention Programs," 1996). Green (1996), discussing the situation in California prisons and noting the disproportional concentration of HIV infection among minority inmates, asserts that

considering the history of genocide in this country, imprisoning targeted groups in an epidemic situation and then withholding treatment and education to stop the spread of the diseases sounds like giving smallpox-contaminated blankets to the Native Americans.

Given recent history, it seems unlikely that state or federal governments will implement progressive policies such as making condoms, bleach, methadone, and sterile injection equipment available to prisoners, as the World Health Organization has suggested (Jurgens, 1996).

Although many Americans and policy makers currently view prisoners as unworthy of compassion, there is a far greater threat posed by the spread of HIV in prison populations. The overwhelming majority of prison inmates will be released at some time, and as Marquart et al. (1999) in a study of women prisoners in the state of Texas note,

> Recent drug control policies, grounded in deterrence and based on harsh legal penalties, have led to the incarceration of numerous offenders who are low criminal risks but represent major public health risks on release. Criminal justice policies penalizing drug users may be contributing to the spread of HIV infection in the wider society. (p. 82)

Are there any signs that any of this will end soon? It is perhaps notable that an overly optimistic and misleading press release from the Office of National Drug Control Policy (ONDCP) was titled "FY 2000 Drug Control Budget Builds on Success—Budget Provides $17.8 Billion for Demand and Supply Reduction." A perusal of the fine print of this press release reveals that, similar to drug control policy in the last two decades in the United States, two thirds of the money is devoted to supply reduction, the bulk of which is composed of additional monies for law enforcement. Only one third of the money is devoted to "demand reduction."

MEDICINAL MARIJUANA— REEFER MADNESS AGAIN

The ONDCP (1997), in its statement on the use of marijuana for medical purposes, asserted that state-level initiatives to allow the use of medical marijuana had

> sent a confusing message to our children that could not have come at a worse time. In recent years, we have seen drug use by our young people increase at an alarming rate. Among 8th graders, the use of illicit drugs, primarily marijuana, has tripled. This increase has been fueled by a measurable decrease in the proportion of young people who perceive marijuana to be a dangerous substance.

Aside from the fact that this statement conveniently neglects the reality that levels of illicit drug use by youth were considerably higher in the late 1970s, it is even more curious in the context of ONDCP's contention in the same document that the "foremost objective" of the office "is to create a national drug control strategy based on *science* rather than *ideology*" [italics added].

In critiquing California's medical marijuana legislation, President Clinton's "drug czar," General McCaffrey, noted that the wording of California's Proposition 215 led to a situation whereby "any other illness would include "recalling forgotten memories, cough suppressants, and writer's cramp." McCaffrey continued, "this is not medicine. This is a Cheech and Chong show" (Mundell, 1998). In response to the California initiative, the Clinton government threatened to prosecute doctors who prescribed marijuana to their patients.

Interestingly, as Grinspoon and Bakalar (1995) pointed out in an editorial published in the *Journal of the American Medical Association*, the Drug Enforcement Administration's (DEA's) own administrative law judge, Francis Young, asserted in 1988 that marijuana in its natural form fulfilled the legal requirements of currently accepted medical use in treatment in the United States. Young added that marijuana was "one of the safest therapeutically active substances known to man" (as cited in Grinspoon & Bakalar, 1995 p. 1875). Interestingly, Young's order that marijuana be reclassified as a Schedule II drug was overruled, not by any medical authority, but by the DEA itself.

There is also evidence that the National Institute of Drug Abuse was instrumental in suppressing a 1997 World Health Organization report suggesting that marijuana was far less harmful than alcohol and tobacco ("The report the WHO tried to hide," 1998). However, the evidence for marijuana's medical uses is mounting. The substance is effective in treatment of more than 100 separate illnesses or diseases (http://www.medicalmarijuana.org), with studies demonstrating marijuana's usefulness in reducing nausea and vomiting, stimulating appetite, promoting weight gain, and diminishing intraocular pressure associated with glaucoma (Zimmer & Morgan, 1997). And despite the contention of ONDCP and other federal drug agencies that similar effects are possible with synthetic tetrahydrocannabinal (THC) or Marinol, studies suggest that smoked marijuana is more effective because it delivers THC to the bloodstream more quickly. In addition, some evidence suggests that the psychoactive side effects of Marinol may actually be more intense than those that are associated with smoking marijuana (Zimmer & Morgan, 1997).

ONDCP and other federal drug agencies have also attempted to dismiss studies of marijuana's effectiveness by claiming that the research is lacking in scientific standards. However, as Grinspoon and Bakalar (1995) note, although it is certainly true that many of the studies examining medical marijuana are not consistent with FDA standards, this is primarily because of the bureaucratic,

legal, and financial obstacles that are put in place by this same federal agency.

It appears as though federal drug agencies have a vested interest in keeping marijuana illegal. Since 1970, approximately 13.5 million Americans have been arrested for marijuana possession, and in 1999 alone, there were 708,480 marijuana-related arrests (Charbeneau, 1998; U.S. Department of Justice, n.d.). Despite popular belief then, there is little question that marijuana is the main focus of the drug warriors. It is worth noting, however, that the federal government's strict prohibitionist position with respect to marijuana is opposed by the American Public Health Association, the Federation of American Scientists, the Physicians' Association for AIDS Care, the Lymphoma Foundation of America, and national associations of prosecutors and criminal defense attorneys. *The New England Journal of Medicine* has supported marijuana's use as medicine, the *Journal of the American Medical Association* published the previously mentioned editorial by Grinspoon and Bakalar, which delivered essentially the same message (Morgan & Zimmer, 1997), and based on a review of the research the Senate Special Committee on Illegal Drugs (2002) in Canada recently concluded that cannabis can be a beneficial therapy for the treatment of specified medical conditions. Despite the fact that 11 states and the District of Columbia have passed legislation allowing for medicinal marijuana, the legal status of using the substance for these purposes is unclear given the federal resistance to recognize the new state policies.

THE WAR ON DRUGS AND DISENFRANCHISEMENT

One of the unanticipated consequences of the war on drugs is the disenfranchisement of a particular segment of society. Although most Americans will not be unduly disturbed by the prospect of convicted felons being unable to vote, the disproportionate impact of felony disenfranchisement on African Americans should be cause for concern.

Historically, the United States limited the right to vote to relatively few, primarily affluent White males, and excluded women, African Americans, and the poor. One other category, convicted felons, were unable to vote as a result of the United States's adopting the European practice of declaring convicted offenders "civilly dead" on conviction (Fellner & Mauer, 1998). The felony disenfranchisement laws gained some additional currency after the Civil War when White Southerners sought to limit Black suffrage with the aid of supposedly race-neutral laws (e.g., grandfather clauses).

Depending on state legislation, convicted felons may not lose the right to vote; or lose it while in prison, on probation, on parole, or even *for life*. Maine, for instance, does not disenfranchise convicted felons; Idaho disenfranchises incarcerated felons; California felons in prison or on parole; Georgia felons in prison, on parole, and on probation; and Alabama, similar to Georgia, also disenfranchises ex-felons (i.e., felons are disenfranchised *for life*) (Fellner & Mauer, 1998). The numbers of disenfranchised people are exceptionally large, but the proportions of certain categories of people are even more disturbing:

- 3.9 million adults are currently or permanently disenfranchised as a result of a felony conviction;
- Florida and Texas have each disenfranchised more than 600,000 people;
- 73% of the disenfranchised are not in prison but are on probation, on parole, or have completed their sentences;
- In Alabama and Florida, 31% of all Black men are permanently disenfranchised;
- 13% of all adult Black men are currently disenfranchised;
- 1.4 million Black men are disenfranchised compared to 4.6 million Black men who voted in 1996 (Fellner & Mauer, 1998).

An important study by Uggen and Manza (2002) recently concluded that felon disenfranchisement may have altered seven recent U.S. Senate elections and at least one presidential election.

> Assuming that Democrats who might have been elected in the absence of felon disenfranchisement had held their seats as long as the Republicans who narrowly defeated them, we estimate that the Democratic Party would have gained parity in 1984 and held majority control of the U.S. Senate from 1986 to the present.... In examining the presidential elections, we find that the Republican presidential victory of 2000 would have been reversed had just ex-felons been allowed to vote. (p. 794)

Unfortunately, if current trends continue, the situation will become worse. Mandatory minimum sentence laws, "three strikes" laws, and the war on drugs will increase the number of disenfranchised people and, most likely, increase the racial disparity in this practice. The long-term consequence of this will be the further attenuation of African American political power. More than a decade ago, Wilson (1987) spoke of *The Truly Disadvantaged*. Not only is work disappearing (see also Wilson, 1996), what little political clout existed has eroded. Urban areas have traditionally been strongholds of minority politicians and politicians sympathetic to minority issues. The disenfranchisement of some of their supporters will lead to a political restructuring of the city. In turn, this will lead to even fewer programs for these populations. Instead, politicians will likely heed the calls for more "law and order" emanating from the remaining electorate. And the vicious spiral will continue.

CONCLUSIONS

Few scholars who study the war on drugs are not aware of some of the problems this war entails for the criminal justice system. In fact, even professionals in the field echo some of the concerns of academicians. Former federal drug czar Barry McCaffrey spoke of "America's internal gulag" when referring to the seemingly ever-growing number of drug offenders in prisons ("Prison boom," 1999, p. 12). The irony of such a development must be overwhelming for Christie, should he be aware of McCaffrey's label.

Some positive developments are occurring at the state level, however. Since late 2000, Republican governors in at least seven states, including George Pataki in New York, Gary Johnson in New Mexico, and Dirk Kempthorne in Idaho, have called for placing more drug offenders into treatment and fewer in prison—although the previous year Governor Kempthorne advocated and passed longer sentences for methamphetamine offenses. Although these developments can be viewed in a positive light, it is important not to lose sight of the opposition of many criminal justice officials in the states where these changes have been suggested and of recent developments at the federal level.

In Arizona and California, citizen initiatives have passed that provide drug treatment instead of prison for persons convicted of first- and second time drug possession offenses when no violent crime is present. Although these laws have faced criticism by prosecutors, police, and judges who assert that the law does not give criminal justice authorities enough power to force offenders into treatment, the research shows that these laws are diverting tens of thousands of persons convicted of possession from incarceration into treatment (`www.drugpolicy-alliance.com, www.prop36.org`).

In the November 2002 elections, the voters of the District of Columbia passed a measure similar to those in Arizona and California. This initiative requires that persons convicted of drug possession for a nonviolent offense receive treatment instead of incarceration. The law contains no funding for implementation of this policy, however.

Recent appointments to key positions in the federal government by President George W. Bush indicate that the war may not yet be over. Former Senator John Ashcroft, appointed U.S. Attorney General, has supported revoking the driver's license of anyone arrested for marijuana possession, even if they were not driving at the time. He also supported evicting entire families from public housing if one of their members was suspected of using or selling drugs, even when the other family members were not involved. Ashcroft also opposes devoting funds to demand-side programs believing that a government that shifts resources to drug treatment and prevention programs instead of police and prisons "is a government that accommodates us at our lowest and least" (as quoted in Lindesmith Center, 2001). President Bush also appointed John Walters to the position of federal drug czar, leading Smith (2002, p. 121) to comment

"Walters' appointment is the clearest sign yet that the Bush administration is committed to a punishment approach to the problems caused by illegal drugs." In 1996, Walters indicated that he opposed needle exchange programs on moral grounds (Smith, 2002); he also fervently opposes the decriminalization of marijuana. Walters actively campaigned against a marijuana initiative in the state of Nevada and in response to a proposal for decriminalization of marijuana in Canada, stated "If Canada wants to become the locus for that kind of activity, they're likely to pay a heavy price" (Bailey, 2003). As Stroup and Armentano (2002, p. 223) suggest, "many of Mr. Walters more egregious claims about cannabis appear to have been lifted straight from the 1936 propaganda film [Reefer Madness]."

The rhetoric in recent federal documents might lead one to believe that there have been some changes, however. Witness, for example, the relative prominence that the prevention and treatment of drug abuse received in the 2001 Annual Report of the National Drug Control Policy,

> Preventing drug abuse in the first place is preferable to addressing the problem later through treatment and law enforcement.... There are approximately five million drug abusers who need immediate treatment and who constitute a major portion of domestic demand.... Accordingly, the *Strategy* focuses on treatment. Research clearly demonstrates that treatment works.... Providing access to treatment for America's chronic drug abusers is a worthwhile endeavor. It is both compassionate public policy and sound investment (Office of National Drug Control Policy, 2001, pp. 4–6).

Unfortunately for the harm reduction effort, such rhetoric is offset by the reality of budgetary appropriations. An overview of the proportions of the budgets devoted to law enforcement and drug treatment during the decade of the 1990s indicates that there have not been major redistributions (Office of National Drug Control Policy, 2001, p. 119). Although there have been some increases in the percentage devoted to treatment, any declarations that the drug war is over are clearly premature.

However, it might be interesting to speculate how the end of the war on drugs would affect the consequences that we identified in this article. Although it seems highly improbable that we will witness such an event, it is theoretically possible that the war will be ended with the stroke of a few legislative, judicial, and executive pens. Even if this were to occur, such an event would not fundamentally change the adverse long-term consequences that have cumulated during the last 17 years. Only a comprehensive and vigorously enforced affirmative action–like program aimed at overcoming the negative consequences of the war would do so.

Incarceration provides one example. The mean time served for a federal drug sentence for a drug offense is 41 months. Even if the war ended today, the most recently admitted convicts would remain in prison an average of well over 3 years. The only escape from this situation would be large-scale pardons for drug offenders. Obviously this will not happen. Furthermore, the internal logic of prison expansion would also necessitate new "raw material" for the cell space that exists. If nothing else, states must pay off the long-term debts that have been encumbered for this unprecedented wave of prison construction. A new war on some other outlawed, or yet to be outlawed, behavior would likely be the end result.

Postconviction employment would continue to be problematic for exoffenders. Given that the average time served is over 3 years and that employment difficulties are most pronounced for the first 3 to 4 years after release, employment difficulties would be with us for almost a decade after the end of the war on drugs. The problems associated with unemployment, such as marital instability and family violence would also exist, and their effects would be passed on to yet another generation.

All of the other negative consequences that we have identified in this study, the growth in HIV/AIDS rates, the prohibition of cannabis for medical uses, and the attenuation of the political power of targeted subordinate racial and ethnic groups, would also continue to exist. Whereas the end of the war might stop the further acceleration of the spread of HIV infection by not sending drug users to prisons, ex-inmates would still be infected and potentially spread the virus to their sexual partners and those with whom some will share needles. Similarly, ex-offenders would still be without franchise in many states, but there would be fewer newly disenfranchised felons and ex-felons. The only remedy for such adverse consequences would be the passage of legislation such as the Civic Participation and Rehabilitation Act of 1999. This bill, along with others not yet filed, could reverse some of these adverse consequences. For this to happen, though, powerful interest groups that lobby on behalf of offenders would have to emerge; a scenario that seems highly unlikely in the United States.

Most criminologists have paid little attention to the societal consequences of the war on drugs to date. We see this article as a wake-up call for the discipline. Social scientists interested in race relations, family issues, political participation, labor force issues, and health care policy have studied the areas we have identified as societal consequences of the war on drugs. Most criminologists, however, have limited their inquiries to Sutherland's traditional definition of criminology: the making of law, the breaking of law, and the societal response to the breaking of law. We would argue that criminologists cannot afford to ignore the societal consequences of the last dimension of Sutherland's definition. Doing so will make us "enablers." Limiting our studies to the making and breaking of law, and its societal responses, will reify the "drug problem" (or more broadly, "the crime problem") as nothing more than that. If we expand our inquiry, however, to the study of the societal consequences of public policies, we begin the process of challenging the assumptions underlying our (society's) proposed solutions.

REFERENCES

American Friends Service Committee. (1971). Struggle for justice: A report on crime and punishment in America. New York: Hill and Wang.

Bailey, E. (2003, February 2). The drug war refugees. *Los Angeles Times*. Retrieved from http://www.latimes.com

Beckett, K. (1995). Fetal rights and "crack moms": Pregnant women in the War on Drugs. *Contemporary Drug Problems, 22*, 587–612.

Belenko, S. R. (1993). *Crack and the evolution of anti-drug policy*. Westport, CT: Greenwood.

Blumenson, E., & Nilsen, E. (1998). Policing for profit: The drug war's hidden economic agenda. *University of Chicago Law Review, 65*, 35–114.

Blumstein, A., & Cohen, J. (1973). A theory of the stability of punishment. *Journal of Criminal Law and Criminology, 64*, 198–207.

Bouley, E. E., Jr. (2001). The drug war in Latin America: Ten years in a quagmire. In J. Gerber & E. L. Jensen (Eds.), *Drug war, American style: The internationalization of failed policy and its alternatives* (pp. 169–195). New York: Garland.

Bullington, B. H., Krebs, C. P., & Rasmussen, D. W. (2000). Drug policy in the Czech Republic. In A. Springer & A. Uhl (Eds.), *Illicit drugs: Patterns of use—patterns of response* (pp. 73–88). Innsbruck, Austria: Studien Verlag.

Bureau of Justice Statistics. (n.d.a.). Retrieved from http://www.ojp.usdoj.gov/bjs

Bureau of Justice Statistics. (n.d.b). *Number of sentenced inmates incarcerated under state and federal jurisdictions per 100,000, 1980–1999*. Retrieved from http://www.ojp.usdoj.gov/glance/incrt.txt

Bureau of Justice Statistics. (1999, November). *HIV in prisons, 1997*. Washington, DC: U.S. Department of Justice.

Bureau of Justice Statistics. (2000a, April). *Prison and jail inmates at midyear 1999*. Washington, DC: U.S. Department of Justice.

Bureau of Justice Statistics. (2000b, August). *Prisoners in 1999*. Washington, DC: U.S. Department of Justice.

Butterfield, F. (2001, February 12). California lacks resources for law on drug offenders, officials say. *The New York Times*. Retrieved from http://www.nytimes.com

Center for HIV Information. (1997). Aids and HIV infection in prisoners. Retrieved from http://hivinsite.ucsf.edu/akb/1997/01pris

Charbeneau, T. (1998). *Might as well face it we're addicted to lies*. Retrieved from www.marijuananews.com

Christie, N. (2000). *Crime control as industry: Towards GULAGS, western style* (3rd ed.). New York: Routledge.

Coates, R. B., Miller, D. D., & Ohlin, L. E. (1978). *Diversity in a youth correctional system: Handling delinquents in Massachusetts*. Cambridge, MA: Ballinger.

Crowley, D. W. (1998). Drug testing in the Rehnquist era. In E. L. Jensen & J. Gerber (Eds.), *The new War on Drugs: Symbolic politics and criminal justice policy* (pp. 123–139). Cincinnati, OH: Anderson/Academy of Criminal Justice Sciences.

del Olmo, R. (1993). The geopolitics of narcotrafficking in Latin America. *Social Justice, 20*, 1–23.

Denq, F., & Wang, H. (2001). The war on drugs in Taiwan: An American model. In J. Gerber & E. L. Jensen (Eds.), *Drug war, American style: The internationalization of failed policy and its alternatives* (pp. 149–167). New York: Garland.

Donzinger, S. (1996). *The real war on crime*. New York: Harper.

Donzinger, S. (1998). Fear, crime, and punishment in the United States. *Tikkun, 12*, 24–27.

Elliott, D.S., & Voss, H. L. (1974). *Delinquency and dropout*. Lexington, MA: Lexington.

Feldman, Lisa, Schiraldi, Vincent & Jason Ziedenberg. (2001) Too Little Too Late: President Clinton's Prison Legacy. *Center on Juvenile and Criminal Justice*. Retrieved from http://www.cjcj.org/pubs/clinton/clinton.html

Fellner, J., & Mauer, M. (1998). *Losing the vote: the impact of felony disenfranchisement laws in the United States*. Retrieved from www.hrw.org/reports98/vote

Garcia, A. F. (1997). Harm reduction at the supply side of the drug war: the case for Bolivia. In P. G. Erickson, D. M. Riley, Y. W. Cheung, & P. A .O'Hare (Eds.) *Harm reduction: a new direction for drug policies and programs* (pp. 99–115) Toronto, ON: The University of Toronto Press.

Green, C. (1996). *HIV+ and in prison: the shadow of death row*. Retrieved from www.igc.apc.org/justice

Greenberg, D. F. (1980). Penal sanctions in Poland: A test of alternative models. *Social Problems, 28*, 194–204.

Grinspoon, L., & Bakalar, J. (1995). Marijuana as medicine: A plea for reconsideration. *Journal of the American Medical Association, 273*, 1875–1876.

Hagan, J. (1994). *Crime and disrepute*. Thousand Oaks, CA: Pine Forge Press.

HIV prevention programs in prisons on the decline. (1996, May 16). *Reuters*. Retrieved from http://www.reuters.com

Inciardi, J. A., McBride, D. C., & Rivers, J. E. (1996). *Drug control and the courts*. Thousand Oaks, CA: Sage.

Irwin, J., & Austin, J. (2001). *It's about time: America's imprisonment binge* (3rd ed.). Belmont, CA: Wadsworth.

Jensen, E. L. (2000). The civil forfeiture of assets: Harms inherent within U.S. policy. In A. Springer & A. Uhl (Eds.), *Illicit drugs: Patterns of use—Patterns of response* (pp. 31–45). Innsbruck, Austria: Studien Verlag.

Jensen, E. L. (in press). Non-criminal sanctions for drug offenses in the U.S.A. In S. Scheerer (Ed.), *Drug prohibition regimes: International perspectives*. Onati, Spain: International Institute of the Sociology of Law.

Jensen, E. L., & Gerber, J. (1996). The civil forfeiture of assets and the War on Drugs: Expanding criminal sanctions while reducing due process protections. *Crime and Delinquency, 42*, 421–434.

Jensen, E. L., & Gerber, J. (1998). The social construction of drug problems: An historical overview. In E. L. Jensen & J. Gerber (Eds.), *The new war on drugs: Symbolic politics and criminal justice policy*. Cincinnati, OH: Anderson/Academy of Criminal Justice Sciences.

Julien, R. (1998, February 27). Lapeer supports thumb prison expansion. *Michigan Live* (Flint ed.). Retrieved from http://www.mlive.com

Jurgens, R. (1996). *HIV/AIDS in prison*. Canadian Aids Society. Ottawa: Health Canada. Lindesmith Center. (2001, January 22). *Judiciary committee to vote on Ashcroft*. Retrieved from www.drugpolicy.org

Maguire, K., & Pastore, A. L. (Eds.). (1998). *Sourcebook of criminal justice statistics—1997*. Washington, DC: Government Printing Office.

Marquart, J., Brewer, V., Mullings, J., & Crouch, B. (1999). The implications of crime control policy on HIV/AIDS-related risk among women prisoners. *Crime and Delinquency, 45*, 82–98.

Mast, B. D., Benson, B. L., & Rasmussen, D. W. (2000). Entrepreneurial police and drug enforcement. *Public Choice, 104*, 285–308.

McDonald, P. (1997). The lockdown of higher education. *Westchester County Weekly*. Retrieved from http://www.westchesterweekly.com

Mundell, E. J. (1998, August 5). Legal expert supports medical marijuana. *Reuters*. Retrieved from http://www.reuters.com

Nacci, P., & Kane, T. (1982). *Sex and sexual aggression in federal prisons*. Washington, DC: Federal Bureau of Prisons.

National Institute of Justice. (1980). *American prisons and jails* (Vol. 1). Washington, DC: Government Printing Office.

Nevada secretary of state questions drug czar's failure to comply with law. (2002, December 5). *Drug Policy Alliance Newsletter*. Retrieved from `http://actioncenter.drugpolicy.org/news`

Office of National Drug Control Policy. (1997). *ONDCP statement on marijuana for medical purposes*. Washington, DC: Government Printing Office.

Office of National Drug Control Policy. (2001). *The national drug control strategy: 2001 Annual Report*. Washington, DC: Government Printing Office.

Overbeck, C. (1997). *Prison factories: Slave labor for the New World Order?* Retrieved from `http://www.parascope.com/articles/0197/prison.html`

Petersilia, J. (2003a, March/April). Prisoner reentry and criminological knowledge. *Criminologist*, pp. 1, 3, 4–5.

Petersilia, J. (2003b). *When prisoners come home: Parole and prisoner reentry*. New York: Oxford University Press.

President's Commission on Law Enforcement and Administration of Justice. (1967). *Task force report: Corrections*. Washington, DC: Government Printing Office.

Prison boom expected to go on for a generation, officials say. (1999, March 7). *Houston Chronicle*, p. 12A.

Quittner, J. (1998, April 22). The incarceration industry: Teeming prison rolls bode well for private jails. *Fox News*. Retrieved from `http://www.iprnet.org/prison/news`

The report the WHO tried to hide. (1998, February 21). *New Scientist*. Retrieved from `http://www.newscientist.com`

Robinson, M. (1998). *The new money machine*. Retrieved from `http://accnt.ashcc.uky.edu`

Rothman, D. (1971). *The discovery of the asylum: Social order and disorder in the new republic*. Boston: Little, Brown.

Rusche, G., & Kirchheimer, O. (1939). *Punishment and social structure*. New York: Columbia University Press.

Ryan, K. (1998). Globalizing the problem: The United States and international drug control. In E. L. Jensen & J. Gerber (Eds.), *The new War on Drugs: Symbolic politics and criminal justice policy* (pp. 141–156). Cincinnati, OH: Anderson/Academy of Criminal Justice Sciences.

Sagatun-Edwards, I. J. (1998). Crack babies, moral panic, and the criminalization of behavior during pregnancy. In E. L. Jensen & J. Gerber (Eds.), *The new War on Drugs: symbolic politics and criminal justice policy* (pp. 107–121). Cincinnati, OH: Anderson/Academy of Criminal Justice Sciences.

Sampson, R. J. (1995). Unemployment and imbalanced sex ratios: Race-specific consequences for family structure and crime. In M. B. Tucker & C. Mitchell-Kernan (Eds.), *The decline in marriage among African Americans: Causes, consequences, and policy implications* (pp. 229–254). New York: Russell Sage.

Sampson, R. J., & Groves, W. B. (1989). Community structure and crime: testing disruption. *American Journal of Sociology, 94*, 774–802.

Sampson, R. J., & Laub, J. H. (1993). *Crime in the making: Pathways and turning points through life*. Cambridge, MA: Harvard University Press.

Schlosser, E. (1998, December). The prison-industrial complex. *Atlantic Monthly*. Retrieved from `http://www.theatlantic.com`

Sellin, T. (1976). *Slavery and the penal system*. New York: Elsevier.

Senate Special Committee on Illegal Drugs. (2002, September). *Cannabis: Our position for a Canadian public policy* (Summary report).

Smith, A. (2002). America's lonely drug war. In M. Gray (Ed.), *Busted: Stone cowboys, narco-lords and Washington's War on Drugs* (pp. 121–124). New York: Thunder's Mouth Press/Nation Books.

Sourcebook of Criminal Statistics. (2001). Retrieved from `http://albany.edu/sourcebook`

Stroup, K., & Armentano, P. (2002). The problem is pot prohibition. In M. Gray (Ed.), *Busted: Stone cowboys, narco-lords and Washington's War on Drugs* (pp. 223–224). New York: Thunder's Mouth Press/Nation Books.

Sutton, J. R. (2000). Imprisonment and social classification in five common-law democracies, 1955–1985. *American Journal of Sociology, 106*, 350–386.

Uggen, C., & Manza, J. (2002) Democratic contraction? Political consequences of felon disfranchisement in the United States. *American Sociological Review, 67*, 777–803.

U.S. Department of Justice. (n.d). *Uniform Crime Reports*. Retrieved from `http://www.ojp.usdoj.gov`

Western, B., & Beckett K. (1999). How unregulated is the U.S. labor market? The penal system as a labor market institution. *American Journal of Sociology, 104*, 1030–1060.

Wilson, W. J. (1987). *The truly disadvantaged: The inner city, the underclass, and public policy*. Chicago: University of Chicago Press.

Wilson, W. J. (1996). *When work disappears: The world of the new urban poor*. New York: Vintage.

Wright, P. (1998). *Business behind bars*. Retrieved from `http://www.speakeasy.org/wfp/29/prison1.html`

Zimmer, L., & Morgan, J. P. (1997). *Marijuana myths, marijuana facts*. New York: Lindesmith Center.

Zimring, F. E., & Hawkins, G. (1991). *The scale of imprisonment*. Chicago: University of Chicago Press.

AUTHOR'S NOTE: Revised version of a paper presented at the annual meeting of the Academy of Criminal Justice Sciences, Orlando, FL, March 9–13, 1999.

<u>Call to Arms</u>

How to Win the Drug War

The drug war has trampled our liberties, broken up families, and done nothing to stop the flow of illegal drugs. So how can people of good will end this pernicious war?

by James Gray

For more than two decades I was a soldier in the War on Drugs. In the course of my career, I have helped put drug users and dealers in jail; I have presided over the breakup of families; I have followed the laws of my state and have seen their results.

At one point, I held the record for the largest drug prosecution in the Los Angeles area: 75 kilos of heroin, which was and is a lot of narcotics. But today the record is 18 tons. I have prosecuted some people, and later sentenced others, to long terms in prison for drug offenses, and would do so again. But it has not done any good. I have concluded that we would be in much better shape if we could somehow take the profit out of the drug trade. Truly, the drugs are dangerous, but it is the drug money that is turning a disease into a plague.

I saw the heartbreaking results of drug prohibition too many times in my own courtroom. I saw children tempted by adults to become involved in drug trafficking for $50 in cash, a lot of money to a youngster in the inner city, or almost anywhere else. Once the child's reliability has been established in his roles as a lookout or gofer, he is trusted to sell small amounts of drugs. Of course, that results in greater profits both for the adult dealer and his protégé. The children sell these drugs, not to adults, but to their peers, thus recruiting more children into a life of taking and selling drugs. I saw this repeated again and again. Like others in the court system, I didn't talk about it.

More than once, I saw a single mother who made a big mistake: she chose the wrong boyfriend, a drug dealer. One day, he offered her $400 to carry a particular package across town and give it to a fellow dealer. She strongly suspected that it contained drugs, but she needed the money to pay her rent. So she did it. And she was arrested, convicted, and sentenced to five years in prison for the transportation of cocaine. Since the mother legally abandoned her children because she could not take care of them, they all came to me, in juvenile court, to be dealt with as abused and neglected children.

I tell these mothers that unless they are really lucky and have a close personal friend or family member that is both willing and able to take care of their children until they are released from custody, their children will probably be adopted by somebody else. That is usually enough to make a mother hysterical.

Taxpayers shouldn't be very happy, either. Not only does it cost about $25,000 to keep the mother in prison for the next year; it also costs about $5,000 per month to keep a child in a group home until adoption. For a family of three, that means that our local government has to spend about $145,000 of taxpayer money for the first year simply to separate a mother from her children. And it falls upon me to enforce this result. I do it, because I am required by my oath of office to follow the law.

But there came a time when I could be quiet about this terrible situation no longer.

I concluded that helping to repeal drug prohibition was the best and most lasting gift I could make to my country. On April 8, 1992, I held a press conference outside the Courthouse in Santa Ana and recommended that we as a country investigate the possibility of change.

Since that time, I have spoken on this subject as often as possible, consistent with getting my cases tried. Most people listen; some agree, and others still want to punish me for my attempts to have an open and honest discussion of drug policy. I remember a short introduction I received before one of my talks, which was along the lines of: "I know you all want to hear the latest dope from the courthouse, so here's Judge Gray."

The major parties will never begin the process of ending the War on Drugs. It takes another party to do that—one that holds dear the principles of liberty.

During the next few years, I worked on a book to expose the evil anti-drug crusade. In 2001, my book, *Why Our Drug Laws Have Failed and What We Can Do About It—A Judicial Indictment of the War on Drugs*, was published by Temple University Press. It was the culmination of my experience as a former federal prosecutor with the United States Attorney's Office in Los Angeles, criminal defense attorney in the United States Navy JAG Corps, and a trial judge in Orange County, California since 1983, experience which had long before convinced me that our nation's program of drug prohibition is not simply a failure, but a hopeless failure.

In February, I took another step to end the War on Drugs. After being a Republican for all of my adult life, I registered as a member of the Libertarian Party. I realized that the major parties will never begin the process of ending the War on Drugs. It takes another party to do that—one that holds dear the principles of liberty. I had taken the "World's Smallest Political Quiz," and discovered that I was already a libertarian. I was frustrated and concerned about our country's lack of principled leadership, the direction of our economy, and the continued subversion of the protections of our Bill of Rights. The Libertarian Party is my natural home. And it is the Libertarian Party's historic mission to begin the peace process in the War on Drugs.

Drug prohibition has resulted in a greater loss of civil liberties than anything else in the history of our country. The United States of America leads the world in the incarceration of its people, mostly for non-violent drug offenses. Statistics show that all racial groups use and abuse drugs at basically the same rate, but most of those incarcerated are people of color. The War on Drugs has contributed substantially to the increasing power, bureaucracy, and intrusiveness of government. And, of course, the sale of illicit drugs is by far the largest source of funding for terrorists around the world. If we were truly serious about fighting terrorism, we would kill the "Golden Goose" of terrorism, which is drug prohibition.

It is important to understand that the failure of these laws is not the fault of law enforcement. It makes as much sense to blame the police and the criminal justice system for the failure of drug prohibition as it would be to blame Elliot Ness for the failure of alcohol Prohibition. The tragic results are the fault of the drug laws themselves, and not those who have been assigned the impossible task of enforcing them.

"We the People" are facing radicals at the controls of government who are impervious to the harm they are causing. When the head of the Drug Enforcement Administration expressly flouts the will of the people as expressed, for example, by California's medical marijuana Proposition 215, that is one thing. He is a policeman, enforcing the law as ordered. But what about when the head of the Department of Justice subverts that will? When John Ashcroft, as the United States Attorney General, directly acts against the expressed will of the people in this area, simply because he disagrees with it, he is not being conservative. We should call this action what it is: extremist. And when various officials of the federal government use our tax money actively to oppose state ballot initiatives all around the country, we should call that what it is: illegal.

The Republican and Democratic parties are invested in the drug war, committed to it. If we wait for them to act against drug prohibition, we will be waiting a very long time. However, we Libertarians are singularly in a position to help. I suggest that the Libertarian Party make the issue of the repeal of drug prohibition the centerpiece issue of all state and federal political campaigns for 2004. R. W. Bradford has made a similar argument in speeches over the past several years, and in an article in the December 1999 *Liberty*, and so possibly have others. The idea is not original with me, but it is a good idea.

I understand that, historically, the Libertarian Party has been largely unsuccessful in putting its candidates into office. But that can change, and in many ways the voters are ahead of the politicians on this issue. If we can make it clear that every vote for a state or federal Libertarian candidate represents a vote to end the War on Drugs and we capture only a third of the votes of people who want drug reform, we will get ten percent of the vote. That would be enough to make us a political force to be reckoned with and to put the drug war into the nation's political debate.

I want to make this very clear. If we focus our campaign on the drug issue, people who agree with us will not worry about "throwing away their vote" on a third-party candidate. For a change, *every* vote will be seen to matter.

Many Americans have seen and suffered through the unnecessary harms perpetrated by our failed drug policy. And many of these people are organized. By the time this article is published, I will have contacted all the drug policy reform groups I know, such as the Drug Policy Alliance, Families Against Mandatory Minimums, Common Sense for Drug Policy, Families Against Three Strikes, the National Organization for the Reform of Marijuana Laws, the Marijuana Policy Project, the Drug Policy Foundations of Texas, Hawaii, and New Mexico. I will call their members to join me and become dues-paying members of the Libertarian Party, and request their friends and family members to do the same.

The people in these groups are frustrated by the absence of a tangible national movement that they can support. In addition, in many ways they have learned through their experiences to share libertarian principles and values. The more people who register Libertarian, the more public attention will be paid to the issue of drug policy reform. This, in turn, will attract additional members, and additional attention. I think this plan will be successful, because most of the people in these groups are active; they are committed; they vote, and they have friends who vote.

Today, most Americans realize that our country is not in better shape with regard to the use and abuse of drugs and all the harm and misery that accompany them than we were five years ago. They also are beginning to understand that since that is the case, we can have no legitimate expectation of being in better shape next year than we are today unless we change our approach. Accordingly, many of our fellow citizens are beginning to realize that it is okay to discuss this subject.

Whether they know it or not, Americans are looking to the Party of Principle for guidance and leadership. Our slogan in 2004 should be "This Time It Matters."

From *Liberty*, May 2003, pp. 33-34, 40. © 2003 by Liberty Magazine.

Tokin' Politics

Making Marijuana Law Reform An Election Issue

"Penalties against drug use should not be more damaging to an individual than the use of the drug itself. Nowhere is this more clear than in the laws against the possession of marijuana in private for personal use." Former U.S. President Jimmy Carter spoke these words in a message to Congress in 1977. Since then, no sitting U.S. President has advocated decriminalizing marijuana, and virtually all have used the "bully pulpit" to advocate for tougher penalties for cannabis users.

Paul Armentano

THIS STARK REALITY LEAVES many American pot-smoking voters in a bind on election day. Few mainstream presidential hopefuls have dared to campaign on a platform of drug law reform, and of those who have suggested changes—most notably former president Bill Clinton (who promised to grant qualified patients federal access to medicinal marijuana) and current president George W. Bush (who said that state governments should be free to decide on the legalization of medical pot without federal interference)—both immediately reversed their positions upon gaining office. Others have simply ignored the marijuana

issue, or worse, promised to crack down even more severely on illicit drug users, à la former presidents Ronald Reagan and George Bush Sr.

The pending 2004 presidential election appears unlikely to buck this trend. Over the past four years, incumbent Republican President George W. Bush has amassed a heinous record regarding marijuana law reform. His administration has overseen more than 700,000 marijuana arrests per year, nearly 90 percent of which have been for simple possession only. Bush and his henchmen have also led an unprecedented domestic crackdown on businesses that sell glass pipes and other items

associated with marijuana smoking, and handed down criminal indictments against their proprietors, including noted actor Tommy Chong. In addition, the President instructed the Department of Education to vigorously enforce a seldom used 1998 law that bars convicted marijuana and drug offenders from receiving financial student aid. As a result, approximately 50,000 citizens—primarily marijuana offenders—have been denied federal student financial aid annually under the Bush presidency.

The President has been no better on the medical marijuana front, launching numerous federal raids against medicinal marijuana patients and dispensaries in states that have legalized its use. In addition, administration officials have aggressively campaigned against local and state proposals seeking to protect patients who use marijuana as a medicine. Bush has also been an international menace, as his administration has levied significant political pressure upon the Parliaments of both Canada and Jamaica to persuade them to reject proposals to decriminalize small amounts of marijuana.

The President's Democratic opponent, longtime U.S. Senator John Kerry, promises only incremental improvement. When asked his opinions on the personal use of marijuana in a November 2003 interview with *Rolling Stone Magazine*, Kerry acknowledged" I've met plenty of people in my lifetime who've used marijuana … [like] some people drink beer or wine or have a cocktail; I don't get too excited by any of that." However, when asked directly if he supported decriminalizing pot, he disappointingly replied, "No, not quite."

"Over the past four years, incumbent Republican President George W. Bush has amassed a heinous record regarding marijuana law reform."

Kerry's position regarding the medicinal use of marijuana is only slightly better. Speaking in January at the New Hampshire College Convention, Kerry said that he opposed the Bush administration's policy of federally prosecuting medical marijuana patients who reside in states that have legalized its use. However, Kerry stopped short of endorsing marijuana's therapeutic use, stating

(as summarized by the Associated Press), "he wanted to wait for the completion of a study to see what other alternatives might be available … before deciding whether to legalize it in all states." Kerry neglected to mention that no such "study" is pending, or that the last federal study to examine pot's medical utility—a 1999 report by the U.S. Institute of Medicine—recommended legalizing the use of medical cannabis for qualified patients.

So what's a marijuana law reform advocate to do on election day? Hold their nose and cast their ballot for the so-called "lesser of two evils" (aka" anybody but Bush"); remain true to their pot smoking principles and vote for a third party candidate (i.e. Green Party, Libertarian Party, etc.) who advocates marijuana law reform, but holds zero chance of winning the presidency; ignore the drug law reform issue altogether and vote for a candidate based on their support for other relevant political policies; stay home?

Recently, this question was posed to several leaders in the U.S. drug law reform movement. Their opinions were equally varied and engaging, a sampling of which is presented below.

"Upon much reflection, I am still in the 'ABB' [anybody but Bush] category. Kerry is a mixed bag at best, although I think he is okay on the medical marijuana issue—if only for the cynical reason that most of the country already support it. … I shudder to think what will happen if the [Bush administration] gets another four years, when they don't have to worry much about another election, and have a Republican controlled Congress.

That being said, if for some reason it looks like a sure thing for Kerry here in Michigan in November, my principles dictate a vote for the Libertarian Party candidate."

"I hear the 'anyone but Bush' cry often and I understand it; I am certainly no Bush fan. Here in New York [state] however, I will still be able to vote for a third party candi-

date without fear of giving anything to Bush because New York is solidly Democrat. Since the electoral votes are all that count and they are going to go to [Democratic nominee John Kerry], I can vote for a [third party candidate] with no worry about helping throw the election to Bush.

Should polls in the state show a close race I might vote Democrat. On the other hand, part of me says 'What's the difference?' Voting Democrat will only delay America's headlong rush to totalitarianism. None of the current contenders impress me in the least. If this is what Americans want, let them have it. When it's here we'll see how many of them like it. I'll probably vote Libertarian.

Check out the situation in your state and vote accordingly. There's no sense encouraging these mediocre candidates by voting for them unless absolutely necessary."

"Having had the opportunity to talk briefly to John Kerry at a campaign event in San Francisco, I was frankly impressed. He radiated charisma, charm and wit, and addressed my questions attentively and responsively. I welcomed him to the 'medical marijuana center' of the U.S. and asked whether he would keep the [federal Drug Enforcement Administration] out of the city's [cannabis] clubs. 'I certainly hope so,' he said. He went on to volunteer that the U.S. had far too many nonviolent prisoners, and that he supported sentencing reform of mandatory minimums. This was more than I asked for. It is also more than Clinton ever promised. I recognize that Kerry does not have a record of standing up for drug reform [as a U.S. Senator]—he even led hearings calling for tougher measures against the drug lords in Colombia. But I feel he offers a real chance of opening the door to reform. If we keep the pressure up, I think he may prove responsive."

"Taking a lesson from the Civil Rights Movement, I vote 'single-issue' all the time. If a candidate refuses to represent my community, then I refuse to vote for them. That's why I didn't vote for [former Democratic presidential candidate] Al Gore in 2000.

Though the democrats haven't quite figured it out, hopefully they'll realize that people stay home or vote for candidates like [Independent candidate Ralph Nader] because the two-party system is failing to represent them. The Democrats, excluding [minority candidate and U.S. Representative] Dennis Kucinich, have failed to adequately address many social issues, including environmental protection, racial inequality, civil unions, and most important to me, failed drug policies. Though I haven't written him off, John Kerry has yet to earn my vote. If marijuana smokers want to be a visible political constituency we have to prioritize marijuana issues as something that will make or break our voting decisions. When politicians realize that they have no choice but to address issues of marijuana law reform, then we will truly be able to 'Smoke the Vote.'"

"I think that Bush [and U.S. Attorney General John Ashcroft] are significantly threatening to the U.S. Constitution and civil rights. [Therefore,] I am firmly in the 'ABB' [anybody but Bush] camp. Although I am a registered Green Party, I will hold my nose and vote for the Democrat this time, and pray that we can hold Kerry to his campaign positions regarding medical marijuana."

"As I look forward to the 2004 presidential election, I am conflicted. On one hand, I decided a couple of years ago that I could never again vote for someone who wants to put me in jail for smoking pot. I understand the reasons for voting for the lesser of two evils, but there is something self-destructive about helping put people in office who want to treat me like a criminal.

However, I live in suburban Virginia which generally votes Republican in presidential elections. Hopefully the fact that I will either not vote for president, or will vote for some marginalized candidate who has a good position on marijuana policy, does not help George

Bush get reelected. If the election were close in Virginia, I might have to reconsider.

Until marijuana smokers in large numbers are willing to withhold their support from those candidates who insist that we are criminals, we will never win our freedom. It's time we came out of the closet and let our elected officials know that they must revise their policy on marijuana smoking or lose our collective votes."

"Don't vote, it just encourages them! I'm only half kidding. ...Ultimately, I think the politics of scale perverts national elections [though] I have voted in local races. [As a result,] part of me still feels it is more effective to vote with the majority who stay at home because they realize our [national] electoral system is terminally ill. But unless we can effectively articulate an alternative, even that act of abstention becomes devoid of meaning. On the other hand, we're all toast if we don't get some 'regime change' in November.

At minimum, I think reformers should push for Instant Runoff Voting [a system that allows voters to rank their candidates in order of preference] so that people can vote their conscience without 'wasting' their vote. Any candidate for office who supports IRV can be assured of one of my votes! Without it, we are stuck eternally with choosing between the lesser of two evils."

"If drug policy reformers decide they are going to vote for Kerry I'd suggest not telling him, and making him earn our votes. Let's not give someone who has been pretty much a drug war hawk our vote for free. Make him work for it! The power of our vote is something he needs, especially since there will be a Libertarian, Green and maybe Independent candidates [on the Presidential ballot] who will each be better on our issue. Indeed, I would hold out and support the minor party/independent candidate until the last minute if I were voting Kerry, and if I were in a non-battleground, safe state I'd vote

for whoever was closest to my views."

•••

While the particulars of individuals' opinions differ, there indeed exists a consensus among drug law reformers that citizens must become more involved in the political process in order to move the pot issue forward. The bottom line: In order to achieve substantive legislative reform, the tens of millions of U.S. marijuana smokers must become an active, visible political constituency whom elected officials from both major parties take notice of and respond to. "Drug policy reformers need to get recognized as an identifiable, voting constituency to have some influence," explains Mikki Norris. "Either use what democratic process we have, or lose it! If we don't vote, we don't count."

> "If a candidate refuses to represent my community, then I refuse to vote for them. That's why I didn't vote for [former Democratic presidential candidate] Al Gore in 2000."

Common Sense for Drug Policy President Kevin Zeese agrees. "The only real way you have power in this country is to vote," he advises. "We can put out all the facts, statistics and emotional horror stories we want, but if we cannot remove drug warriors from office and replace them with reformers, we will never succeed."

The best way to achieve this? Get involved in the political process at both the national and local level and encourage other like-minded reformers to do the same. "The facts have been on our side for a long time, political power has not been," says Zeese. "So not only should you vote, but you should get politically active. Join a local political club of any of the major or minor parties; help register voters; help educate voters; run for office; help people who are running for office with time and money. This is where the rubber meets the road—electoral politics."

Indeed, political reform almost always grows from the ground up, but only after having sufficiently watered the grassroots. Marijuana law reform is no different. This November, make your voice heard. Tell America's politicians: We're here, we smoke, we vote!

Paul Armentano is the Senior Policy Analyst for The NORML Foundation in Washington, DC. To learn more about NORML or to register to vote via NORML's online "Smoke the Vote" campaign, please visit the NORML website at: **http://www.norml.org** or call (888) 67-NORML to make a donation.

Drug Legalization

Four Points About Drug Decriminalization

DOUGLAS HUSAK

Philosophers have been strangely silent about the topic of illicit drugs, even though it is a gold mine of philosophical questions. It is distressing to see how few of the dozens of books now available on current moral and social issues contain sections on drug issues. It seems far more pressing to question the punishment of drug users than the execution of murderers—mostly because there are so many more of them. Approximately 80 to 90 million people have used illicit drugs at some point in their lives. There are well over 400,000 drug offenders in jail, about 130,000 for possession alone. Unlike the case of capital murderers, it is plausible to suppose that drug users should not be punished at all, and this is what I want to argue here.

I suspect that the best single explanation for the philosophical neglect of this topic is that it is has a considerable empirical content. When I raise this issue with my undergraduate classes, and ask why we should or should not punish drug users, less than a minute is needed before someone makes a controversial empirical claim about the effects of given drugs on users or on society in general. No one can hope to address the set of moral and legal issues about drug decriminalization without knowing a lot of facts about drugs and drug users. Contrast this with abortion, in which the relevant facts can be learned fairly quickly. Philosophers understandably tend to shy away from topics with a heavily empirical component.

Yet without the input of philosophers, the field has been left largely to scholars in criminal justice, nearly all of whom profess to have no theory of criminalization, but seem mostly to be consequentialists. They prepare cost-benefit analyses of the relative merits of criminalization and decriminalization. Many have concluded that our current drug laws are ineffective and counterproductive. They are probably correct, but that is not the line of inquiry I want to pursue here. As philosophers, I think we should be more interested in examining arguments of *principle*.

I The Meaning of Decriminalization

First, there is absolutely no consensus among those of us who work in criminal theory about the meaning of such terms as *legalization* or *decriminalization*. So I resort to stipulation. What I mean by the use of the term "decriminalization" in this context is that the use of a given drug would not be a criminal offense. I take it to be a conceptual truth for which I will not argue here that criminal offenses render persons liable to state punishment. Thus anyone who thinks that the use of a given drug should be decriminalized believes that persons should not be punished merely for using that drug.

I am aware that there is enormous confusion about this topic. In polls, many respondents report that they do not want to see a given drug decriminalized, but do not favor punishing people who merely use that drug. If my account of decriminalization is accepted, this response is incoherent.

For a number of reasons, this definition of decriminalization is deceptively simple. First, there really is little punishment for use today. In most but not all jurisdictions, what is punished is possession rather than use. Technically, then, drug use is generally not criminalized. But I take the fact that statutes punish possession rather than use to be relatively unimportant. Possession is punished rather than use because it is easier to prove. In what follows, I ignore this complication and continue to suppose that decriminalization pertains to drug use. Except perhaps in fantastic cases, no one can use a drug without possessing it.

Second, there is no clear understanding of what kinds of state responses amount to punishments. Many reformers argue that drug users should be fined rather than imprisoned, and they call this idea decriminalization. Others argue that drug users should be made to undergo treatment, and they also call this idea decriminalization. Whether these proposals are compatible with what I mean by decriminalization depends on whether fines or coerced treatment are modes of punishment rather than alternatives to punishment. I think both fines and coerced treatment are modes of punishment. Even though they are probably preferable to what we now do to drug users, these responses are ruled out by decriminalization as I construe it. But that is a quibble I hope not to worry about. Simply put, whatever you take punishment to be, that is what decriminalization forbids the state from doing to people who merely use drugs.

Third, decriminalization as I propose to define it has no implications for what should be done to persons who *produce* or *sell* drugs. Therefore, it is not really a comprehensive drug policy that can rival the status quo. The considerations that I think work in favor of decriminalizing use are somewhat different from those that apply to the decriminalization of production and sale, so I propose to put production and sale aside in this essay. This is bound to disappoint some people. Many thinkers are attracted to decriminalization, or reluctantly driven to support it, because they hope to end the violence, black market, and involvement of organized crime in drug transactions today. These sound like worthwhile objectives, but drug decriminalization per se does not achieve them. I think we should start by clarifying what should happen to drug users, and *then* move to the issue of whether or how production and sale should be regulated. Again, I am aware that many thoughtful people believe that these topics should all be tackled simultaneously, but I think it is easier to proceed one step at a time.

Finally, I admit that there is something odd about my understanding of decriminalization. What I call decriminalization in the context of drugs is comparable to what was called prohibition in the context of alcohol from 1920 to 1933. During those memorable years, production and sale were banned, but not the use or mere possession of alcohol. If we replicated that approach in our drug policy, I would call it decriminalization. That is admittedly odd, but it underscores the fact that our response to illicit drug users today is far more punitive than anything we ever did to drinkers.

II The Best Reason to Decriminalize Drug Use

With these preliminaries out of the way, let me proceed to the basic question to be addressed. In my judgment, the fundamental issue is not whether to *decriminalize* the use of any or all drugs, but whether to *criminalize* the use of any or all drugs. The status quo must be defended. If this is the right question to ask, I would now like to offer what I believe to be the most plausible answer to it: The best reason not to criminalize drug use is that no argument in favor of criminalizing drug use is any good—no argument is good enough to justify criminalization. I want to make three points about this general strategy for decriminalization.

First, I recognize that this approach is not very exciting. My reason to oppose criminalization does not invoke any deep principle worth fighting about like freedom of speech or religion. I am not sure that there is any deep principle that *all* drug prohibitions violate. In particular, my approach does not invoke the principle that some libertarians cite: the "freedom to do whatever you want to your own body." I do not invoke this principle because I do not believe it is true. I am not a libertarian. Whether you have a right to do something you want to your body depends on what happens when you do it.

Then again, *some* drug prohibitions seem to violate deep principles that philosophers should care about. This becomes more apparent when you pause to consider exactly what it is that drug proscriptions are designed to prevent. Most drugs have a legitimate use, so drug consumption per se is rarely prohibited. Instead, the use of most drugs is prohibited only for a given purpose. To get directly to the heart of the matter, the proscribed purpose is usually to produce a state of intoxication or a drug "high." In case there is any doubt, let me cite the California criminal statute regulating nitrous oxide. This statute makes it a crime for "any person [to possess] nitrous oxide … with the intent to breathe [or] inhale… for purposes of causing a condition of intoxication, elation, euphoria, dizziness, stupefaction, or dulling of the senses or for the purpose of, in any manner, changing… mental processes."[1] The ultimate objective of this statute is to prevent persons from breathing something in order to change their mental processes. It is hard to see why this objective is legitimate in a state committed to freedom of thought and expression.[2] I am not sure that *all* drug prohibitions so transparently jeopardize our right to freedom of thought. In any event, I do not believe we need to appeal to any deep principle to resist drug prohibitions generally.[3]

Second, my case is necessarily inconclusive. I am in the unenviable position of trying to prove a negative. How can I hope to show that no argument in favor of criminalizing drug use is good enough? All I can ever aspire to do is to respond to the best arguments that have been given. I am reminded of a remark made by Hume. "Tis impossible to refute a system, which has never been explain'd. In such a manner of fighting in the dark, a man loses his blows in the air, and often places them where the enemy is not present."[4] This is the predicament someone faces in trying to defend drug decriminalization. I am usually asked to go first on panels convened to debate drug decriminalization, but I think I should go last so that I can respond to what others think are good reasons for criminalization.

Third, my case for decriminalization has the advantage of making minimal assumptions about justice. I assume that no one should be punished unless there are excellent reasons for doing so. Punishment, after all, is the worst thing our state can do to us. The imposition of punishment must satisfy a very demanding standard of justification.[5] It is hard to imagine that anyone would reject this assumption.

The fundamental issue is not whether to decriminalize the use of any or all drugs, but whether to criminalize the use of any or all drugs.

Thus my case against criminalization depends on the claim that no case for criminalization has been adequately defended. It is utterly astounding, I think, that no very good argument for drug prohibitions has ever been given. When I am asked to recommend the best book or article that makes a philosophically plausible case for punishing drug users, I am embarrassed to say that I have little to suggest.[6]

Let me then cut directly to my own conclusions. No single argument for decriminalization responds to all arguments for criminalization. We must respond argument-by-argument, and, I think, drug-by-drug. We may have good reasons to criminalize some drugs, but not others. For example, I do not know anyone who wants to punish persons who use caffeine. Surely this is because of empirical facts about caffeine—how it affects those who use it and society in general. I can certainly *imagine* a drug that people should be punished for using. Such drugs are easy to describe; they are vividly portrayed in great works of fiction. Consider the substance that transformed Dr. Jekyll into Mr. Hyde. If a drug literally turned users into homicidal monsters, we would have excellent reasons to prohibit its consumption. Fortunately, no such drug actually exists. In fact, I have never seen a persuasive argument for punishing persons who use any drug that I am aware is widely used for recreational purposes.

III   Criminalization

Any good reason to criminalize a kind of behavior invokes a theory of criminalization. We cannot decide whether we have a good reason to punish persons who use drugs in particular unless we know what would count as a good reason to punish anyone for anything. We do not really have a theory of criminalization in the real world, unless "more is always better" qualifies for a theory.[7] I want to pause briefly to describe what passes for a theory of criminalization in our constitutional law today.[8] Most laws limit or restrict liberties. When the constitutionality of these laws is challenged, courts respond by dividing liberties into two kinds: fundamental and non-fundamental. The constitutionality of legislation that restricts a fundamental liberty is subjected to "strict scrutiny" and is evaluated by applying the onerous "compelling state interest" test. Virtually all criminal laws, however, limit non-fundamental liberties, and they are assessed by applying the much less demanding "rational basis" test. Under this test, the challenged law will be upheld if it is substantially related to a legitimate govern-

ment purpose. The legitimate government purpose need not be the actual objective of the legislation—only its conceivable objective. Since only those laws that lack a conceivable legitimate purpose will fail this test, courts almost never find a law to be unconstitutional when non-fundamental liberties are restricted. As a result, the state needs only some conceivable legitimate purpose to enact the great majority of criminal laws on the books today—most notably, drug prohibitions, which are always evaluated by applying the rational basis test. So persons who break these laws can be punished simply because the state has a rational basis to do so.

What is remarkable about this approach is its complete indifference to the distinction between criminal and non-criminal legislation.[9] It is one thing to enact non-criminal laws that pass the rational basis test. But it is quite another when criminal legislation is assessed by that same standard. Criminal law is different—it is importantly dissimilar from other kinds of law. Many of the arguments I have heard for drug prohibitions do a perfectly good job explaining why rational persons might well decide not to use illicit drugs, or why the state may have good reasons to discourage people from using drugs, but I fear they do not provide a justification for punishing drug users.

If our theory of criminalization in the real world is so bad, one would have thought that the most distinguished criminal theorists of our day would have had lots to say to rectify the situation. But they have said surprising little. They mostly continue to argue about the *harm principle*. But debates about whether to accept the harm principle in our theory of criminalization do not get us very far when trying to decide whether to punish drug users. We have excellent reasons to punish people who commit theft or rape. These offenses harm others by violating their rights. But this rationale cannot explain why drug users should be punished. I do not think there is any sense of harm or any theory of rights that can be invoked to show that I harm someone or violate his rights when I inject heroin or smoke crack. At most, I risk harm to myself or to others when I use a drug. I conceptualize offenses that create only a risk of harm that may or may not materialize as *inchoate* offenses—similar to attempt, solicitation, or conspiracy. If I am correct, the criteria we should apply to assess the justifiability of drug proscriptions are those we should apply to assess the justifiability of inchoate offenses. Unfortunately, we have no such criteria. Almost no theorist has tried very hard to extend a theory of criminalization to conduct that creates a risk of harm rather than harm itself.[10]

Notice, however, the enormous burden an argument for criminalization would have to bear. As I have said, there are about 80 or 90 million Americans who have used an illicit drug at some point in their lives. That is approximately 42 percent of our population aged 12 and over. About 15 million Americans used an illicit drug last year, on literally billions of occasions. Very few of these occasions produced any harm. Longitudinal studies do not indicate that the population of persons who ever have used illicit drugs is very different from the population of lifetime abstainers in any ways that seem relevant to criminalization. So any argument for punishment would have to justify punishing the many, whose behavior is innocuous, for the sake of some objective that results in a very tiny percentage of cases. Many attempted murders result in successful murders, which are harms, but very few instances of drug use bring about any result we should describe as significantly harmful.

When you cannot possibly punish all of the people who commit a crime, you can only punish some. Inevitably, those who get arrested, prosecuted, and sentenced are the least powerful. Drug prohibition would have vanished long ago had whites been sent to prison for drug offenses at the same rate as blacks. Although minorities are no more likely to use illicit drugs, they are far more likely to be arrested, prosecuted, and punished when they do. This is one of the features of drug prohibitions that should outrage us all. Some people try to package drug prohibitions as a benefit to minorities, but there is plenty of evidence that they devastate minority communities and will continue to do so as long as enforcement is so selective. And yet enforcement will always be selective, since every offender cannot possibly be punished.

If drug prohibitions are so bad for minority communities, one may wonder why minority leaders are not more outspoken about the drug war. In fact, blacks are more ambivalent than whites about drug policy.[11] Overall, blacks tend to have more negative opinions about drugs (both licit and illicit) than whites. At the same time, blacks are less likely than whites to believe that the solution to the problem is to enforce prohibition with severe punishments. Black mothers who are staunchly anti-drug are not enthusiastic about policies that lock up their sons and daughters for lengthy periods of time. But why are blacks not even more critical of the status quo? No one explanation can be given. But my own hypothesis cites the role of religion on attitudes about drugs. Although opinions about drug policy vary somewhat with age, education, income, and gender, no variable correlates with anti-drug attitudes more closely than religion and, at least in the United States, protestant Christianity in particular.

IV   Predictions: A Bad Reason to Criminalize

I have space to provide a brief critique of only one argument, and I apologize in advance if I neglect the reader's own candidate for the best reason to criminalize drug use. I will not comment on drugs and kids, drugs and health, drugs and crime, or drugs and morality. But I think the argument I discuss here may be the most common. It rests on predictions that the use of drugs would soar if we stopped punishing persons who use them. This argument, I think, flounders on both empirical and normative grounds.

I begin with the empirical considerations. My conclusion is that we simply do not have any good basis to predict how the amount of harm caused by drugs would change if we did not punish those who use them. Many persons find my uncertainty to be unwarranted. Economic models indicate that the frequency of use is a function of costs: decriminalize use, and the monetary and non-monetary costs of drugs will go down. The trouble is that all predictions about how rates of consumption will rise after use is decriminalized assume that nothing else will change. One thing we can predict is that many other things will change if drug use is decriminalized. Let me mention just a few things that might very well change, and that make all such predictions perilous.

I begin by challenging the claim that decriminalization will cause the monetary price of drugs to plummet. Why assume that decriminalization will make illicit drugs significantly more affordable? Decriminalization itself, as I have emphasized, need not allow illicit drugs to be sold with impunity. If decriminalization does not extend to sale, it need not have much affect on the monetary cost of drugs. But even were sale decriminalized, illicit drugs would become subject to taxation. I will not try to estimate the optimal rate of taxation. Whatever the exact amount, we can be sure that taxes would add enormously to the price of newly decriminalized drugs.

Another factor influencing the price of decriminalized illicit drugs is very difficult to estimate. If illicit drugs are anywhere near as harmful as many people believe, some mechanism must be created to compensate victims for the harms they suffer when drugs are used. These harms might befall users themselves, or be suffered by others. One way to compensate victims for each of these kinds of harms is by allowing lawsuits against producers of illicit drugs. We have been reluctant to allow such lawsuits in the cases of tobacco, alcohol, or firearms; powerful lobbies have fought against them for years. But we need not be so reluctant if we establish a new system of sale for illicit drugs. Producers could be made to pay for the costs of the various harms that their customers cause to themselves or to others. Producers would be able to pay these costs, and remain in business, only if they could pass them along to buyers by raising their prices. How much of an increase in price would be needed to compensate all of the victims for the harms they suffer when illicit drugs are used? No one can be sure. We cannot begin to answer this question unless we know how dangerous illicit drugs really are. I believe that the dangers of illicit drugs tend to be grossly exaggerated. Even if I am mistaken about the dangers of illicit drugs today, we can be confident that illicit drugs would be less dangerous in a world in which production and sale had been decriminalized. In such a world, suppliers would have enormous incentives to make their drugs as safe as possible in order to limit the amount of money they would be required to pay when harm was caused by the use of their product. If a given drug is very dangerous, we might even find that no company could hope to make a profit by selling it, and the drug would disappear from the lawful market. We simply do not know how dangerous illicit drugs will turn out to be after decriminalization, but financial incentives are bound to make them less harmful.

Illicit drugs would be less dangerous in a world in which production and sale had been decriminalized.

As a result of these two factors, we have almost no basis for estimating how the monetary price of decriminalized drugs would differ from their price in today's black market—if, that is, decriminalization were extended to production and sale. We do not know how much states will decide to tax the sale of drugs. In addition, we do not know how much sellers will have to charge in order to survive when lawsuits are brought against them. If this latter figure is high, drugs will be expensive, and fears about cheap drugs will be put to rest. If this figure is low, the price of drugs will decrease. But if the amount sellers must charge as a result of these lawsuits is low, it means that drugs will turn out to be less dangerous than we thought. If drugs turned out to be less dangerous than we thought, we will come to wonder why we were so worried about making them more affordable in the first place.

However uncertain we may be about how decriminalization will affect the monetary price of drugs, it will clearly eliminate the non-monetary cost of use. People will no longer fear arrest and prosecution. To the extent that this fear has helped to keep illicit drug use in check, we can anticipate that decriminalization would cause the incidence of drug use to rise. But to what extent? How will consumption change if drug users need not worry about punishment? No single piece of evidence on this point is decisive. But several factors suggest that the threat of punishment is not especially effective in curbing drug use. In what follows, I will describe a number of reasons to doubt that the removal of criminal penalties would cause a significant increase in the use of illicit drugs.

One source of evidence is obtained through surveys. People who have never used drugs are asked to explain their reasons for abstaining, and to speculate about how their willingness to experiment would be affected by a change in the law. Very few respondents cite their fear of punishment as a substantial factor in their decision not to try drugs.[12] The more dangerous the drug is perceived to be, the smaller the number of respondents who mention the law when asked to explain their reluctance to use it. Other surveys ask former users why they decided to quit. Those who once used drugs are asked why they do not continue to do so today, and to explain why their behavior has changed. Very few respondents report that fear of arrest and prosecution led them to stop using drugs. They cite a bad experience with a drug or some new responsibility, like a job or a newborn, but rarely mention the risk of punishment.[13] Of course, the value of these kinds of surveys is questionable. We may doubt that people have accurate insights into why they behave as they do, or what might lead them to behave differently. Surely, however, these surveys provide better evidence than mere conjecture. These surveys suggest that the fear of punishment is not a major factor in explaining why drug use is not more pervasive than it is.

For further evidence about how the fear of punishment affects the incidence of drug use, we might examine how trends in illicit drug use over the past thirty years are correlated with changes in law enforcement. If the fear of punishment were a significant factor in deterring illicit drug use, one would expect that rates of consumption would decline as punishments increased in frequency and severity. There is no correlation, however, between the frequency and severity of punishment and trends in drug use. If we look at the decade from 1980 to 1990, a case could be made that punishments were effective in deterring use. The incidence of illicit drug use, which peaked in 1979, steadily decreased throughout the 1980s. But frequent and severe punishments have not caused further declines during the 1990s; drug use has remained relatively flat in the past decade. We reach the same conclusion when we examine the data on a state-by-state basis. States with greater rates of incarceration for drug offenders tend to experience higher rates of drug use. Prohibitionists who predict a massive increase in drug use after decriminalization must struggle to explain these data. If punitive drug policies keep drug use in check, why do actual trends in drug consumption prove so resistant to the massive efforts we have made to punish drug users?

There is no correlation between the frequency and severity of punishment and trends in drug use.

Additional evidence can be gleaned from the experience of other countries, where the fear of arrest and prosecution for the use of given drugs is practically nonexistent. Most European countries have lower rates of illicit drug use, even though given drugs are often higher in quality, lower in price, and less likely to result in punishments. American teenagers consume more marijuana and most other illicit drugs than their European counterparts, although European teens are more likely to smoke cigarettes and drink alcohol. Consider the Netherlands, which is known for its relatively permissive drug laws. Although marijuana prevalence rates are roughly comparable in the two countries, about twice as many residents of the United States have experimented with other kinds of illicit drugs. In general, data from other parts of the world provide better evidence for an inverse than for a positive correlation between severities of punishments and rates of illicit drug use. Admittedly, however, this evidence is inconclusive. No country in the world has implemented decriminalization as I have defined it here.

The history of the United States provides further reason to doubt that fear of punishment plays a major role in reducing the use of illicit drugs. We must keep in mind that, for all practical purposes, drug prohibition did not begin until the early part of the twentieth century. In the nineteenth century, purchases of opium, morphine, cocaine, and marijuana were subject to almost no restrictions. Americans could buy these drugs in many different varieties from several different sources, including by mail order. But even though criminal penalties were not imposed for the use of opiates and cocaine, these drugs were probably less popular than today. Admittedly, however, the verdict of history is mixed. Most Americans agree that our era of alcohol prohibition was a dismal failure. By most accounts, however, per capita consumption of alcohol decreased throughout prohibition, and did not return to pre-prohibition levels for many years. This finding has led some social scientists to conclude that prohibition "worked" after all—if a reduction in use is the most important criterion of success. Others are skeptical. Curiously, however, even those social scientists who insist that alcohol prohibition was effective almost never recommend that our country should reinstate that policy.

Trends in the use of *licit* drugs provide yet another source of evidence. Prohibitionists tend to point to a reduction in illicit drug use over the last twenty years as a reason to believe that severe punishments have been effective in curbing drug use. Comparable declines in the use of alcohol and tobacco, however, have taken place over this same period of time, even without the threat of criminal liability. Rates of monthly illicit drug use in the United States peaked at about 14 percent in 1979, steadily declined to a low of just above 5 percent in 1992, and slowly increased thereafter to about 6 percent in 2001. Trends in alcohol and tobacco use exhibit more similarities than dissimilarities with these patterns. The overall use of alcohol and tobacco declined throughout the 1980s, and rebounded somewhat during the 1990s. We have ample evidence that the use of licit drugs can be decreased without the need to resort to criminal sanctions. We should assume that the same is true of illicit drugs.

If changes in the certainty and severity of punishment are not major factors in explaining trends in illicit drug use, what *does* account for these patterns? This is one of the most fascinating and difficult questions that arises about drug use, and I confess to having no good answer to it. Trends in the use of both licit and illicit drugs are as baffling and mysterious as trends in fashion. Unless we have better theories to explain why people use drugs, our forecasts about the future are bound to be simplistic. No one has a convincing explanation of why the use of a given drug increases or decreases within a given group in

a given place at a given time. By 2001, the popularity of crack in inner cities had waned enormously. Crack is no longer regarded as "cool" or "hip." Why? No simple answer can be given. Most experts believe that a heightened consciousness about health contributed to the reduction in the use of licit drugs during the 1980s. But what caused this growing concern about health, and why did it not lead rates of drug use to fall still further throughout the 1990s? Again, no answer is clearly correct. But credibility is strained if we suppose that a factor is important in accounting for decreases in the consumption of alcohol and tobacco but unimportant in accounting for decreases in the consumption of illicit drugs, especially when the patterns of these decreases are roughly comparable. In any event, we have little reason to believe that punishments play a central role in explaining trends in drug use.

The state may adopt any number of devices to discourage drug use, as long as these devices are not punitive.

I have provided several reasons to doubt that punishment is needed to keep rates of illicit drug use within reasonable bounds. But skepticism about the efficacy of punishment as a deterrent to drug use is only a small part of the reason why predictions about drug use after decriminalization are so tenuous. Recall the terms of decriminalization that I have offered here. The only change that this policy requires is that the state would not *punish* anyone simply for using a drug for recreational purposes. The state may adopt any number of devices to discourage drug use, as long as these devices are not punitive. Even more important, institutions other than the state can and do play a significant role in discouraging drug use. After decriminalization, some of these institutions might exert even more influence. Private businesses, schools, insurance companies, and universities, to cite just a few examples, might adopt policies that discriminate against drug users. Suppose that employers fired or denied promotions to workers who use cocaine. Suppose that schools barred students who drink alcohol from participating in extracurricular activities. Suppose that insurance companies charged higher premiums to policy holders who smoke tobacco. Suppose that colleges denied loans and grants to undergraduates who use marijuana. I do not endorse any of these ideas; many seem unwise and destined to backfire. Removing drug-using kids from schools, for example, seems destined to *increase* their consumption. I simply point out that such institutions could have a far greater impact than our criminal justice system on people's decisions to use drugs.

Predictions about drug use after decriminalization are confounded by yet another phenomenon—the "forbidden fruit" effect. Many people, adolescents in particular, are attracted to an activity precisely because it is forbidden or perceived as dangerous. Much of the thrill of illicit drug use stems from its illegality and the culture of deviance that surrounds it. Might the use of some illicit drugs actually *decrease* because they are no longer forbidden? If we change the law, the appeal of illicit drugs will be changed as well. To what extent? No one knows. Although many scholars have noted the forbidden fruit effect, serious research has yet to demonstrate its real significance.

Alarming predictions about future use assume that the drugs of tomorrow will resemble the drugs of today. This assumption seems extraordinarily naïve. The development of new and different substances makes predictions about consumption enormously speculative. Even though many illicit drugs—heroin and LSD, for example—were originally created by pharmaceutical companies, reputable corporations have tried hard to disassociate their drug products from illicit drugs. Decriminalization may lead pharmaceutical companies to expend their talent and ingenuity to create better and safer recreational drugs. One can only wonder about the products that might be developed if the best minds were put to the task. If more enjoyable and less dangerous drugs could be perfected, consumption might boom. But the development of better and safer drugs would make the increase in consumption less of a problem.

Whether or not better drugs appear on the market, no one can predict how users will substitute newly decriminalized drugs for existing licit drugs. After decriminalization, consumers will have lawful alternatives that we take for granted in other contexts. We simply do not know whether and to what extent users will substitute newly decriminalized drugs for those licit drugs they now tend to prefer. If a great deal of substitution takes place, the enormous social harm presently caused by tobacco and alcohol might decline considerably. So the total amount of harm caused by *all* categories of drugs might actually *decrease*, even if the consumption of illicit drugs were to *increase*. I do not find this conjecture so implausible. Over time, one would expect that users would tend to gravitate toward those drugs that could be integrated more easily into their lifestyles. In particular, we should welcome a possible reduction in alcohol use. As any college administrator knows, alcohol is the drug implicated in most of the date rapes, property damage, and violent behavior on campus. A possible decrease in alcohol consumption is one of the silver linings on the feared black cloud of drug decriminalization.

For all of these reasons, we should avoid predictions about how the decriminalization of drugs will affect rates of consumption. An even more important point is that these empirical conjectures are not especially relevant to the topic at hand. We are looking for a respectable reason to criminalize drug use. Predictions about how decriminalization will cause an increase in drug use simply do not provide such a reason. Indeed, this reason could be given against repealing virtually any law, however unjus-

tified it may be. Let me illustrate this point by providing an example of an imaginary crime that I assume everyone would agree to be unjustified. Suppose that the state sought to curb obesity by prohibiting people from eating pizza—an offense that would pass the rational basis test, by the way. Suppose that a group of philosophers convened to discuss whether we should change this law and decriminalize pizza consumption. Someone would be likely to protest that repealing this law would cause the consumption of pizza to increase. I imagine they would be correct. But surely this prediction would not serve to justify retaining this imaginary prohibition. If we lacked a good reason to attack the problem of obesity by punishing pizza eaters in the first place, the effects of repeal on pizza consumption would not provide such a reason. And so with drugs. Unless we already have a reason to punish pizza consumption, the prediction does not provide a good reason to *continue* to punish it.

If there is a good reason to criminalize illicit drug use, we have yet to find it. We need a better reason to criminalize something other than predictions about how its frequency would increase if punishments were not imposed. These predictions are dubious both normatively and (in this case) empirically. Despite my uncertainty about the future, there is *one* prediction about which we can be absolutely confident. After decriminalization, those who use illicit drugs will not face arrest and prosecution. The lives of drug users would not be devastated by a state that is committed to waging war against them. Punishment, we must always be reminded, is the worst thing a state can do to us. The single prediction we can safely make about decriminalization is that it will improve the lives of the hundreds of thousands of people who otherwise would be punished for the crime of using drugs for recreational purposes.

NOTES

[These comments are drawn from two books I have written about drug prohibitions. See Douglas Husak: *Drugs and Rights*, Cambridge: Cambridge University Press, 1992; and *Legalize This! The Case for Decriminalizing Drugs*, London: Verso Press, 2002.]

1. *Cal. State Penal Code*, § 381(b) (2002).
2. This point is made nicely by Richard Boire. see his http://www.cognitiveliberty.org.
3. I would be happy to be mistaken about this. Anyone who is more confident in his ability to identify and defend deep principles that are violated by all drug prohibitions is welcome to enlighten and assist me.
4. David Hume, *A Treatise of Human Nature*, (Selby-Bigge ed, 1968), Book III Section 1 p. 464.
5. See Douglas Husak: "Limitations on Criminalization and the General Part of Criminal Law," in Stephen Shute and A.P. Simester (eds), *Criminal Law Theory: Doctrines of the General Part*, Oxford: Oxford University Press, 2002, p. 13.
6. When I lecture about this topic, I try to anticipate and respond to an argument that I think people in the particular

audience are likely to hold. Invariably, among the first points raised in the ensuing discussion is: You did a fine job with the argument you addressed, but you did not respond to some other argument. Of course, the argument to which I did not respond is the very argument which I addressed in a previous lecture, when someone in the audience protested that I neglected the argument to which I am now responding. This is all very frustrating. Again, I find myself in the predicament described by Hume.

7. William Stuntz, "The Pathological Politics of Criminal Law," *Michigan Law Review* 100 (2001), p. 508 n.5.

8. For a more detailed elaboration, see Erwin Chemerinsky, *Constitutional Law: Principles and Policies*, New York: Aspen, 1997, pp. 414-17, 533-45.

9. See Sherry Colb, "Freedom from Incarceration: Why Is This Right Different from All Other Rights?" *New York University Law Review* 69 (1994), p. 781.

10. But see Douglas Husak: "The Nature and justifiability of Nonconsummate Offenses," *Arizona Law Review* 37 (1995), p. 151.

11. U.S. Department of Justice, Bureau of Justice Statistics: *Sourcebook of Criminal Justice* (29th ed., 2001), Table 2.49.

12. See Robert J. MacCoun and Peter Reuter, *Drug War Heresies*, Cambridge: Cambridge University Press, 2001, pp. 82-84.

13. See Mitch Earlywine, *Understanding Marijuana*, New York: Oxford University Press, 2002, p. 247.

Douglas Husak, author of *Philosophy of Criminal Law*, is Professor of Philosophy at Rutgers University.

From *Criminal Justice Ethics*, Winter/Spring 2003, pp. 21-29. Copyright © 2003 by Institute for Criminal Justice & Ethics. Reprinted by permission.

On the Decriminalization of Drugs

Sher negates writer Douglas Husak's claim on his paper "Four Points About Drug Decriminalization" that none of the standard arguments for criminalizing drugs are any good. It is important to continue to criminalize prohibited drugs since many individuals prescribed from using them will be deterred from harming themselves, hurting others, and wasting their own lives.

GEORGE SHER

In his lively and provocative paper, "Four Points About Drug Decriminalization,"[1] Douglas Husak advances two main claims: first, that none of the standard arguments for criminalizing drugs are any good, and, second, that there is little evidence that drug laws deter drug use. In these comments, I will not take up the second claim (though I must admit to some skepticism), but I do want to take issue with the first. My strategy will be, first, to sketch three pro-criminalization arguments that I take to have real weight; second, to respond to an objection of Husak's that, if sound, would tell against all three of my arguments; and, third, to confront the related objection that we cannot consistently support the criminalization of narcotics without also supporting the criminalization of alcohol.

I Three Arguments for Criminalization

I begin with two ritual disclaimers. When I say that there is a good case for continuing to attach criminal penalties to the use of narcotics, I do not mean that that case extends to any particular schedule of penalties or to any special list of drugs. I am sure that many drug sentences, both past and present, are far too harsh. I am also willing to concede that the harms and bads associated with some drugs—marijuana is the obvious example—may not be significant enough to justify attaching even minor penalties to their use. I do think, however, that the harms and bads associated with many other drugs are sufficiently weighty to justify their continued criminalization. The drugs of which I take this to be true include heroin, cocaine, methamphetamine, LSD, and ecstasy, among others.

What, then, are the main arguments for criminalizing these drugs? They are, I think, just the familiar ones: drug users harm themselves, they harm others, and they do not live good lives. At the risk of sounding like an eighth-grade teacher, or a drug czar, I will briefly sketch each argument.

(1) *The paternalistic argument*

The nature of the harms that drug users risk is of course a function of the drugs they use. Thus, to borrow a point from Peter de Marneffe, heroin harms the user by sapping his motivation and initiative.[2] Also, because heroin is addictive, using it now forecloses the option of comfortably not using it later. By contrast, cocaine and methamphetamine do not have only these effects (though "crack" is by all accounts highly addictive), but their regular use also significantly increases the risk of heart attack and stroke. Furthermore, by drastically enhancing self-confidence, aggression, and libido, these drugs elicit behavior that predictably culminates in high-speed collisions, shootouts in parking lots, and destroyed immune systems. Other drugs have still other destructive effects: LSD can trigger lasting psychosis; ecstasy harms the brain, impairs the memory, and, taken with alcohol, damages the liver; and so on. Thus, one obvious reason to continue to criminalize these drugs is simply that many persons deterred by the law from using them will thereby be spared serious injury.

(2) *The protective argument*

Just as drug use can harm the user, so, too, can it harm others. Drug use harms strangers by involving them in the collisions, shootouts, and other catastrophes to which the impaired and overly aggressive are prone. It harms family members by depriving them of the steady companionship and income of their addicted partners. It harms fetuses by exposing them to a toxic and permanently damaging prenatal environment. It harms children by subjecting them to the neglect and abuse of their drug-addled parents. Thus, a second obvious reason to continue criminalizng drugs is that many persons deterred by the law from using drugs will thereby be prevented from harming others.

(3) *The perfectionist argument*

Just as there is broad agreement about what constitutes harm, so, too, is there broad agreement about many factors determining both good and bad lives. Most would agree that it is bad when people stumble through life with a blurred and distorted view of reality; bad when they cannot hold a thought from one moment to the next or follow a simple chain of reasoning; bad when they drift passively with no interest in pursuing worthwhile goals; and bad when they care more about the continued repetition of pleasant sensations than about the needs and interests of those who love and depend on them. Many would agree, too, that it is doubly bad when the reason people live this way is simply because they have squandered the chance to live better. Thus, a third main argument for retaining the drug laws is that many persons whom they deter are thereby prevented from wasting their lives.

II Criminalization and the Risk of Harm

There may be other arguments for continuing to criminalize drugs, but the three just mentioned are surely among the most influential. However, although Husak concedes that some such arguments may indeed explain "why rational persons might well decide not to use illicit drugs, or why the state may have good reasons to discourage people from using drugs," he denies that any of them "provide a justification for *punishing* drug users."[3] Why, exactly, does he deny this?

As Husak agreeably acknowledges, his opposition to criminalization is not a matter of deep principle. He emphasizes that he is not a libertarian, and allows that he can easily imagine drugs so harmful that they should be criminalized: "[i]f a drug literally literally turned users into homicidal monsters, we would have excellent reasons to prohibit its consumption."[4] However, according to Husak, no actual drug satisfies this description because no drug causes harm in more than a small proportion of cases. As Husak points out, "[a]bout 15 million Americans used an illicit drug last year, on literally billions of occasions," but "[v]ery few of these occasions produced any harm."[5] Because the antecedent likelihood of harm is small on any given occasion, Husak maintains that there

is no "sense of harm ... that can be invoked to show that I harm someone ... when I inject heroin or smoke crack. At most, I risk harm to myself or to others when I use a drug."[6] This is said to undermine the case for criminalization because "[a]lmost no theorist has tried very hard to extend a theory of criminalization to conduct that creates a risk of harm rather than harm itself."[7]

Although Husak's official aim in these passages is only to cast doubt on those defenses of the drug laws that appeal to the harm principle, his reasoning can also be extended to the paternalistic and perfectionist arguments. To extend it, we need note only that just as no single occasion of drug use is likely to harm anyone other than the user, so, too, is no single occasion likely either to harm the user himself or to reduce significantly the goodness of his life. Because the (un)likelihood of each effect is roughly equal, the threats that Husak's reasoning poses to our three arguments seem roughly equal as well. This, of course, makes it all the more urgent to ask whether the reasoning can in fact be sustained.

Whatever else we say, we surely must insist that all reasonable theories of criminalization *do* allow governments to criminalize behavior simply on the grounds that it is too risky. We must insist on this not only for the boring reason that all reasonable theories permit governments to attach criminal penalties to drunk driving, discharging firearms in public places, and innumerable other forms of endangerment, but also for the more interesting reason that any decision to criminalize a form of behavior must be made *before* any occurrence of that behavior for which anyone can be punished. Such a decision must be based on an ex ante judgment about how risky the behavior is. Husak can hardly be unaware of this, and so his point can hardly be that we are *never* justified in criminalizing behavior merely on the grounds that it is risky. Instead, I take him to be making only the more modest (but still relevant) point that we are not justified in criminalizing behavior merely on the grounds that it imposes a risk of harm *that is as small as the risk imposed by a single instance of drug use.*

Should we accept this version of Husak's claim? We might have reason to accept it if the relevant forms of low-risk behavior could all be assumed to be rare, for then the amounts of harm we would tolerate by tolerating them would also be small. However, drug use is of course not rare—Husak puts its frequency at billions of occurrences per year-so even if the risk on any given occasion is small, the total amount of harm must still be large. Even if, say, cocaine users harm no one but themselves in 999 out of 1000 cases, ten million uses of cocaine will still harm non-users ten thousand times. If there is any reason to take this number of harms less seriously when they result from ten million uses of cocaine than when they result from only ten thousand uses of some more reliably harmful drug, I must confess that I do not see what it is. Thus, if criminalizing the more reliably harmful drug to prevent this number of harms to non-users is legitimate—as it surely would be if each harm were on average as severe as the average harm done by cocaine—then criminalizing cocaine to prevent this number of harms must be legitimate too.

Even were prevention of harm to others the only legitimate rationale for criminalizing any form of behavior, the aggregative nature of the harms associated with drug use would pose a serious problem for Husak's claim about risk. However, if, as I believe, the state may also legitimately criminalize behavior for paternalistic and perfectionist reasons, then aggregation will pose problems for his claim in at least four more ways. First, just as the infrequent but serious harms that drug users do to others are bound to add up, so are the infrequent but serious harms they do to themselves. Second, if each use of a given drug does a small amount of harm to the user's brain or heart, then his frequent and repetitive use of that drug is likely to do his brain or heart a lot of harm. Third, even if no single instance of drug use has much impact on the goodness of a person's life, a life entirely given over to drug use may be very bad indeed. And, fourth, just as there can be aggregation within each category of harm or bad, so, too, can there be aggregation across the categories. If the cumulative harm that drug users do to themselves is one reason to criminalize drugs, and the cumulative harm they do to others is another, and the cumulative badness of their lives is still another, then the cumulative weight of the three cumulative reasons must surely be greater than the weight of any single one alone.

III If Narcotics, Why Not Alcohol?

Given all this, I am unconvinced by Husak's suggestion that the risks associated with drugs are too small to warrant their criminalization. However, another objection to their criminalization—an objection which Husak does not make explicit but which hovers near the edge of much of what he says—bothers me more. This is the objection that every argument that speaks for the criminalization of drugs speaks with equal strength for the criminalization of alcohol. If this objection can be sustained, then those who favor criminalizing drugs but not alcohol—as I do—are simply giving their preferred intoxicant a free pass.

The reason for treating drugs and alcohol differently will be that we can hold the relevant harms and bads below the threshhold by legally permitting one or the other but not by permitting both.

Although the parallels between drugs and alcohol are pretty obvious, it may be useful to make a few of them explicit. To bring these out, we need only remind ourselves that alcohol, too, is famous for causing people to do things that culminate in fiery collisions, parking-lot shootouts, and destroyed immune systems; that alcoholics are well known for neglecting their partners and abusing their children; that alcohol creates an environment that is toxic and permanently damaging to fetuses; that being drunk cuts a person off from, reality and prevents him from thinking clearly; and that alcohol harms the brain, impairs the memory, and, taken with ecstasy, damages the liver. We may remind ourselves, as well, that although most instances of alcohol use have no such effects, its use is so common—Americans drink alcohol billions of times per year—that the overall amount of harm and degradation that it causes is very large indeed.

Given these impressive similarities, the arguments for criminalizing the two intoxicants appear to stand or fall together. Thus, having claimed that the arguments succeed for drug criminalization, I may seem also committed to the view that they succeed for alcohol. However, because I find a world without beer too grim to contemplate, I want to resist this conclusion if possible. Is there any wiggle room here?

Given the structure of the pro-criminalization arguments, I think there may be. The salient feature of each argument is that it appeals to a kind of harm or bad that is (relatively) infrequent but whose overall total exceeds some crucial threshhold. Thus, all three of my arguments leave open the possibility that the reason drugs take us past the threshhold is that alcohol has already gotten us part of the way there. It may be the case, in other words, that either alcohol or the use of drugs by itself would *not* produce more harms or bads than a reasonable society can tolerate, but that in combination they would produce harms and bads that surpass the threshhold. If anything like this is true, then it will not be at all inconsistent to advocate the criminalization of drugs but not alcohol. The reason for treating drugs and alcohol differently will be that we can hold the relevant harms and bads below the threshhold by legally permitting one or the other but not by permitting both; the reason for continuing to criminalize drugs but not alcohol will be that this is easier and less costly than switching—easier because it avoids divisive legislative battles and the uprooting of entrenched traditions, less costly because it does not require the dismantling of a multi-million-dollar industry.

Is what I have just described anything more than a bare logical possibility? Would the decriminalization of drugs, together with the continued non-criminalization of alcohol, really take us beyond some crucial threshhold of harm and badness? I must admit that I do not know. I do not know how to conceptualize the relevant threshhold, how to quantify the harms and bads to which it applies, or (therefore) how to decide whether drugs plus alcohol would add up to one legal intoxicant too many. But although I am sure that I do not know these things, I am also sure that those who favor drug decriminalization do not know them either. Thus, as long as there is *some* level of harmfulness and badness beyond which criminalization becomes reasonable, the question of whether we should legalize both intoxicants, or one of the two, or neither will remain unsettled. Although the status quo is not easy to defend, it is not clear that Husak's relaxed alternative is really any easier.

NOTES

1. Douglas Husak, "Four Points about Drug Criminalization," *Criminal Justice Ethics*, 22 (this issue, 2003), pp. 3-11.

2. Peter de Marneffe, "Against the Legalization of Heroin," *Criminal Justice Ethics*, 22 (this issue, 2003), pp. 16-22.

3. Husak, "Four Points about Drug Criminalization," p. 6.

4. *Id.*

5. *Id.*, p. 7.

6. *Id.*, p. 6.

7. *Id.*

George Sher, author of Beyond Neutrality: Perfectionism and Politics, *is Herbert S. Autrey Professor of Philosophy at Rice University, Houston, Texas.*

Against the Legalization of Heroin

PETER DE MARNEFFE

The case against drug legalization rests on the empirical premise that drug use would increase in the absence of drug control laws. Everything I know about human nature and the effects of drugs supports this. People use drugs because they are pleasurable, and because they are an effective antidote to anxiety, frustration, and feelings of inadequacy. Were drugs legal, they would be socially destigmatized and they would become easier to acquire, cheaper to purchase, and safer to use. Given the genuine psychological benefits of drug use, we can be sure that it would increase were drugs legalized.

The predictable increase in drug use alone, however, does not justify drug laws, nor does it provide a convincing argument against legalization. For one thing, drinking might decrease as a result of increased drug use, which would be a good effect if drinking is more harmful. Even if increased drug use would not have this indirect benefit, drug laws impose substantial burdens. They impose risks of criminal liability on those tempted to deal drugs, especially young men in poor urban neighborhoods; they create incentives for gang membership and gang violence; they cost money in law enforcement; they result in outlaw groups abroad having more money and influence than they otherwise would, with dangerous political consequences; they increase the risk of overdose and other health risks commonly associated with drug use; and, of course, they make an enjoyable recreational activity illegal. Given these burdens, the benefits of keeping drug use down must be substantial in order to justify drug control. What are these benefits? This depends on the drug in question. Here I focus on heroin.[1]

The strongest argument against heroin legalization, in my opinion, is its predictable effect on the life prospects of young people in poor communities. A person who is ill-educated, whose skills are not in demand, who does not feel admired or respected by society, who has no clear path to social success or financial security, is likely to feel self-doubt and frustration in large measure. Such feelings can be relieved by heroin. Given the intense pleasure and temporary relief that heroin provides, many of those who try it in any community, rich or poor, are likely to use it again and some are likely to develop a habit. Why would this be bad? Habitual heroin use typically lowers a person's expectations of himself and decreases his concern with what others expect of him; it typically weakens a

person's motivation to accomplish things and to meet his responsibilities to others. A general increase in the availability of heroin would therefore increase the risk to children of inadequate parenting, and would make it more likely that young persons disposed to drug abuse will not do what they need to do in order to get a decent education, develop good work habits, develop relationships with mentors, and so on.

By "drug abuse" I mean drug use that has negative consequences for the user or others that are sufficiently bad to make this use either imprudent or irresponsible. Poor people are not uniquely susceptible to drug abuse. Life is difficult, especially in adolescence. Heroin brings pleasure and relief. We can therefore predict that adolescents in every economic group would begin using it regularly if it were legalized. Some, perhaps most, would "mature out" of a habit, but drug abuse during crucial stages of a person's mental and emotional development, whether by oneself or one's parents, will typically have lasting consequences that are difficult to correct. The greater availability of heroin might distract some young people from problem drinking, but the impact of heroin abuse on a person's development is arguably more severe because the degree of indifference it produces toward tasks and mentors is arguably greater. If it is, then the impact of legalization on poor communities is especially worrisome because an increase in drug abuse there would further clog already narrow opportunities for achievement and success.[2] Legalization would no doubt pose less of a threat were wealth distributed more equally, but this is no argument for legalization until it is.

Perhaps I am wrong. Perhaps the legalization of heroin would not result in an increase in drug abuse. Perhaps an increase in drug abuse would not have a disproportionately negative impact on the poor. I am convinced, however, that these effects would occur. So I wish to consider the justifiability of heroin laws on these assumptions in order to make a philosophical point about the morality of drug control. I argue that if drug laws are morally objectionable, this is not because of some general principle of political morality such as Mill's principle of antipaternalism[3] or Dworkin's principle of neutrality;[4] it is because the burdens they impose on individuals outweigh the benefits they bring to them as a matter of fact.

A coercive government policy violates a person's moral rights, in my view, if and only if it violates a principle I call *the burdens principle*. This principle prohibits the government from adopting a coercive policy that burdens someone unless (a) someone would bear a burden in the absence of this policy that is at least nearly as great, and (b) there is sufficient epistemic reason for government officials to believe that someone would bear this burden in the absence of this policy. To say that a person is burdened by a policy is to say there is good reason for her to prefer her situation without this policy, that her situation is objectively better in some way without the policy. To say a person is burdened by the absence of a policy is to say there is good reason for her to prefer her situation with this policy in place, that it objectively improves her situation in some way.[5] A coercive government policy violates a person's moral rights, then, if the reasons for her to prefer her situation in the absence of this policy have substantially greater objective moral weight than any reason a person has to prefer her situation under this policy.

A natural objection is that this account of rights rules out all criminal laws since the burden imposed on those who are caught and punished for breaking a criminal law is generally worse than the worst burden someone would bear in the absence of this law. The burden of being imprisoned seems worse, for example, than a greater risk of being robbed. However, the situation relevant to assessing whether a criminal law violates the burdens principle is not the situation of the person who has been caught or who is already in prison; it is the situation of the person contemplating doing something illegal. With respect to laws against theft, the question is whether the reasons we have to want our possessions made more secure by law are at least as weighty as the reasons a person has to want the legal freedom to take from others whatever he wants when he wants it. In a society in which no one must steal to survive, this is true, and laws that prohibit theft therefore satisfy the burdens principle.

In my opinion, current heroin laws violate our moral rights because they license penalties for early offenses, and this makes the risk of imprisonment too great for those tempted to buy or sell heroin. Furthermore, some penalties are draconian and unfair because disproportionate. Current policy, however, is not the only form that drug control might take. Penalties for manufacture, sale, and possession of heroin might be gradual and proportionate: no one serves prison time for first or second offenses, provided he meets the conditions of probation, and prison terms after multiple offenses remain proportionate in length to the potential harm involved.[6] Suppose a system of penalties like this one, if reliably enforced and effectively targeted at assets, would reduce drug consumption roughly as much as current policy does. This is not utterly fanciful, since criminologists take seriously the possibility that softer penalties—reliably enforced—are more effective than harsh penalties enforced erratically.[7] If current laws reduce heroin abuse substan-

tially, then, I think, a moderate system of penalties like this one might better satisfy the burdens principle and so respect our moral rights.[8]

If drug laws are morally objectionable, it is because the burdens they impose on individuals outweigh the benefits they bring to them as a matter of fact.

Of course it is commonly objected that drug laws "don't work," in which case an alternative policy that works just as well will not work either. The "don't work" objection, however, might mean at least three different things. It might mean that drug laws do not *eradicate* drug use. It might mean that they do not decrease drug use *at all*. Or it might mean that they do not decrease it *enough* to justify the burdens they impose. Certainly drug laws do not eradicate drug use. Neither do property laws eradicate theft. This is no argument for their abolition. On the other hand, no informed student of drug policy supposes that drug laws do *nothing* to lower drug use. Since they make drugs scarcer, more expensive, more dangerous to use, and reinforce social norms against use, they predictably reduce consumption, a prediction supported by the best available evidence.[9] The "don't work" objection should therefore be taken seriously only if it means drug laws do not reduce consumption *enough* to justify the burdens they impose. This may be true, but if the alternative policy I have sketched would reduce heroin abuse in poor communities roughly as much as current policy does, and current policy does reduce this drug abuse substantially,[10] then I think it is not true.

The burden of criminal liability is not the only burden imposed by drug laws. Among other things, they make an enjoyable recreational activity more difficult, costly, and dangerous. A complete defense of any drug law must consider the greatest total burden it imposes on any individual and explain why this burden is justified by its greatest benefit to someone. My aim here is not to provide a conclusive defense of drug laws. It is to explain how they might be justified as compatible with respect for our moral rights. Drug laws are compatible with our rights, I maintain, if they satisfy the burdens principle. But some may think that drug laws are wrong because they are paternalistic or fail to be neutral toward different conceptions of a good life. Thus I should explain why I think a policy that satisfies the burdens principle is not open to criticism on these grounds.

Drug laws are compatible with our rights if they satisfy the burdens principle.

I have given two arguments in favor of heroin laws. The first is that they would reduce the risk to children of inadequate parenting by reducing the likelihood that their parents will abuse heroin. The second is that heroin laws would reduce the risk to young people of developing a habit that undermines their own opportunities for future achievement and well-being.[11] The first justification is not paternalistic in the way liberals have traditionally opposed, since it limits the liberty of adults to prevent harm to children. The second justification, however, may seem objectionably paternalistic in aiming to deter young adults from heroin abuse that undermines *their own* life prospects. Heroin addicts commonly oppose drug legalization when asked about it.[12] This is noteworthy since the paternalism Mill opposes in *On Liberty* consists in policies that limit a person's liberty for his own good *against his will*,[13] and if a person supports a coercive policy, then the coercion it involves is not against his will in the relevant sense. But I will assume for the sake of argument that the policy I am considering can be fully justified only as benefiting some young adults who oppose it, and that it is therefore paternalistic in the way Mill opposed.

Paternalistic interference with a person's liberty is wrong in my view only when it violates the burdens principle with respect to that person. A policy violates the burdens principle with respect to a person only if the (objective) reasons for her to want the government not to limit her liberty decisively outweigh every (objective) reason she has to want the government to limit it.[14] When this is not the case—when a person's reasons for wanting the government to limit her liberty in some way outweigh her reasons for wanting the government not to do so—paternalistic interference with her freedom does not violate the burdens principle, at least not with respect to her, and so does not violate her moral rights. My argument for heroin laws assumes that the reasons why some individuals want the manufacture, sale, and possession of heroin to be illegal *do* outweigh their reasons to want it to be legal. If so, then heroin laws do not violate their rights even if paternalistic.

A persistent objection is that if this kind of paternalism is permissible, there is no limit to the kind of paternalism the government may engage in. If the government is justified in prohibiting heroin because its habitual use is bad for the user, it must also be justified in prohibiting alcohol, tobacco, gambling, and fatty foods. Where will it all end? I will remain neutral here on the justifiability of alcohol prohibition,[15] but I will concede that if the burdens principle permits the government to restrict the possession and sale of every product that provides an opportunity for self-destructive use, then it licenses too much government interference with our liberty. I should now explain, then, why I do not think the burden's principle implies this.

I believe a person's reasons for wanting the legal freedom to buy fatty foods decisively outweigh his reasons for wanting not to have this legal freedom, and that the burdens principle therefore prohibits paternalistic interference with a person's freedom to buy fatty foods. To be sure, there are good reasons for a person who is tempted to eat himself into an early grave to want to have greater difficulty in acquiring unhealthy foods. But since the length of a person's life is not the only factor in happiness, and eating, preparing, and sharing fatty foods is part of what makes life enjoyable, and a general legal discretion over what foods to buy is valuable in other ways, I believe that paternalistic interference with the freedom to buy fatty foods is not in fact justifiable. My argument for heroin prohibition would suggest the opposite if our reasons to want the legal freedom to buy heroin were as weighty as our reasons to want the legal freedom to buy fatty foods, and our reasons to want not to have the legal freedom to buy fatty foods were as weighty as our reasons to want not to have the legal freedom to buy heroin. But I think this claim about the relative weight of reasons is incorrect. My argument for drug prohibition is that drug legalization would further dim the life prospects of young people in poor communities. The main reason to prohibit the sale of fatty foods is to discourage behavior that tends to shorten a person's life. I think the reasons for a young person to want to be deterred from engaging in conduct that closes important opportunities to achieve the good things in life going forward have objectively greater moral weight than the reasons a person has to want to be protected from engaging in conduct that will shorten his life. This is because a person will have already had most of the opportunities he will have to achieve and enjoy these good things by the time that eating fatty foods will have the effect of shortening his life. This is not to deny that obesity closes desirable opportunities, but these are not so numerous or important, it seems to me, as those closed by a failure to become educated and to develop self-discipline in adolescence and early adulthood, which I assume is a common consequence of habitual heroin use. It thus makes sense, in my view, to hold that while the burdens principle prohibits fatty food paternalism it permits paternalistic drug laws.

> *My argument for drug prohibition is that drug legalization would further dim the life prospects of young people in poor communities.*

Here it is perhaps natural to ask: on what principle do I distinguish permissible from impermissible forms of paternalism? The formal answer is, on the basis of the burdens principle. But, some may wonder: on what more specific principle do I distinguish those forms of paternalism that violate the burdens principle from those that do not? The answer is, none. Judgments about whether a government policy violates the burdens principle rest on judgments about the relative weight of the relevant reasons. Judgments of this kind are not based on further principles; rather they are the basis on which more specific principles of liberty are justified. How, then, does one know whether a particular form of paternalism violates the burdens principle? By thinking carefully about the relevant reasons, checking for consistency and coherence, and discussing the matter with others. If this seems insufficient to ground a knowledge claim about our rights, it is important to recognize that no claim about our rights can be justified without relying on this process of reflection at some point. Thus while one might justify a rights claim by reference to whatever principle of liberty would be chosen in John Rawls's "original position,"[16] the argument for this principle from the original position must itself rely on assumptions about the relative weight of individuals' interests in liberty and other goods that are justified by this same process of reflection.

If someone's reasons for wanting the government to prohibit him from buying fatty foods have at least as much moral weight as any reason he has to want to be free to do so, then, it is true, the burdens principle does permit this form of paternalism, assuming it could be adopted and enforced at a tolerable cost to others. Some may conclude the burdens principle permits too much paternalistic interference and it is therefore a poor account of our rights. But on this assumption about the relative weight of reasons, it is not possible to identify anything wrong with this form of paternalism. If no one's reasons to want the government to reject a policy have greater moral weight than anyone's reasons to want it accepted, then no one has a decisive complaint against this policy, and if no one has a decisive complaint against a policy, it does not violate anyone's moral rights. It is thus only on the assumption that a form of paternalism does violate the burdens principle—whether it limits our freedom to buy fatty foods, cigarettes, or chances to win at the casino—that it makes sense to think it is wrong.

I have just explained why I do not think the paternalistic character of drug laws provides a decisive reason for objecting to them. Another general principle of political morality that drug laws might be thought to violate is the liberal principle of neutrality toward conceptions of a good life. Drug laws may seem to violate this principle because they make it more difficult to pursue certain conceptions of the good—those conceptions of good that endorse recreational drug use. But the principle of neutrality cannot be understood to rule out policies that make some conceptions of a good life more difficult to pursue as a matter of fact since every defensible system of laws will make some conceptions of the good more difficult to pursue: those that require a system of slavery, for example. The principle of neutrality therefore must be interpreted to rule out only policies that cannot be fully justified by neutral reasons. Any policy that satisfies the burdens principle can be justified by neutral reasons, I would argue. So heroin laws do not violate the principle of neutrality, properly understood, if they can be justified in the way I propose.

Some advocates of neutrality may, of course, oppose all forms of paternalism, but it is important to make a distinction here between those kinds of paternalism that clearly violate the principle of neutrality as intuitively understood and those that do not. Among the paternalistic reasons that seem clearly non-neutral are "perfectionist" reasons: the reason to prohibit an activity or pursuit because it is intrinsically bad, for example, or degrading, ignoble, or worthless. Not all paternalistic reasons are perfectionist in this way, and some that are not seem relatively neutral, like the paternalistic reason of safety to require motorists to wear seatbelts. The argument I have given for heroin laws is paternalistic but not perfectionist. It holds that drug laws are justified by the negative effects the easy availability of drugs will have on the life prospects of the least advantaged. This is a neutral reason in my view because improving the life prospects of the least advantaged is a neutral goal. It is a "political value" in Rawls's sense, one that might be appealed to in defending drug control while fully adhering to his idea of public reason.[17]

The argument I have given for heroin laws is paternalistic but not perfectionist.

I have just explained why I do not think heroin laws—justified in the way I have proposed—are wrong in being paternalistic or non-neutral. Some may think they are still wrong in sacrificing the liberty of the many for the benefit of the few. My argument does not suppose heroin laws are to everyone's benefit. It does not suppose that most people who use heroin are likely to abuse it. Nor does it suppose that heroin poses such a serious threat to a person's autonomy, by short-circuiting his capacities for rational self-governance and thereby turning him into a zombie, that the protection of everyone's autonomy requires its prohibition. Indeed, my argument for heroin laws allows that they make some people worse off: those recreational users for whom pleasure is a good reason to use it, who would not abuse it if they did use it, but for whom the price, difficulty, and danger of its use is increased sharply by its illegality. For this reason it would be inaccurate to criticize my argument as involving an illegitimate generalization from worst-case scenarios. To the contrary, it supposes that the genuine risk to some individuals due to the substantial losses that would accompany an increase in heroin use suffices to justify limiting the liberty of everyone. But this may seem to make my argument even worse. I should therefore explain why I do not think it does.

The burdens principle is individualistic in nature, not aggregative. It requires that we evaluate policies by making a one-to-one comparison of the burdens on individuals. Only if the burden some individual would bear in the absence of a policy is great enough to justify the worst burden this policy would impose on anyone can this policy be justified. Aggregative considerations properly come into play only when the worst burdens that individuals would bear with and without this policy are roughly equivalent, and the numbers must be appealed to in order to break a tie.

Individualism cuts in two ways against aggregative arguments. If individualism prohibits enslaving a minority to benefit the majority, it also permits restraining the majority in other ways to benefit the minority, at least in principle. The mere fact that a policy burdens more people than it benefits is no objection; a policy is morally objectionable only if the burden it imposes on the many is at least nearly as great as the benefit it provides the few. Anti-discrimination laws, for example, limit the liberty of more people than they directly benefit, but this does not mean that they are wrong. They are permissible because the burden of being discriminated against is substantially worse than the consequent burden of having less associational freedom.

Consider in this connection how the burdens principle bears on the common objection that drug laws are costly. Suppose that heroin laws cost each of us an average of $50 a year in police, court, prison, and military expenditures, and foreign aid. Whether this is a decisive objection depends on how this cost is distributed and on whether the policy improves the situation of someone enough to justify this cost to everyone. To assess this from an individualistic perspective, one asks whether the benefit to someone is great enough to justify the loss to each of us of whatever money an equitable tax would impose on us, in addition to whatever other burdens this policy imposes. We do not aggregate here in comparing benefits and burdens; we compare the total burden on each individual one to one. If the reduced risk to someone of losses associated with drug abuse is worth at least as much to her as the amount that any individual is required to pay, then this expense is compatible with the burdens principle and so with the individualism essential to taking rights seriously, provided that it does not make the total burden on anyone too great.

One might still argue on purely individualistic grounds that drug laws unjustifiably deprive some individuals of the opportunity to enjoy heroin legally. The enjoyment of life is a good thing, and moderate drug use promotes it. But I think the government is justified in restricting this particular source of enjoyment, given the existence of so many other sources, *if* doing so is necessary to secure goods of greater moral importance. Successful emotional and intellectual development in adolescence and early adulthood are goods of greater moral importance. So if prohibition would substantially reduce the risk to someone of losing these goods, this can justify the consequent loss of this legal opportunity for enjoyment.

My argument against heroin legalization rests on a number of empirical assumptions. First, that legalization would result in an increase in heroin abuse with a disproportionate negative impact on the opportunities of individuals in poor communities. Second, that heroin use could be kept at its current levels by laws reliably enforced by a proportionate and fair system of penalties that targets assets effectively. Third, that the financial cost of enforcing these laws could be equitably distributed

through a progressive tax without substantially reducing anyone's standard of living. Many other empirical assumptions must be added to provide a conclusive case against heroin legalization. It must be assumed that the risks of gang violence can be kept at acceptable levels by effective neighborhood policing without drug legalization. It must be assumed that the health risks created by drug control can be reduced to acceptable levels by the distribution of public information and sanitary needles. It must be assumed that drug control can be effectively enforced without destabilizing governments in other countries and without greatly increasing the risk of terrorist violence here and elsewhere. And these assumptions are only the beginning.

The fact-dependence of this argument naturally raises the question of burden of proof: how much evidence must one have before being morally justified in supporting drug prohibition? I suppose a person is justified in supporting a coercive policy for a reason only if there is sufficient epistemic justification for her to accept the proposition that provides this reason. Whether this is true of the empirical assumptions I have made here is open to debate. What I have done is sketch an individualistic framework within which drug laws might be justified, consistent with taking our rights seriously. If this framework is sound, and my empirical assumptions are correct, and we are justified in believing them, the government may therefore prohibit heroin without violating anyone's moral rights.

NOTES

[I thank Andrew Koppelman, Daniel Shapiro, and Leif Wenar for comments on drafts.]

1. I intend my argument here to apply also to morphine, heroin's less popular sibling, with the exception mentioned in note 8.
2. Acceptance of this argument, or something like it, provides the most plausible explanation, in my view, of why leaders of poor urban communities typically support drug laws, a fact that casts doubt on the charge that such laws are "racist."
3. See J. S. Mill, *On Liberty*, ed. Elizabeth Rapaport, Indianapolis: Hackett Publishing Co., 1978, p. 9.
4. See Ronald Dworkin, "Liberalism," *A Matter of Principle*, Cambridge, MA: Harvard University Press, 1985, p. 191.
5. Some may find it unnatural to say that a person is burdened by the absence of a coercive policy, but since I think that individuals would be burdened by the *repeal* of some coercive policies, like laws against theft, I think it makes sense to say that individuals can be burdened by the *absence* of a policy.
6. In allowing penalties for *possession* I do not directly disagree with the claim that use should not be criminalized, which Douglas Husak argues ("Four Points About Drug Decriminalization," *Criminal Justice Ethics*, 22 [this issue, 2003], pp. 3-11). The goal of the drug prohibition I defend here is not to reduce use per se, but to reduce certain kinds of abuse by reducing drug availability and by making drug use more burdensome legally and socially. If drug

abuse would be substantially reduced in these ways, by a gentle system of penalties for possession combined with stiffer penalties for manufacture and sale, I would defend penalties for possession on this ground. By a "gentle" system of penalties, I mean one that gives everyone convicted the probationary opportunity to avoid imprisonment by accepting some form of treatment, performing community service, or both. For some considerations that weigh against legalizing possession completely, see James Q. Wilson, "Heroin," *Thinking About Crime*, New York: Basic Books, 1975, pp. 144-52.

7. See, for example, James Q. Wilson & Richard J. Herrnstein, *Crime and Human Nature*, New York: Simon and Schuster, 1985, p. 62.

8. Another objection to current policy is that it makes illegal the medical use of heroin for the treatment of pain. This objection is compelling only if heroin is more effective than morphine. If not, then the current policy of permitting the medical manufacture, sale, and possession of morphine suffices to meet the medical needs of patients. If heroin is more effective, then it should be treated by the law in the same way morphine is now. For an expression of doubt about the greater effectiveness of heroin, see John Kaplan, *The Hardest Drug*, Chicago: The University of Chicago Press, 1983, p. 6.

9. Three facts are commonly cited as evidence that heroin use varies in proportion to availability, which, it is assumed, drug prohibition reduces to some degree. First, the percentage of American troops who used heroin in Vietnam, where it was easily available, is much higher than the percentage of the same group who used the drug before and after their service there. Second, opiate use is much higher among medical professionals, who have much greater access to opiates, than it is in the general population. Third, alcohol consumption fell substantially during Prohibition. All three arguments are endorsed by Erich Goode, *Drugs in American Society*, 4th ed., New York: McGraw-Hill, Inc., 1993, pp. 375-76. See also Kaplan, *The Hardest Drug*, p. 113, for an endorsement of the first two arguments.

10. It is sometimes said that since heroin is already available in poor urban communities, drug laws do little to reduce drug consumption there, but this reasoning is flawed in at least three ways. First, while heroin is relatively available in some poor urban communities, it is not nearly as safe, plentiful, and affordable as it would be if sold legally along with liquor or candy at the corner store (Kaplan, *The Hardest Drug*, pp. 123-24). Second, although heroin is now quite available in *some* poor urban communities, it is much less available in others (*id.*, p. 88). Third, even in those

poor communities in which heroin is now quite available, the expense, unreliability, danger, and inconvenience of supporting a habit remain a strong incentive to stop using it (*id.*, p. 125).

11. Note that in both cases the relevant burden is the greater risk of loss under a policy of legalization, and not the actual loss that results. If the relevant comparison were of the actual losses from prohibition and legalization, then drug laws would surely violate the burdens principle because, to make just one comparison, death from drug-related gang violence is worse than inadequate parenting.

12. Wilson, "Heroin," p. 135.

13. Mill, *On Liberty*, p. 9.

14. Note that I do not say that the burdens principle is violated if the reasons someone has to want the government not to limit her liberty outweigh every reason she has to want it to do so. I think this claim about reasons holds for many recreational drug users, but the burdens principle is violated only if their reasons to want drugs to be legal decisively outweigh everyone's reasons to want it to be illegal, a claim that I believe to be false.

15. Perhaps it is worth observing here that while alcohol prohibition might be permitted by the burdens principle, the argument I have given for heroin laws does not alone warrant the conclusion that it is. This is because the legal prohibition of a drug is likely to be far more effective in reducing abuse where its use is already generally believed "wrong." This is now the case with heroin but not with alcohol. Although the (greater) deterrent benefits of reducing heroin abuse might now be sufficient to justify continuing heroin prohibition, the (lesser) benefits of reducing problem drinking might not be sufficient to justify a return to alcohol prohibition, even if drinking is equally harmful. The reason I remain neutral on the justifiability of alcohol prohibition is that I suspect that problem drinking is more harmful on average than heroin abuse is, especially to others.

16. See John Rawls, *A Theory of Justice*, Cambridge, MA: Harvard University Press, 1971, pp. 11-15.

17. See John Rawls, *Political Liberalism*, New York: Columbia University Press, 1993, pp. 223-24. For another argument for drug prohibition that would be supported by Rawls's liberal political values on different empirical assumptions, see Samuel Freeman, "Liberalism, Inalienability, and Rights of Drug Use," in Pablo De Greiff, ed., *Drugs and the Limits of Liberalism*, Ithaca: Cornell University Press, 1999, esp. pp.128-30.

Peter de Marneffe is Associate Professor of Philosophy at Arizona State University, Tempe.

U.S., Canada clash on pot laws

Parliament's plan to decriminalize possession creates rift

By Donna Leinwand
USA TODAY

The Bush administration is hinting that it could make it more difficult for Canadian goods to get into this country if Canada's Parliament moves ahead with a proposal to drop criminal penalties for possession of small amounts of marijuana.

The proposal, part of an effort to overhaul Canada's anti-drug policies, essentially would treat most marijuana smokers there the same as people who get misdemeanor traffic tickets. Violators would be ticketed and would have to pay a small fine, but they no longer would face jail time.

Canada's plan isn't that unusual: 12 U.S. states and most of the 15 nations in the European Union have eased penalties on first-time offenders in recent years. That's a reflection of how many governments have grown weary of pursuing individual marijuana users.

But U.S. officials, while stressing that they aren't trying to interfere in Canada's affairs, are urging Canadians to resist decriminalizing marijuana.

In a lobbying campaign that has seemed heavy-handed to some Canadians, U.S. officials have said that such a change in Canada's laws would undermine tougher anti-drug statutes in the USA, lead to more smuggling and create opportunities for organized crime. Bush administration aides note that marijuana is an increasing problem along the Canadian border, where U.S. inspectors seized more than 19,000 pounds of the

leaf in 2002, compared with less than 2,000 pounds four years earlier.

In December, U.S. anti-drug czar John Walters stumped across Canada, criticizing the decriminalization plan. He told business groups in Vancouver, where police allow public pot-smoking in some areas, that they would face tighter security at the U.S. border if Canada eased its marijuana laws.

The backlash was immediate across Canada, where surveys have shown that nearly 70% of the country believes that possessing a small amount of marijuana should be punishable only by a small fine. Canadian newspapers accused the USA of being arrogant and called Walters paranoid.

For years, the USA and Canada have squabbled over border issues like longtime friends with a few habits that annoy each other. U.S. officials dislike Canada's looser immigration laws and limited regulation of prescription drugs, particularly pseudoephedrine, used to make methamphetamine.

Canadian officials complain that Colombian cocaine and Mexican heroin often enter Canada via the USA. Canadians argue that the USA should do more to curb Americans' demand for illegal drugs, because restricting the supply only increases prices.

Canada's full Parliament is likely to consider a decriminalization proposal soon.

Committees in the House of Commons and the Senate have issued reports

that say police should not arrest people for smoking marijuana, adding momentum to the decriminalization effort. Early versions of the proposal say those caught with no more than 30 grams—about an ounce—of marijuana for personal use would be ticketed and fined an undetermined amount.

'Drug tourist' penalties

Marijuana possession in Canada now is a criminal offense that can carry jail time. Although people convicted of such an offense rarely are sent to jail, they do end up with a criminal record. In the USA, states generally prosecute marijuana-possession offenses, and sentences vary from mandatory jail time to fines. Under federal sentencing guidelines, a person convicted of possession could be sentenced to a year in jail.

Canada would keep criminal penalties for marijuana offenses that pose a significant danger to others, such as illegal trafficking, selling to minors or driving while under the influence of the drug. To prevent "drug tourists," Canadian officials say they would consider special penalties for sales to non-Canadians.

Walters and other U.S. officials said they are worried that such a policy change would make marijuana more available in Canada, leading to more smuggling. They say drug gangs, sensing a more tolerant climate, probably would move their operations near the Canadian-U.S. border, and more Ameri-

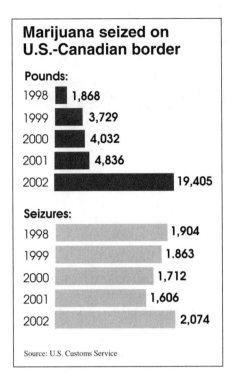

Marijuana seized on U.S.-Canadian border

Pounds:

Year	Pounds
1998	1,868
1999	3,729
2000	4,032
2001	4,836
2002	19,405

Seizures:

Year	Seizures
1998	1,904
1999	1.863
2000	1,712
2001	1,606
2002	2,074

Source: U.S. Customs Service

can teens would cross the border to smoke pot.

Looser marijuana laws in Canada would make it "probable we will have to do more restrictive things at the border," Walters said.

For Canadians who have been slowed by security checks imposed by the USA since the Sept. 11, 2001, terrorists attacks, that would mean more delays in crossing the border, he said. That could damage Canadian business; trade with the USA accounts for 70% of Canada's exports.

Canadian Sen. Pierre-Claude Nolin, head of the panel that released the Senate report and a supporter of eased penalties, doubts that a new marijuana policy in Canada would lead U.S. officials to hinder trade.

Walters "should have respect for our courts and our public," Nolin says. "He cannot stop 8,000 semitrailers at the Windsor (Detroit) border every day. He's saying that, but he will not do that."

Marijuana use in the USA has risen during the past decade. A 2001 study by U.S. government and university researchers indicated that 49% of high school seniors had smoked pot, up from 32.6% in 1992.

In Canada, authorities say their studies indicate that about 30% of Canadians ages 12 to 64 have used marijuana at least once. Although drug use generally is presumed to be rising, Canadian officials say they do not have accurate data they could use to plot a trend.

Canadians say America's rising demand for marijuana makes smuggling appealing to criminal organizations. They also cite the dozen U.S. states that have cut penalties for marijuana possession in recent years—Alaska, California, Colorado, Maine, Minnesota, Mississippi, Nebraska, Nevada, New York, North Carolina, Ohio and Oregon—and say the U.S. government should focus more attention on them.

"It is up to each country to get its own house in order before criticizing its neighbor," a Canadian Senate report said. In the USA, state and local prosecutors handle most marijuana cases. Federal prosecutors usually handle cases that involve large amounts of the leaf or that involve suspects who cross state or national borders.

Asa Hutchinson, a former head of the U.S. Drug Enforcement Administration who now is a top official at the Department of Homeland Security, said last year that "we have to accept responsibility, and we're trying to reduce demand. But without being critical of Canada, we're simply stating a reality: The decision of the Canadian government will have a consequence in this country."

More from Mexico

U.S. Customs agents say the amount of marijuana entering the USA for Canada is dwarfed by that from Mexico. The Royal Canadian Mounted police says 800 tons of marijuana circulates in Canada each year. It's grown mostly in British Columbia, Ontario and Quebec—all of which border the USA. Canadian and U.S. officials say they do not know how much Canadian pot reaches the USA.

"B.C. Bud," the potent, hydroponically grown marijuana from British Columbia, and its eastern counterpart, "Quebec Gold," sell for as much as $4,500 a pound, the DEA says.

If Canada decriminalizes marijuana, U.S. Customs officials expect to see more marijuana coming over the northern border, Customs spokesman Dean Boyd says. "It doesn't take a rocket scientist to come to that conclusion."

Canadian Justice Minister Martin Cauchon, who soon will present the government's plan for decriminalization, says he wants to bring Canadian law in line with public opinion and with judicial rulings favoring lighter penalties for marijuana possession. "We're not talking about being weak. We want to have tougher law enforcement. Our policy toward trafficking will remain the same.

UNIT 7

Prevention, Treatment, and Education

Unit Selections

49. **Drug Treatment: The Willard Option**, Melvin L. Williams
50. **Strategies to Improve Offender Outcomes in Treatment**, Faye Taxman
51. **Marijuana: Just Say No Again: The Old Failures of New and Improved Anti-drug Education**, Renee Moilanen
52. **Binge Drinking: Not the Word of Choice**, Fern Walter Goodhart, Linda C. Lederman, Lea P. Stewart, and Lisa Laitman
53. **A New Weapon in the War on Drugs: Family**, Alexandra Marks
54. **National Survey Finds Strong Public Support for Treatment**, Alcoholism & Drug Abuse Weekly
55. **Addicted, Neglectful Moms Offered Treatment, Custody**, Henri E. Cauvin
56. **Consumer Direction, Self-Determination and Person-Centered Treatment**, Alcoholism & Drug Abuse Weekly
57. **SACHR: An Example of an Integrated, Harm Reduction Drug Treatment Program**, Bart Majoor and Joyce Rivera

Key Points to Consider

- As you read the following articles, attempt to identify additional questions and issues that mold public opinion and shape public policy on drugs. Some examples worthy of discussion are: How serious is the drug problem perceived to be? Is it getting worse?

- What are the impacts of drugs on children and schools? How do drugs drive crime? What are the impacts of drugs on policing, the courts, and corrections?

- How are public opinion and public policy affected by public events, drug education campaigns, announced government policies, and media coverage?

 **Links: www.dushkin.com/online/**
These sites are annotated in the World Wide Web pages.

The Drug Reform Coordination Network (DRC)
http://www.drcnet.org

Drug Watch International
http://www.drugwatch.org

United Nations International Drug Control Program (UNDCP)
http://www.undcp.org

Marijuana Policy Project
http://www.mpp.org

Office of National Drug Control Policy (ONDCP)
http://www.whitehousedrugpolicy.gov

D.A.R.E.
http://www.dare-america.com

Hazelden
http://www.hazelden.org

There are no magic bullets for preventing drug abuse and treating drug-dependent persons. As one commentator stated, "Drug addicts can be cured, but we're not very good at it!" History is replete with accounts of the diverse attempts of frustrated societies to reclaim or reject their fallen members. Addicts have been executed, imprisoned, and treated with ambivalent indifference. In some circles, the debate still rages as to whether addicts suffer from a pernicious disease or simply a weak character. The evolution of processes used to rehabilitate addicted persons and prevent future abuse has been slow and filled with paradox. Yet the case is not lost. On the contrary, great new strides have been made in not only understanding the various genetic, physiological, psychological, and environmental frameworks that combine to serve as a basis for addiction but in using these frameworks successfully to treat and prevent dependency. Research continues to establish and strengthen the role of treatment as a critical component in the fight against drug abuse. Some drug treatment programs have been shown to reduce dramatically the costs associated with high-risk populations of users. For example, recidivism associated with drug abuse has been shown to decrease 50 percent after treatment. Treatment is a critical component in the fight against drug abuse but it is not a panacea. Society cannot "treat" drug abuse away just as it cannot "arrest" it away.

Drug prevention and treatment philosophies subscribe to a multitude of modalities. Everything seems to work a little and nothing seems to work completely. The articles in this unit illustrate the diversity of methods utilized in prevention and treatment programs. Special emphasis is given to treating the drug problems of those who are under the supervision of the criminal justice system. All education, prevention, and treatment programs compete for local, state, and federal resources.

Education: One critical component of drug education is the ability to rapidly translate research findings into practice, and today's drug policy emphasizes this more than ever. Although funds budgeted for drug education were reduced in some areas, such as those enacted for the U.S. Department of Education's 611 million dollars in 2005 (down from 624 million dollars in 2004) the overall commitment to research and education is strong. In 2005, for example, over one billion dollars was committed to the National Institute of Drug Abuse to continue important drug-related research. This research supports important education, prevention, and treatment programs such as The National Prevention Research Initiative, Interventions and Treatment for Current Drug Users Who Are Not Yet Addicted, the National Drug Abuse Treatment Clinical Trial Network, and Research Based treatment Approaches for Drug Abusing Criminal Offenders.

Prevention: A primary strategy of drug prevention programs is to prevent and/or delay initial drug use. A secondary strategy is to discourage use by persons minimally involved with drugs. Both strategies include (1) educating users and potential users, (2) teaching adolescents how to resist peer pressure, (3) addressing problems associated with drug abuse such as teen pregnancy, failure in school, and law breaking, and (4) creating community support and involvement for prevention activities.

Prevention and education programs are administered through a variety of mechanisms, typically amidst controversy relative to what works best. Schools have been an important delivery apparatus, as have local law enforcement agencies. Based upon research, the effectiveness of the D.A.R.E. program of drug education is being questioned more than ever before. Currently, however, it is still a cornerstone in the delivery of drug education to children in elementary school. Also significant to school programs is 25 million dollars in federal grants for student drug testing. These grants support the development of student drug-testing programs, and subsequent assessment, referral, and intervention processes in situations where parents and educators deem it necessary. Additionally, 80 million dollars in grant funds has been made available as part of the federal Drug-Free Communities Program which provides funds at the community level to anti-drug coalitions working to prevent substance abuse among young people. Additionally, there are community-based drug prevention programs sponsored by civic organizations, church groups, and private corporations. All programs pursue funding through public grants and private endowments. Federal grants to local, state, and private programs are critical components to program solvency.

The multifaceted nature of prevention programs makes them difficult to assess categorically. School programs that emphasize the development of skills to resist social and peer pressure produce generally varying degrees of positive results. Research continues to make more evident the need to focus prevention programs with specific populations in mind.

Treatment: Like prevention programs, drug treatment programs enlist a variety of methods to treat persons dependent upon legal and illegal drugs. There is no single-pronged approach to treatment for drug abuse. Treatment modality may differ radically from one user to the next. The user's background, physical and mental health, personal motivation, and support structure all have serious implications for treatment type. Lumping together the diverse needs of chemically dependent persons for purposes of applying a generic treatment process provides confounding results at best. In addition, most persons needing and seeking treatment have problems with more than one drug—polydrug use. Current research also correlates drug use with serious mental illness (SMI). The federal Substance Abuse and Mental Health Services Administration (SAMSHA) reports that adults with a drug problem are 3 times more likely to have a serious mental illness. The implications of this dual diagnosis are serious, as it is estimated that there are 30 to 40 million chemically dependent persons in this country. The existing harmful drug use and mental health nexus is exacerbated by the fact that using certain powerful drugs, such as methamphetamine, push otherwise functioning persons into the dysfunctional realm of mental illness. Providing treatment services to dually diagnosed persons is one of the most difficult and troubling aspects of the treatment equation. According to SAMHSA, only 11.8 percent of persons with a drug problem and a serious mental illness receive treatment for both.

Although treatment programs differ in methods, most provide a combination of key services. These include drug counseling, drug education, pharmacological therapy, psychotherapy, relapse prevention, and assistance with support structures. Treatment programs may be outpatient-oriented or residential in nature. Residential programs require patients to live at the facility for a prescribed period of time. These residential programs, often described as therapeutic communities, emphasize the development of social, vocational, and educational skills.

The number of available treatment programs is a continual political controversy with respect to federal and state drug budget expenditures. The current trend is to increase the availability of treatment programs. One key component of federal drug strategy was to fund a new 600 million dollar treatment initiative in 2004 which provided drug treatment to individuals otherwise unable to obtain it. In 2005, over 1.6 billion dollars was committed to this program. It is hoped that this program will allow a more flexible delivery of services that will target large populations of dependent persons not reached through other treatment efforts. Drug treatment is costly but not providing it is more costly.

DRUG TREATMENT:
The Willard Option

BY MELVIN L. WILLIAMS

If there was an easy answer to drug addiction, everyone would use it. Since the evolution of the 1960s, the nation has been faced with the ever increasing use of illegal drugs in society. Of course, this also corresponds with the increase of legal pharmaceutical drugs. In fact, there are drugs for everything from growing hair to improving a person's sexual life. Americans are taught from a very young age that if there is a problem, there is a drug to fix it; yet when unacceptable drugs are used or found, as a nation, citizens become offended and develop high criminal penalties to eradicate this nuisance.

The ever resounding question is, "What is there to do?" The United States uses the latest military technology to protect its borders and drug use still increases. There are drug awareness programs in schools, nationally televised programs in household living rooms and drug treatment centers throughout many communities. Yet, people still are being sent to prison for long periods of time for drug charges. Sometimes it appears that correctional staff are so tied up with the law enforcement part of the job that treatment is forgotten. Many people hope that drug abuse will become somebody else's problem or it will simply go away, yet when they open their eyes, they see millions of people who are affected—families are broken and lives are destroyed.

There are certain things about drug abuse that must be understood:

- It is a personal choice, no matter what events led up to it;

- It is a bane on American life and is creating a culture that is subversive and criminal; and

- Throwing money and resources at the problem does not help—a stealth bomber may locate illegal drug sources by using infrared, but if people still want drugs, they will get them.

In drug treatment, everyone, including the client, must recognize that drug abuse is a personal issue. Oftentimes, society needs to place blame on something else—faulting poor neighborhoods, schools, awful parents—yet no one forces a person to continually put drugs into his or her system.

In corrections, by the time a client with a drug problem is incarcerated, the addiction has probably existed for years; it is a developed behavior. There may be many drugs involved and many different types of abuse. This usually results in criminal behavior in the form of obtaining or using drugs, or attempting to get money to buy more drugs. Community treatment centers have been built with the hope that that drug abusers could simply be shown the error of their ways, counseled and the problem would disappear. Thus, overnight the client would become a law-abiding citizen with a wonderful job, and the world would be great. When this did not work out, however, the drug abusers were then incarcerated for long periods of time. What this accomplished was the removal of these offenders from the community, but they still had the urge to continue to abuse drugs even while incarcerated. Also, valuable taxpayer revenue was being used to incarcerate many people who still had a problem when they were released. There must be a better way.

In corrections, jails and prisons cannot pick their clients—the clients are sent to them. However, correctional staff must recognize that often, clients are medically and sometimes mentally unstable, they have been abusing drugs and themselves for a long period of time, and many simply enjoy the "street scene" and using drugs.

EFFECTIVE DRUG TREATMENT

In reviewing these basic factors, treatment staff also recognize that their goals may be different from their clients'. Knowing this, how does corrections proceed? If the nation has laws that make it a criminal offense to possess, sell or use drugs, there must be consequences. Without treating individuals and their drug abuse, the revolving door will continue. The country's prisons are full of these offenders. It would seem that given the nation's history and corrections' observations of the past 40 or so years, many viable treatment programs are available. An accountable treatment approach should include:

- Taking offenders out of the community for a short period of time and putting them in a secure treatment environment;

- Returning clients, after a specific time, to in-patient treatment in the community from which they came;

- Ensuring follow-up after the client completes in-patient treatment; and

- Establishing goals that are attainable and measurable.

By taking offenders out of the community, they will be removed from their environment, which protects not only the clients, but also the community. In addition, by putting the client in a secure environment, the street scene and easy access to addictive drugs are removed, allowing a client's behavior to be addressed. A simple but very important thing can also be accomplished—the client's health can be assessed and improved, both physically and mentally. Through eating controlled, balanced meals, and physical therapy, the client can vastly improve his or her physical health, because without working on the body, one cannot work on the mind. Also, with assessment, the client's mental health needs can be addressed since it is common knowledge that the nation's streets and correctional facilities are filled with people with mental health issues.

A client's stay at a secure environment should be measurable through his or her progress toward achievable goals. Not only do treatment staff want to make their clients' health important, they want to make them more amenable to treatment. Often, a client's greatest incentive for treatment is knowing that by refus-

ing treatment there will be consequences such as prison.

Following their specific treatment program during their short stay in the secure environment, offenders should progress to an in-patient drug treatment program in the community from which they came. This puts them back into the community, which offers certain benefits, including family support, employment opportunities and a continuum of treatment. The program must be licensed and accredited, as well as specific in treatment with attainable goals for the clients. This involves not only getting into their heads, but also dealing with other issues such as job training and life skills. Throughout treatment, clients must take personal responsibility and be held accountable for their actions. They also must have a plan and, after release, follow-up, whether it is parole or some other type of system that ensures that the clients continue to meet expectations.

WILLARD DRUG TREATMENT PROGRAM

One program that has all of these attributes is the Willard Drug Treatment Program in Willard, N.Y. Its mission is to prepare chemically impaired individuals for work release and to reduce recidivism. Run by the New York State Department of Correctional Services in conjunction with the New York State Division of Parole and licensed by the Office of Alcohol and Substance Abuse Services, the program was mandated by the New York State Legislature in 1995 through an initiative by Gov. George Pataki.

Glenn S. Goord, commissioner of New York State Department of Correctional Services, chose a site and model for the program, using a shock-based model with enhanced treatment. Shock-based is a highly structured program that includes military training and discipline. Everyone who comes to the facility is either judicially sanctioned directly from the courts or a parole violator,

and is a second-time, nonviolent felony offender.

This highly structured program mandates 90 days of intensive substance abuse treatment followed by an individualized continuing care plan, which includes intensive parole supervision and continuing treatment needs with providers licensed by the Office of Alcohol and Substance Abuse. The program is designed to assist participants to achieve, develop and maintain recovery.

Phase 1 of the Willard Program is designed to provide treatment for parolees using the disease model of recovery, intensive substance abuse treatment, cognitive-behavioral and motivational enhancement, as well as the military protocol and therapeutic community structure of the Shock Incarceration Program.

Phase 2 of the Willard Program occurs upon release. All parolees who successfully complete the 90-day residential component at the Willard Drug Treatment Campus (DTC) are released to a period of intensive parole supervision and placed in a community-based treatment program also licensed by the Office of Alcohol and Substance Abuse Services.

Willard DTC clients actively participate in all alcohol and drug treatment, individual and group counseling, physical fitness, academic and GED preparation, vocational job skills, network decision-making classes, drill and ceremony, and other parole transition activities.

Self-discipline is an important component in overcoming addictions. Participants are expected to know and comply with all the program rules and those of the Division of Parole and the Department of Correctional Services. The major focus of this program is on simplicity of lifestyle and clarity of thought through disciplined behaviors. Parolees are expected to demonstrate responsibility for themselves and for the treatment environment.

This unparalleled program, designed by Cheryl L. Clark, director of the Shock Incarceration Program with assistance from Ronald Moscicki, supervising superintendent of Shock Facilities, uses treatment teams comprised of alcohol and substance abuse counselors and program assistants, teachers and drill instructors from the Department of Correctional Services, and parole officers and parole substance abuse counselors from the Division of Parole. Staff are responsible for providing specific treatment duties for their assigned caseloads. These duties include individual counseling, group sessions, treatment planning, discharge planning, weekly evaluations of treatment progress and assessment duties. Staff facilitate the ancillary programs, which include education, vocational programming, networking and therapeutic work crews.

All Willard DTC staff go through an intensive four-and-a-half-week training program, whether a secretary or the superintendent—everyone is trained. This allows all staff members to understand the entire Willard Program so they can best facilitate it to the parolees. They also are involved with the participants' treatment process, working together to institute this multifaceted, holistic approach to addressing addiction and recovery.

SHOCK MODEL

One might ask, how is it possible to do anything in 90 days? Certainly, that is a good question. The answer is, first treatment staff have to have their attention. At Willard, this is done through the military style of the shock model. Parolees are awakened at 5:30 a.m. and march outside to the physical training deck at 5:55 a.m. For the next hour, they participate in group exercises and a company run, which gets them motivated and ready for the rest of their treatment day. After breakfast and showers, there is morning formation and then off to programs. Each group of parolees, or platoon, is involved in all aspects of the program, with a different program for

the day, which may include school, vocational training, alcohol/substance abuse treatment, confrontation (the process of helping participants face and change their own nonproblem-solving behaviors), network training, individual counseling, group meetings or therapeutic work program.

The Willard Program was designed to process as many as 3,600 clients per year. Of the 900 beds at the facility, approximately 800 are for males and 100 are for females. All parolees housed in each unit form a platoon. Females are programmed and housed separately from the males, thus alleviating any potential problems.

There is also a medical platoon comprised of many men who have significant medical, physical and/or psychological issues often requiring medication and/or routine monitoring by medical staff. Programming these men on a separate unit allows full exposure to treatment activities while limiting more stringent physical aspects of the program.

Willard accepts adult male and female parolees of any age who are second felony nonviolent offenders, and may have a multitude of physical issues. Willard parolees are sent there for their actions and are expected to dedicate themselves to their treatment.

By working together, staff, both uniform and nonuniform, have created an environment in which treatment can take place. Some people, when they see the shock model, are concerned and confused. They remember images from television of uniformed boot camp facility staff abusing clients. This is not the case in New York. Although staff will confront and hold parolees accountable, they do not put their hands on them. In order for treatment to take place, the parolees must be focused. The shock model, through its military approach, obtains this cooperation and attention in a short period of time. By having platoons work together, there is no time for individual acting out. Everyone wears the

same uniform, has the same haircut and goes through the same program.

Through the use of the military approach, parolees form structure and discipline in their lives, which prepares them for treatment. Willard is not easy nor is it meant to be. Outside treatment providers, where Willard parolees go when they leave, consistently say that Willard graduates are the most prepared for treatment and the most successful.

Twelve percent to 14 percent of those who come to Willard DTC either change their mind once they are there or cannot complete the program and are sent to a correctional facility to complete their sentences. In addition, if during the review process a parolee is found not to be living up to the expectations, he or she could appear before an evaluation review committee. There are a variety of sanctions, including keeping them for a longer period of time so that they have a chance to be successful in the program.

ASSESSMENT AND TREATMENT

When parolees first arrive at Willard, they go through an assessment. During that time, a preliminary treatment plan is devised, which each parolee signs. Parolees also sign a memo of agreement. An assigned treatment staff member completes an admission assessment and a treatment assessment of each parolee to determine or confirm the existence of alcoholism or substance abuse conditions based on criteria in the *Diagnostic and Statistical Manual of Mental Disorders*, the psychiatry compendium. Additionally, this assessment addresses clients' medical/psychiatric, educational, legal and general/psychosocial issues. It prepares the groundwork for the preliminary treatment plan and the substance treatment and discharge plans. The preliminary treatment plan addresses treatment needs for the clients' first 30 days in the program, which prepares parolees for entrance into the treatment phase of the program and provides the foundation for continuing care. Parolees are apprised of their program plan and general expectations.

After assessment and reception, parolees are assigned to a regular platoon. Once there, they are oriented by their drill instructor and their new treatment team. Clients live in dormitory-style housing and attend programming seven days a week. They are evaluated weekly in four areas: alcohol and substance abuse/parole, education, network, and drill and ceremony. One day each week they meet with members of their assigned treatment team and are given feedback on how they are doing. Goals have been set and they are expected to meet them.

Within 30 days of completion of the preliminary treatment plan, a comprehensive treatment plan is completed for each parolee. The treatment plan is filled out by the assigned treatment team members, and reflects goals and objectives for treatment needs as determined in both the treatment assessment and the preliminary treatment plan, as well as any new information that has presented itself concerning the parolee's addiction. The purpose of the treatment plan is to develop appropriate and specific long- and short-term goals for each parolee, providing a foundation for ongoing recovery.

The treatment plan is reviewed and signed by the parolee and the assigned treatment team member. The completed treatment plan also must be approved by a qualified health professional or senior coordinator. All parolees receive a copy of their individual treatment plan and become responsible for their recovery process. To assist or remind parolees of their agreed upon goals, they bring their treatment plan copy to their individual and case conference sessions and are expected to report on individual progress/challenges.

Treatment areas in each completed treatment plan must contain at least one individualized short-term objective for each problem area. The type and frequency of counseling must be identified in each short-

term objective, as appropriate. This applies to both individual and group counseling. All parolees also must have alcohol/drugs and legal areas addressed in the complete treatment plan, as well as supportive services (i.e., education, vocational) needs.

A weekly case conference meeting attended by the primary and secondary treatment teams is scheduled for all parolees. Medical staff also are encouraged to attend. Staff discuss each parolee's program participation and treatment plan progress, and case conference notes are completed and signed by each parolee. Weekly case conference summaries indicate type and duration of program participation and a rating in each area. Staff comments reflect a parolee's progress toward his or her treatment plan objectives. This weekly case conference also may be used to address parolees who have been having difficulty in the program as evidenced by their ratings and comments on their weekly evaluation form. The treatment team may refer parolees to the learning experience committee or evaluation review committee as behavior warrants. The learning experience committee meets with parolees who have demonstrated continued negative behavior and assign useful learning experiences, which may be a physical task or process. The evaluation review committee meets parolees whose poor evaluations have shown they are having difficulty with the program or who choose not to address their poor behavior.

PREPARING FOR RELEASE

Parolees begin the community reintegration process and adjustment to parole supervision as soon as they enter the Willard DTC. This process begins with orientation and continues through out the 90-day program. The treatment team assists parolees at every level.

The assigned treatment team member has specific responsibilities regarding this process. Treatment staff coordinate with the parole sub-

stance abuse counselor and the community-based parole officer. This ensures that parolees are tied into the community-based treatment program that is best suited to their needs with no interruption in the continuum of care and treatment.

The treatment team and parole substance abuse counselor work together to make sure that parolees have a clear understanding of the community-based treatment program and scheduled appointments. The treatment team parole officer also ensures that parolees have a clear understanding of the rules and regulations regarding parole supervision and that these standards are adhered to throughout program participation. Each parolee's progress is shared with the community-based parole officer who, in turn, has made the necessary contacts and is ready to take over the reins of parole supervision and assist the parolees upon their re-entry into the community without an interruption in treatment services and with the best possibility of maintaining a healthy, law-abiding lifestyle.

The assigned parole officer meets with parolees to ascertain their desired residence/employment plans upon release. Any shortcomings are discussed and parolees are counseled about any possible problems within the desired residence that could impact negatively on their adjustment. Parolees' past employment history and future vocational/educational goals also are reviewed at this time. If a parolee has no job offers or realistic vocational aspirations, he or she is counseled relative to other job opportunities as well as vocational/educational programs within his or her areas.

At this time, the above information is forwarded to the community-based parole officer for investigation and input. Willard parole staff maintain ongoing contact with the community parole officer to ensure that the proposed parole plan is appropriate and to include the parolee in any needed modifications.

No parolee leaves Willard DTC without a release plan in place. All aspects of that plan are discussed with the parolee prior to graduation. In addition, specific written instructions are provided to parolees to ensure their understanding and best assure a positive reintegration to the community. Immediately after their release, parolees are directed to make an arrival report to the community-based parole officer, at which time both immediate and long-term residence and employment planning are discussed. By working with parole and having parole staff on site, a program continuum is established—from Willard to outside treatment and care.

NINETY DAYS TO HEALTH

Certainly, no one will stop their addictive behavior until they decide they want to. Nothing can be accomplished without hard work and Willard parolees and staff do, indeed, work hard, with the goal of addressing addictive behavior. A lot of time is spent having parolees look at themselves and the addictive behavior, which has brought them to where they are now. In only 90 days, parolees become healthier, both in mind and body, and begin the long process of treatment. Through discipline, confrontation, education and care, much can be accomplished.

Melvin L. Williams is superintendent of the Willard Drug Treatment Campus in Willard, N.Y.

Strategies
To Improve Offender Outcomes In Treatment

By Faye Taxman

Is drug treatment effective? Research studies consistently show that drug-dependent offenders in drug treatment programs have reduced drug use, reduced criminal behavior and increased employment. Essentially, participation in drug treatment services reduces the likelihood of drug use by a minimum of 20 percent, and the longer the duration of treatment, the better the outcomes.[1] More successful treatment occurs when offenders are provided a continuum of care or a minimum of two levels of care that include outpatient and inpatient treatment. The continuum can occur from prison to the community or from intensive treatment community to less intensive services—both increase offenders' involvement in treatment, provide an opportunity for offenders to test their new recovery skills and

strengthen offenders' commitment to a substance-abuse-free lifestyle.

The question is not whether drug treatment services are effective, but how can services be delivered to achieve improved outcomes on the part of offenders. The manner in which services are implemented in the correctional system or how offenders are referred to drug treatment programs available through the public health settings affects offender outcomes. The key to success in drug treatment programs generally involves two main ingredients: selecting a target population of appropriate offenders that will benefit from the services and using a manualized treatment curriculum (one that has been empirically tested in the field) to improve treatment outcomes. These topics are often discussed in

literature, and yet, they continue to present tremendous challenges to the field as organizations strive to develop and implement treatment programming in prison, in the community or in transition.

Selecting Appropriate Offenders

The offense versus offender dilemma prevails in most decisions about the suitability of an offender for a treatment program offered through the judicial or correctional system. This dilemma represents a difficult tension in the criminal justice system where preference is often given to using the offense that the offender is convicted of (or arrested for, depending on the stage of the criminal justice system) as the criteria for eligibility. The offense is fre-

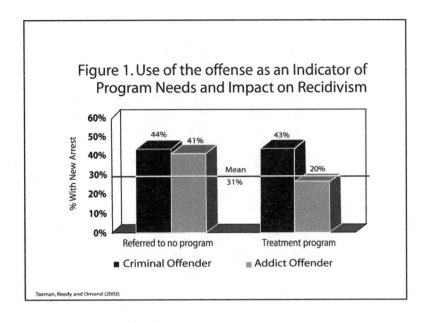

Figure 1. Use of the offense as an Indicator of Program Needs and Impact on Recidivism

quently used as a selection criteria because it is easily available and serves as a symbolic indicator of the offender's behavior. The charge or convicted offense is recorded in official criminal justice documents that render it easily available to the system. The offense also characterizes the nature of the offender's behavior—it is presumed that violent offenders will have offenses of person-to-person crimes, assaults, etc., whereas addicts will have mostly drug possession offenses. Yet, this is not always the case. Although it may be easy for the criminal justice system to use the offense to characterize offender traits, the offense does not lend itself to be a measure of behavioral characteristics.

The offender perspective (as compared with offense) focuses on understanding the criminogenic and social-psychological needs of an offender that affects functioning in society and involvement in criminal behavior. The key to the offender focus is to distinguish between static and dynamic measures. Static measures refer to past behaviors, or actions of the offender that are historical or unchanging such as if the offender has ever used drugs and the number of times he or she has been arrested. Dynamic factors refer

to traits that are current or subject to change such as how often the offender used alcohol or drugs during the past 30 days, how much alcohol or drugs the offender consumes at one time and whether the offender has a place of residence. An understanding of dynamic factors allows for an assessment of the areas in which the offender currently needs to make changes to become pro-social and improve the odds for achieving law-abiding behavior. For example, through an assessment of dynamic factors, the criminal justice system will determine whether the offender is a user of illicit substances (i.e., has ever used) or an abuser/addict (i.e., has compulsive behavior, patterns of binging or currently consumes). Similarly, for mental health function, a review of dynamic factors will determine whether the offender has ever had mental health issues (similar to nearly 20 percent of the American adult population) or currently is experiencing impaired functioning due to a mental health condition. An assessment of dynamic factors can assist the system in distinguishing between past and current behavior, which provides the ability to target offenders to treatment programs that can address some of the current social and psy-

chological issues that affect criminal conduct.

Figure 1, which illustrates the impact of poor offender assessment on outcomes, is from a study of offenders ordered to treatment programs as part of the conditions of release or community supervision. The determination was based on offense: Did the offender have a drug-related offense? This is the result of an offense-based system where, based on the nature of the offense, the offender was ordered to treatment programming in the community. Yet, using dynamic assessment tools in the research protocol, it was determined that some offenders were "criminals" and others were "addicts." Those determined criminal had an entrepreneurial nature by their involvement in the drug trade, whereas the addicts were offenders who compulsively consumed drugs and used crime as a means to obtain drugs. When addict offenders are assigned to a treatment program, there is a reduction in the rearrest rates (from 41 percent without treatment to 26 percent with treatment); however, when addict offenders are not provided treatment, there is no difference as compared with the criminal offenders.[2] More important, criminal offenders in treatment programs have similar outcomes to like criminal offenders who did not attend treatment. These findings are the result of offenders being placed in treatment that is not appropriate for their needs—a drug treatment program addresses the offender's use of alcohol and/or illicit substances and does not address the criminogenic values of an offender. Targeting the appropriate offenders to treatment programs can improve the outcomes of the treatment programs and, more importantly, use the scarce treatment resources for those offenders who will benefit from the services.

To improve outcomes, systems must use an assessment protocol that separately examines both the offender's risk and need factors. As part of this assessment, the goal is to determine the degree to which the offender's behavior is currently affected by use of drugs or alcohol (and/or mental health functioning) and the degree to which the use contributes to criminal behavior. For the addict offender, the distinction is whether the offender is a user or abuser, and the type of drug that the offender is most often likely to use such as heroin, cocaine, methamphetamines or marijuana. The goal is to determine whether the offender's use is consequential to criminal behavior or one of the driving factors. These are not necessarily distinctions that can be made by examining the offense. A standardized assessment tool or protocol can assist in making this determination, and then systems can assign offenders to treatment programs that are likely to benefit them.

Manualized Treatment Curriculums

During the past two decades, treatment has advanced from open "talk" therapy to skill-development forms of interventions. Many of the therapies that have been empirically tested fall under the rubric of cognitive or behavioral

therapies where the goal is to assist the offender in acquiring new skills to address thinking or behavioral issues. Different therapies are designed to provide the offender with different skills, ranging from social skill development to thinking/cognitive processing. The emphasis of this set of therapies is on assisting the offender in acquiring new skills to develop intrinsic controls and providing alternative strategies for substance-abusing behaviors. The advancement of treatment has resulted in improved outcomes from treatment programs, and researchers continue to demonstrate that offenders tend to have better outcomes from involvement in treatment programs that focus on skill development through cognitive and/or behavioral interventions.

Recent studies on the delivery of drug treatment services to offenders reveal a number of concerns that historically challenged the effectiveness of treatment for offenders.[3] These concerns include the purpose of the treatment, goals of the services, ability of the services to be provided in a correctional setting, appropriateness of the content of the therapy to change offender behaviors and ability of the treatment staff to work with offenders. All of these "doubts" are referred to as program failures that seem to loom in the minds of administrators, correctional officers and criminal justice staff. The question for the criminal justice system is how to structure services to improve the ability of the treatment programs to facilitate change in the offenders. One of the advances in the field has been the use of specialized curriculums that serve as a guide for the contents of a treatment program. The curriculum approach advances the field by moving away from the perception of treatment as a "soft" method of offender change to a more directive method. Plus, the curriculum outlines the different components of the treatment program and illustrates how the treatment can assist the offender in improving behavior. A curriculum provides

interested parties, such as criminal justice actors, judges and correctional officers, a visual process by which offenders progress to make changes in their lives. A number of curricula have been empirically tested and, therefore, have been shown to improve offender outcomes.

The manualized curriculum approach provides a framework for offender change that eases the ability to deliver the services. Systems that adopt a manualized curriculum usually find that the approach has certain advantages, such as:

- Defining the philosophy about the change process that frames the nature of the treatment intervention;

- Providing specific goals and objectives for each treatment session that can be measured to determine whether the offender is making changes as a result of obtaining new skills;

- Providing material that can be presented by qualified staff;

- Providing exercises and skill-development tools that offenders can use as "homework" or enhancements to the formal therapy sessions;

- Focusing on adult-learning styles where the sessions can be more interactive as a result of the offender learning techniques of self-diagnosis and self-management; and

- Ensuring that the treatment program builds on the skills incrementally (from self-awareness to self-diagnosis to self-management) as the offender goes through the process of change.

The manualized approach serves to enhance outcomes by providing a map of the offender change process and then assisting the offender in walking through these different skill development components to achieve the most desired outcomes.

From a management perspective, the manualized approach also has certain other advantages. Many correctional systems have difficulty obtaining and retaining counseling staff, or the manner in which treatment is delivered relies upon contractual staff who merely administer the treatment program but have no other responsibility in the prison or community program. A manualized approach provides a framework to ensure quality assurance of the treatment process by providing a mechanism to address staff-related issues. It also allows managers to be aware of the treatment sessions. If staff leave or are not available for a session, it is possible to have a replacement that can begin at the same place. While this does not address the issue of the counselor's familiarity with the offenders in the group, it does provide a vehicle to ensure the continuity in the treatment program. Further, the manualized approach allows for management to determine how much the offenders are progressing in the treatment program by using tools and exercises to assess treatment progress. This can only occur if the treatment recovery process is clear.

Another advantage of the manualized approach is that many of the curricula have been empirically evaluated prior to the distribution of the curricula. That is, there are studies that can illustrate the potential outcomes if the treatment programs are administered as planned. This can also help the correctional system obtain support for the treatment programs by illustrating the potential outcomes from participation in the treatment programs. For example, the National Institute on Drug Abuse (NIDA) has sponsored numerous studies on the efficacy of certain treatment curricula to address substance-abusing behaviors. The studies demonstrate the effectiveness of the treatment programs. An example of some of the treatment curricula that have been tested are available for use on the Web site www.nida.nih.gov/DrugPages/ Treatment.html. They are: "A Cognitive-Behavioral Approach: Treating Cocaine Addiction," "A Community Reinforcement Approach," "An Individual Drug Counseling Approach," "Drug Counseling for Cocaine Addiction," and "Brief Strategic Family Therapy for Adolescent Drug Abuse." Other NIDA-funded researchers also make their empirically tested curricula available for the public. One example is Texas Christian University (www.ibr.tcu. edu/resources), where it has several manuals readily available such as "Partners in Parenting," "Straight Ahead: Transition Skills for Recovery," and "TCU Cognitive Interventions."

Moving to a manualized curriculum approach, as in any clinical component, requires the system to adopt good quality assurance and control strategies. The first one is that the staff must be thoroughly trained and skilled in the delivery of the treatment sessions. An important part of the training is that staff are able to handle both the education-oriented parts of the training as well as the processing sessions. The processing sessions, or where the offenders have to role-play and rehearse the skills learned in treatment, are an important part of the treatment intervention. These are the parts that distinguish between "talk" therapy and skill development. Systems need to ensure that counseling staff are skilled in the ability to conduct and run processing sessions. Second, the system should provide for a means for clinical staff to develop an expertise in the curriculum. Clinical oversight and feedback are usually essential to achieving further outcomes.

Conclusion

Improving offender outcomes from participation in treatment programs can occur from both ensuring that appropriate offenders are targeted to the program and ensuring that the type of treatment services provided to the offenders are targeted to improving their specific behaviors that affect abuse of substances and criminal conduct. Good assessment tools are critical to ensuring that drug-involved offenders are placed in treatment programs. Without the assessment that focuses on dynamic factors, the treatment sessions cannot be oriented to changes in these dynamic factors that can assist the offender in improving outcomes. Stated simply, the manualized treatment programs tend to address contemporary issues that affect current offender behavior. A good assessment tool can identify these issues, and then in the treatment sessions, the offenders can develop skills to attend to these issues. Improving offender outcomes is more likely to occur when the system ensures that the appropriate offenders are participating in the appropriate treatment programs.

Other System factors that have been well-articulated in the studies are the importance of a continuum of care (more than two phases of treatment) and the importance of duration of treatment. These concepts are similar—learning new skills requires time to acquire the skills. This cannot occur in 30 or 60 days. Instead, treatment requires several phases that allow offenders an opportunity to practice, rehearse and acquire the skills. Increased time and several phases of the treatment enhance the outcomes by giving offenders the time to acquire and rehearse the skills they have learned in treatment. Together, the formula for improving outcomes requires making sure that the appropriate offenders are placed in the appropriate services and that the services are of sufficient duration to allow them to acquire these skills.

ENDNOTES

1. Taxman, F.S. 1999. Unraveling "what works" for offenders in substance abuse treatment services. *National Drug Court Institute Review*, II(2):92-134.

2. Taxman, F.S., D. Reedy and M. Ormond. 2003. *Break the cycle: Fourth year implementation*. College Park, Md.: University of Maryland.

3. Taxman, F.S. and J. Bouffard. 2003. Substance abuse counselors' treatment philosophy and the content of treatment services provided to offenders in drug court programs. *Journal of Substance Abuse Treatment*, 25(2003):75-84.

Taxman, F.S. and J. Bouffard. 2003. Drug treatment in the community: A case study of study integration. Federal Probation, 67(2):4-15.

Faye Taxman, Ph.D., is director of the University of Maryland Bureau of Governmental Research, College Park, Md.

Marijuana: Just Say No Again: The Old Failures of New and Improved Anti-drug Education

Renee Moilanen

I'M AT THE February 2001 Teens at the Table conference, a feel-good event sponsored by a coalition of Los Angeles youth organizations and high schools. It's designed to boost self-esteem and teach teenagers how to make smart decisions. In one of the sessions, a group of students is about to learn how easy it is to stay off drugs. It doesn't require anything as lame as red ribbons or "Just Say No" chants. It just takes knowing what constitutes a healthy decision—one that is all your own—coupled with a little real-life practice.

The kids test their skills with a role-playing skit. The scenario: Two girls are walking home from a party late at night when a car full of boys pulls up to offer them a ride. "The boys have been drinking and smoking," the script reads. "Trouble is imminent."

Here is where the teenagers are supposed to call on their newfound decision making skills in choosing whether to get into the car. They're asked to think about their options, weigh the consequences, and decide what to do based on what would be best for them—no judgments, no right or wrong, none of that thoughtless Just Say No stuff from the 1980s and early '90s. Today's drug prevention lessons, scientifically crafted and tested, are supposed to be all about teaching teenagers how to make choices, not telling them what to do; respecting their autonomy, not treating them like ventriloquist's dummies.

So the teenagers choose. If they don't get into the car, they walk home and everything is fine. But if they do …

Boys: Hop in girls!

(Eventually the boys get out of hand and come on to the girls.)

Girls: Stop it!

Boys: Come on, it will be fun!

Girls: No!

(Car accident.)

The teachers say there's a choice here, but these kids aren't stupid. They can stay out of the car and live, or get in the car and die. So … just say no.

Dare to Keep Your Kids off DARE

That three-word mantra "Just Say No" became a national punch line for a reason: It didn't keep kids away from drugs.

Drug use among teenagers dropped steadily from the early 1980s until 1992, mirroring a decline in drug use among adults. But this downward trend began before the anti-drug curricula developed in the 1980s, exemplified by Drug Abuse Resistance Education (DARE), could have had any impact. The drop was detected in surveys of students who had never heard of DARE or Just Say No. And by the early 1990s, when students who were exposed to DARE and similar programs in grade school and middle school reached their late teens, drug use among teenagers was going up again. In the 2002 Monitoring the Future Study, 53 percent of high school seniors said they had used illegal drugs, compared to 41 percent in 1992. Past-month use rose from 14 percent to 25 percent during the same period.

Meanwhile, the leading model for drug education in the United States has been DARE, which brings police officers into elementary and middle school classrooms to warn kids away from drugs. DARE claims to teach kids how to resist peer pressure and say no to drugs through skits, cartoons, and hypothetical situations. Founded by Los Angeles Police Chief Daryl Gates in 1983 and organized as a nonprofit corporation (DARE America) in 1987, DARE is still used in around three-quarters of the nation's school districts. At the annual DARE Officers Association Dinner a few years ago, Bill Clinton's drug czar, Barry McCaffrey, declared that "DARE knows what needs to be done to reduce drug use among children, and you are doing it—successfully." But as McCaffrey should have known, the effectiveness of DARE has never been demonstrated, a fact DARE America itself implicitly conceded when it announced, half a year after the drug czar's praise, that it was revamping its program.

During the last decade DARE has been widely criticized as unproven and unsophisticated. In one of the most damning studies, published in 1999, a team of researchers at the University of Kentucky found that 10 years after receiving the anti-drug lessons, former DARE students were no different from non-DARE students in terms of drug use, drug attitudes, or self-esteem. "This report adds to the accumulating literature on DARE's lack of efficacy in preventing or reducing substance use," the researchers noted. In a 2003 report, the General Accounting Office reviewed six long-term evaluations of DARE and concluded that there were "no significant differences in illicit drug use between students who received DARE … and students who did not." The surgeon general, the National Academy of Sciences, and the U.S. Department of Education also have declared DARE ineffective.

Determined not to repeat past mistakes and prodded by a federal government that lately has been demanding accountability in education, teachers today are turning to prevention programs backed by "scientifically based" claims of effectiveness. In 1998 the Department of Education, concerned that money was being wasted on a mishmash of ineffective programs, decided to fund only those proven by "scientifically based research" to reduce or prevent drug use. Testimonials and we-think-it's-working assurances like those cited by DARE would no longer pass muster. Every prevention program now needed hard numbers, objective experiments, and independently reviewed conclusions based on long-term follow-ups to prove they worked.

In 2000 the Department of Education convened an expert panel that judged nine prevention programs "exemplary" for their proven effectiveness and 33 others "promising." Comprised mostly of educators and health professionals, the panel gave the "exemplary" or "promising" nod only to programs backed by at least one scientific evaluation of effectiveness (DARE did not make the cut). Schools using programs that were not on the list would risk losing their slice of the Department of Education's $635 million drug prevention budget. In 2001 President George W. Bush included the "scientifically based research" criterion for drug education in his No Child Left Behind Act, signing into law what had previously been only administrative practice.

But the officially endorsed alternatives to DARE aren't necessarily better. Once you remove the shiny packaging and discard the "new and improved" labels, you'll find a product that's disappointingly familiar. The main thing that has changed is the rhetoric. Instead of "Just Say No," you'll hear, "Use your refusal skills." The new programs encourage teachers to go beyond telling kids that drug use is bad. Instead, they tell teenagers to "use your decision making skills" to make "healthy life choices." Since drugs aren't healthy, the choice is obvious: Just say no.

The persistence of this theme is no accident. Prevention programs can get the federal government's stamp of approval only if they deliver" a clear and consistent message that the illegal use of drugs" is "wrong and harmful." But this abstinence-only message leaves teenagers ill-equipped to avoid drug-related hazards if they do decide to experiment.

After examining some of the new anti-drug curricula and watching a sampling of them in action, I strongly doubt these programs are winning many hearts and minds.

The Class Struggle Against Drugs

In September 2001, I join a class of middle schoolers in the upscale Los Angeles suburb of Palos Verdes Estates as they run through a series of hypothetical scenarios ostensibly designed to put their decision making skills to work. The program, called Skills for Adolescence, is used in about 10 percent of the nation's 92,000 K-12 schools. The curriculum, which the Department of Education deems "promising," "teaches the social competency skills young adolescents need for positive development," according to program literature.

Clustered into small groups, each student fingers a wallet-size blue card. The card—titled "Will it lead to trouble?"—lists the five questions adolescents should ask themselves when confronted with a difficult choice.

It's laminated, presumably so teenagers can keep it in their back pockets and whip it out whenever they're faced with a tough decision and need a quick reminder about how to make one.

If the answer to any of these questions is yes, the students are supposed to say no: "Is it against the law, rules, or the teachings of my religion? Is it harmful to me or to others? Would it disappoint my family or other important adults? Is it wrong to do? Would I be hurt or upset if someone did this to me?"

The questions clearly are designed to elicit a complete rejection of drug use. Is it against the law? Yes, drugs are against the law. Therefore, you must reject them. Is it harmful? Yes, they can be harmful. Reject them. Would it disappoint my family or other adults? Yes, reject. There's no way to make any other decision. "If the only decision that's the right decision is the decision to say no, you've effectively cut off the discussion again," observes Marsha Rosenbaum, director of the West Coast office of the Drug Policy Alliance and author of Safty First: A Reality-Based Approach to Teens, Drugs, and Drug Education.

Another program praised by the Department of Education is Project ALERT, which it calls "exemplary." A series of anti-drug and anti-tobacco lessons used in about a fifth of the nation's 15,000 school districts, Project ALERT boasts that it "helps students build skills that will last a lifetime," including "how to identify the sources of pressure to use substances," "how to match specific resistance techniques with social pressures," "how to counter pro-drug arguments," and "how to say 'no' several different ways."

Eliminate the psychobabble, and Project ALERT's message is almost indistinguishable from that of the 1980s anti-drug programs that teachers now roundly scorn: Peer pressure is bad. Drugs are bad. Just say no.

In a room plastered with posters titled "Pressures" and "Ways to Say No," I join a class of Los Angeles middle schoolers in November 2002 as it breaks into small groups to plod through an anti-drug lesson from Project ALERT. The adolescents have just finished watching a video about smoking cigarettes featuring former teenaged smokers who say things like, "Life is too short. I'm not eager to die."

Each of the four groups is assigned a different question to answer: How can you help people quit? What's good about quitting? How do people quit? What gets people to quit?

There is little discussion. The kids know what the teacher expects. How can you help people quit? Tell them smoking is dumb. Don't hang out with them anymore.

When asked if she knows anyone who smokes, one girl nods.

Do you think any of this helps?

"No," she says without hesitation.

Why not?

The girl barely lifts her eyes from the paper, where she is decorating the "Smoking is dumb" and "Don't hang out with them anymore" list with bright red hearts. She shrugs. "Some people just don't care," she says.

The students are asked why they think kids use drugs.

They respond in unison, "Peer pressure"—the answer they know is expected. When asked to explain what this means, the students conjure up images of older kids hassling younger ones. "Sometimes they're your friends, but sometimes they're crazy people that come up and ask if you want some;" one boy says, drawing on concepts that prevailed during the Just Say No era but have little basis in real life.

One boy defines peer pressure as other students "trying to force you, trying to convince you to do it." When asked if he's ever experienced peer pressure, he shakes his head. He's waiting for a group of sinister strangers to thrust drugs in his face. Drug education apparently has not helped him realize that peer pressure is far subtler, like wearing the same clothes as your friends or sharing inside jokes. And the teachers, by continuing to portray peer pressure as a palpable evil, fail to protect their students from anything.

Everything Old Is New Again

Today's anti-drug programs claim to have replaced all the scare tactics of years past with good, solid information about the physiological effects of drug use. But these programs, which are based on the same flawed "scientific" information that adults have been using for years to keep kids off drugs, are a lot like anti-alcohol propaganda from the late 19th and early 20th centuries.

Back in the late 1800s, health lessons endorsed by the Woman's Christian Temperance Union (WCTU) and its Department of Scientific Instruction portrayed alcohol as a wicked poison that created an uncontrollable appetite for more: "Many persons who at first take only a little beer, cider, or wine, form a great desire for them.... The appetite for alcoholic liquors usually grows rapidly, and men who use but little at first often become drunkards in a short time." This selection comes from The House I Live In, a schoolbook written in 1887 and heartily endorsed by the WCTU.

A century later, another popular textbook offers a similar perspective on drug use. This passage comes from Making Life Choices (1999), lauded by teachers for its scientific content: "Attachment to the drug becomes almost like a great love relationship with another person. The only sure way to escape drug addiction is never to experiment with taking the drugs that produce it."

In the popular classroom video Marijuana Updates, produced in 1997, teenagers and Leo Hayden, a former college football player turned drug counselor, describe how pot ruined their lives. They say the drug made them feel invincible, tired, hungry, and numb. Soon they were slacking off in school, shirking responsibilities, and turning to harder drugs for a better high. Their testimonials, which suggest that pot turns people into useless zombies eager to snort cocaine and shoot heroin, draw on two major themes in anti-marijuana propaganda: "a motivational syndrome" and the "gateway effect."

A century ago, kids heard the same warnings about tobacco, another target of the so-called temperance movement. Our Bodies and How We Live (1904) warned that "the mind of the habitual user of tobacco is apt to lose its capacity for study or successful effort." According to the 1924 Primer of Hygiene, a smoker "forgets the importance of the work he has to do, and idles away his time instead of going earnestly to work to finish his task." The Essentials of Health (1892) worried that cigarettes would lead to harder stuff: "It is to be feared that if our young men continue the use of cigarettes we shall soon see, as a legitimate result, a large number of adults addicted to the opium habit."

The scientific studies allegedly proving the effectiveness of the new drug education programs aren't much more impressive than the tired rhetoric. Consider Life Skills Training, a fast-growing program that reaches about 2 percent of the nation's 47 million schoolchildren and tops the list of "exemplary" programs. Generally touted as the future of drug education, Life Skills Training purports to cut tobacco, alcohol, and marijuana use by up to 75 percent; to reduce the use of multiple drugs by two-thirds; and to decrease the use of inhalants, narcotics, and hallucinogens. These claims aren't based on testimonials or case studies about 12-year-old Johnny turning his life around after a few Life Skills Training lessons. The program's supporters cite actual scientific studies, reported in journals published by the American Medical Association and American Psychological Association.

But the lead scientist on those evaluations, Cornell University epidemiologist Gilbert Botvin, is the creator of Life Skills Training and the one profiting from its success. Botvin also sits on the expert panel that deemed his prevention program "exemplary." He is not the only program developer sitting on the expert panel; two other panelists have participated in rating prevention programs they helped develop. All of their programs have received "exemplary" marks.

Such conflicts of interest aren't proof that the conclusions are flawed. But independent researchers such as Joel Brown at the Center for Educational Research and Development in Berkeley have found problems with the Life

Skills Training studies. Brown charges that the evaluations often focused only on positive outcomes and omitted results indicating that teenagers who went through the prevention program were more likely to use drugs or alcohol than their peers.

You Gotta Believe

In a 2001 analysis published by the Journal of Drug Education, Brown noted that a six-year evaluation of Life Skills Training reported data only from students who had completed 60 percent or more of the curriculum, just two-thirds of the original 2,455-student sample. The students left out were the ones who missed many of the anti-drug lessons—probably students who skipped class a lot or were less motivated. Such students, other research suggests, would be especially prone to drug use. Carving them out of the picture inflated the program's apparent effectiveness, Brown's study shows.

Brown also found that when students completed anything less than 60 percent of the Life Skills Training curriculum, even 59 percent, their drug use was no lower, and in many cases higher, than that of students who did not participate in any lessons at all. Since the researchers don't give a good reason for using 60 percent as the cutoff point (only saying it was "a reasonably complete version of the intervention"), it seems they simply chose the point at which the outcomes turned positive.

Furthermore, Brown says, real students in real class-rooms are unlikely ever to see 60 percent of the curriculum, because most teachers simply pick out lessons and squeeze them in whenever possible. The Life Skills Training research reinforces this caveat: Even under pristine condi-tions, with teachers getting constant training and monitoring, one-third of the students failed to reach the 60 percent mark. And those kids, Brown's research shows, were more likely to use drugs than the students who did not participate at all.

The National Academy of Sciences found similar gaps in drug education research in its 2001 report Informing-America's Policy on Illegal Drugs: What We Don't Know Keeps Hurting Us. Too many studies omit negative results, exclude students from the original sample, and inflate statistical evidence, the report concluded. But because the federal government only requires a prevention study to demonstrate a single positive outcome, programs backed by weak evidence stay in business.

Another problem with many of the new "science-based" prevention programs is that they continue to rely on statistics measuring student attitudes toward drugs. Project ALERT celebrates outcomes such as these: "Anti-drug beliefs were significantly enhanced," among them "inten-tions not to use within the next six months," "beliefs that one can successfully resist pro-drug pressures," and "beliefs that drug use is harmful and has negative consequences." But whether a student intends to abstain or believes he can resist drugs does not tell us whether he actually will do so.

DARE officials likewise tried to counter bad publicity by falling back on beliefs, trumpeting that 97 percent of teachers rated DARE as good to excellent, 93 percent of parents believed DARE teaches children to avoid drugs, and 86 percent of school principals believed students would be less likely to use drugs after DARE. With only beliefs to cite, DARE was left off the federal government's list of "exemplary" and "promising" prevention curricula in 2000. Many schools have dropped it from their anti-drug lineups or scaled it back to the point of irrelevance, a fact that DARE officials concede while refusing to release numbers on the decline.

Desperate to retain its dominance in the prevention market, DARE has embarked on a dramatic retooling of its lessons to keep up with the current emphasis on scientific research, decision-making skills, and resistance techniques. The Robert Wood Johnson Foundation has given DARE a $13.7 million grant to create a new middle school curriculum, which teachers began testing last fall. DARE officials said the new curriculum was drastically different.

"It's not just say no, it's not Nancy Reagan," says Charlie Parsons, executive director of DARE America. "We're teaching kids how to say no."

It remains to be seen how this revamped DARE curriculum is going to be any different from the old one—or, for that matter, how any of the new prevention programs are different from the old DARE. Many of the DARE tactics now scorned by educators are quite similar to those used in the new, supposedly revised programs. Project ALERT and Life Skills Training have "Ways to Say No" almost identical to the ones taught in DARE.

Drug Education as if Reality Matters

What all of these programs continue to ignore is the most crucial piece in the drug prevention puzzle—the kids, and their stubbornly independent reactions to propaganda. They aren't fooled by "decision making" skills or "healthy choices." They know what the teachers expect: Just say no.

"They make you feel as bad as they can if you do it," says one Los Angeles teenager. Still, he says, "almost every person I know has tried marijuana. Even good people."

At Mira Costa High School in Manhattan Beach, California, a 10th-grade summer health teacher, Guy Gardner, recognizes his difficult position. About one in four Manhattan Beach students are "current" (past-month) marijuana users, according to the district's own studies, which puts them near the national average. "A lot of them know more than I do," Gardner confesses. Yet he plays the game, rattling off a list of warnings—cocaine will rot out your nose, marijuana could kill you, there's no such thing as recreational drug use—even as most of his students know how unlikely or just plain wrong it all is.

In one lesson, Gardner asks students to name the first thing that comes to their minds when they hear the word drugs. "Don't give me answers I want to hear, give me your answers," he urges.

A couple of kids call out: Crime. Death. Stupid. Something that alters your mind and screws up your body.

But a few offer another point of view.

"I think it's bad, but people have the choice to do it, and if they do it, it's their problem," says one boy.

"If you really want to do it, you're going to do it," says another, even going so far as to advocate legalizing drugs. "We'd be so much more chill in the nation."

That may be, but saying so is untenable in the abstinence-only world of drug education. Gardner pulls back the debate. You can't legalize drugs, he tells the students, because they're harmful. "The ultimate message" of legalization, he says, "is it's OK to do drugs." And that, he implies, just isn't true.

In the end, meaningful drug education reform probably won't come from educators. It will have to come from those who have far more at stake when it comes to drug use by teenagers: their parents. They are the ones who see their kids stumble home with bloodshot eyes, who can't fall asleep when their kids are partying the night away, who know their kids are experimenting with drugs and want, above all, for them to be safe.

That's why drug experts such as Safety First author Marsha Rosenbaum are calling for a truly new approach to drug education, one that abandons the abstinence-only message and gives kids the unbiased, factual information they need to stay safe, even if they choose to experiment. Such information could include now-forbidden advice on real but avoidable hazards such as driving under the influence, having sex when you're high, mixing alcohol with other depressants, and overheating while using Ecstasy.

One possible model is Mothers Against Drunk Driving (MADD), which recognized that if it couldn't stop young people from drinking, it could at least stop them from getting behind the wheel while intoxicated. MADD's efforts, which made designated driver a household term, seem to have worked: Since 1982, according to the National Highway Traffic Safety Administration, the number of teenagers killed in drunk driving accidents has plunged 57 percent. MADD thus helped prove that we can make drug use safer without eliminating it entirely.

"There are kids who are not going to use drugs for religious reasons, because they're athletes, because they're focused on school, because they don't like the way they feel," Rosenbaum notes. "These kids don't need a program to tell them no. They're already not using. But for the kids who are amenable to the experience, it doesn't matter how many DARE programs they sit through; they're going to do it anyway.… If we can't prevent drug use, what we can prevent is drug abuse and drug problems. But we have to get real."

Renee Moilanen (rmoilanen@adelphia.net) is a freelance journalist studying drug policy at UCLA.

A product of Nancy Reagan's 1980's, RENEE MOILANEN was solidly on board with the "Just Say No" bandwagon until high school, when she and her peers began to see those dire warnings as propaganda. As an education reporter for the Torrance, California, Daily Breeze, she felt a sense of déjà vu as she watched today's "new and improved" drug prevention programs in action. In "Just Say No Again", she reports on the still-dull cutting edge of drug education. Moilanen is currently earning a master's degree at UCLA's School of Public Policy and Social Research, where she studies drug policy.

Binge Drinking: Not the Word of Choice

Abstract. Educators and researchers strive to use terms that reflect a replicable measure of behavior. A term commonly used to describe drinking of a problematic nature is *binge drinking*. Binge drinking defines behavior by a number of drinks of an alcoholic beverage consumed in a space of time. The authors argue that the term does not describe drinking behavior that students believe is problematic. They claim that students define problem drinking not in terms of quantity, but rather by the outcome (and occasionally by frequency), and attribute different negative connotations to the term *binge*. They suggest using a term that has shared meaning with students, such as *dangerous drinking*, to describe the drinking behavior that results in undesirable or unintended consequences.

By Fern Walter Goodhart, MSPH, CHES; Linda C. Lederman, PhD;
Lea P. Stewart, PhD; and Lisa Laitman, MSEd

A rose by any other name may smell as sweet, but to college students, the term *binge drinking* may not mean the same behavior as it does to researchers and educators. *Binge drinking* is now a common term used to describe college drinking that is problematic. It emerged in the 1990s, initially in the work of the Harvard School of Public Health.[1-3]

A large and growing body of literature documents drinking patterns and drinking-related problems on college campuses.[4-7] Many authors agree that some college students who drink do so in ways that are more problematic than the students themselves comprehend. However, those authors differ on strategies to reduce drinking-related behaviors among college students and use different terms to describe similar drinking behavior. If researchers and health educators want students to take our educational messages personally so that the messages are meant for *them*, we believe that researchers and educators must pay attention to the terms used to describe students' drinking behavior.

Weschler and associates[8] report that the students whose drinking patterns match their criteria for binge drinkers have a self-serving reason for not agreeing with the research definition of binge drinking because the students do not think they have a drinking problem. However, are they considering the connotations of the word *binge* to these student drinkers? Why would students be motivated to change their drinking behavior if they neither relate to the terms used to describe their behavior nor agree that their drinking is problematic?

The drinking-related phenomenon the word *binge* describes is 5 or more drinks in a setting for a man and 4 or more for a woman. Previously, the same drinking behavior was referred to in the literature as *at-risk drinking*.[3,7,9,10]

We researchers and educators may be unwittingly contributing to students' denial of problematic drinking by using the word *binge* to describe drinking on campus. We found that 92% of the students did not think of themselves as binge drinkers, even though 35% of those students drank at levels that researchers use to define binge drinking.[11] Our work at Rutgers University convinced us that students not only do not identify with *binge drinking* as a phrase that describes drinking 5 or more drinks for men or 4 or more for women. They also laugh when they think of it as describing their own or their friends' behavior.

We propose replacing *binge drinking* as a term with *dangerous drinking* to describe the drinking behavior that results in unintended or undesirable consequences. Rutgers students tell us that they think about frequency rather than just quantity as the measure of someone's having a problem with alcohol.[11,12] To them, daily drinking, regardless of amount, is seen as more problematic than 8 drinks on one occasion once a semester. Our students did not categorize drinking as a problem until they got "buzzed," "plastered," or "out of it."

Neither *at-risk drinking* nor *binge drinking* are words that our students themselves use to describe their own drinking. In fact, a study at a major midwestern university found that calling drinking *risky* was appealing to students, as students at that institution liked to think of themselves as risk-takers.[13] Milgram and Anderson[14] argue that *binge* actually refers to a situation in which an individual consumes alcohol to the point of intoxication over a long period of time (eg, 2 or 3 days).[14] They point out that when *binge* is used to refer to a set number of drinks, it fails to take into account such external factors or individual differences of size or composition of drink, weight of drinker, or food consumption.

If students do not relate to the word *binge* as describing their own behavior, if that word has different meanings and connotations for them than 5 or more drinks at a time, are health educators making it too easy for them to dismiss reports of binge drinking as what "happens to other people" and to view binges as more extreme behaviors than those they identify with? One way to help students personalize messages about drinking is to change the use of the word *binge* to a term that more closely describes their behavior and that is one to which they can relate.

Students know a great deal about drinking on campus from their own and others' drinking-related behavior—it is part of their college experience.[8,11] In addition to learning what they do and how they think, as health educators, we also need to learn why they think and behave as they do. For example, we see that some university students who drink do not usually characterize their drinking as problematic (for some, it is not, but for others, it is). Many of them do not think that 5 or more drinks is too much to drink, and most do not believe that they have a problem with drinking unless they drink every day. Some students also think that no matter how much they drink, others drink more.[4,8,15]

We also hear students telling us that they measure their drinking by what happens to them, rather than by the number of drinks they consumed. Students describe drinking behavior in terms of consequences or outcomes, such as when drinking caused physical, emotional, or academic harm to themselves or to others. Students, even those who drink heavily, are aware of some, if not all, of the consequences of their drinking behavior, such as the relational consequences of being taken advantage of (sexually or socially), getting into sexually intimate relationships too quickly, embarrassing themselves, or getting into situations that are violent.

If the quantity of alcohol consumed does not seem to affect what students define as a problem, they are not going to pay attention to limiting the amount they drink. Instead, they speak of limits in terms of impaired judgment and the resulting negative consequences or illness.

If the students we health educators most need to reach are students who are least likely to want to learn that their drinking is problematic, the words we choose to describe students' drinking need to be carefully thought out. The word *binge* lets students off the hook; it is easy for them to think of binges as something that other people do, to associate it with alcoholics, and to think of alcoholism as something to avoid rather than as a disease. For many students, the word *alcoholic* still carries with it the stigma that many educators and counselors try to eliminate. Despite the fact that their families may contain people suffering from alcoholism, the word *alcoholic* has negative connotations, and as long as they do not have to use that word to describe themselves, they think they have no problems with alcohol. This means, of course, that when they go out to party and get "smashed," they may be ignorant of the real dangers associated with what they are doing. These dangers go beyond what they know about drinking and its associated problems.

We propose *dangerous drinking* as an alternative to the term *binge drinking* for several reasons. Students think it more appropriate because it focuses on outcomes of drinking. They reject other terms as follows:

- *Binge drinking*—students do not identify with it.
- *High-risk drinking*—some students would think that high risk was cool.
- *Responsible drinking*—it is judgmental, members of the community who have serious alcohol problems would be labeled irresponsible, which seems like blaming the victim of a disease.

The term *dangerous drinking* places the focus on the type of drinking to address—that which is dangerous—in an arena that perhaps most students and administrators can agree with. Instead of students being at odds with administrators about the problem of drinking, we may be more likely to agree on what is a problem if we are both discussing drinking that is a problem. If a male student has 5 to 6 drinks during a party that starts at 1 PM and ends at 4 AM, consumes food and spaces his drinks out over this period, this is not necessarily problem drinking. Yet if a student has too much to drink in a short time and needs to be taken to the hospital with alcohol poisoning, this should be defined as dangerous drinking.

The challenge is to use a clear definition of dangerous drinking by a term that makes the drinking problematic, so that health educators have a replicable measure of behavior and outcomes. If administrators want to alert students to a problem, first we have to get the students' attention. The word *binge* does not do it. Let us see if *dangerous drinking* can be a more effective way for students to be better able to reflect on their own drinking-related choices.

And let us ask researchers to find a better way to describe or quantify the types of consequences that describe dangerous drinking so that we can all be talking about the same rose.

ACKNOWLEDGMENT

Research reported in this Viewpoint was funded, in part, by grants from the US Department of Education Safe and Drug Free Schools Program, US Department of Education Fund for the Improvement of Post Secondary Education, Rutgers University Health Services, and Rutgers University Department of Communication. We wish to express our appreciation to Adrienne Coleman for her careful reading and suggestions about this article.

NOTE

For comments and further information, please address communications to Fern Walter Goodhart, MSPH, CHES, director, Department of Health Education, Rutgers University Health Services, 319 Hurtado Health Center, 11 Bishop Place, New Brunswick, NJ 08901-1180 (e-mail goodhart@rci.rutgers.edu).

REFERENCES

1. Meilman PW, Cashin JR, McKillip JR, Presley CA. Understanding the three national databases on collegiate alcohol and drug use. *J Am Coll Health*. 1998;46(4):68.

2. Weschler H. Alcohol and the American college campus: a report from the Harvard School of Public Health. *Change*. 1996;28(4):20–25.

3. Weschler H, Dowdall GW, Maenner G, Gledhill-Hoyt J, Lee H. Changes in binge drinking and related problems among American college students between 1993 and 1997. *J Am Coll Health*. 1998;47(2):57–68.

4. Haines MP. *A Social Norms Approach to Preventing Binge Drinking at Colleges and Universities*. Washington, DC: US Department of Education, Education Development Center, Inc; 1996. Publication ED/OPE/96-18:1996.

5. Jeffrey LR, Negro P. *Contemporary Trends in Alcohol and Other Drug Use by College Students in New Jersey*. New Jersey Higher Education Consortium on Alcohol and other Drug Prevention and Education; 1996.

6. Lederman LC, Stewart LP, Kennedy L, et al. The role of communication theory and experiential learning in addressing dangerous drinking on the college campus. In: Lederman LC, Gibson WD, eds. *Communication Theory: A Casebook Approach*. Dubuque, IA: Kendall Hunt; 2000.

7. Perkins W, Wechsler H. Variation in perceived college drinking norms and its impact on alcohol abuse: a nationwide study. *J Drug Issues*. 1996;(4):961–974.

8. Wechsler H, Lee JE, Kuo M, Lee H. College binge drinking in the 1990s: a continuing problem: results of the Harvard School of Public Health 1999 college alcohol study. *J Am Coll Health*. 2000;48(5):199–211.

9. Carey KB. Alcohol-related expectancies predict quantity and frequency of heavy drinking among college students. *Psychol Addict Behav*. 1995;9(4):236–241.

10. Pasavac EJ. College students' views and excessive drinking and the university role. *J Drug Education*. 1993;23(3): 237–245.

11. Lederman LC, Stewart LP, Kennedy L et al. Using qualitative and quantitative methods to triangulate the research process: the role of communication in perpetuating the myth of dangerous drinking as the norm on college campuses. In: Herndon SL, Kreps GL, eds, *Qualitative Research: Applications in Organizational Communication*. 2nd ed. Cresskill, NJ: Hampton Press; 2000.

12. Lederman LC, Stewart LP, Kennedy L, Powell R, Goodhart F. Self report of student perceptions: an alcohol awareness measure. *Communication and Health Issues Research Series: Report #2*. New Brunswick, NJ: Communications and Health Issues Partnership for Education and Research, School of Communications, Information and Library Studies. Rutgers University; 1998.

13. Workman TA. Constructions from within the collegiate drinking culture: an analysis of fraternity drinking stories. Presented at: Annual Meeting of the National Communication Association; New York, 1999.

14. Milgram GG, Anderson DS. Action planner: steps for developing a comprehensive campus alcohol abuse prevention program. Fairfax, VA: George Mason University; 2000.

15. Lederman LC, Stewart LP. Addressing the culture of college drinking through correcting misperceptions: using experiential learning theory and Gilligan's work. *Communication and Health Issues Research Series: Report #4*. New Brunswick, NJ: Communication and Health Issues Partnership for Education and Research, School of Communication, Information and Library Studies, Rutgers University; 1998.

Fern Walter Goodhart *is director, Department of Health Education at the Rutgers University Health Services, New Brunswick, New Jersey, where* ***Linda C. Lederman*** *and* ***Lea P. Stewart*** *are professors in the Department of Communication and directors, Communication and Health Issues Partnership for Education and Research; and* ***Lisa Laitman****, is director, Alcohol and Other Drug Assistance Program for Students (ADAPS) in the Student Health Service.*

From *Journal of American College Health,* Vol. 52, No. 1, July/August 2003. Reprinted by permission of the Helen Dwight Reid Educational Foundation. Published by Heldref Publications, 1319, Eighteenth St., NW, Washington, DC 20036-1802. Copyright © 2003.

MICHAEL DARBY'S JOURNEY

A new weapon in the war on drugs: family

A New York program that focuses on drug treatment through family support is a revolutionary new model.

By Alexandra Marks
Staff writer of The Christian Science Monitor

NEW YORK—Michael Darby has five new reasons to stay off drugs and out of jail: His girlfriend, Denise Ruiz, and her four daughters.

It's the family the 24-year-old parolee has always wanted. And despite the challenges and frustrations that come with such close relationships, he's determined to work to keep them.

"It's crazy because she and the girls got here right on time," says Mr. Darby, who was paroled in September and moved in with Ms. Ruiz shortly thereafter. "I always prayed for a family and someone who could love me a much as I loved her."

The new Darby/Ruiz family is part of what's being touted as a "revolutionary" approach to drug treatment and probation. Called La Bodega de la Familia, it's proven to have significant success in reducing substance abuse and a return to crime among parolees such as Darby. The reason: It looks at the parolee not as an individual but part of a whole family that has its own set of separate issues that need to be addressed for real healing and recovery to take place.

It sounds like simple common sense. And in fact, many of the private treatment centers for middle-class addicts that have insurance make working with the whole family a priority. But because most poor people get their drug treatment through the criminal-justice system, families are usually an afterthought at best.

WE ARE FAMILY: Denise Ruiz and two of her four children helped parolee Michael Darby stay off drugs by particpating in a program started by Carol Shapiro.

"It is one of those things that is so intuitive, but its never really been used," says Carol Shapiro, the founder of La Bodega de la Familia.

"Government in poor people's lives tends to discount the power and influence of family; it tends to think they have all the answers."

A study by the Vera Institute for Justice released in Washington on Tuesday found that illegal drug use by participants in La Bodega declined from 80 percent to 42 percent, significantly more than in the comparison group. La Bodega participants were also less likely to be arrested again and they, along with their families, reported an "enhanced sense of well-being" as a result of the increased access to—and use of—support services.

Principles with policy implications

The findings have caught the attention of policymakers in a wide range of fields from drug treatment to public housing. The reason: using La Bodega's systematic approach to family healing can be taught to social workers and case managers in any field. And with an estimated 600,000 people being released from prison each year and the worst budget crisis in generations—the hope is that any government agency can tap and leverage the power of the family to help in recovery.

An expanded program

In 2001, Miss Shapiro started a new nonprofit called Family Justice which is designed to teach La Bodega's principles to thousands of people in the criminal justice system around the country.

"Considering that we have limited resources, we're always looking for what works," says Rick Levy, New York City's first deputy commissioner of probation. There are currently about 60 probationers in the program and he would like to expand that number.

When La Bodega was started in 1996 as an experimental project in an old bodega on New York's predominantly Hispanic Lower East Side, Shapiro and the other founders thought that family involvement would help participants stay in drug treatment longer. So researchers were stunned to see the significant drop in drug use with no correlating increase in the use of treatment. They went back to try understand why.

"It wasn't the formal treatment," says Chris Stone, the director of the Vera Institute of Justice. "But it appears people were adjusting their behavior because of their changed and stronger relationships with their families."

One of things that distinguishes La Bodega's approach is the program's definition of "family."

The family case managers make it a point of going beyond just the immediate family to provide support by asking their participants about other figures in their lives. As a result the "family" grows to include girlfriends and even close neighbors from childhood.

In Michael Darby's case, it included Ms. Ruiz and her children. They'd met while he was in prison. Ruiz was a born-again Christian. She'd gone to visit Darby as a favor to his grandmother. The two eventually became romantically involved.

Building a support network

When Darby first arrived home after spending most of the past six years in prison primarily for drug dealing, he had a difficult time adjusting to his new freedom and responsibilities. Ms. Ruiz had expected that he'd immediately get back to work. The two clashed, and the relationship almost ended.

"I had my downs and I went real down, but I didn't know how to stop," says Darby. "I almost lost her."

He easily could have been sent back to prison for violating his parole. Instead, his case manager Amy Alverez worked closely with Darby and also helped Ruiz gain a new understanding of the challenges her boyfriend was facing.

"It helped me understand that I have to be patient," she says.

"I expected a lot from him quick, but jail is all he's ever really known, he hasn't really been in a healthy, structured environment."

The two are committed to building a life together. And Darby is ready now, because his life no longer feels like a "black hole" filled with pain, but something that's blessed and is his own.

National Survey Finds Strong Public Support for Treatment

Faces & Voices of Recovery (FAVOR), the national recovery support organization, last week released results from a groundbreaking survey that found overwhelming public support for addiction treatment.

The survey found that addiction has affected most people's lives, often through family members, and found great support for insurance coverage of treatment.

The surprisingly strong findings should give great credence to the public awareness campaigns that are in the planning stages by FAVOR, the National Council on Alcoholism and Drug Dependence (NCADD) and others.

Sixty-three percent of the 801 American adults surveyed by telephone said there had been a great deal or some impact on their own lives as a result of grappling with addiction. For 72 percent of these people, the addiction resided with a family member.

Lead poll researcher Allan Rivlin told *ADAW* that the 63 percent is "a remarkable number—it tells us that this is a disease that affects a lot of people." Rivlin is a senior vice president with Peter D. Hart Research Associates, the national polling firm that conducted the survey.

The survey found that the public shows a strong preference for policies that treat addiction as a health issue rather than a law enforcement issue. More than eight out of 10 people (81 percent) say they would be more likely to vote for a Congressional candidate who favored reallocating what the government spends on the war on drugs to place more emphasis on drug prevention, education, treatment and recovery programs. This attitude was bipartisan—85 percent of Democrats and 81 percent of Republicans felt this way.

"The poll signals a sea change in the way America believes policymakers should be addressing addiction issues," said Rivlin.

The survey also found that:

- Seventy-six percent are more likely to vote for a candidate who proposed a law that required health insurance companies to cover the treatment for addiction to alcohol and other drugs the same as other conditions (substance abuse parity). This included 66 percent of Republicans and 87 percent of Democrats.

- Seventy-five percent of respondents were more likely to vote for a candidate who called for an increase in federal government funding for programs to prevent and treat addiction and support recovery.

- By 63 percent to 28 percent, respondents supported changing the law that bans students who have been arrested for drug possession from receiving student loans.

- "This reflects a tremendous change in attitude towards addiction—a strong support for changes in policy," Pat Taylor, FAVOR's campaign coordinator, told *ADAW*. "It starts with the concept that addiction is a health issue rather than a law enforcement issue."

- "There is a tremendous amount of public commitment to changing the way we deal with addictions, both from the perspective of providing opportunities for people to get well to removing barriers that keep them from getting a job and moving back into society," said Taylor.

Stigma

Two-thirds of survey respondents believe that a stigma exists toward people in recovery from addiction to alcohol or other drugs.

A significant minority of respondents (27 percent) admitted that they would be less likely to hire someone who was in longterm recovery from addiction to alcohol or other drugs. Eighty percent of respondents said that addiction discrimination in the workplace was a problem and 75 percent said that health insurance coverage for people seeking recovery was a problem.

"The poll strongly illustrates the barriers and roadblocks that people face as they strive to improve their lives and participate in community life," said Taylor. "Discrimination is very much a factor in the lives of millions of Americans who are in recovery—those who have been addicted to alcohol or other drugs but are now free of their addiction."

Addicted, Neglectful Moms Offered Treatment, Custody

By Henri E. Cauvin
Washington Post Staff Writer

For many of the drug-dependent mothers who end up in D.C. Superior Court, charged with neglecting their children, the choices are rarely good.

Going into residential treatment might be their best hope for curing their destructive addictions, but it would often leave their children languishing for months in foster care, far from the one person they depend on.

A program launched yesterday by the D.C. courts and the city's social services agencies aims to give at least a few troubled mothers a better choice.

Instead of being forced to choose between treatment and their children, a few dozen mothers will enter a six-month drug rehabilitation program with their children, under the supervision of the District's new Family Treatment Court.

In a city with just 100 District-funded residential treatment slots for an estimated 60,000 addicts, the 18 beds that the new program will add will be precious.

By housing the children with their mothers and keeping them in the schools they were attending, officials hope to avoid the anxiety and depression that young children frequently feel when they are separated from the people and places they know best.

At the facility, the mothers will have help caring for the children but still will be expected to feed and dress them.

Anita Josey-Herring, the Family Court judge who will preside over Family Treatment Court, said she was skeptical about the proposal at first. "I actually had to be convinced that having kids accompany the parent into residential treatment was a good idea," she said.

The initiative, a pilot project, is modeled after efforts in Virginia, Florida and elsewhere. Seeing those programs at work persuaded Josey-Herring that they can give parents "an incentive to stop using drugs. They could see their child. They could hold their child."

Krista Evans, coordinator of women's programs at the city's Addiction Prevention and Recovery Administration, said that children and their mothers typically benefit from the new setting.

"In most cases, it's a better environment, because it's highly structured and there's a lot of support," Evans said.

"The child was probably, in most cases, parenting themselves, and now, being in a safe environment, they are able to react as children," she said.

The District's child welfare system has long been criticized as among the country's most dysfunctional. For years, it has struggled, often unsuccessfully, to deal effectively with a large caseload.

With more than 2,000 neglect cases in the court system as of Jan. 1 and more than half of those affected by drug use, the Family Treatment Court for now will reach a small number of mothers.

In all, 36 women will be chosen to participate, 18 of them in the next few days and 18 more six months from now, after the first group has completed its treatment program and moved into after-care. Officials declined to say where the privately run residential facility will be located, saying they need to protect the privacy and ensure the safety of participants.

At the center of the new initiative is Family Court, created by Congress in 2001 after reform. The court faces new local and federal mandates to resolve a child's fate in abuse and neglect cases within 18 months.

Josey-Herring said the Family Treatment Court will give judges an important tool. Finding stable, permanent homes for the children in these cases is the overriding goal, she and others said.

If a mother overcomes her drug habit, completes the program and demonstrates progress toward becoming a good parent, her chances of being reunited with her children are good. But a parent who fails to do so, in spite of the intensive support and supervision, risks having her child or children put up for adoption and other consequences.

"We're not guaranteeing that the children will be returned to the parents," Josey-Herring said. "What we're saying is: If you are successful, it enhances your chances. But it does not guarantee it."

The project, about a year in the planning, is a collaboration by D.C. Superior Court; the Department of Health; the deputy mayor for children, youth, families and elders; and the Child and Family Services Agency, which will foot the $1.4 million bill for the treatment and supervision of participants.

Officials set up a plan to identify candidates for the program. Once a neglect case has been identified by a police officer or social worker, the city will conduct an initial screening to determine whether a mother and her children might be eligible.

Within a couple of days, a more exhaustive screening by social workers from the court and the Addiction Prevention and Recovery Administration would take place.

A few days later, the candidate could be before Josey-Herring, who will make the final decision on who enters the program, which is voluntary and requires participants to sign a contract.

Not every drug-addicted mother will be a candidate. Only those accused of neglect are eligible; mothers accused of abuse will not participate. Mothers with severe psychiatric problems or histories of violent behavior also will be excluded.

Along with their drug treatment, the women will be counseled on education, health and nutrition, with yoga a planned part of the program.

While in the program, they will appear every two weeks before Josey-Herring for progress reports.

"You're rebuilding people, essentially," she said. "You're helping them to understand that they are valuable and they have a life worth living."

Consumer direction, self-determination and person-centered treatment

John de Miranda

The Substance Abuse and Mental Health Services Administration (SAMHSA) is hosting a Consumer Direction Summit on March 22-23 that will convene substance abuse and mental health field leaders. The purpose of the gathering is to "make strategic recommendations" to SAMHSA for the development of "new programs, technical assistance initiatives, supports, consultation to states and communities, and collaboration between federal, state and local government agencies and between government, foundations, providers and advocacy groups." SAMHSA plans to "develop an agenda for change and the tools that will help states develop more consumer-directed models of care."

While self-determination and consumer direction have long been central principals in the disability services and mental health fields, the alcohol and drug prevention and treatment communities tend to be program-centered rather than person-centered.

Thinking about potential clients as empowered, autonomous individuals competent to make decisions in their best interests runs counter to a substance abuse treatment system that values subtle (an angry spouse) or overt (a drug court judge) coercion and bestows societal acceptance only after some level of abstinence-based recovery is established. In the official prevention arena, young people are offered limited choices and usually presented with information about drugs that focuses only on the downside of use.

The concept of consumer direction in the disability and mental health sectors at the individual level means real choice and control over services, making decisions without undue external influence and self-directed recovery. At a systems level, it means developing and implementing programs utilizing direct consumer involvement and ownership. The disability community's slogan "Nothing about us, without us," captures the sentiment.

On a governance level, having a board of directors comprised of a majority of current or former consumers implements the principal at the operational level. In theory, at least, power and control are vested in the consumer.

The addiction treatment community tends to vest power in the treatment program and twelve-step support systems. Clients in treatment or pretreatment are viewed as lacking good decision-making skills and the emotional equilibrium to make appropriate choices.

"You may not want this program, but you need it," captures this approach used by many addiction professionals, when faced with the ambivalence and denial of active addiction. Believing that we know what is best for the addict can be seen by some as realistic, while others might view this as paternalism or a by-product of treatment's persistent alliance with the criminal justice system.

How to square self-determination and consumer direction principles with current practice will be a challenge for summit participants. While there may be general agreement that substance abuse services could be more person-centered, how to evolve in this direction without missteps will not be easy.

If providers are to move away from a captive, coerced and somewhat secure client base and to compete for customers in a free market, what is to stop some entrepreneurs from presenting their programs as the cheapest, easiest, quickest way to get "treated?"

The administration's Access To Recovery voucher program is a major driver. Similar to school vouchers, the program will provide vouchers to consumers for the purchase of substance abuse treatment and recovery support services. According to the program's promotional materials, "With a voucher, people in need of addiction treatment and recovery support will be able to choose the programs and providers that will help them the most. Increased choice protects individuals and encourages quality."

One mechanism to increase the ability of consumers to make appropriate choices is the use of pre-treatment counseling and education groups. The CAM (Consumer Advocacy Model) Program at Wright State University in Dayton, Ohio has developed an approach that utilizes a motivational approach to individuals considering its outpatient services.

The CAM program is also unique in assisting clients with substance use disorder who have another co-occurring disability such as traumatic brain injury, sensory and/or developmental disabilities.

Pre-treatment counseling focuses on assisting the client to determine readiness for treatment, the benefits they can expect as well as orienting them to the activities of a treatment and recovery regime. This approach has evolved from CAM's roots in the disability world. CAM was chosen last year as one of eight promising programs for dual disorder treatment in the country.

According to Dennis Moore, Ed.D. director of Substance Abuse Resources and Disability Issues, CAM's parent organization, "CAM differs from other treatment programs in that it provides wholistic, person-centered care that considers multiple domains of need, not just immediate substance abuse issues."

If SAMHSA's initiative can help the field become more consumer-oriented, the upcoming summit will pay large dividends.

For further information about the CAM program, contact Dennis Moore at (937) 775-1484.

John de Miranda, Ed.M., is executive director of the National Association on Alcohol, Drugs and Disability, Inc., 2165 Bunker Hill Drive, San Mateo, CA 94492-3801; phone (650) 578-8047; fax (650) 286-9205; or e-mail at **solanda@sbcglobal.net**. The opinions expressed are those of the author and not necessarily the organization he represents.

From *Alcoholism & Drug Abuse Weekly*, Vol. 16, Issue 11, March 15, 2004, pp. 5-6. Copyright © 2004 by Manisses Communications Group, Inc. Reprinted by permission.

Discussion

SACHR: An example of an integrated, harm reduction drug treatment program

Abstract

In this article, we report on our work at St. Ann's Corner of Harm Reduction, a multi-service agency committed to implementing effective public health strategies in disenfranchised communities from a harm reduction perspective. Based on our experiences, we hope to contribute to the ongoing dialogue about the definition of harm reduction, while proposing to integrate harm reduction and abstinence-oriented treatment modalities into a model of comprehensive drug prevention and care. The five components of our harm reduction service provision are discussed, and a vignette is provided. We conclude with a plea for close collaborations between innovative researchers and harm reduction agencies, and a call for the full integration of harm reduction approaches into the substance abuse field at large. © 2003 Elsevier Inc. All rights reserved.

Bart Majoor*, Joyce Rivera

1. Introduction

This paper, which draws upon the grassroots clinical experience of the writers with active drug users in both the Netherlands and the United States, is primarily focused on the presentation of the five components of the harm-reduction service model provided in our program, the St. Ann's Corner of Harm Reduction (SACHR), located in The Bronx, NY. This presentation is followed by a clinical vignette that demonstrates selected components of behavior change that are applied in the harm reduction approach to substance users in disenfranchised minority communities. Throughout the paper, harm reduction is presented as a drug treatment approach that could become the foundation for a system of integrated drug care that honors the multiple need profiles of participants from our target group. We chose the term 'participant' for the community members who take part in our services. The more usual terms 'patient' or 'client' reflect too much of an uneven power relationship between worker and client/patient. Harm reduction approaches the participant as the expert of their story, respecting their solutions

and pace. This paper aims at contributing to a professional dialogue that enhances the integration of harm-reduction and abstinence-oriented treatment modalities into a model of comprehensive drug prevention and care.

2. Toward a definition of harm reduction in the United States

Although a definition of Harm Reduction has yet to find consensus, the focus remains on defining the Harm Reduction *approach* or *strategy* in a manner that contains some of the core characteristics generally agreed upon in the literature (MacCoun, 1998: Riley et al., 1999; Wodak, 1999). This is complicated by the fact that harm reduction may take a variety of forms in different cultures and subcultures. The diversity of meanings and activities is enormous, and much still remains to be written about the actual practice of harm reduction as it is conducted across the United States, Brazil, and the Southern Cone (Argentina, Chile, and Uruguay). For example, the North American Syringe Exchange Network (NASEN), now 12 years in existence, identified in its 2000 United States Syringe Exchange Program Survey 127 needle exchanges operating in 35 states (Des Jarlais, McKnight, Eigo, & Friedmann, 2000). Of these, 101 were either legal or quasi-legal (illegal but tolerated); all of this indicates a robust pioneering of harm reduction practice at the local level (Des Jarlais et al., 2000).

---

*Corresponding author. Tel.: +1-718-585-5544: fax: +1-718-585-8314.
E-mail address: sachr@aol.com (B. Majoor).

Given all of these developments and the fact that the field is in the midst of a paradigm shift (Kuhn, 1970), a simple and clear definition of harm reduction has not been possible. However, for us, harm reduction practice involves the mediation of substance use through the provision of self-management strategies that are immediately effective in reducing personal and communal harm.

3. Interventions: A continuum of improvement

The drug users who are seen in our program are frequently faced with all of the insults and indignities that come from living in an area full of poverty, violence, disease, and discrimination. The use of substances is connected, at least initially, to a range of motivations. These include a desire for pleasure (in a situation where the range of available pleasures are limited), an attempt to feel alive, as a way of connecting with others, as a method of reducing the pain related to constant frustration and deprivation, to cope with the effects of ongoing and or past violence, and as a form of self-medication for anxiety, depression, and other forms of psychic pain. Over time, the drugs themselves become a problem as the cycle of physical dependence becomes a motivator as well.

Within this context, there are two core themes that underlie our approach: (1) the centrality of affirming relationships; and (2) the ability of our program participants to become the creative directors of their own lives. This last includes developing their strengths and inner resources so that they can move from the position of victim, or reactor, to one in which they are self-directed and can take an "agentic" approach to life (McAdams, 1993).

Through teaching poor and working-class substance users alternative survival strategies, a model of comprehensive care responds to the complex web of their needs and poor resources. When total abstinence is unattainable, there remain many good objectives that can still be achieved. Better management of drug use and safer drug use—achieved by syringe exchange, substitution, or moderation interventions—are examples of good treatment objectives when the participant does not have the social resources to be abstinent.

A continuum of prevention and care can be created in which harm-reducing (including abstinence) interventions are closely working together. Substance users experience mastery over their addiction when they are taught to analyze the demanding role of the drug, at specific emotional moments, within specific settings. Addiction specialists, using Motivational Interviewing (Miller & Rollnick, 1991), are then poised to support the participant's understanding by locating presented problem behaviors within a Stages of Change model (Prochaska, DiClemente, & Norcross, 1992). These two taken together—"drug, set, setting" (Zinberg, 1984) and stages of change (Prochaska et al., 1992)—increase the substance users' personal capacity for change and are translated into a treatment plan that can be monitored. The development of a range of harm reduction interventions gradually builds a repertoire of more feasible alternatives for the participant, both in terms of concrete changes in distinct life areas and in enhancing the self-efficacy of the participant (Majoor, 1996; Murphy & Vuchinich, 2002).

4. Five components of harm reduction service provision

Our clinical practice is at St. Ann's Corner of Harm Reduction (SACHR) in the South Bronx, New York. There are five components to the syringe exchange/harm reduction services that we provide, and our intent is to be a comprehensive program. Recognizing that the present system of care suffers from fragmentation and discontinuity, harm reduction services are organized around a one-stop shopping module. Not only does our program offer multiple services, but also our approach includes seeing the participant in a complex and multi-dimensional manner. As will be seen, our services address many of the levels in Maslow's Hierarchy of Needs (Maslow, 1970). Our approach is holistic; this means that our interventions concern body, mind, and spirit, and, in some cases, the heart. McAdams' (1993) work emphasizes the importance of both a personal sense of agency (the "agentic") and connections to others (the communal) in life and personality, and these aspects of the self are nurtured in our program. Lastly, we interact with our participants along a number of different social dimensions. They are seen as individuals and as members of families, groups, social networks, and communities.

4.1. Palliative care

These are the low-threshold services that take care of the basic and acute needs of participants. Meeting survival needs with food, showers, a hot drink, syringes, condoms, clothes, boots, sleeping bags, and a roof to sleep under brings a sense of safety and self-worth that lay the cornerstones for the changing of high-risk behaviors. In the example of Zoraya, discussed below, the offered palliative care was her portal into service provision, and she developed a connection to our program by establishing a regular pattern of visits to the center.

Using Maslow's perspective, this first component is addressing the physiological needs of drug users. With the possible exception of methadone maintenance treatment, harm reduction is unique in the drug-treatment field for its emphasis on addressing these basic survival needs. Holistically, the body is central, and the interventions are focused on the individual.

To help ensure that drug users will see our program as a positive resource that they will want to become a part of, all of the services are provided freely with no demands placed on the participants. The ability to offer services that are anonymous and free (i.e., grant-funded) is a essential component of the engagement and retention process.

4.2. Stress reduction

Participants from this target group live a life of stress that finds relief in seeking thrills in a cycle of immediate gratification followed by dysphoria. Bodily levels of stress have become mingled with this ongoing thrill-seeking behavior and get conditioned to that state. The development of bodily relaxation, for our participants, is a pre-condition to looking at their reality in a way that might enable them to make changes in behavior. A typical harm-reduction center will have a team of holistic health staff that is able to introduce alternative approaches to health and well-being.

Acupuncture, acupressure, massage, yoga, and the teaching of self-relaxation techniques are concrete interventions here. Even the creation of a 'sanctuary' space in the center where the participants can sit in silence or listen to quiet music will make the link to another world and other possibilities. The experience of not being chased or abused, but simply being respected and left by yourself to nod out after a night of bartering sex for drugs in a crack house, can be important to create the security, as well as the confusion or dissonance that anticipates behavior change.

From Maslow's perspective, the creation of a sanctuary is an attempt to address the safety needs of addicted individuals. Holistically, there is a continued emphasis on the body. Instead of just meeting its needs, there is now an effort to begin to heal and renew the body. These techniques and disciplines may also begin to stir the spiritual aspects of the participants. While still individually focused, they are, perhaps, somewhat more interactive. They may also serve to create the foundation that will lead to further development of both the agentic and the communal.

4.3. Education and information

Essential to the harm reduction approach is the provision of a wide range of information. If the goal is to make the participant his/her own change agent, awareness is a major prerequisite. To make informed choices about the issues they face, there is a deep need for education and information. Realizing that families cannot solely rely on personal networks for managing the complexity of their choices, harm reduction agencies focus on building information resources that make a difference in the every day decision-making of their participants. Up-to-date knowledge that helps them navigate their difficulties and addresses their concerns is presented in various modalities and in a linguistically and culturally appropriate way.

While the educational intervention does not fit into the Maslow hierarchy as clearly as the others, nevertheless, in a holistic way, it is addressing the mind. It is also an attempt to build up the agentic aspect of the person as knowledge is intertwined with choice and action. It also serves the program's fundamental goal of participant empowerment.

4.4. Healing and empowerment

In the later stages of the harm reduction working alliance, the service component that supports healing from past wounds and gathering power for upcoming changes becomes essential. Open support groups are available for several target groups (i.e., men, women, transgender persons, recent ex-convicts, sex workers, and HIV and Hepatitis C-positive people). Mental health services are important in this component for reasons of crisis intervention, assessment of psychiatric disorders, and, especially, to gain more self-awareness through regular counseling. Social skills are trained within this context of growth because social learning theory teaches that changing cognitions (beliefs, expectations) by educating participants and developing the skills to do something with what they have learned, are essential to the process of changing high-risk behaviors (Marlatt & Gordon, 1985).

These groups certainly address what Maslow (1970) called the belongingness and love needs, and, in some situations, they may begin to address the esteem needs of the individual. This last would be true if the participants are able to begin to master new skills and these changes are then recognized and applauded. As can be seen from our group list, many of the participants in our program are "social outcasts." They are typically seen as undesirable people. The world of dysfunctional drug use may have provided them with a home, a dangerous one, but a home nonetheless. As they begin their journey away from the world of dysfunctional drug use, these groups can serve as niches where they can break out of isolation and their emerging self-transformations have the possibility of being affirmed and confirmed. When all goes well, our participants are beginning to form their new, alternative community. From a holistic perspective, these groups are speaking to the mind and perhaps to the heart. From a focus that was primarily individual, the interventions are becoming more relational.

4.5. Social integration

The fifth component of harm reduction service provision is the cluster of interventions that are aimed at reintegrating the participant back into society. The microcosm of internal and relational security that the participant has built up over time working with the agency has to result in the launching of a self-regulating individual into society. A great deal of support is needed to accomplish this. Case management is essential here to monitor the participant's style and pace of change, and to help him or her negotiate with an environment that may not be receptive to their needs. The most essential component is the support of "natural" groups, like the family. This means that the harm reduction agency has to be a "family" center to be effective in its mission to support participants in their journey back into society (Murphy & Vuchinich. 2002).

This is, of course, one of the more difficult transitions to make. The drug user begins to give up the role of service participant and gradually takes on the one of the independent and self-directed individual. They will be challenged to see if they can now find healthy ways to meet the needs we have already discussed, and, perhaps, even their needs for self-actualization. In some sense, all of the spheres, levels, and dimensions are at play here, and, ideally, there is an integration of the communal and the agentic so that the recovering person is both supported and empowered.

Harm reduction values community-based work because behavior change occurs within the context of a social milieu. Optimally, this is a two-way process. Through the change process, the social network of participants is an important resource for supporting the behavior changes that they are attempting to make. It is one that can be reconstructed or replaced, but it cannot be ignored. In turn, Harm Reduction agencies are also operational in creating positive changes on the communal level because, when successful, they are helping to transform and reintegrate these participants back into the community.

4.6. "Zoraya": A vignette

As an example of how our 'clinic' actually operates, we have provided a vignette that exemplifies the kind of change process that we frequently see. A typical participant for harm reduction in our program is "Zoraya," a 38-year-old Latina with three children and a husband in jail for drug sales. She is HIV positive and has multiple economic and drug-related problems. Zoraya arrived at our offices as a result of her familiarity with the volunteer director. "Enya." Enya knew Zoraya, her family, and her children, and reached out to her in response to Zoraya's increasing complaints about "female problems". Enya also knew that Zoraya, an active IV drug user, had experienced stigma and shame within established medical centers and had grown averse to medical intervention (Finkelstein & Ramos, 2002). Enya began the pretreatment intervention by engaging Zoraya in palliative care program services such as syringe exchange, nutritional workshops, safer sex supplies, and, finally, case management. After a few visits during which multiple members of the care planning team were enlisted to meet with Zoraya and help her with her needs (including financial entitlements, mental health counseling, and school problems with her children), she was able to feel supported and comfortable enough to confide to the case manager that she was suffering from chronic vaginal itching. The team met to discuss the best method of approaching her, and, conscious of her deep distrust of medical doctors, assigned a staff member who not only coordinated the details of the visit, but also personally accompanied her to a local medical care facility. This staff member was introduced to Zoraya by Enya, and Zoraya agreed to talk with this female staff member. One of the outcomes of this conversation was that she decided to get a full physical work up that included HIV testing. This carefully orchestrated and respectful palliative care plan serves to relieve participants of long-held fears of medical intervention while safely connecting them to care in an active and comprehensive way. Up to this point, Zoraya had consistently exchanged used syringes for new ones, a practice that suggested stabilization. As her confidence with the program grew, Zoraya began to voice ambivalence regarding her relationship with drugs. Nine months later she was on methadone and AIDS medication, and was playing an active role in the women's group.

Zoraya's story demonstrates the continuum of improvement that the harm reduction approach offers to its participants in a non-obtrusive, client-centered way. Their priorities and capacity to change are respected in a working alliance that may take months before the first significant outcomes emerge. Her story is exemplary of the complex issues that these participants present: active multiple substance use, mental health symptoms, severe medical condition (i.e., HIV positive status), and many problematic life areas (i.e., homelessness, no benefits/income, no health insurance, and social isolation). A core ingredient of the harm reduction approach is a secular, non-doctrinaire acceptance of the situation, including participant's drug use, as a strategy for incremental change in the areas they want to change (Majoor, 1995). A low-threshold approach to Zoraya also requires a culturally appropriate environment (i.e., the center is located in a familiar community, staff is Spanish-speaking, printed information is available in Spanish, and even the meals are prepared by a Puerto Rican cook).

Zoraya's optimal autonomy—the ultimate treatment goal in the harm reduction approach—was defined by her as she grew more confident with her regained (and sometimes new-found) ability to take care of herself and manage her medical and social needs. This includes her ongoing participation in a methadone maintenance program and her life-long monitoring of her medical status. Zoraya's quality of life has significantly improved, according to her reports, and she now assists others in their steps toward self-improvement.

5. The role of research

Paradoxically, while one part of our program has received a great deal of scrutiny, the rest has received none. Between 1991 and 2000, eight government-funded reports unanimously concluded that syringe exchange reduced HIV transmission, and not one study found the programs to cause an increase in drug use (General Accounting Office, 1993; Health and Human Services, 2000; Lurie & Reingold, 1993; National Commission on AIDS. 1991; National Institutes of Health Consensus Panel, 1997; National Research Council, 1995; Office of Technology Assessment of the U.S. Congress, 1995; Satcher, 1993). Despite its own findings, and in defiance of the scientific support for these interventions, the Federal government still prohibits the use of government funding for syringe exchange.

Given these, at best, ambivalent feelings towards the funding of needle exchange programs, it is not surprising that there have been no studies of comprehensive programs like St. Ann's Corner of Harm Reduction. Instead, integral, separately funded program components like prevention case management have received the acclaim of the United States Conference of Mayors as a best-practice model (USCM, 2000). While we have clinical confidence in the effectiveness of our program, there is no empirical evidence in the American context, other than that noted above, to support what we are doing at present.

Looking to the future, harm reduction agencies should seek to connect with innovative research groups; groups that are comfortable with quantitative, qualitative, and quasiexperimental methods and designs. Together they have the potential to create a feedback loop in which the clinical experiences of the harm-reduction service providers are compared with empirically derived process and outcome measures. Not only could these findings help improve the quality of care, but also they could be used to help persuade policymakers, funding sources, and the general public that harm reduction programs are of value because they offer such advantages as optimal autonomy for the participant, healthier communities, and a humane and cost-effective solution for society.

Given the grassroots background of these organizations, the process approach to participant change, the acceptance of resistance and relapse, and the emphasis on relationship, the indices examined, the measures used, and the design chosen must all be formulated very carefully. It is vitally important that researchers truly understand the harm reduction model, that the outcome variables reflect the vision and the goals of the program, and that sufficient time is provided in the research design for these outcome measures to be attained.

6. Conclusion

In this paper we have presented what we feel are the merits of working on the problem of substance use from a harm reduction approach. At its core, we believe that dysfunctional substance use is mediating a cluster of personal challenges that neither abstinence nor incarceration can eliminate. We have presented the SACHR model as one that allows for both meeting immediate needs and building toward long-term goals. It has been our clinical experience that this kind of endeavor can have a powerful impact in a very desperate situation. For these kinds of programs to prosper, it would be ideal for there to be a significant increase in funding, an interest among researchers to collaborate in developing creative and relevant research projects, and the full integration of harm reduction services into the substance abuse field at large.

Acknowledgments

Bart Majoor is clinical director and Joyce Rivera is executive director and founder of St. Ann's Corner of Harm Reduction, Bronx, NY.

This paper is adapted from a presentation that was given at a conference entitled, "The Great Debate: Abstinence versus Harm Reduction in Addiction Treatment" that was held at The New School University on April 6, 2001. This conference was conceptualized by the Division on Addictions Executive Committee of the New York State Psychological Association.

We give our special thanks to McWelling Todman and the Masters Program in Mental Health and Substance Abuse Counseling at The New School University for their help. Support for this work was received from the Division on Addictions of the New York State Psychological Association for their assistance. We thank Scott Kellogg for his sensitive patience and considerable editing work. Our work at St. Ann's Corner of Harm Reduction is made possible by grants from the AIDS Institute/New York State Department of Health, Division of HIV Prevention of the New York City Department of Health, Cicatelli Associates, and the Tides Foundation. We thank our friends and colleagues, and our linkage partners, all contributing to the dynamic synergy of a great team, our courageous participants, and a tolerant community.

References

Des Jarlais, D., McKnight, C., Eigo, K., & Friedmann, P. (2000). *2000 United States Syringe Exchange Program Survey*. New York: North American Syringe Exchange Network and The Baron Edmond de Rothschild Chemical Dependency Institute.

Finkelstein, R., & Ramos, S. (Eds.) (2002). *Manual for primary care providers: Effectively caring for active substance users*. New York: The New York Academy of Medicine.

General Accounting Office. (1993). *Needle exchange programs: Research suggests promise as an AIDS prevention strategy*. Washington, DC: US Government Printing Office.

Health and Human Services. (2000). *Evidence-based findings on the efficacy of syringe exchange programs: An analysis from the Assistant Secretary for Health and Surgeon General of the scientific research completed since April 1998*. Washington, DC: Department of Health and Human Services. 2000.

Kuhn, T. S. (1970). *The structure of scientific revolutions* (2nd ed.). Chicago: The University of Chicago Press.

Lurie, P., & Reingold, A. L. (1993). *The public health impact of needle exchange programs in the United States and abroad*. San Francisco: University of California.

MacCoun, R. (1998). Toward a psychology of harm reduction. *American Psychologist, 53*, 1199–1208.

Majoor, B. (1995, March). *The art of accepting*. Paper presented at the 6th International Conference on the Reduction of Drug Related Harm. Florence, Italy.

Majoor, B. (1996). *The funnel model: New approaches in drug care*. Amsterdam: European Addiction Training Institute/The Jellinek Institute.

Marlatt, G. A., & Gordon, J. R. (Eds.) (1985). *Relapse prevention: Maintenance strategies in the treatment of addictive behaviors*. New York: Guilford Press.

Maslow, A. H. (1970). *Motivation and personality* (2nd ed.). New York: Harper & Row.

McAdams, D. (1993). *The stories we live by: Personal myths and the making of the self*. New York: Guilford Press.

Miller, W. R., & Rollnick, S. (1991). *Motivational interviewing: Preparing people to change addictive behavior*. New York: The Guilford Press.

Murphy, J. G., & Vuchinich, R. E. (2002). Behavioral theories of choice and substance abuse: Implications of behavioral theories for substance abuse treatment. *The Addictions Newsletter, 9* (2).

National Commission on AIDS. (1991). *The twin epidemics of substance abuse and HIV*. Washington, DC: National Commission on AIDS. pp. 3, 12–14.

National Institutes of Health Consensus Panel. (1997). *Interventions to prevent HIV risk behaviors*. Kensington, MD: National Institutes of Health Consensus Program Information Center.

National Research Council and Institute of Medicine. (1995). J. Normand, D. Moses, & L. Moses (Eds.). *Preventing HIV transmission: The role of sterile syringes and bleach*. Washington, DC: National Academy Press.

Office of Technology Assessment of the U.S. Congress. (1995). *The effectiveness of AIDS prevention efforts*. Springfield, VA: National Technology Information Service.

Prochaska, J. O., DiClemente, C. C., & Norcross, J. C. (1992). In search of how people change: Applications to addictive behaviors, *American Psychologist, 47*, 1102–1114.

Riley, D., Sawka, E., Conley, P., Hewitt, D., Mitic, W., & Poulin, C. (1999). Harm reduction: Concepts and practice. A policy discussion paper, *Substance Use & Misuse, 34*, 9–24.

Satcher, D. (1993). *The Clinton administration's internal reviews of research on needle exchange programs*. Atlanta, GA: Centers for Disease Control.

United States Conference of Mayors. (2000). *Best practices models*. Washington DC: USCM Annual Publication.

Wodak, A. (1999). What is this thing called harm reduction? *International Journal of Drug Policy, 10*, 169–171.

Zinberg, N. E. (1984). *Drug, set, and selling: The basis for controlled intoxicant use*. New Haven, CT: Yale University Press.

Index

A

accumbens, 41, 43

acetamenophen, 124

acetycholine, 50, 52

Adderall, 5, 32

Addiction Prevention and Recovery Administration, 210

African Americans, social consequences of war on drugs and, 150, 151–152, 154–155

AIDS. *See* HIV

AKT molecule, 50, 51

alcohol: defining terms for use of, in research, 204–206; health impacts of, 51, 71–73; women and, 69–70

alcohol abuse, privatization of public costs of, 29–30

alcohol tolerance gene, 62

Alzado, Lyle, 104

Alzheimer's disease, alcohol and, 51

amygdala, 41, 43

Anabolic Steroid Control Act, 106

anabolic steroids, 19–20, 101; "designer", 105–107. *See also* performance-enhancing drugs

androstenedione, 76, 77

anti-depressants: children and, 3–4, 5, 139–140; controversy over addiction to, 82–85

anti-drug education programs, 199–203

anti-social behavior, methamphetamine users and, 113

apoptosis, 50

aristolochic acid, 76, 77, 79–80

Arizona, anti-smoking campaign in, 8–9

Armstrong, Lance, 17, 108

Ashcroft, John, 155

Athens Olympics, performance-enhancing drugs and, 108–111

athletes, 15–23; Athens Olympics and, 108–111; BALCO and, 16, 21, 101–102, 103–104; baseball and, 103–104

at-risk drinking, 204

attention deficit hyperactivity disorder (ADHD), 3, 6, 7, 31

B

Barton, Elisabeth, 15, 22

baseball, performance-enhancing drugs and, 16, 20, 21, 103–104

Bay Area Laboratory Co-Operative (BALCO), performance-enhancing drugs and, 16, 21, 101–102, 103–104, 108, 109

Best Pharmaceuticals for Children Act (BP-CA), 12

binge drinking, 204–205

bipolar disorder (BPD), 3, 4

bitter orange, 77, 80

blacks. *See* African Americans

blood doping, 101

Blumer, Jeffrey, 10, 11

Bonds, Barry, 16, 20, 103, 104

Botvin, Gilbert, 201

brain, reward circuitry in, and addiction, 40–44

Brown, Joel, 201–202

buprenorphine, 117; as treatment for opiate addiction, 47–49

burdens principle, argument against legalization of heroin and, 179–182

Bush, George W., 109, 155–156, 184; marijuana law reform as election issue and, 162–165

BuSpar, 13

C

California, anti-smoking campaign in, 9

Caminiti, Ken, 20

Canada: decriminalization of marijuana in, 184–185; growth of marijuana in, 88–92

Canseco, Jose, 20–21

change, quitting addictions and, 37–39

chaparral, 76, 77, 80

child abuse and neglect (CAN) teams, children found at methamphetamine labs and, 135

children: drug research and, 10–14; effect of parental heroin use on, 179–180; methamphetamine labs and, 134–136; smoking and, 8–9; use of drugs to treat mood disorders in, 3–7

chloropheniramine, 124

cigarettes. *See* smoking

club drugs, 96–97

cocaine, 112

comfrey, 76, 77

community re-entry, decline in prisons and, 26

"compelling state interest" test, 168

Concerta, 5, 32

Consumer Advocacy Model (CAM) Program, 211–212

consumer direction, drug treatment programs and, 211–212

Conte, Victor, 21, 101, 108

Coricidin HBP Cough and Cold, 123, 124

corporate accountability, privatization of public costs of alcohol abuse and, 29–30

Costas, Bob, 103–104

cough medicine, over-the-counter, 123–125

creatine, 17

CREB (cAMP response element-binding protein), 42, 43

criminalization, theory of, and decriminalization, 168–169

cycling, use of performance-enhancing drugs in, 108

D

dangerous drinking, 204, 205

Darby, Michael, on war on drugs, 207–208

DARE (Drug Abuse Resistance Education), 199–200, 202

date rape drugs, 97, 141–143

Davis, Susan, 80–81

Day, Nancy L., 72

decriminalization, 166–173, 174–177, 178–183, 184–185

delta FosB, 42, 43

Depakote, 5

"designer" steroids, 105–106

dextromethorphan (DMX), 123–125

diabetes, alcohol and, 72

Dietary Supplement Health and Education Act, 76

Dilaudid, 32

Diprivan, 13

disenfranchisement, social consequences of war on drugs and, through loss of voting rights, 154–155

dopamine, 41, 112

"drug, set, setting," 214

Drug Abuse Resistance Education (DARE), 199–200, 202

Drug Abuse Treatment Act of 2000 (DATA), 48

Drug Enforcement Agency (DEA), 63

Drug Identification Bible, The, 33

drug offenders, decline of, 24–28

drug prevention programs, 199–203

drug research, children and, 10–14

drug treatment: buprenorphine as, for opiate users, 47–49; change and, 37–39; using consumer direction, self-determination, and person-centered treatment for, 211–212; family and, 207–208; harm reduction, 213–217; public support for, 209; strategies for improving offender outcomes and, 194–198; Willard approach to, 189–193

drug-endangered children (DEC) program, children found at methamphetamine labs and, 135–136

Durbin, Richard, 80–81

dynorphin, 42

E

East Germany, steroid use and, 19

ecstasy, 96

Effexor, 4, 5

18–MC (18–methoxycoronaridine), 45–46

elections, marijuana law reform and, 162–165

emergency medical technicians (EMTs), children found at methamphetamine labs and, 135

ephedra, 76, 78

erythroprotein (EPO), 17, 19

ethics, drug testing on children and, 10

F

Faces & Voices of Recovery (FAVOR), 209

families, war on drugs and, 207–208

Family Justice, 207, 208

family structure, social consequences of war on drugs and changes in, 152

Family Treatment Court, 210

Federal Trade Commission, 80

fetal drug exposure, 72–73, 137

flunitrazepam, 97, 141

Food and Drug Administration (FDA), 10, 12, 47, 48, 83; prescription drug abuse and, 117–118; supplements and, 76, 78, 79–80

Food and Drug Administration Modernization Act of 1997 (FDAMA), 11

frontal cortex, 43

G

Gamma-hydroxybutyrate (GHB), 97, 142

Gardner, Guy, 202

Gates, Daryl, 199

gays, methamphetamines and, 112–114

gene therapy, for performance enhancement, 15, 18, 22–23

germander, 76, 77

Giambi, Jason, 103

glandular extracts, 77

GlaxoSmithKline (GSK), withdrawal from Paxil and, 53, 54, 55, 56

Glick, Stanley, 45–46

glutamate, 43

Goldenheim, Paul D., 64

Grando, Sergei A., 50, 51

Gray, James, on war on drugs, 159–161

H

habenulo-interpeduncular pathway, 46

Harkin, Tom, 81

harm principle, criminalization and, 169, 175–176

Hatch, Orrin, 81

heroin, 48, 112; increased availability of, 94–95; against legalization of, 178–183; in Ohio, 93–95

high-risk drinking, 205

hippocampus, 41, 43

HIV, social consequences of war on drugs and, 153, 156

Hoberman, John, 18–19

homosexuals, methamphetamines and, 112–114

human growth hormone (hGH), 101

hydrocodone, 63

I

ibogaine, clinical trials of, 45–46

ibuprofen, children and, 11

IGF-1 (insulinlike growth factor-1), 15, 22

Instant Runoff Voting, 164

insulinlike growth factor-1 (IGF-1), 15, 22

Internet: sex sites on, 113; sites for psychologists on, 49

Iowa, anti-smoking campaign in, 9

J

Johnson, Brooks, 17

Jones, Marion, 16–17

Josey-Herring, Anita, 210

Journal of the American Medical Association, 72

Joyner, Florence Griffith, 20

J-shape curve, alcohol and, 72

K

Kauffman, Ralph, 11, 12

kava, 76, 77, 79

Kerry, John, 163

ketamine, 96–97, 142–143; fetal exposure to, 137

L

La Bodega's systematic approach, to family healing, 207–208

legalization. *See* decriminalization

levo-alpha-acetly methadol (LAAM), 47

Lewis, Carl, 17

Libertarian Party, 160

Life Skills Training, 201–202

Lithium, 5

"live high, train low" method, to sports training, 17

lobelia, 77

long-term potentiation, 43

Lorcet, 32, 63

Lortab, 32, 63

Luvox, 13

M

manualized curriculum approach, to drug treatment, 196–197

marijuana: drug prevention programs and, 199–203; growth of, in Canada, 88–92; increasing strength of, 86; reform of laws on, and elections, 162–165; use of, by Queen Victoria and drug policy, 147–148

marriage, social consequences of war on drugs and, 152

McCaffrey, Barry, 154, 155

McGwire, Mark, 16, 20

McIntire, Steven, 62

Medco Health Solutions, 31

medicalization, 163; use of marijuana by Queen Victoria and, 147–148; social consequences of war on drugs and, 153–154

mental illness, fetal drug exposure and, 137

mesolimbic dopamine pathway, 46

Metabolife International, 78

methadone, 47

methamphetamine labs, children found at, 134–136

methamphetamines, 129–130; gay men and, 112–114

methylenedioxymethamphetamine (MDMA), 96

Methypatch, 5

METRICH task force, 93

Mexico, 88

Mill, John Stuart, 180

minorities, disproportionate effect of criminalization on, 169

modafinil, 16, 101

mood disorders, use of drugs to treat, in children, 3–7

Moses, Ed, 17

Mothers Against Drunk Driving (MADD), 203

mothers, treatment for addicted and neglectful, 210

motivational interviewing, 38–39, 214

mu receptors, 47, 63

Murphy, Dianne, 10, 12, 13

mushrooms. 102

N

Netherlands, 170

Neurontin, 11, 13

neutrality, principle of, and drug laws, 181

New York program, of drug treatment through family support, 207–208

nicotine, effects of, 50–52

nitrous oxide, 167

Nixon, Richard, 27

nucleus accumbens, 41, 43

nutraceuticals, 21

O

Office of National Drug Control Policy (ONDCP), 153–154

Oklahoma, children found at methamphetamine labs and, 135–136

On Liberty (Mill), 180

opiates, 63–65; buprenorphine as treatment for addiction to, 47–49

organ extracts, 77

"original position," of Rawls, 181

over-the-counter (OTC) drugs, 11; cough medicine, 123–125

OxyContin, 32, 64, 65, 95, 117, 119–123

P

painkillers, abuse of, 63–65. *See also* specific painkillers

patents, drug, 12

paternalism, criminalization of drugs and, 174, 180–181

Paxil, 4, 5; controversy over, 82–85; withdrawal from, 53–57

PC SPES, 79

pediatric exclusivity provision, of FDAMA, 11–12

Pediatric Pharmacology Research Unit (PP-RU) Network, 13

"pediatric rule," of FDA, 11, 12–13

peer pressure, drug prevention programs and, 201

pennyroyal acid, 77

Percocet, 32

Percodan, 32

perfectionist argument, for criminalization, 175

performance-enhancing drugs, 15–23; Athens Olympics and, 108–111BALCO and, 101–102, 103–104; baseball and, 103–104

person-centered treatment, drug treatment programs and, 211–212

potassium channels, alcohol tolerance genes and, 62

Pound, Richard, 18, 19, 21–23, 109–111

poverty, disproportionate effect of drugs on poor and, 178–179, 180

predictions, of future drug use, as bad reason for continued criminalization, 169–172

pregnancy: alcohol use during, 70, 72–73; mental illness and use of drugs during, 137

prescription drug abuse, 31–33, 117–118

prison capacity, drug policy and, 150–153

privatization, of public costs of alcohol abuse, 29–30

Project ALERT, 200–201, 202

protective argument, for criminalization, 174–175

Prozac, 82, 83, 84; children and, 5, 139, 140

pseudoephedrine, 124

Q

Quick, Richard, 17

R

"rational basis" test, 168

Rawls, John, 181

Reagan, Ronald, 27

Relaxin, 79

residential treatment, 210

responsible drinking, 205

reward circuitry, of brain, and addiction, 40–44

Ritalin, 5, 31, 32

Rohypnol, 97, 141

Rose, Pete, 18

Ryan, Bob, 21

S

St. Ann's Corner of Harm Reduction (SA-CHR), 213–217

Sallee, Floyd R., 13

Schilling, Curt, 20

Schuster, Charles, 48

scullcap, 77

selective serotonin reuptake inhibitors (SS-RIs), 83, 85; children and, 139. *See also* specific selective serotonin reuptake inhibitors

self-administration, addiction and, 41

self-determination, drug treatment programs and, 211–212

sensitization, addiction and, 42

sexual abuse, OxyContin use and, 120

Sheffield, Gary, 103

shock model, drug treatment and, 191

skin, effect of nicotine on, 50, 51

slo-1 gene, alcohol tolerance and, 62

Smith de Bruin, Michelle, 18

smoking, 29; children and, 8–9; quitting without assistance, 37–38

social bonds, social consequences of war on drugs and, 152

social integration, drug treatment and, 215

Sosa, Sammy, 16, 20

Stages of Change model, 214

steroids, 19–20, 101; "designer", 105–107. *See also* performance-enhancing drugs

Stockwell, Tim, 69

Strattera, 5

stress reduction, drug treatment and, 214–215

Suboxone, 48

Substance Abuse and Mental Health Services Administration (SAMSA), 211–212

suicide: anti-depressant use by children and, 139–140; among gay methamphetamine users, 113

supplements, 76–81; for performance enhancement, 17

Sweeney, H. Lee, 15, 22

T

teenagers, 116; alcohol and, 73

tennis, use of performance-enhancing drugs in, 108

Theo-Dur, 80

theophylline, 80

Thermorexin, 80

THG (Tetrahydrogestosterone), 16, 18, 101, 104, 105, 108

tolerance, addiction and, 42

Torres, Dara, 17

trial-and-error approach, to drug testing on children, 11

tumors, alcohol and, 51

Tylox, 32

U

unemployment, social consequences of war on drugs and, 152, 156

United States Anti-Doping Agency (US-ADA), 17, 108

Urquhart, John, 84

V

Valium, 32

vascular endothelial growth factor (VEGF), 51

ventral tegmental area (VTA), addiction and, 41–42, 43

Versed, 11, 13

Viagra, methamphetamines and, 113

Vicodin, 32, 63

Victoria, queen of England, cannabis use by, and drug policy, 147–148

vitamins, 81

voting rights, social consequences of war on drugs and loss of, 154–155

W

Wadler, Gary, 15

Walters, Gary, 184

Walters, John, 155–156

war on drugs, 159–161, 207–208; disproportionate effect of, on minorities, 169; social consequences of, 149–158

warfarin, 79

water, alcohol use by women and, 69

weight control supplements, 81

White, Kelli, 16

Why Our Drug Laws Have Failed and What We Can Do About It — A Judicial Indictment of the War on Drugs (Gray), 160

Willard Drug Treatment Program, 189–193

withdrawal: 18–MC and, 45–46; methamphetamines and, 113

women, alcohol use and, 69–70

Woods, James, 48

World Anti-Doping Agency (WADA), 15, 17, 18, 21–23, 109–111

X

Xanax, 32

Xenadrine, 78, 80

Y

yohimbe, 76, 77

Z

Zantac, 11

zero-tolerance policies, toward GHB, 113

Zoloft, 5, 82

Zyprexa, 5

Test Your Knowledge Form

We encourage you to photocopy and use this page as a tool to assess how the articles in *Annual Editions* expand on the information in your textbook. By reflecting on the articles you will gain enhanced text information. You can also access this useful form on a product's book support Web site at *http://www.dushkin.com/online/*.

NAME: _____ DATE: _____

TITLE AND NUMBER OF ARTICLE: _____

BRIEFLY STATE THE MAIN IDEA OF THIS ARTICLE: _____

_____

LIST THREE IMPORTANT FACTS THAT THE AUTHOR USES TO SUPPORT THE MAIN IDEA:

_____

WHAT INFORMATION OR IDEAS DISCUSSED IN THIS ARTICLE ARE ALSO DISCUSSED IN YOUR TEXTBOOK OR OTHER READINGS THAT YOU HAVE DONE? LIST THE TEXTBOOK CHAPTERS AND PAGE NUMBERS:

_____

LIST ANY EXAMPLES OF BIAS OR FAULTY REASONING THAT YOU FOUND IN THE ARTICLE:

_____

LIST ANY NEW TERMS/CONCEPTS THAT WERE DISCUSSED IN THE ARTICLE, AND WRITE A SHORT DEFINITION:

We Want Your Advice

ANNUAL EDITIONS revisions depend on two major opinion sources: one is our Advisory Board, listed in the front of this volume, which works with us in scanning the thousands of articles published in the public press each year; the other is you—the person actually using the book. Please help us and the users of the next edition by completing the prepaid article rating form on this page and returning it to us. Thank you for your help!

ANNUAL EDITIONS: Drugs, Society, & Behavior 05/06

ARTICLE RATING FORM

Here is an opportunity for you to have direct input into the next revision of this volume.
We would like you to rate each of the articles listed below, using the following scale:

1. **Excellent: should definitely be retained**
2. **Above average: should probably be retained**
3. **Below average: should probably be deleted**
4. **Poor: should definitely be deleted**

Your ratings will play a vital part in the next revision.
Please mail this prepaid form to us as soon as possible.
Thanks for your help!

RATING	ARTICLE	RATING	ARTICLE
	1. Medicating Young Minds		34. Warning Label: Teens Find a Dangerous, Cheap High in Over-the-Counter Cough Medicine
	2. Too Many Kids Smoke		35. Policing a Rural Plague
	3. Drug Research and Children		36. About Face Program Turns Lives Around
	4. In Pursuit of Doped Excellence: The Lab Animal		37. Drug-Endangered Children
	5. Is the Drug War Over? The Declining Proportion of Drug Offenders		38. Fetal Exposure to Drugs
	6. So Here's to Privatizing the Public Costs of Alcohol Abuse		39. FDA Was Urged to Limit Kids' Antidepressants
			40. Date Rape Drugs
	7. A Prescription for Abuse		41. Queen Victoria's Cannabis Use: Or, How History Does and Does Not Get Used in Drug Policy Making
	8. The Surprising Truth About Addiction		
	9. The Addicted Brain		42. Social Consequences of the War on Drugs: The Legacy of Failed Policy
	10. The End of Craving		
	11. A New Treatment for Addiction		43. How to Win the Drug War
	12. More Than a Kick		44. Tokin' Politics: Making Marijuana Law Reform An Election Issue
	13. The Down Side of Up		
	14. Finding the Future Alcoholic		45. Drug Legalization
	15. Research Finds Alcohol Tolerance Gene		46. On the Decriminalization of Drugs
	16. In the Grip of a Deeper Pain		47. Against the Legalization of Heroin
	17. Alcohol's Deadly Triple Threat		48. U.S., Canada Clash on Pot Laws
	18. When Drinking Helps		49. Drug Treatment: The Willard Option
	19. Binge Drinking Holds Steady: College Students Continue to Drink Despite Programs		50. Strategies to Improve Offender Outcomes in Treatment
			51. Marijuana: Just Say No Again: The Old Failures of New and Improved Anti-drug Education
	20. Dangerous Supplements Still at Large		
	21. Addicted to Anti-Depressants?		52. Binge Drinking: Not the Word of Choice
	22. Stronger Pot, Bigger Worries		53. A New Weapon in the War on Drugs: Family
	23. Inside Dope		54. National Survey Finds Strong Public Support for Treatment
	24. Heroin Hits Small-Town America		
	25. What You Need to Know About Club Drugs: Rave On		55. Addicted, Neglectful Moms Offered Treatment, Custody
			56. Consumer Direction, Self-Determination and Person-Centered Treatment
	26. Blowing the Whistle on Drugs		
	27. Baseball Takes a Hit		57. SACHR: An Example of an Integrated, Harm Reduction Drug Treatment Program
	28. Designer Steroids: Ugly, Dangerous Things		
	29. Ever Farther, Ever Faster, Ever Higher?		
	30. Life or Meth?		
	31. Teens Tell Truth About Drugs		
	32. Prescription Drug Abuse: FDA and SAMHSA Join Forces		
	33. Adolescent OxyContin Abuse		

(Continued on next page)

NO POSTAGE
NECESSARY
IF MAILED
IN THE
UNITED STATES

BUSINESS REPLY MAIL
FIRST CLASS MAIL PERMIT NO. 551 DUBUQUE IA

POSTAGE WILL BE PAID BY ADDRESEE

McGraw-Hill/Dushkin
2460 KERPER BLVD
DUBUQUE, IA 52001-9902

ABOUT YOU

Name _____ Date _____

Are you a teacher? ❏   A student? ❏
Your school's name _____

Department _____

Address _____ City _____ State _____ Zip _____

School telephone # _____

YOUR COMMENTS ARE IMPORTANT TO US!

Please fill in the following information:
For which course did you use this book?
_____

Did you use a text with this ANNUAL EDITION? ❏ yes ❏ no
What was the title of the text?
_____

What are your general reactions to the *Annual Editions* concept?
_____

Have you read any pertinent articles recently that you think should be included in the next edition? Explain.
_____

Are there any articles that you feel should be replaced in the next edition? Why?
_____

Are there any World Wide Web sites that you feel should be included in the next edition? Please annotate.
_____

May we contact you for editorial input? ❏ yes ❏ no
May we quote your comments? ❏ yes ❏ no